SOUTHERN BALKANS

PLACE

80 100 M.

BELGRADE

•SOFIA

•SKOPJE

CONSTANTINOPLE

M A C E D O N I A

KORÇE   •FLORINA   SALONICA

Lesbos

E U B O I A

Chios   SMYRNA

Levkas
Ithaca

Andros   Samos

ATHENS

TRIPOLIS

D O D E C A N E S E

SPARTA

Kastellarizo

Rhodes

Kythera

C R E T E

C Y P R U S

H.E. GUNTHER, 1960

SOUTHERN EUROPEANS IN AUSTRALIA

CHARLES A. PRICE

Published in association with
The Australian National University

MELBOURNE
OXFORD UNIVERSITY PRESS
LONDON   WELLINGTON   NEW YORK

1963

Oxford University Press, Amen House, London, E.C.4

GLASGOW NEW YORK TORONTO MELBOURNE WELLINGTON
BOMBAY CALCUTTA MADRAS KARACHI LAHORE DACCA
CAPE TOWN SALISBURY NAIROBI IBADAN ACCRA
KUALA LUMPUR HONG KONG

Registered in Australia for transmission by post as a book
PRINTED IN AUSTRALIA BY HALSTEAD PRESS, SYDNEY

CONTENTS

TABLES

MAPS

APPENDIXES*

* Published as *The Method and Statistics of 'Southern Europeans in Australia'* by the Publications Committee of The Australian National University, on behalf of the Research School of Social Sciences (see p. xiv below).

FOREWORD

SINCE World War II Australia has received many more settlers from the British Isles and the mainland of Europe than in any equivalent period in her past history. Although the annual net intake of 83,240 (1947-61) has been little more than a tenth of that enjoyed by the United States at the turn of the century, it has been relatively large in terms of Australia's total population. As a consequence, public and academic interest in problems of migration and settlement have developed considerably, and investigations into them have grown apace. Some of these studies, such as Rabbi L. Goldman's *Jews in Victoria in the Nineteenth Century*, have been the work of ethnic social scientists and historians seeking to understand and make known the story of their own people settled in Australia. Others have derived from such public bodies as the Federal and State Departments of Immigration or the resettlement divisions of the World Council of Churches and Roman Catholic Church, which are anxious to discover what is happening to the migrants they sponsor and what their relationships are with native Australians. Yet others have come from the universities, from scholars interested in examining the story of migration and settlement, in improving methods of studying the complex problems involved, and in making their discoveries known to the general and academic public.

This book, which belongs to the third, the academic group, is based on the premise that a great deal of post-war migration and settlement—especially southern European—has been built upon foundations laid by pre-war settlers and can only be understood when related to those foundations. Moreover, the history of pre-war southern Europeans in Australia is itself a fascinating subject, and deserves to be written about irrespective of its relations with post-war migration.

Primarily, this book is the work of a social historian, for though it uses techniques and concepts evolved by the social sciences—notably those of demography and sociology—its point of view is historical: its aim is to tell a story of growth and development as clearly and accurately as possible.

The focus of the work partly explains why it contains so many slices of personal history, anecdotes of pioneering days, sketches of events and customs in southern Europe, and stories about immigrant societies. These are intended not only to illustrate the point under discussion—and provide colourful interludes—but also to put the reader more closely in touch with the realities of the human situation. Non-typical illustrations, of course, must always be treated with caution—though the analysis of such material within a general demographic framework has considerable merit. Indeed, often it is not the careful scientific analysis but the brief personal anecdote or fleeting description (frequently to be found in the works of unscientific writers such as E. A. Steiner: see, for example, *On the Trail of the Immigrant* and *The Immigrant Tide*) that brings the sudden flash of light and reveals the general contours of the scene. The writings of R. E. Park have this illuminating quality. They are the work of a great scholar and one whose disciplined and scientific activity stems from the deep waters of genuine understanding and intuitive perception; these, in turn, gathered slowly but surely from his experiences as a journalist, his intense interest in the human situation, and his vast acquaintance with the people and the cities he describes. I owe him a deep debt of gratitude.

A similar tribute is due to those great ethnic historians who become so steeped in the letters, diaries, and chronicles of bygone days that they recreate the colourful immigrant societies of the past in terms so vivid that the modern reader feels as if he is watching ethnic group life pass before his eyes. T. C. Blegen, in his monumental history of the Norwegians of Canada and the United States, is an example here.

This work is not a complete history of southern European settlement in Australia; some of the main features of that story have already been covered by writers such as J. S. Lyng and W. D. Borrie, and there is no need to traverse the ground they have already covered so well. Furthermore, the field is so vast that its proper exploration requires not only demographers, historians, and sociologists but also anthropologists, economists, geographers, linguists, social psychologists, and many others. This work simply stresses the social features of the story and those that seem to have been of unusual importance, or to have been hitherto ignored, or for which the material has only recently become available.

Though such limitations are inevitable and necessary, I have felt bound to cover as many topics as possible, simply to maintain a rational perspective. Indeed, one of the main themes is the impossibility of assessing migration and settlement without examining the way in which numerous forces and trends intertwine themselves in the 'peculiar' histories of diverse migrant groups from different parts of Europe settled in different places in Australia. A work of this size cannot cover the complex histories of all the groups it mentions—rather it is a survey of general trends, using selected incidents from the histories of various groups by way of illustration. To show how complex the intertwining of general forces and personal careers can be, and how important it is to understand such complexity, the final chapter contains a brief consecutive history of one migrant group—the Macedonians from north-western Greece.

Because of this complexity, and of the impossibility of understanding general patterns and trends without reference to particular places, individuals, and incidents, this work is heavily weighted with numerous names, both personal and geographical. It cannot be too strongly emphasized, however, that places of origin and settlement provide the key to the story and that frequent reference to them is one way of keeping the minds of both writer and reader anchored firmly to the realities of migrant history instead of letting them soar into the treacherous currents of oversimplified generalization. The Greek and Slav placenames have all the charm but also the bewildering complexity of the exotic—not least in their spelling. I have therefore anglicized them, following Lippincott's *Gazetteer*, with the exception that, where recent political changes in Macedonia have replaced Serbo-Croatian spellings with Macedonian, I have adopted these for all names in Yugoslav Macedonia.

Although the main topic of the book is southern European settlement in Australia, there are frequent references to southern Europeans in Canada, New Zealand and the United States of America. These countries have many social institutions and activities similar to those of Australia, so that comparison helps to set the Australian story in a more general context. Nevertheless, despite references to the great pioneering studies in this field of ethnic history in North America, this work makes no attempt at systematic and comprehensive comparison. Both comparisons and references appear when, and only when, they seem to throw light on the Australian scene.

Canberra,   C.A.P.
July 1962

APPENDIXES

In order not to impede the flow of the narrative, all the purely demographical and sociological analyses and statistics, except where these are essential to an understanding of the main story and are incorporated in the text, have been grouped into a separate volume entitled *The Method and Statistics of 'Southern Europeans in Australia'*.* The contents of this separate volume, therefore, act firstly as supporting Appendixes to this present, or main volume, and references to particular paragraphs of each Appendix are given throughout the main volume in the form—see Appendix 1:2, etc. The contents, however, have a second function: to make available to scholars statistical and analytical details that are of great potential use but are more extensive than the documentation of the main volume requires.

* Published by the Publications Committee on behalf of the Research School of Social Sciences, The Australian National University, Canberra, 1963.

ACKNOWLEDGEMENTS

In completing what has turned out to be an eight-year task there remains only to say that I am deeply grateful for the help of several institutions. The Rockefeller Foundation, through its Fellowship system, enabled me to visit Canada and the United States in 1958-9 to do research amongst southern European settlements comparable with those of Australia. On this visit the Citizenship Branch of the Canadian Department of Citizenship and Immigration gave me much help and good advice. In Australia the Commonwealth Archives and Department of Immigration have been of very great assistance, while my detailed field investigations in Griffith, N.S.W., in 1954-5 owe much to the encouragement of officers of the Irrigation Research and Extension Committee, especially Dr Joan Tully and Mr Alan Grasby.

I also owe much to all those southern European families in Australia, Canada, and the United States who helped me with life histories, translations, interpretation of statistics, and so on: in particular to Messrs Grbelja, Lulich, and Mijat of Osborne Park, Perth; J. Kolieff and P. Marinoff of Adelaide; C. Altis, A. Chris, F. Demetrie, A. Nicolaides, A. Pappastergiou, P. Peshut, P. Polites, E. Shannos, A. Stamos, G. Tollis, P. Varvaregos, E. Vlass of Melbourne; J. Cassidy, A. Grivas, L. Leondis, S. Niketich, A. Perish, G. Potiri, J. Raftopoulos, G. Sartara, T. Sticka, and the late Archbishop Evangelides of Sydney; F. Norman and P. Panto of Canberra-Queanbeyan; J. Uylacki of Berri; A. Mototek of Mildura; G. Vlassis of Ottawa; H. Dranis, A. Ginou, C. Kokkinos, P. Meanchoff, Mrs J. Harris, Mrs P. Janetakis, Father Andrews, Father Elieff, and Father Mihailoff of Toronto; A. Eterovich, C. Marinovich, N. Misevich, Mrs M. Franicevich, and Mrs G. Kulich of Berkeley and San Francisco.

To four persons and their families I owe a particular debt, both for having me to stay as a guest in their homes—so giving me an insight into problems of migration and assimilation not attainable even from lengthy interviews and detailed examination of records—and for providing a great mass of information: Dr K. K. Barris of Sydney, and Messrs C. De Luca, R. Snaidero, and P. Calabria of Griffith, N.S.W.

Others have very kindly given much of their time reading the manuscript and making helpful suggestions: my father, Dr

A. Grenfell Price, of Adelaide; Professor E. P. Hutchinson of the University of Pennsylvania; Professor O. H. K. Spate, Mr L. F. Fitzhardinge, Drs Bolton, Brookfield, and Zubrzycki of The Australian National University. Mrs L. Nicolson and Mrs L. Wilson did much of the tedious statistical analyses and tables, and Mrs N. Kuskie and Mrs M. Mansfield did much of the statistical checking; Mr Hans Gunther, of the Geography Department cartographic section, drew my maps for reproduction; and the Editorial section of the Publications Committee of the University has spent much time and energy in improving the manuscript. Finally, to Professor W. D. Borrie, Head of my own department, I owe a special debt for all the time, advice, and encouragement he has given since the project began.

I willingly make the traditional disclaimer: though all the people and institutions mentioned have been so helpful, none but myself can be held responsible for any of the statements, statistics, or conclusions of the book.

C.A.P.

CHAPTER I

INTRODUCTION

The wild Albanian kirtled to his knee,
With shawl-girt head and ornamented gun,
And gold embroider'd garments, fair to see;
The crimson-scarfèd men of Macedon;
The Delhi with his cap of terror on,
And crooked glaive; the lively, supple Greek;
And swarthy Nubia's mutilated son;
The bearded Turk, that rarely deigns to speak,
Master of all around, too potent to be meek.

Such be the sons of Spain, and strange her fate!
They fight for freedom who were never free.

The Tiber winds, and the broad ocean laves
The Latian coast where sprung the Epic war,
'Arms and the man,' whose re-ascending star
Rose o'er an empire:—but beneath thy right
Tully reposed from Rome;—and where yon bar
Of girdling mountains intercepts the sight
The Sabine farm was till'd, the weary bard's delight.

> Byron, *Childe Harold's Pilgrimage*, Canto
> II, 58; I, 86; IV, 174

THIS work is about southern Europeans in Australia—such persons as those mentioned in Byron's verse above. In a sense we are about to take a journey covering the same realm and meeting the same folk as did Childe Harold in his wanderings, and it is not inappropriate to start each chapter with a quotation from his pilgrimage. The Byronic view of the Mediterranean world, however, is rather too romantic and elevated for a study such as this. It may be wiser, therefore, to start the discussion by quoting some earthier views of southern Europeans—views very relevant to the Australian story since they were expressed by Australians themselves.

The league has been advised that Maltese are the cheapest semi-white labourers known and, like Chinese, are very ready to work long hours for a low wage.[1]

[1] Letter to the Prime Minister of Australia from the British Immigration League, Sydney, Tasmanian *Herald*, 23 July 1912.

B

The Greek residents of North Queensland are generally of an undesirable type, and do not make good settlers . . . Their admission to Queensland can be of no possible benefit to the country.[2]

The trouble with those b—— dagoes is that they stink of garlic and live on the smell of an oily rag.[3]

These remarks express, comparatively mildly, the opinions numerous British Australians have held—and in many cases still hold—about immigrants from the southern parts of Europe. Such opinions, though strongly held, are usually very vague. Many Australians, for instance, use the word 'dago' quite indiscriminately to embrace any migrant from the Mediterranean; only a few use it in the American sense as a term to describe Spaniards, Portuguese, and Italians, and still fewer use it in the original sense and limit it to persons of Spanish origin. (It derives from 'Diego', a Portuguese-Spanish word for James (*Oxford English Dictionary*), and was used by northern European settlers in the southern regions of North America when they came in contact with central Americans of Spanish descent. The term probably came to Australia in the gold-rush period when many persons left the diggings of California to try their luck in Victoria and New South Wales.)

Many Australians are also very vague as to what precisely is a 'southern European'. For some the term covers all Spaniards, Portuguese, Italians, Yugoslavs, Albanians, Greeks, and Maltese;[4] others tend to leave out northern Italians and Yugoslavs and confine the term to the remaining peoples. The latter usage seems to be connected with some vague feeling that northern Italians and Yugoslavs are predominantly Nordic and Slav in origin and have managed to escape the 'racial inferiority', or at any rate 'racial deterioration', which supposedly afflicted the peoples farther south. The statement of J. S. Lyng that 'in Southern Italy and Sicily . . . the once pure Mediterranean blood has been impoverished by an infusion of inferior African and Asiatic blood' is typical of this feeling,[5] as is the widespread opinion that British-Australian girls have no objection to marrying the 'tall blonde males' who come from northern Italy but

[2] T. A. Ferry 'Report of the Royal Commission to inquire into . . . the Social and Economic Effect of Increase in Numbers of Aliens in North Queensland', Qld *Parliamentary Papers*, 1925, vol. 3, pp. 38-9 (No. A28, pp. 12-13) (henceforth cited as 'Ferry Report').

[3] Remark uttered in 1955 in an Australian country town where Italian farmers are rapidly buying out older settlers.

[4] See, e.g., J. S. Lyng, *Non-Britishers in Australia*, pp. 100, 135.

[5] Ibid., p. 93.

are much less ready to marry the 'short, dark, greasy males' from Calabria, Sicily, Malta, and Greece. That these opinions are not altogether true will appear later.

In this book the term 'southern European' will be used to denote persons whose family origins lie in the Mediterranean islands, in the Iberian, Italian, and Balkan peninsulas, and in the continental zones connecting these peninsulas: Portugal, Spain, southern France, Italy, Yugoslavia, Bulgaria, Albania, Greece, Malta, and Cyprus.[6] The reason for this choice is partly geographic—all these places lie within the Mediterranean climatic zone or else in the mountainous hinterland of Mediterranean Europe—but it is also ethnic, a point which requires further explanation.

In the past the term 'ethnic division' has carried a variety of meanings, ranging from a collection of human beings grouped together primarily by physical characteristics—height, size and shape of skull, colour of skin, colour of hair and eyes—to one grouped together primarily by cultural characteristics such as language, religion, social customs, or political traditions. The term adopted here is used in the broad sense to mean a collection of persons who, for physical, geographical, political, religious, linguistic, or other reasons, feel themselves, or are felt by others, to constitute a separate people.[7]

In southern Europe some major ethnic divisions—Greeks, Italians, and Albanians, for example—are clearly discernible. At first sight it would seem simple to describe these ethnic groupings as 'nations', especially as each conforms to the old meaning of the word—an aggregate of persons bound closely enough by descent, language, history, or political institutions to form a distinct race or people (O.E.D.)—as well as to the more modern meaning of a number of persons occupying a separate political state with a particular legal nationality or citizenship. Unfortunately, these two meanings do not always coincide. The Slovenes, Croats, and Serbs of Yugoslavia, as do the Czechs and Slovaks farther north, generally feel that though they belong to the one political state and have a common nationality they are nevertheless quite distinct peoples. Many, indeed, intensely disliked the political union they received after World War I,

[6] In official British documents and in Australian census and migration statistics Cyprus counts as part of Asia. Here it is counted as a part of southern Europe, because the majority of its inhabitants are of Greek origin.

[7] Caroline Ware, 'Ethnic Communities', in *Encyclopaedia of Social Sciences*.

strove vigorously to obtain independent nation-states, and for a time, during World War II, actually achieved separate status. Such feelings can become very important abroad: fervent Croats or Slovaks have refused to become naturalized because they would have to renounce their 'Yugoslav' or 'Czechoslovak' nationality, something they resolutely refuse to admit they possess since it was the 'invention' of their Serb or Czech 'oppressors' and 'exploiters'. To some extent the present political state of Yugoslavia recognizes the situation by refraining from naming any one official language and by describing itself as a federation of autonomous republics.

Still more difficult are peoples such as the Basques and Catalans of Spain. These belong to a political unit that has one official language and a long tradition of administrative unity under one central government. Yet their long, if sporadic, struggle for political autonomy, their distinctive social customs, and their distinctive languages and literatures entitle them to be treated as major ethnic units. In this sense they are not dissimilar from the Welsh, Scottish, Irish, and English peoples in the United Kingdom.

Perhaps the most difficult ethnic groupings to discuss are those whose claims to be treated as separate peoples have aroused tremendous argument. Foremost amongst these are the Macedonians. It is, indeed, hardly surprising that strenuous efforts have been made, and are still being made, to deny the existence of a separate Macedonian people: before World War I, in the interests of their own territorial and cultural ambitions, Greece, Serbia, and Bulgaria usually found it convenient to claim that the bulk of the Slav-speaking persons who were living in the area stretching from Lake Ohrid west to the River Struma, and from Salonica north to Skopje, were only slightly different varieties of Greeks, Serbs, or Bulgarians. We are not concerned to adjudicate between these claims here; what matters is that a considerable number of immigrants to Australia, as well as to America, have strenuously denied that they are Greeks or Serbs and, while admitting close religious and linguistic affinities with the Bulgarians proper, have asserted that for reasons of history, language, and custom they are part of the unrecognized Macedonian people. Since we are dealing with the settlement of migrants in Australia rather than with political ambitions in Europe, it seems proper to respect their claims and treat them separately as the Macedonians or, as some writers describe them, the Macedo-Slavs. (Here again modern Yugoslavia has recognized an autonomous Macedonian republic.)[8]

It is in discussing ethnic groupings such as these that the discrepancy between the two common meanings of the term nation becomes most apparent. To refrain from calling them nations in a work on ethnic history quite wrongly suggests that ethnically and in their behaviour overseas they differ from peoples with separate political status; to call them nations on a par with Italians, Greeks, and Albanians immediately confuses the modern concept of nationality with the arbitrary usage that has crept in with organizations such as the League of Nations and United Nations.[9]

It therefore seems advisable to confine the terms nation and nationality to their modern legal sense and find another term for these ethnic divisions. No English term is entirely suitable, but the word Folk is probably as free from ambiguity as any. In this sense each of the peoples mentioned above—Greeks, Albanians, Croats, Catalans, etc.—make up a particular Folk and the ethnic settlements they may form overseas are Folk settlements.[10] The form has several advantages. First, it is not altogether out of line with some of the many meanings given it by modern sociologists, especially those that stress the cultural and social life of a people in contrast to their political activities. Second, it leaves the term 'nationalism' to describe the feelings and activities that led many Folk to fight for political autonomy or a separate nation-state, whether that fight were successful or not; equally it leaves that term free to describe the process whereby an artificial nation-state such as Yugoslavia or Spain has intentionally or unintentionally used its control of central

[8] See also pp. 310-24 below.

[9] Arbitrary in the sense that though the nations or peoples of the world are represented in such organizations, the unit of representation is not the people (nation in the old sense) but political units that may sometimes cover more or less than one distinctive people. The concepts 'nation' and 'nationality' are much more complex than is suggested by the simple distinction drawn above between the two common meanings of the word 'nation'. 'Nationality' is a comparatively recent concept and has varied from country to country. For the sake of simplicity, however, this discussion is confined to this simple distinction and leaves the more complex aspects of nationality, citizenship, allegiance, domicile, denization, etc. to experts in international law. See, E. K. Francis, 'Minority Groups—A Revision of Concepts', *British Journal of Sociology*, II (1951), iii, 219-29.

[10] The word is capitalized throughout this book wherever it is used in this special sense. It thus avoids infringing on general usage and leaves the specialized meaning given it by sociologists.

government to create a kind of supra-Folk nationalism and to foster loyalty and affection for the political unit as a whole (these two kinds of nationalism, when contrasted, are called 'Folk-nationalism' and 'state-nationalism'). Third, it overcomes the difficulty raised by changing political boundaries and changing legal nationalities: the Croatian population of the Dalmatian town of Zadar, for instance, were 'Austrians' before World War I, 'Italians' between the wars, and 'Yugoslavs' after World War II; yet they belonged to the same ethnic grouping, the same Folk, throughout. And so with many other parts of the old Hapsburg and Ottoman empires.

The last and perhaps greatest advantage of using Folk rather than nation is that the former unequivocally takes account of persons born beyond the territorial area occupied by the majority of the ethnic grouping in question. Persons of Greek origin may be born as French subjects in Algiers, British subjects in Cyprus, Russian subjects in Odessa, or Greek subjects in Greece. Furthermore, they may have children who are Australian citizens by birth while they themselves may or may not become Australian citizens by naturalization. Yet they may all think of themselves as ethnic Greeks and live in ethnic Greek settlements in Australia. Whether and when such families lose their Greek identity and become Australian by assimilation is a major problem to be discussed later. Clearly the term Folk covers such persons, at any rate in the years before assimilation is well advanced, more satisfactorily than the terms nation and nationality.

There are, as it happens, smaller ethnic divisions than the Folk. Regional differences, such as those existing between the Calabrian and Piedmontese regions of Italy, have been very pronounced and have covered many aspects of social life, including dialect, family customs, and religious opinions. Indeed, in the decades before and after World War I, when the migrants we are concerned with were coming to Australia, marked differences often existed in the dialects and customs of districts geographically very close to one another—as, in southern Greece, between the district of Mani and the rest of the Peloponnesus. These distinctions have at times been very great, leading migrants from one district or region to think of themselves as so different from persons from another district or region that they have little to do with them and form quite distinct ethnic group settlements abroad.[11]

Some authorities may argue here that regional differences be-

[11] For definition of 'group settlement' see pp. 223-6 below.

tween Calabrians and Piedmontesi are so great that these peoples
should be treated as separate Folk, in the way that Serbs are
treated as a separate Folk from Croatians. It is sometimes very
difficult to draw a clear line between Folk and regional peoples,
but the cases above present no real trouble: the cultural differences between Serb and Croat are so great that each is clearly
conscious of belonging to different Folk even when families have
been living together in the same district for centuries, as in parts
of Bosnia and Herzegovina. So also with the Basque and non-
Basque peoples of the western Pyrenees. With the regional
peoples of Italy, except perhaps the Sardinians, the lines of de-
marcation are much less clear. In dialect, customs, and attitudes, Calabrians shade almost imperceptibly into Basilicatans,
and Basilicatans into Apulians. It is only when Calabrians are
contrasted with persons from a region some distance away—say,
Lombardy or Piedmont in the north of Italy—that the regional
distinctions become so clear that it is plain we are dealing with
quite different ethnic groupings. For this reason district and
regional peoples are best thought of as ethnic subdivisions of
the one Folk.

There are, of course, cases of cultural fusion between different
Folk, and these give much the same appearance as the gradual
merging of one regional people into another—the border areas
of Slovenia and Croatia, for instance, or of Catalan and non-
Catalan territory in Spain. Somewhere, however, a line must be
drawn: so one can only endeavour to assess the sum total of
cultural characteristics and to decide, arbitrarily, where and
at what moment of time it becomes necessary to think of one
ethnic grouping as a Folk and another as a regional people.
The importance of the distinction, especially in relation to the
much more definite cultural differences involved in the concept
of Folk, will emerge more and more as the work proceeds.

There are, however, even larger ethnic units than the Folk.
In southern Europe, where physical characteristics are very
mixed and the concept of race, or physical type, requires careful
treatment, the most satisfactory larger division is based on
language. There are, for example, places in Australia where
Portuguese, Catalan Spaniards, and Venetian Italians have
formed a single group settlement, primarily because they found
that, with some adjustment, they could understand each other.
Likewise with Bulgarians, Macedonians, Serbs, and Croats. This
has not often happened when numbers from various districts,
regions, or Folk have been large enough to permit the formation

of separate settlements, but rather it has happened where a few families from different places of origin have settled in the same part of Australia and have found themselves thrown together by the exigencies of life in a predominantly British country. The fact that it has happened, even occasionally, shows the reality of ethnic divisions based on similar languages.

In this sense the Folk fall into certain major ethnic divisions. The Portuguese, Castilians, Catalans, southern French, and Italians form a 'Latin' grouping. The Slovenes, Croats, Serbs, Macedonians, and Bulgarians make up the South Slav peoples, cut off from their Slav relatives in the north by a belt of non-Slav-speaking peoples, the Austrians, Magyars, and Rumanians. Finally, there are the remnants of certain Folk once much more widely spread than at present—the Basques, Albanians, Greeks, and Maltese. All these, whether living in southern Europe itself or settled elsewhere in Europe, Asia, or Africa, make up the southern European peoples discussed in this work. (Turkish people from European countries such as Yugoslavia, Greece, Bulgaria and Cyprus are, for ethnic and linguistic reasons, treated as Asiatics and not as southern Europeans; very few of these have emigrated to Australia.)

Having defined the southern Europeans it is now possible to mention their relationship with other migrants to Australia, who constitute several broad ethnic categories. First, there are the British, those whose parents, grandparents or remoter ancestors were born in England, Scotland, Ireland, Wales, or the Manx and Channel Islands; in this sense the Maltese and Cypriots, though they may possess British nationality and have to a limited extent adopted the English language, cannot be counted as British. Second, there are the Jews. In any work on migration to Australia it is important to separate Jews from persons with the same birthplace or legal nationality, since the whole pattern of Jewish migration and settlement has been so different from that of other peoples that the few Jewish migrants who have come to Australia from the old Jewish communities in southern European towns such as Barcelona, Marseilles, and Trieste have been treated as Jews and excluded in this book from the analysis and discussion of southern European settlement. Third, there are the north-western Europeans—the Scandinavians, Dutch, Germans, Austrians, Swiss, Belgians, and northern French. Finally, there are the north-eastern European groups: the Finns and Estonians; the Latvians and Lithuanians; the Poles, Czechs and Slovaks; the Ukrainians, Russians and White (or Bielo- Russians; the Rumanians and Hungarians. Speaking strictly these broad categories, together with the southern Europeans, make up the total of European migration to Australia: in this work, however, the terms Europe and European will exclude the British —a procedure that is not only convenient but conforms to normal usage in Australia, where some 85 per cent of the people are still of British descent.

The first noticeable feature about European settlement in Australia is that until very recently it has been relatively slight in comparison with British settlement. Until 1891 the ratio averaged about one European settler to every ten British, and in the next fifty years, 1891-1940, about one European to every five British. Only since 1947 has the balance tipped the other way, with the ratio at two European to every one British settler.[12] As a result, the non-British section of the white population of Australia has risen somewhat slowly: some 7 per cent in 1861, 9 per cent in 1901, 11 per cent in 1947, and perhaps 15 per cent in 1954.[13] Nevertheless, one-tenth or so of a population is no negligible proportion; it is quite sufficient to produce substantial ethnic groups and all the problems associated with them.

The second noticeable feature is that until the last quarter of the nineteenth century settlers from southern Europe were relatively insignificant. Even by 1891 only 6,000 or so had arrived, compared with more than 70,000 from the north-west, about 2,000 from the north-east, and some 4,000 European Jews. Persons from the north-west, in short, dominated nineteenth-century migration from Europe to Australia, keeping southern Europeans to a mere 8 per cent of the non-Jewish total. Between 1891 and 1940, however, the whole picture changed. During this period, in addition to some 15,000 European Jews, some 10,000

12 These, somewhat generalized, ratios are based on statistics of net migration and the census birthplace figures. For details see Appendix 1 of this work; W. D. Borrie, *Italians and Germans in Australia*, Chapter IV; C. A. Price, 'The Effects of Post-War Immigration. . . .', *Australian Quarterly*, XXIX (1957), 28-40.

13 It is impossible to calculate completely accurate proportions. The above figures have been estimated by taking the birthplace proportions which existed in 1861, applying these to the natural increase between 1861 and 1891, and adding on to each birthplace group the relevant net migration 1861-91. The intercensal periods 1891-1901, 1901-11, 1911-21, 1921-33, 1933-47, 1947-54 have been similarly treated. These proportions make interesting comparison with the 2% produced by the census report of 1947, which is based not on descent but on nationality at birth—a highly misleading concept when applied to the study of ethnic minorities.

migrants arrived from the north-west and about 6,000 from the north-east, but nearly 50,000 arrived from the south—an increase in southern European migrants from 8 per cent to 75 per cent of total non-Jewish immigration from Europe during this fifty-year period.

There is here a marked and important difference between United States and Australian immigration. As in Australia, persons from the north-west dominated migration from Europe to the United States before the 1890s and then fell rapidly in relation to other peoples—from 1820 to 1890 they comprised at least two-thirds of the non-Jewish total whereas from 1891 to 1940 they made up considerably less than one-third. But whereas in Australia the southern Europeans surged ahead into the lead, in the United States they had to share the honours with migrants from north-eastern Europe—the ratio, after discounting Jews, being a little better than 1:1 in favour of the southern Europeans.[14] The corresponding Australian ratio was 8:1, a fact that goes far to explain why, in Australia, migrants from southern Europe have been singled out for so much attention and odium.

At this point it is appropriate to consider the ethnic composition of the southern European population of Australia as shown in the three census years 1891, 1921, and 1947. Not only are these years roughly one generation apart, but the census of 1947—the only one taken between 1933 and 1954—is both the one census that reveals the immigration of the late 1930s and also the last to show the European population of Australia as it existed before the great post-war movement to Australia got under way.

The first thing to note is that Table I is based on broad ethnic groupings. It endeavours to correct some of the anomalies outlined earlier when discussing the inadequacy of 'nation' and 'nationality' to reveal ethnic identity and so differs considerably from the nationality statistics published by the Commonwealth Bureau of Census and Statistics. It also endeavours to correct similar anomalies in published birthplace statistics, which can be nearly as deceptive as nationality statistics, because all they show for a great many persons is nationality at birth, and therefore not only fail to distinguish between the different Folk and regions of the one national state but sometimes count the dependent territories of European powers as part of the European country concerned. Between 1920 and 1946, for example, the

14 See *Reports of the Immigration Commission*, 1907-10; W. F. Willcox, *International Migrations*.

Greek inhabitants of the Dodecanese islands were counted as Italian-born because the islands belonged to Italy from 1920 until after World War II.

TABLE I

ESTIMATED SOUTHERN EUROPEAN POPULATION OF AUSTRALIA*

(Excluding Australian-born generations)

Grouping	1891		1921		1947	
	No.	%	*No.*	%	*No.*	%
Basques, Catalans ⎫ Other Spanish ⎪ Portuguese ⎬ Southern French ⎭	1,000	16·7	1,700	10·7	1,500	2·5
Italians:†						
North	2,400	40·0	4,520	28·5	17,000	28·1
Central	450	7·5	520	3·3	2,000	3·3
South	150	2·5	300	1·9	6,500	10·8
Insular	900	15·0	1,910	12·0	8,200	13·6
Total	3,900	65·0	7,250	45·7	33,700	55·8
South Slavs:						
Slovenes	20	0·3	40	0·3	240	0·4
Croats	250	4·2	720	4·4	5,020	8·3
Serbs	20	0·3	40	0·3	340	0·6
Macedonians	..	..	50	0·3	1,900	3·1
Bulgarians	10	0·2	110	0·7	550	0·9
Total	300	5·0	960	6·0	8,050	13·3
Greeks	600	10·0	4,600	29·0	12,500	20·7
Albanians	..	..	10	0·1	1,400	2·3
Maltese	200	3·3	1,350	8·5	3,300	5·4
TOTAL	6,000	100·0	15,870	100·0	60,450	100·0
North-west	66,400		40,000		24,000	
North-east	1,300		3,900		7,500	
European Jews	3,400		5,500		16,500	

* For the way in which these estimates have been reached, see Appendix 1: 17, 18.

† For Divisions of Italy, see Appendix 1:17.

For an estimate of the second generation, see Appendix 4:8, 12. They raise the southern European population of Australia to nearly 100,000, or some 1·3 per cent of the total Australian population in 1947.

The figures in Table I are estimates derived by relating census nationality and birthplace totals to other evidence. Nonetheless, they give a better picture of the general ethnic composition of Australia's southern European population than other statistics. They also show changes in the general ethnic composition of southern European immigration, as, for instance, the early supremacy of northern Italian migration and the gradual catching up by Italian migrants from the islands and the south; or the steady increase of the South Slav peoples—mainly Dalmatian Croats and Slav Macedonians—and the relative decline of the Basques, Catalans, Portuguese, and southern French.[15]

It would be a great mistake, however, to imagine that broad ethnic groupings, even allowing for their superiority over official nationality or birthplace divisions, are sufficient in themselves for an adequate analysis of migration and settlement: such groupings are too wide for detailed work and may at times suggest superficial and misleading conclusions. Broad ethnic groupings, for instance, tend to encourage somewhat loose, over-generalized, thinking about Folk or 'national' character. Certainly the use of crude stereotypes—the proud disdainful Spaniard, the noisy sociable Greek, or the phlegmatic patient Slav—may be restricted, but it may be difficult to refrain from discussing in somewhat more sophisticated terms a 'typical' Slovene, Maltese, or Albanian. Indeed, many books describing the European background to migration start by discussing the so-called 'national character' and then suggest that Slovene, Maltese, Albanian or other settlers abroad tend to behave in a 'typical' way. For example, H. P. Fairchild, in his *Greek Immigration to the United States* (pp. 21-8) states that the Greeks are 'passionate, quick-tempered and excitable . . . voluble and very fond of noise . . . courteous, polite and hospitable . . . dishonest and quarrelsome . . .' and so on. Despite Fairchild's own warning against generalized statements, his thinking clearly oversimplifies and is far from precise.

The second difficulty about this kind of description has already been indicated in the reference to regional and district sub-divisions. Generalized description may fairly portray the average member of a broad ethnic division such as a Folk, but it suggests that migrants have come as a well-distributed scatter from the

---

[15] Before World War I the United States tried to discover ethnic groupings by asking the immigrants themselves—the official U.S. Immigration reports of this time are therefore most revealing. After the Versailles Treaty, however, this admirable practice lapsed.

broad ethnic division as a whole and have not come in a concentrated stream from one or two particular places or sections
within it; or that, if they have done so, there exist no appreciable
differences between these places. But if, in fact, migrants do tend
to come in concentrated streams, and there do exist marked differences of dialect, customs, and traditions between the areas of
origin, then any conclusions based on broad ethnic character
may be most misleading. This is a weakness in those works
which outline general trends in migration and settlement and
illustrate by a limited number of case histories; unless the reader
is careful he tends to generalize from the particular migrant
career mentioned to all migrants of that class and ethnic grouping, irrespective of whether the case is representative of the
main classes and districts of origin.

Now southern Europeans settling in Australia have not come
as a broad scatter from each main ethnic grouping; they have
tended to come in concentrations from restricted areas of origin,
areas producing large numbers of migrants being interspersed
with vast areas producing practically no migrants at all. The
endpaper map makes this very plain—there the dots, each of
which represents 100 males (occasionally 60-100 where numbers
are scarce), embrace some 92 per cent of men migrating from
areas shown.[16] Possible exceptions to this are Portugal, Spain,
and southern France; and even here, though detailed information is at present lacking, there seem to be few important sources
of origin apart from the districts containing Marseilles and
Barcelona and the district east of Bilbao in the Basque province
of Viscaya.[17]

As the map shows, we are examining not a scattering of
migrants from all over southern Europe but concentrations of
migrants from particular localities: not with North Italians as
a whole, but with northern Italians from the relatively restricted
areas of the Monferrato, the Bergamasque Alps, and the Venetian slopes and mountains; not with Croatians as a whole but
with Croatians from the restricted regions of central Dalmatia,
the Rijecka area and isles, and the Medjumurje; not with

16 The endpaper map is set out in tabular form in Table II.
17 Of the small sample of 60 Spanish families who had settled in various
parts of Australia between 1900 and 1940, 51% came from Catalonia (including 32% from places near Barcelona and 15% from coastal villages near
Palamos in Gerona), 29% from the Basque provinces (22% from the district
round Munguia in E. Viscaya), and 20% from Valencia, Andalusia, and
Castile.

Greeks as a whole but with Greeks from a relatively small number of islands, ports, and inland districts; and so with the Albanians, Macedonians, Bulgarians, and southern Italians. When there are marked differences of dialect, traditions, and social customs between these restricted areas of origin—and in many cases there are—then clearly we may fall into serious error if we think solely in terms of broad ethnic groupings.

The only proper way to proceed, therefore, is to examine the areas concerned as closely as possible, preferably by visiting them for some length of time, and to study carefully the life stories of migrants who have come from those particular districts. In this way the scholar comes to know the background and characteristics of the principal migrant groups, and is to some extent protected from making irrelevant generalizations about the broad Folk or ethnic division to which any particular migrant group belongs. Moreover, this procedure allows the collection of much detailed information which subsequently assists in understanding the process of migration from particular districts, as well as the process of settlement and adaptation in the country of reception. Only after areas have thus been examined in detail should any general statements about the migration and settlement of southern Europeans in Australia be formulated.

As it happens, the areas of origin of the southern Europeans and their places of settlement in Australia are more than enough to make the visiting of every district and the collecting of a representative sample of migrant life histories a very formidable task. Certainly there are a few detailed studies available, but these are quite insufficient to build up a general picture of southern European settlement in Australia.[18] Nor will there be enough studies completed in the next few years to make it worthwhile holding back a general survey of the kind contemplated in this work. Furthermore, as long as no general survey exists, people will be tempted to generalize from the one or two particular studies available, to assume that what has happened in those instances is true of all southern European groups in this country, and to make unsafe comparisons with events in other countries.

[18] E.g. C. Gamba, *The Italian Fishermen of Fremantle*; Borrie, *Italians and Germans in Australia*, more particularly the parts relating to Sicilians and Piedmontesi in North Queensland; J. Bromley, The Italians of Port Pirie (MS.); C. A. Price, *Italian Population of Griffith*; J. S. McDonald, Migration from Italy to Australia (MS.); J. A. Hempel, *Italians in Queensland*; J. M. Bertei, Innisfail (MS.); J. A. Petrolias, Post-War Greek and Italian Migrants in Melbourne (MS.).

In these circumstances it seems desirable to discover, if possible, some set of records which cover the topic—both areas of origin in Europe and places of settlement in Australia—in sufficient detail to outline the general situation, at any rate provisionally; particular studies may then take place within the general framework, either as illustrations of trends already perceived or else as samples intelligently chosen. So far as areas of origin are concerned the position is not desperate: local and regional studies of various kinds do exist, and these, together with background information obtained from migrants in Australia, provide enough material for anyone who has visited southern Europe and has some idea of the problems involved; some remoter and less well documented districts will inevitably suffer, but on the whole the material should be adequate for a preliminary survey. Representative migrant life histories and details of the various places of settlement in Australia present greater difficulties, particularly as the published census and migration statistics are inadequate in that they fail to show ethnic divisions and particular places of origin; in any case these have been well worked over by writers such as J. S. Lyng and W. D. Borrie, who have set out with great clarity the general conclusions which emerge from this type of material.[19] Probably the best records available are the old naturalization papers, which go back to the early days of each Australian colony and give full details concerning village or town of birth, date of arrival, occupation, and place of residence in Australia; some of the later papers, in fact, also give details of parents, marriage, children, dates and places of settlement in Australia, and ability to read and speak English. In short, the papers give a condensed biography of each migrant up till the time of naturalization—for most southern Europeans, from ten to fifteen years after arrival. The information provided by the 10,500 naturalization papers examined, together with additional material obtained from selected migrant groups and individuals, provides the basis for the Australian part of this book; it also throws much light on the European end of the story—the endpaper map, for instance, is based on this material, as are the statistics set out in Table I.[20]

What, then, is the outline that emerges from this type of survey? Does it permit us to make any useful generalizations about

[19] Lyng, *Non-Britishers in Australia*; Borrie, *Italians and Germans in Australia*.

[20] For further details of the naturalization records, together with an assessment of their representativeness and reliability, see Appendix 1.

pre-war southern European settlers as a whole? Essentially, these are the questions this book sets out to answer. The logical beginning is with the geographic and social background.

The first matter of geographical interest to emerge is that only approximately 4 per cent of settlers came from the great plains—the Po valley, the Danube-Drava plains, the Catanian plain in Sicily; the remainder came from the coast, the coastal slopes, or from inland hills and mountains (see migration areas on end-paper map and Table II). This pattern is of considerable importance to any understanding of the nature of southern European migration and settlement in Australia.[21]

The second matter of interest (see map) is that slightly more than half the total of settlers have come from small islands or the coast (defining 'coast' as a belt of land varying from five to seven miles inland from the sea), the rest have come from districts farther inland. This high proportion of islanders and coastal peoples—apparently very much higher than in southern European migration to America[22]—is of considerable significance: not only may persons living near the coast lead a somewhat different economic and social existence from those farther inland but they often tend to take up trading and sailing—a tendency of paramount importance in the early stages of migration to a country as remote as Australia.

The third important matter is that, when migrants are divided into those who come from 'villages' (or 'small towns') of less than 10,000 inhabitants and those who come from 'towns' or 'cities' of 10,000 persons and more, some 82 per cent of pre-war southern European settlers seem to have come from villages and small towns and only 18 per cent or so from towns and cities, and of the latter about two-thirds—12 per cent of the total—came from coastal towns and ports.[23] This means that southern European migration to Australia contained relatively few labour-

[21] For an elaboration of 'habitation districts' see Chapter II.

[22] The European migrant stream to America contained a relatively high proportion of persons from the inland districts of Abruzzi-Molise, Basilicata, Arcadia, and elsewhere.

[23] A 'village' of 10,000 may seem unduly large in Australia or the United States, where the terms of C. P. Loomis and J. A. Beagle may be more appropriate—a village is less than 1,000; a town between 1,000 and 2,500, a city more than 2,500 (*Rural Social Systems*). But the multifarious administrative conditions of Europe and the tendency of the agricultural population to form very large residential centres—there are, for example, some towns in Apulia of 50,000—preclude any such division in this book, where the distinction between village (or small town) and towns or cities, though perhaps sociologically crude, is preserved.

ers, tradesmen, and professional men from the large industrial and commercial towns but was essentially a 'peasant' migration from coastal and inland villages.[24] The consequences of this are important—so important that they require special consideration. Indeed, it would probably be as well at this point to make a much more detailed analysis of the whole social and geographic background.

There is, however, a general difficulty about background chapters that is of great importance in works on migration: the difficulty of describing the physical or social structure in its entirety, with the result that some writers, often influenced by personal recollections and interests, tend to select only a few of the characteristics concerned. Strictly speaking, every physical and social trait of the place of origin has some relevance in the country of settlement: the dilemma is to find and expose that relevance within reasonable confines. Unfortunately, the dilemma is not solved in this book—anthropologists, geographers, or economists will no doubt find missing things they consider important enough for special mention; it claims only to have attempted to cover those background characteristics of the districts of origin that seem to the writer relevant to this particular survey.

Before embarking on a detailed description of these areas of origin it may be as well to recollect precisely what they are by consulting the endpaper map and Table II, which tabulates all the places of origin except districts of origin of the Portuguese, Spanish, and southern French, since precise information on them is at present lacking. Likewise, in the discussion following the table the proportions and generalizations will relate to the southern European total less these three countries of origin. More detailed information on Portugal, Spain, and South France is unlikely to upset these generalizations, however, partly because Portuguese, Spanish, and southern French have been so small a part of the total migration from southern Europe—approximately $2\frac{1}{2}$ per cent by 1947—and partly because the information we do have about migrants from these countries matches the generalizations induced from migration from other countries.

---

[24] The term 'peasant' has here no special restricted meaning such as is given it by some economists, lawyers, and anthropologists; it is used simply in its general and historical sense to denote members of the labouring class who do not have urban occupations—i.e. the class distinct from urban labourers on the one hand and country gentry on the other. In this sense it covers most of the migrants we have noted as coming from villages and small rural towns—at least 75% of Australia's pre-war southern European total.

C

TABLE II

MALE SETTLERS IN AUSTRALIA 1890-1940

Districts of Origin						No.	%
NORTH ITALIANS							
Bergamasque Alpine Valleys							
Valtellina (Sondrio)	..	..	..	..	..	3,700	7·8
Val Camonica (Brescia)	..	..	..	..	..	900	1·9
Val Seriana (Bergamo)	..	..	..	..	..	400	0·8
					Total	5,000	10·5
Venetian Alps and Foothills							
Trentino	..	..	..	..	..	300	0·6
Cadore	..	..	..	..	..	320	0·7
Feltre area ..	..	..	..	..	..	300	0·6
Asiago plateau	..	..	..	..	..	600	1·3
Mt Lessini ..	..	..	..	..	..	150	0·3
Foothills of Verona, Vicenza, Treviso ..			..	..	..	2,050	4·3
Friuli foothills	..	..	..	..	..	750	1·6
					Total	4,470	9·4
Other Alpine Areas							
Piedmontese	..	..	..	..	..	420	0·9
Other	..	..	..	..	..	180	0·4
					Total	600	1·3
Monferrato-Langhe Hills							
Monferrato	..	..	..	..	..	1,355	2·8
Langhe	..	..	..	..	..	190	0·4
					Total	1,545	3·2
Emilian Hills ..	..	..	..	..	..	180	0·4
Northern Plain							
Piedmont	..	..	..	..	..	100	0·2
Lombardy ..	..	..	..	..	..	550	1·2
(Ostiglia	..	..	..	..	..	270	0·6)
Veneto	..	..	..	..	..	200	0·4
Friuli	..	..	..	..	..	250	0·5
Emilia	..	..	..	..	..	55	0·1
					Total	1,155	2·4
Coastal Regions							
Ligurian	..	..	..	..	..	250	0·5
Emilian	..	..	..	..	..	10	..
Venetian	..	..	..	..	..	200	0·4
					Total	460	1·0
					TOTAL NORTH	13,410	28·1

Districts of Origin	No.	%

CENTRAL ITALIANS

Apuan Alps	710	1·5
Other inland	360	0·8
Coastal	310	0·6
(Elba	180	0·4)
TOTAL CENTRAL	1,380	2·9

SOUTH ITALIANS

Abruzzi-Campanian Hills

Abruzzi Valleys	300	0·6
Gargano Promontory	290	0·6
Campanian Hills	420	0·9
Viggiano Valley	250	0·5
Total	1,260	2·6

Campanian-Apulian Coast

Campanian..	300	0·6
Apulian	665	1·4
(Molfetta	620	1·3)
Total	965	2·0

Calabrian Inland

Sila area	130	0·3
Le Serre— } N. Aspromonte }	1,335	2·8
Total	1,465	3·1

Calabrian Coast

Reggio province	960	2·0
Other	90	0·2
Total	1,050	2·2
TOTAL SOUTH	4,740	9·9

INSULAR ITALIANS

Lipari Isles (officially in Messina province, Sicily)

Lipari	650	1·4
Salina	850	1·8
Stromboli, Alicudi, Filicudi, Panarea	500	1·0
Total	2,000	4·2

Districts of Origin							No.	%
INSULAR ITALIANS—*Continued*								
Sicily								
Nth Messina	..	..	..	..	..	..	1,135	2·4
(Coast	..	..	..	..	..	..	935	2·0)
Mt Etna (Nth Catania)	..	..	..	..	..		1,850	3·9
(Coast	..	..	..	..	..	..	1,700	3·6)
Mt Iblei (Sth Catania-Syracuse)			..	..	..		400	0·8
Poggioreale (Trapani)	..	..	..	..	..		150	0·3
Other inland	..	..	..	..	..	..	160	0·3
Other coastal	..	..	..	..	..	..	220	0·5
						Total	3,915	8·2
Sardinia								
Inland	..	..	..	..	..	..	75	0·2
Coastal	..	..	..	..	..	..	160	0·3
						Total	235	0·5
					Total Insular		6,150	12·9
TOTAL ITALIANS	..	..	..	..	..	..	25,680	53·8
(Coastal	..	..	..	..	..	..	7,800	30·4)
(Inland	..	..	..	..	..	..	17,880	69·6)
ISLAND GREEKS								
Ionian Isles								
Levkas (Santa Maura)	..	..	..	..	..		250	0·5
Ithaca	..	..	..	..	..	..	860	1·8
Kythera	..	..	..	..	..	..	2,200	4·6
Others	..	..	..	..	..	..	180	0·4
						Total	3,490	7·3
Cyclades (Kiklades)								
Syros	..	..	..	..	..	..	80	0·2
Andros	..	..	..	..	..	..	60	0·1
Paros	..	..	..	..	..	..	60	0·1
Others	..	..	..	..	..	..	60	0·1
						Total	260	0·5
Aegean Isles								
Lemnos	..	..	..	..	..	..	140	0·3
Lesbos (Mytilene)	..	..	..	..	..		300	0·6
Chios	..	..	..	..	..	..	240	0·5
Samos	..	..	..	..	..	..	310	0·6
Icaria (Nicaria)	..	..	..	..	..		100	0·2
Others	..	..	..	..	..	..	140	0·3
						Total	1,230	2·6

Districts of Origin							No.	%
ISLAND GREEKS—*Continued*								
Dodecanese Isles								
Symi	..	..	..	..	..	..	120	0·3
Rhodes	..	..	..	..	..	..	200	0·4
Karpathos (Scarpanto)	..	..	..	..	..	60	0·1
Kastellorizo (Megiste)	..	..	..	..	..	1,290	2·7
Others	..	..	..	..	..	..	90	0·2
						Total	1,760	3·7
Evvoia (Euboea)	..	..	..	..	..	..	340	0·7
Crete (Kriti)	..	..	..	..	..	..	190	0·4
Cyprus ..	..	..	..	..	..	..	495	1·0
					Total Islands		7,765	16·3
MAINLAND AND OTHER GREEKS								
Peloponnesus (Morea)								
Argolis	..	..	..	..	..	..	65	0·1
Vatika Bay	..	..	..	..	..	..	130	0·3
Sparta area	..	..	..	..	..	..	115	0·2
Tripolis basin	..	..	..	..	..	..	175	0·4
Akrata	..	..	..	..	..	..	160	0·3
Aigion (Aegium)	..	..	..	..	..	45	0·1
Others	..	..	..	..	..	..	100	0·2
						Total	790	1·7
Other Mainland								
Athens-Piraeus	..	..	..	..	..	..	600	1·3
Salonica	..	..	..	..	..	..	60	0·1
Kozani, Edessa, etc.	..	..	..	..	..	50	0·1
Epirus	..	..	..	..	..	..	90	0·2
Others	..	..	..	..	..	..	120	0·3
						Total	920	1·9
Turkey, etc.								
Turkish Thrace	..	..	..	..	..	..	110	0·2
Constantinople	..	..	..	..	..	..	120	0·3
Smyrna	..	..	..	..	..	..	190	0·4
Other Asia Minor	..	..	..	..	..	145	0·3
Syria	..	..	..	..	..	..	20	..
Egypt	..	..	..	..	..	..	130	0·3
Rumania	..	..	..	..	..	..	40	0·1
Russia	..	..	..	..	..	..	30	0·1
						Total	785	1·6
	Total Mainland and Other Greeks						2,495	5·2
TOTAL GREEKS	..	..	..	..	..	..	10,260	21·5
(Coastal	..	..	..	..	..	..	9,640	94·0)
(Inland	..	..	..	..	..	..	620	6·0)

Districts of Origin	No.	%
SOUTH SLAVS		
Slovenia		
Trieste	60	0·1
Other	90	0·2
Total	150	0·3
Croatia-Slavonia		
Istria	90	0·2
Isles	80	0·2
Rijecka (Fiume)	60	0·1
Other coastal	150	0·3
Medjumurje	200	0·4
Other inland	60	0·1
Total	640	1·3
Northern Dalmatia		
Zadar area (Zara)	40	0·1
Šibenik area (Sebenico)	130	0·3
Prvić isle	105	0·2
Total	275	0·6
Central Dalmatia		
Split area	95	0·2
Makarska area	690	1·4
Vrgorac area	425	0·9
Metković area	70	0·1
Pelješac peninsula	180	0·4
Hvar isle	185	0·4
Vis isle	190	0·4
Korčula isle	600	1·3
Brač	70	0·1
Other isles	170	0·4
Total	2,675	5·6
South Dalmatia		
Dubrovnik area	170	0·4
Kotor area (Cattaro)	110	0·2
Total	280	0·6
Boznia-Herzegovina	90	0·2
Montenegro	140	0·3
Serbia	80	0·2

Districts of Origin	No.	%
SOUTH SLAVS—*Continued*		
*Macedonia**		
Bitola-Ohrid	190	0·4
Florina area	670	1·4
Kastoria area	370	0·8
Other	60	0·1
Total	1,290	2·7
Bulgaria		
Tirnova	210	0·4
Shumen (Kolarovgrad)	70	0·1
Others	110	0·2
Total	390	0·8
TOTAL SOUTH SLAVS	6,010	12·6
(Coastal	3,730	62·1)
(Inland	2,280	37·9)
ALBANIANS		
Gjinokastër area	175	0·4
Korçë area	1,080	2·3
Other inland	25	..
Total	1,280	2·7
MALTESE		
Malta and Gozo	2,600	5·4
SPANISH, PORTUGUESE, Sth FRENCH	1,900	4·0
Coastal	25,130	52·7
Inland	22,600	47·3
GRAND TOTAL	47,730	100·0
Islands (excluding Sicily and Sardinia)	14,300	30·0
Islands (excluding Sicily, Sardinia, Crete, and Cyprus) ..	13,615	28·5

Note: For the derivation of these statistics see Appendix 1: 19-21. The proportions in this table are given to the nearest place of decimals and are designed to show what proportion each place of origin contributed to the total of southern European settlers in Australia. Consequently they are not artificially rounded; percentages for particular places therefore do not always add to the sub-total percentage. Coastal and inland percentages are designed to show what proportion of the migration stream from any main area of origin came from coastal and inland districts; consequently these are not based on the Grand Total but on the relevant sub-total and under each heading add to 100.

* For reasons why these areas are grouped as Macedonia and not as parts of Bulgaria, Greece or Yugoslavia see pp. 4-5.

CHAPTER II

GEOGRAPHICAL BACKGROUND[1]

The horrid crags, by toppling convent crown'd,
The cork-trees hoar that clothe the shaggy steep,
The mountain-moss by scorching skies imbrown'd,
The sunken glen, whose sunless shrubs must weep,
The tender azure of the unruffled deep,
The orange tints that gild the greenest bough,
The torrents that from cliff to valley leap,
The vine on high, the willow branch below,
Mix'd in one mighty scene, with varied beauty glow.

Childe Harold's Pilgrimage, I, 19

OF pre-war immigrants from southern Europe some 20 per cent
came from industrial and commercial towns and only 4 per cent
came from the great plains; the rest, over three-quarters of the
total, were villagers from rugged mountains and hills or from
steep coastlines and islands. This is not really surprising, for
by and large southern Europe is a rugged broken land. In some
places great earth movements of the past have forced up high
mountain chains, as in the Alpine regions of northern Italy,
where subsequent erosion has produced broken plateaux and
slopes, steep mountain valleys, or long narrow U-shaped valleys
with relatively flat surfaces hemmed in by enormous cliffs on
either side: about 10 per cent of pre-war southern Europeans in
Australia came from the plateaux, valleys, and foothills of the
Venetian Alps, and well over 10 per cent from the great ice-cut
valleys of the Bergamasque Alps in north-eastern Lombardy—
the Valtellina, Val Camonica, and Val Seriana. Farther south
these earth movements created the Appenines of central and
southern Italy and the Dinaric, Pindus, and Balkan mountains
of the Balkan peninsula: from the broken plateaux and valleys

[1] This chapter is based mainly on the official censuses and annual statistics
of the countries concerned, the Geographic Handbooks Series produced by
the Royal Naval Intelligence Division during the 1940s (hereinafter called
R.N.G.H.S.), and interviews with numerous migrants now settled in Australia.
A useful general survey is M. I. Newbigin, *Southern Europe*.

of these regions came some 15 per cent of southern European
immigrants—notably from the Apuan Alps of Tuscany, from the
Gargano Promontory and the hills of Campania and Basilicata,
from the Sila and Aspromonte mountains of Calabria, from
the wild country round Lakes Ohrid and Prespa in south-eastern
Albania and south-western Macedonia, and from the Balkan
uplands of Bulgaria.[2] Elsewhere these earth movements forced
up stretches of limestone in which subsequent faulting and
erosion have hollowed out large sink-basins—flat-floored basins
almost entirely surrounded by high steep hills—as at Aquila and
Sulmona in the Abruzzi region of central Italy, at various places
in the 'karst' country of Yugoslavia, and at Tripolis in the
Peloponnesus of Greece. Though the bulk of migrants from these
constricted areas have gone to America, a number, perhaps 1 per
cent of the southern European migrant total, have come to
Australia.

Great mountain building movements of the past have often
been accompanied or succeeded by submergence, which has resulted in the Mediterranean region in steep-sided gulfs, bays,
and promontories, as well as the numerous peninsulas and
islands, the survivors of ancient peaks and chains. Occasionally
volcanic eruptions have accompanied these activities, forcing
up islands such as the Lipari isles of north-eastern Sicily, and
Thera and Lesbos in the Aegean, or building up vast coastal
mountains such as Vesuvius and Etna. The destruction to lives
and property caused by earthquakes and volcanoes is one reason
why many southern Europeans have left their homeland for the
United States and Australia. From certain districts of these
broken shores and islands came many thousands of pre-war
migrants to Australia. Some 24 per cent came from the narrow
coastal shelves and slopes of the mainland and larger islands—
Sardinia, Sicily, Crete, and Cyprus—principally from the coastal
strip of Messina and Catania in north-eastern Sicily, the coastal
areas of Reggio Calabria, the Adriatic fringes of central Apulia
and central Dalmatia, and from the coastal regions of Spain,
southern France, and Greece. Even more—about 28 per cent in
all—came from the smaller archipelagos and islands, mainly
from the Lipari isles off Sicily, from the British possessions of
Malta and Gozo, from the isles of central Dalmatia, from the
Ionian islands of Ithaca and Kythera, and from the microscopic
little Dodecanese island of Kastellorizo off the south-western

2 For the exact figures of these and other districts see Table II.

corner of Turkey. Altogether, well over half Australia's pre-war southern European population was derived from the Mediterranean coasts and islands.

In the districts with which we are concerned the principal rocks have been hard resistant limestones, occasionally schists and gneisses. Erosion has worn away less resistant rocks, so that the terrain is often inhospitable—great tracts of rugged country interspersed with small fertile areas sheltered in some relatively small valley, basin, or bay. At times the cultivable area is extended by terracing, as on the steep hillsides of the Valtellina and other Alpine valleys, on the coastal slopes of Calabria, Sicily, and Dalmatia, and on many of the islands. But even expedients such as these cannot extend the productive land indefinitely, as is clear from the statistics of land under cultivation. Apart from a few exceptional islands such as Samos, Rhodes, Malta, and one or two of the Lipari isles, the majority of the eastern Mediterranean islands have less than one-fifth of their surface under cultivation; similarly with the central Dalmatian coast and islands and the Alpine and Pindus mountains. Messina and Reggio Calabria are somewhat better off, in some places having one-third or more under cultivation. Nevertheless the general picture is clearly one of restricted areas of fertility, or 'habitation-districts', separated from each other by broken mountainous country often highly unsuitable for roads and railways.

To these generalizations there are two principal exceptions. The Monferrato hills of Piedmont in north-western Italy, from which came some 3 per cent of southern European migrants including many of the Italian settlers of northern Queensland, are gently rounded hills of clays and marls; at least half the region is under cultivation for cereals or vines and much of the remainder is grassed for pasture. The second exception is the Mount Etna region of Catania, where fertile volcanic soil has enabled cultivation to extend some 4,000 feet up the mountain and has provided a more extensive region of habitation than the relatively narrow coastal strip of Messina farther north. Another possible exception is the strip of country in the Veneto where the Alpine outliers meet the plain; here about half the territory of the communes of origin is on the relatively barren limestone mountains and half on the more productive lower slopes and plain.

Despite geological differences, these three regions have features in common with the other districts and regions under consideration.[3] The most noticeable is the smallness of cultivation fields or plots, which derives from the terrain itself. Terracing, for example, especially when contained by numerous stone walls as protection against erosion, inevitably restricts the size of any one cultivation plot. In part, however, it derives from the system of inheritance prevalent throughout all the districts of origin during the years under review: on the death of a landed proprietor his property was divided equally between his children. This system was by no means uniform everywhere in our districts of origin: it usually held in the Medjumurje, but in Kythera, as in other places where family responsibilities to the daughters were discharged when they were provided with a handsome dowry of money or movable goods, the land was usually divided between the male children only; and on the central Dalmatian coast it was possible—though apparently not very frequent—for a father to leave his land to one son only and compensate the remainder in other ways. Nevertheless, the effect was much the same throughout: land tended to become subdivided with each generation until in all our districts of origin, except perhaps the Korçë-Florina districts of Albania and Macedonia and the Basque lands of northern Spain, well over two-thirds of the properties were less than seven acres and many, as in the Aegean and Dalmatian islands or in the Valtellina, Reggio Calabria, and north-eastern Sicily, were less than three acres. Furthermore, the system led to further fragmentation because it normally required that each heir should receive a fair share of good arable, poor arable, orchard, vines, vegetable land, meadow flat, and so on, thereby producing a situation where one farmer might have

[3] In this work certain words are strictly used to denote the place from which migrants have come. 'Village' or 'town' denotes a particular hamlet, village, or town of origin. 'District' refers to a relatively small area that is centred on some market or administrative town or delimited by clear natural boundaries: small mountain areas such as the Monferrato hills or Apuan Alps, most Alpine valleys, limestone sink-basins such as Tripolis, peninsulas, and all islands (except Sicily, Sardinia, Evvoia, Crete and Cyprus, which are large enough to be treated as regions). 'Districts', so defined, often override administrative boundaries: the Mount Etna district of origin, for example, includes the villages in the south-east corner of Messina province as well as the townships of north Catania. 'Regions' refer to areas containing several districts and distinguished by larger differences of geography, history, dialect, social customs, etc. Groups of islands—e.g. the Ionian, the Lipari, or the Dodecanese—count as regions, as do the larger islands mentioned above; so also do areas such as the Greek Peloponnesus, or larger mountain regions such as the Alps of Lombardy or the mountains and foothills of the Veneto or Friuli. When some general term for place of origin is necessary, the words 'place', 'area', 'locality', are used.

several plots of half an acre or less scattered over a considerable area.

Closely connected with this fragmentation of cultivation plots is the 'garden' method of agriculture, which nearly all our districts of origin have had in common. For districts within the Mediterranean climatic zone (roughly delineated on the end-paper map by the line entitled northern limit of the olive) garden cultivation means the cultivation on small plots of annual crops such as cereals and vegetables, together with perennial fruit-trees and shrubs whose roots go deep enough to reach water during the dry season. These are principally vines, citrus, almonds, figs, and olives. Elsewhere it means the cultivation on small plots of cereals and vegetables in conjunction with perennial trees and shrubs capable of withstanding prolonged frost, principally vines, mulberries, apples, peaches, pears, and plums; or, as on the slopes of Mount Etna and in many parts of Dalmatia and Greece, of annual crops grown in plots separate from the vines and trees; or, in such places as the Veneto and Friuli, of cereals and vegetables grown in amongst the trees (*coltura promiscua*). Whatever the method used, the effect is much the same: the typical farmer or labourer, working on a small holding subdivided into still smaller cultivation plots, had a great variety of plants to tend and relatively little room in which to work; his technique, therefore, was that of a gardener—his principal tools, the spade and the pick, his primary source of power, himself. One Italian, indeed, commenting on this phenomenon, has suggested that when his fellow-countrymen migrated to America they readily turned to railway building since it involved little else but the pick and shovel, the implements on which they had been reared from childhood and with which they were happily familiar.[4] As one old Italian proverb puts it: 'The plough has a colter of iron but the spade has an edge of gold.'[5]

Methods of agriculture other than garden cultivation are common throughout southern Europe, particularly in the larger plains and in much of the plateau country of Spain, southern Italy, Sicily, and the Balkan states. But Australia, before 1940, received practically no migrants from areas such as these. The one important region of origin where the garden system might be said not to predominate is in the mountainous country around Korçë and Florina. Yet even here, despite the high proportion of cereals grown as compared with fruit, the subdivision of plots

4 C. M. Panunzio, *The Soul of an Immigrant*, p. 77.
5 Quoted by R. F. Foerster, *The Italian Emigration of our Times*, p. 116.

and the relatively large quantities of vegetables and grapes produced by many holdings demonstrate the importance of garden
agriculture.

Agricultural proprietors and labourers in the principal districts of origin did not, however, confine their activities exclusively to cultivating the soil. Most farmers kept poultry near the
home, as well as a number of cows, sheep, goats, and pigs, which
they grazed in special meadow plots or in the forests, scrub, and
poorly-grassed rocky areas beyond the zone of cultivation. This
form of grazing is very important in the mountains, though it
is only the more healthy members of the family—especially in
harder regions such as the Bergamasque Alps and south-western
Macedonia—who can survive the long periods of living in the
mountains, where they must follow the pasture grounds and
sleep in rude huts or out in the open.[6] Furthermore, many farm
proprietors and labourers spent part of their time fishing, more
particularly on the sea-coasts but also in the inland lakes and
rivers. Along the Adriatic coast, for example, many villagers living two or three miles from the sea regularly came down to the
beach and, in exchange for half the catch, helped to set and
haul in the nets. Many of them set night lines or indulged in
rock fishing during the off seasons in farming.

These extra activities—grazing, fishing, and keeping poultry—
may have been important, but they did not often oust cultivation
from its primary position. Rarely indeed were they important
enough to bring into existence substantial numbers of full-time
herdsmen, fishermen, or poultry farmers. In the 1930s, for instance, despite the lengthy coastlines, only $0 \cdot 47$ per cent of the
Italian and $0 \cdot 6$ per cent of the Greek working population were
engaged as full-time fishermen, most of them in areas beyond
those under review. In fact, of the districts in question the only
ones containing appreciable numbers of full-time fishermen
were Greek islands such as Syros, Kastellorizo, Symi, and Evvoia,
a few small towns and villages on the north coast of Messina in
Sicily, and the coastal towns round Molfetta on the Adriatic
shores of Apulia.[7] It is significant that from Symi and Evvoia
have come most of the Greeks who run the deep-sea fisheries of

[6] Mountain grazing, when it involves departure from the village for whole
seasons, becomes part of the general pastoral movement known as 'trans-
humance': see R.N.G.H.S., *Jugoslavia*, vol. III, App. II.

[7] Molfetta contains 40,000 inhabitants. Migrants from there are included
in the 18% from the larger towns, and are discussed here purely for convenience.

the Great Australian Bight from the little South Australian port of Thevenard; from North Messina and Molfetta, the bulk of those engaged in the deep-sea fisheries operating from Fremantle; from Molfetta, practically all the members of the large fishing community centred on Port Pirie in Spencer's Gulf. Back in the Mediterranean, however, even these groups of professional fishermen were often closely connected with the land, a number having small plots which they cultivated during the off seasons of fishing.

As with fishing so with herding. There were, however, numbers of shepherds and herdsmen not connected with the farming life of agricultural villages, perhaps the most interesting being the Vlachs, those Rumanian-speaking nomads who drive their flocks over the wild country of southern Albania, southern Macedonia, and northern Greece, living in permanent mountain villages during summer and in movable tent villages in the lowlands during winter. But Australia has received very few migrants from the Vlach country, except from the hills around Korçë, in south-eastern Albania, and even from here few Vlachs seem to have accompanied their Albanian neighbours to Australia.

The general picture, then, seems clear. Apart from one or two exceptional areas, all the districts under review have been places where cultivation of the land, usually by the garden system, played a most important part in the life of the villages and smaller towns and of almost every inhabitant. Most of the local artisans and tradesmen owned strips or plots of land, while in many smaller villages—more particularly in Greece—the postman, policeman, and other local officials were little more than small-scale agricultural proprietors or labourers supplementing their landed income by extra activities.[8]

A detailed description of the complicated social organization, values, and ambitions associated with this essentially 'peasant' background is unnecessary here.[9] It is sufficient to note that in such conditions there is often a tremendous desire for family self-sufficiency, for becoming independent landholders, for consolidation of property, for improving an estate that will be handed down from generation to generation. Not only has this

[8] R.N.G.H.S., *Greece*, vol. I, p. 338. In some parts of Greece even the local clergy supplemented their income by cultivating small properties: ibid., p. 333.

[9] For definition of 'peasant', see Chapter I, n. 24.

desire very largely determined the way European families have settled in Australia but it has lain behind much of the temporary emigration that paved the way for permanent settlement abroad. Some of the first southern European migrants to Australia were young men anxious to earn money for a year or two and then return home to rebuild the family farmhouse, put a new roof on the barn, clear their indebtedness, or purchase adjacent strips of land and so round off the family holding. Not all of these early migrants came intending to work in Australia. Some were young coastal and inland villagers who thought they could acquire the money needed by signing on for two or three years as a seaman on a long-distance sailing vessel. Several early Dalmatian, Greek, and Lipari island settlers first visited Australia in this way, virtually by accident; only after they had spent some weeks ashore while their ships were re-fitting did they think of earning money on the continent itself.[10]

Seafaring and trading are important features of life in our southern European places of origin. Despite those writers who stress the importance of 'peasant subsistence farming' in southern Europe, few of the districts we are examining were areas of rural self-sufficiency: most, indeed, were part of a highly organized exchange economy. Production for international trade may have been small—little more than wine, currants, fruit, olive oil, or cheese—but the districts themselves were engaged in active local trade. Those in the Mediterranean climatic zone, though they grew cereals alongside the vines and trees, found it necessary to import anything up to two-thirds of their cereals, as well as sugar, rice, coffee, and any industrial goods they could afford; in exchange they exported wine, fruit, olive oil, vegetables, and at times honey, butter, and cheese. Beyond the Mediterranean zone the districts imported cereals and other goods in exchange for wine, fruit, vegetables, chestnuts, cheese, livestock, or silk thread. The Monferrato hills and the Korçë-Florina region were more or less self-sufficient in cereals, so their exports were somewhat different: principally wine, cereals, and vegetables from the Monferrato hills and cereals and livestock from the Korçë-Florina region. (It is of interest here to note that not even these two regions of origin conformed to what some writers regard as the standard southern and eastern European pattern—'one-crop commercial agriculture, chiefly in the form of extensive cultivation of grain-crops'—which demonstrates the danger of endeav-

10 From interviews with descendants of these early settlers.

ouring to assess particular districts in terms of continental, national, or even provincial averages.)[11]

This local exchange system means that most villagers were more or less familiar with the rudimentary processes of marketing and exchange. In most districts there was one market-town, to which one or more members of each family tended to make regular expeditions to barter or to sell. In Kythera, for example, the villagers came from many parts of the island every Sunday to the little town of Potamos to sell vegetables, poultry, livestock, cheese, olives, or grapes in exchange for flour and other goods; in some ways the occasion was as much a social gathering as an economic activity. Similarly, on the central Dalmatian coast and in the hill country of south-eastern Albania and south-western Macedonia the villagers came regularly into Makarska, Zaostrog, Korçë, Bitola, Florina, or Kastoria, carrying or driving their produce as far as ten or twelve miles. In parts of South Italy, such as the Gargano Promontory in Apulia or the Viggiano district of Basilicata, where the population of the district lived in one large town rather than in villages distributed around a market centre, the position was somewhat different: market activities took place within the one urban concentration.

Market-towns do not control the entire trade of these areas—itinerant hawkers, for instance, or travelling dealers in skins and hides were common in many parts of southern Europe. But whatever the exchange system the important fact remains: by and large the rural population of our districts of origin had some experience of buying and selling, of striking a bargain, or handling money. The rustic in these southern European districts, as in so many other parts of the world, may have been crude and uneducated, but he was not necessarily simple or inexperienced in matters of trade.

One of the most fascinating aspects of trade in southern Europe deserves further attention—coastal trading along the shores of the Mediterranean. This, of course, is not a recent phenomenon. The long indented coastlines, the unusually large number of islands, the difficulty of travelling by land over rough mountainous country: all these have influenced the Mediterranean peoples from the very earliest days and have encouraged,

11 W. E. Moore, *Economic Demography of Eastern and Southern Europe*, p. 94. The importance of this work is its insistence on the wide spread of commercial agriculture, not subsistence agriculture, in the so-called 'peasant countries' of Europe.

indeed enforced, the development of vigorous trading between the villages and small townships of the coastal regions.[12] Sometimes this has been little more than a part-time activity—fishermen on periodic trips to coastal market-towns, the unloading of larger vessels, the ferrying of passengers—but sometimes, especially before steamships and motor-boats undermined the supremacy of small vessels, it was quite an important business. Particularly well known were some of the small villages and towns of the Greek islands. Andros and Ithaca, neither of which has townships containing more than 5,000 persons,[13] became quite famous for large-scale seafaring activities during the nineteenth century and even in 1938, in terms of tonnage registered, were still second and fifth respectively in the list of all Greek ports. Kastellorizo, too, exploiting its position as the only safe harbour between Beirut and Makri (on the mainland opposite Rhodes), developed a considerable small-scale entrepôt trade, principally the exchange of wood, charcoal, and pine-bark from the nearby ports of Asia Minor for rice, sugar, coffee, grain, and textiles from Egypt and elsewhere. In much the same way the small coastal villages and towns on the Dalmatian islands of Hvar, Vis, and Korčula developed considerable coastal trading—an activity they trace back to their days as the ancient Greek colonies of Pharos, Issa, and Corcyra Nigra. Many of the small coastal towns of north-eastern Sicily and the Lipari islands also have long histories of local sailing and trading.

Despite their considerable coastal trade, these small coastal villages did not contain large numbers of people devoted exclusively to commerce and sailing. The trading and seafaring population, like the fishing and artisan population, tended to retain its mixed character—families devoting themselves partly to agriculture and pasturing and partly to trading and sailing; even full-time sailors on overseas vessels tended to retain their ties with the land.

Kastellorizo is one of the exceptions to these generalizations. An island of four square miles, less than one-quarter of which is under cultivation, is not likely to carry a population of nearly 10,000 persons without an appreciable number losing their ties with the land; and there is evidence to suggest that a large

[12] On 'village' and 'small town' see p. 16 above.
[13] At the 1928 census the largest townships on Ithaca and Andros contained 3,265 and 2,069 persons respectively—a slight fall from the population present early in the century, largely because of emigration.

proportion of Kastellorizan migrants to Australia came from families devoted to seafaring and the entrepôt trade.[14]

Not unlike Kastellorizo were the medium-sized coastal towns —between 10,000 and 25,000 in population—which have so far not been discussed because they do not fall within our definition of 'villages' and 'small towns'. Milazzo in Messina (Sicily), Palmi in Reggio Calabria, Šibenik, Makarska, and Dubrovnik in Dalmatia; Mytilene (Lesbos), Chios, Syros, and Rhodes on various islands of the Aegean Sea, belong in this class. Taken by and large they have developed a small industrial population—mainly engaged in processing agricultural produce—and an appreciable merchant and seafaring class. Perhaps the most famous are Syros and Dubrovnik. Before the comparatively recent rise to importance of the Athenian port of Piraeus, Syros was for many centuries the principal port of Greece, the meeting-place of sea-routes from the western Mediterranean to the Black Sea and from Salonica and Constantinople to Crete and Africa; it was also, like the ancient town of Delos, the centre of the entrepôt trade of many Aegean islands. Dubrovnik, perhaps better known as Ragusa, was founded in the seventh century A.D. by refugees from barbarian raids farther south; it subsequently developed into so important a centre for shipbuilding and commerce that it was able to maintain virtual independence from both Venetian and Turkish empires and send its vessels into all parts of the world. So wealthy did the town become that English sailors of the sixteenth and seventeenth centuries became accustomed to call any of its well-laden vessels an 'Aragusa' or 'Argosy'.

From such medium-sized coastal towns have come some 5 per cent of Australia's pre-war southern European population—a little over one-quarter of the migrants who originated in places other than villages and small townships. Not all migrants from such places came from industry, trade, or seafaring, however. But to discover this it is necessary to find out whether the migrants have come from the town itself or from the rural areas surrounding it. Until recent years the towns were usually small walled citadels containing the factories, warehouses, and homes of the industrial and seafaring classes, but the administrative

14 The N.S.W. marriage records show that of all Kastellorizan migrants married in that state between 1900 and 1940 over 52% gave their father's occupation as 'seaman' or 'sea-captain'—about three times as high a proportion as any other Greek place of origin. This confirms the statements of Kastellorizans interviewed in N.S.W.

boundaries of the city or commune usually took in much of the surrounding countryside, with its cultivation plots, orchard terraces, pasture grounds, local fisheries, and all the people engaged therein. Thus, for example, the town of Šibenik contained about 18,000 persons in 1931, but the whole commune contained 37,000 or more.

The same considerations apply to medium-sized inland towns. Casale Monferrato, for instance, has an urban population of about 25,000 but a commune population of nearly 40,000. In addition to the rural populace, such inland communes contained an appreciable industrial class—primarily engaged in manufacturing wine, paper, cork, silk, or shoes—and a commercial and administrative class which controlled the trade and administration of the surrounding villages and townships. Inland cities such as these did not contribute greatly to Australia's pre-war southern European population—probably about 2 per cent of the whole.

Yet one step further away from the small villages and townships are the large commercial and industrial towns of more than 25,000. Of these the coastal towns were more important—Barcelona, Marseilles, Genoa, Leghorn, Naples, Molfetta, Venice, Trieste, Rijecka (Fiume), Split, Athens-Piraeus, Salonica, Constantinople, Smyrna, Valetta, Alexandria, and Port Said. These have given Australia nearly 8 per cent of its southern Europeans, the most prolific (excluding Barcelona and Marseilles) being Molfetta, Athens, and Valetta. Large inland cities such as Turin, Alessandria, Milan, Brescia, Vicenza, Adrianople, Zagreb, and Belgrade provided less than 4 per cent of pre-war southern Europeans, but there are signs that they have been contributing more strongly to the flow of migrants since 1947.

At this stage there is little to note about these larger towns except that many persons born in them were not of old city stock but were the children of parents recently moved in from remoter districts. Milan, Brescia, Vicenza, and other towns of northern Italy contained many families who had been moving in from the Alpine valleys and foothills over several decades. Athens, Constantinople, Smyrna, and Port Said, too, often housed families from islands such as Kythera, Ithaca, Rhodes and Kastellorizo. This phenomenon—which manifested itself strongly during the late nineteenth and early twentieth centuries when many towns were growing unusually rapidly at the expense of other areas—was at times of considerable importance to southern European migration: persons moving to urban zones tended to maintain close contact with their relatives in the country and occasionally joined, or even initiated, a migrant stream flowing to the outer world from some particular rural district. In this sense the 12 per cent of migrants who came from the great cities of southern Europe were made up of two streams: those from old city families who were influenced by generations of city life, and those from rural families not long in the city and who carried the associations and influences of life in the country. For this reason it is important, though usually very difficult, to group migrants from large urban centres not only by their own place of birth but by the birthplace of their parents also.

The remainder of Australia's pre-war immigrants—those from inland agricultural villages and townships—were numerically few but they include two most interesting groups. One is from the Medjumurje, the small triangle of country lying between the rivers Mur and Drava in north-western Croatia, where the land is devoted to mixed farming—cereals, dairy, fruit, and vines —and where garden cultivation predominates because the inheritance system has enforced subdivision into numerous small holdings. The great majority of migrants from this area have settled as horticultural farmers on the irrigation blocks of the River Murray between Mildura in Victoria and Barmera in South Australia. The other interesting group is from the commune of Ostiglia on the River Po, in Mantua province, Lombardy. This township and district was primarily concerned with the production and processing of rice, sugar-beet, wheat and livestock, and differed from most of the other areas of origin in that there were numerous large holdings where cultivation could proceed on a capitalistic basis quite unlike the garden system prevalent elsewhere. The great majority of these migrants have settled on sugar-farms in the Ingham-Halifax district of Queensland.

This general discussion of villages and cities of origin has so far ignored the fact that there are different kinds of villages and cities: the compact settlement where numerous families live very close to one another, the small village or hamlet of a few adjacent homes,[15] the wide scatter of isolated homesteads, and so on. These differences, however, may sometimes be important in the

15 The sociological and precise numerical significance sometimes attributed to 'hamlet' in England and America (see e.g. C. P. Loomis and T. A. Beegle, *Rural Social Systems*; Stanley Baron (ed.), *Country Towns in the Future England*) are not preserved in this book, where the word is used to indicate a small village of less than 200 inhabitants.

story of migration, since there is a not infrequent connection between the mode of settlement in Europe and the way in which migrants react to conditions in Australia. The whole topic of settlement is, however, a gateway to the multifarious territory of social customs, political background, cultural traditions, which are discussed in detail later.

CHAPTER III

SOCIAL AND POLITICAL BACKGROUND

Ne city's towers pollute the lovely view;
Unseen is Yanina, though not remote,
Veil'd by the screen of hills: here men are few,
Scanty the hamlet, rare the lonely cot . . .

There is a pleasure in the pathless woods,
There is a rapture on the lonely shore,
There is society where none intrudes,
By the deep Sea, and music in its roar.

Childe Harold's Pilgrimage, II, 52; IV, 178

NUCLEAR SETTLEMENT

Byron's preference for the wilder parts of Italy and Greece, the rugged peaks and savage glens, the lonely woods and empty shores, was not, for domestic purposes at any rate, shared by the inhabitants of those places prolific of migrants for Australia. Many pre-war southern European migrants, so far from leaving lonely cottages dispersed amongst the hills, came from places where the countryside is virtually devoid of any home because the population has gathered itself together in 'nuclear settlements': compact residential areas of relatively small extent.

There are other kinds of habitation in southern Europe: in quite extensive parts of central Italy and of the Italian and Dinaric Alps isolated homesteads are the norm and villages are often little more than collectivities of farmhouses dispersed over several miles square. Very few pre-war migrants, however, came from these regions of dispersed habitation; the great majority derived from areas where nuclear processes had been operating strongly for many centuries.

There are, it is true, certain intermediate or 'mixed' types of settlement, part way between the dispersed and the nuclear, and from these Australia derived a small proportion of its migrants. In the islands of Andros, Vis, and Salina, and in Lipari (see Fig. 1) and in parts of the Valtellina, coastal Catalonia, and the Basque lands it is usual to find compact towns, villages, or hamlets interspersed with numerous farmhouses standing in their

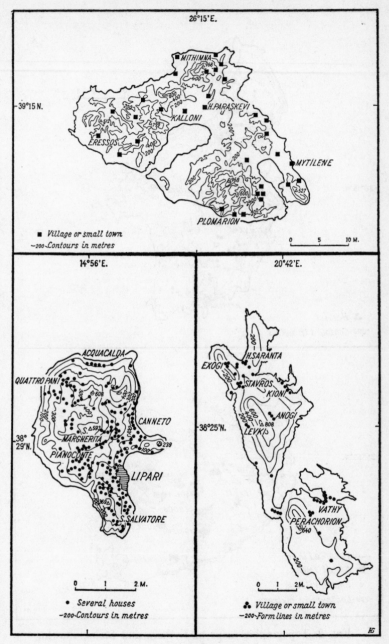

FIG. 1—Topographic maps of Lesbos, Lipari and Ithaca, showing patterns of settlement.

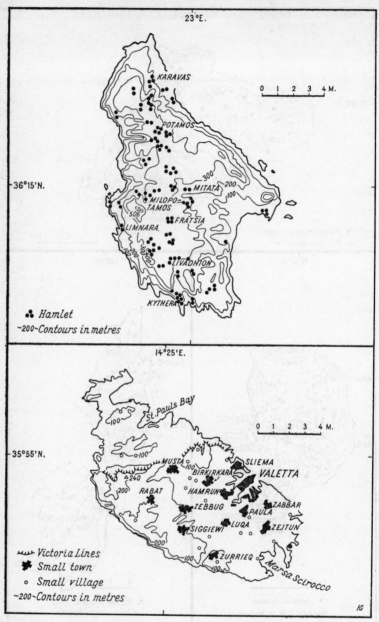

FIG. 2—Topographic maps of Kythera and Malta, showing patterns of settlement.

own grounds. Perhaps some 15 per cent of migrants came from areas such as these.

Much closer to the nuclear pattern are districts where the settlement is technically 'mixed' but where the properties are so small and the houses so frequent that they form an almost continuous zone of habitation. This occurs in the districts around Capo d'Orlando and Milazzo on the north coast of Messina, Sicily, in the almost unbroken strip of habitation down the coast of east Messina and north-east Catania, or in the very densely settled district round Valencia in coastal Spain. In these areas the density of population rises to well over 1,000 per square mile, and in social proximity and intercourse the settlements are virtually identical with compact villages or towns. About 5 per cent of migrants came from districts of this kind.

The simplest nuclear settlements are in areas where the population live in small compact villages or hamlets, each separated by some appreciable distance. The island of Kythera—see Fig. 2 —is an interesting example; it contained over one hundred small villages, most of which, between 1890 and 1940, had less than 100 inhabitants. Kythera town itself, the capital of the island, had less than 1,000 inhabitants in 1928. Other districts of origin—notably the Dalmatian coast to the south of Dubrovnik and parts of the Asiago Plateau and the Cadore in the Venetian Alps—have a few larger villages or towns dotted amongst the numerous small nuclear villages and hamlets. About 10 per cent of migrants came from these or similar districts.

The remainder of Australia's rural southern Europeans (some 50 per cent of all the migrants) derived from places where small villages have been less important and numerous than substantial and compact villages and towns. Most of the Greek islands fall into this category—cf. Lesbos and Ithaca (Fig. 1)—as do Malta, Macedonia, the Medjumurje, the greater part of the Dalmatian coast and isles, the bulk of the Italian Alpine valleys and foothills, the Monferrato, and the greater part of southern Italy, Sicily, Catalonia, and other parts of Spain. An extreme form of this kind of nucleation is the Apulian region of Italy; around Molfetta, for example, the population of nearly 110,000 occupies a roughly rectangular area of some eighty square miles and is collected into the five residential centres: Molfetta (49,000), Bitonto (27,000), Terlizzi (17,000), Giovinazzo (12,500), and Sovereto (about 2,000).

Thus, if the 18 per cent of migrants from larger towns and cities are included, some 75 per cent came from substantial nuclear villages or towns, 10 per cent from areas dominated by small nuclear settlements, and 15 per cent from districts where numerous isolated homes are interspersed among the nuclear villages and towns.

The reasons for this predominance of substantial nuclear settlements are highly interesting and not at all irrelevant to migration. The first can be summed up in three words: banditry, piracy, war. In the turbulent conditions that preceded and followed the break-up of the Roman Empire people naturally came together for protection, usually on small defensible hillsites easily surrounded by walls and protected by castle-towers; ancient walled towns of this kind abound throughout our areas of origin. Nor did this turbulence subside so very long ago—except perhaps in northern Italy and southern France. Indeed, Australians and Americans, looking on Europe as the source of an ancient and relatively stable civilization, often fail to realize how large a part the forces of disruption have played in the social life of southern Europe, even in very recent times. Banditry flourished in Calabria and Sicily until well into the twentieth century, though in its later years it was perhaps less a scourge of the local peasantry than a weapon used by the more rebellious peasants against corrupt officials and rapacious middlemen.[1] In the Balkans, too, banditry was almost universal in the early nineteenth century, and in places such as Macedonia survived well into the twentieth century. In these countries, however, to the extent that banditry was associated with patriotic resistance to the Turks it became guerrilla warfare against foreign invaders, to which the Turks responded in kind by allowing the Spahis and other bands of irregular cavalry to roam the countryside looting and pillaging at will. Naturally, these continual disturbances made the peasantry reluctant to leave the protection of compact settlements, many of those, in the Danubian basin, coming into existence only during the last three centuries, largely as a safeguard against wandering bands of Spahis.

Near the coast there were other and more formidable foes than bandits, brigands, or armed irregulars. Today, when 'piracy' is virtually confined to historical romances and children's games, it is sometimes difficult to remember that only a few decades ago the Mediterranean seas floated numerous pirate craft for which the capture of a well-laden merchantman was only one activity: equally profitable were sudden descents on coastal

---

[1] Cf. Norman Douglas's description of the famous Calabrian bandit, Musolino, in *Old Calabria*.

settlements to loot homes, capture men for ransom, and abduct
women and children into slavery. Piracy has a long tradition in
the area. Pompey temporarily broke up the great pirate fleets
of the eastern Mediterranean in classical times, but many coastal
sites were gradually abandoned during subsequent centuries
when piracy was again rampant and anything but a strongly defended coastal town offered an inviting target. Accordingly, the
pattern of settlement along the Mediterranean littoral became
one of occasional fortified sea-towns interspersed with compact
towns or villages far enough inland to discourage any but the
most reckless pirates. As a result the coastal plains and slopes
were normally cultivated from villages farther inland while
local traders and fishermen could do little more than leave their
boats in some sheltered cove near the village; sometimes one of
these landing-places developed a few small wharves and sheds
and became known as a village port—*skala* in Greek, *marina* in
Italian.

In the western Mediterranean piracy reached its height in the
sixteenth and seventeenth centuries, after the pitiless expulsion
of the Moors from Spain led many of them to join the Barbary
corsairs and wreak revenge on Christendom from their haunts
at Algiers, Oran, Tunis, Tripoli and other points of vantage on
the north coast of Africa. These corsairs raided Ireland and Ice-
land, devastated the Madeiras, established a permanent post at
Ulcinj (south of Kotor) from which to ravage the Dalmatian and
Apulian coasts, and—in the words of a knowledgeable Christian
writer of the day—'utterly ruined and destroyed Sardinia, Cor-
sica, Sicily, Calabria, the neighbourhoods of Naples, Rome and
Genoa, all the Balearic islands, and the whole coast of Spain'.[2]
It was during this period that Sidi ben Muza, son of one of the
last Moorish defenders of Granada, nearly captured Pope Leo X
when that sea-breeze-loving pontiff was walking along a coastal
road near Rome. The people of Malta were somewhat better
protected, at any rate after 1530: in that year the Knights of St
John the Hospitaller (those dedicated enemies of the Prophet
who had recently been driven from their home in Rhodes by a
Sultan goaded beyond endurance by their incessant raids on
Turkish shipping) occupied the islands and relieved the hard-
pressed villagers by building massive forts and walls round the
harbour settlements and erecting along the coasts solid stone
watchtowers, from which the coastguards could give warning of

[2] Diego de Haedo, *Topographia e historia de Argel*, quoted S. Lane-Poole,
The Barbary Corsairs, p. 202.

corsair raids, not only to the villagers themselves but to the war-galleys ready at Valetta (see Fig. 2). Eventually the power of the Barbary corsairs declined, though they were still a distinct menace as late as 1830 when the French invasion of Algeria effectively closed most of their bases.

In the eastern Mediterranean piracy took a somewhat different course, being very largely a by-product of the disturbed conditions wherein Venetian and Genoese adventurers battled with the Byzantine—and later the Ottoman—Empire for control of the islands and coastal plains. Eventually, in the seventeenth and eighteenth centuries, the Greek islanders themselves took to piracy and during these centuries acquired the experience, the vessels, and the resources that enabled them to play so prominent a part in winning the Greek War of Independence, 1821-32; it also enabled them to lay the foundations of those mercantile activities already mentioned.[3] During all these troublous times the inhabitants of coastal regions remained in their fortified towns and compact villages.

When these disturbed conditions eventually died away—both on the coast and in the interior—the local population were free to spread themselves in more dispersed forms of settlement. Then, however, other factors became evident, notably malaria, a dread disease that was widespread throughout most of southern Europe—and until recently so difficult to control. Until the end of the nineteenth century the nature of the disease and the role of its carrier, the anopheles mosquito, remained unknown: the disease was often attributed to some poisonous air—*mala aria*, as the Italian has it—given off by the soil, usually at night and more particularly by the damp marshy soils associated with low-lying basins or plains. Crude though it was, this poisonous air theory reflected the experience of generations of people living in tropical, sub-tropical, and warm temperate climates: low-lying areas, particularly at night, did seem subject to infection; villages and towns built on higher ground, especially if exposed to strong prevailing or local winds, did seem to offer a certain amount of protection. 'Whoever would live long must see neither the rising nor the setting sun' runs a proverb of the people of Sybaris, an early Greek colony in coastal Calabria; these people

---

[3] See p. 33 above. Individual Greeks had, of course, taken to piracy long before this. The two most famous Barbary corsairs—Uruj and Kheyr-ed-din, the Barbarossa brothers—were natives of Lesbos who during the sixteenth century embraced Islam and piracy as more profitable pastimes than Christianity and agriculture.

also, it seems, believed that cities built in the hills offered shelter from the pestilential climate of the lowlands—hence their later colony at Paestum.[4]

No doubt the need for defence against marauders originally caused people to crowd together in hill villages and towns, but these opinions provided a very strong reason for staying there, particularly when disturbances died away and the population were freer to disperse. The many regions where dispersion has occurred are either regions where malaria has never been prevalent—as in the Alps, the northern and central Apennines, and one or two favoured Greek and Italian isles[5]—or else regions where *Anopheles superpictus* (the malarial mosquito which can penetrate hilly country) is so predominant that it is immaterial whether the inhabitants live in hill-towns or not. There are, of course, other forces at work, but it seems clear that this has been a major force in maintaining the system whereby much of the population of southern Italy and Sicily—where *A. superpictus* is relatively scarce—continue to live in hill-top towns and descend each day to work in the lower country round about. The recent discoveries relating to malarial control have only just begun to affect this pattern of life.[6]

Another reason for the continued importance of nuclear settlement is that, once free to leave their compact hill villages, people have often settled in a new compact settlement rather than in a widely dispersed one. The cessation of piracy, for instance, has encouraged inhabitants of many hill villages to come back to the shore, where they have simply turned the village's *skala* or *marina* into a compact little town that contains the homes, not only of traders and fishermen, but also of those cultivating coastal farms and plots. Sometimes the original *skala* or *marina* has become larger and more important than the original hill village it served—as have Plomarion on Lesbos isle (see Fig. 1), and Siderno Marina on the west coast of Reggio Calabria. A considerable number of migrants have come from places such as these.

Many other reasons contribute to the continuation of nuclear settlement: sheer human inertia; the love some people undoubt-

4 Douglas, *Old Calabria*, pp. 295-6.

5 It is of interest here to contrast a map of malaria mortality in Italy in the 1880s with a map of dispersed settlement. Cf. the maps in the R.N.G.H.S., *Italy*, vol. II, pp. 476, 507.

6 For details of the various malarial mosquitoes and the districts they dominate see R.N.G.H.S. (*Italy*, vol. II, p. 476; *Jugoslavia*, vol. II, p. 365; *Greece*, vol. I, p. 271; *Albania*, p. 122; *Spain*, vol. I, p. 150).

edly develop for the close communal life which compact settlement entails; the absence in many areas of such positive incen-
tives for dispersal as exist under the *mezzadria* system of central
Italy—the system whereby the sharefarmer cultivates such a
variety of crops that he has to live on the farm all the time. But
whatever the reason the net effect is clear: some 85 per cent of
Australia's pre-war southern European migrants came from areas
where nuclear settlement has been dominant for many generations. It is necessary, then, to look more closely at the social life
this form of habitation enjoins.

The first characteristic of life in nuclear settlements is high
population density, a relatively large number of persons occupying a relatively small area of land. This holds for both the towns
and small villages, though it is more obvious in the towns,
especially in the older parts. There, in ancient two- or three-
storeyed buildings in dark, narrow streets, hundreds of people
live like rabbits in a warren: in Partinico, in Sicily, some 20,000
persons occupy about one-third of a square mile; in Valetta city,
despite the number of public buildings, the population density
has at times reached nearly 100,000 per square mile; in Kastellorizo, in its heyday, many more than 8,000 persons squeezed
themselves into an area little more than one-tenth of a square
mile.[7] Obviously, living space is often very limited: in Valetta
city, for instance—on the basis that overcrowding exists where
there are 3 or more persons in one room, 5 or more in two, 7 or
more in three, and 9 or more in four rooms—between 35 and 40
per cent of the population have been living in overcrowded conditions from the late nineteenth century until quite recent times.[8]
Though less conspicuous, the same situation existed in most of
our villages of origin before the 1930s: cottages of one, two or
three rooms might house 9 or 10 persons who shared very primitive conditions and in some places slept in one room on rugs
on the floor. At times, when the men were away with the livestock, or remained overnight in the fields during busy periods in
the off season of malaria, the home accommodation became less
cramped: for the men, however, crowded together in small agricultural shelters or shepherds' huts, the pressure not infrequently
became even greater.

The second characteristic of nuclear settlement is close com-

[7] These figures have been calculated from the statistics of city population
and from large-scale maps of the city areas.

[8] Proportions for 1891, 1901, and 1911 estimated on the assumptions of the
1921 and 1931 censuses for Malta and Gozo.

munal life. Usually, the small towns and villages are centred upon a market-place—frequently with the church near by—and this *agora*, or *piazza*, acts as a social centre where the local population gather in the evenings, on Sundays, or on special market and festival days. Here, in the local cafés and inns, the inhabitants drink coffee, wine, or spirits amidst the din and noise of many tongues and footsteps. For the women there are often other occasions for social intercourse: the gossip in the market-place; the gathering at the well to draw water for the daily round; the communal washing of clothes at the fountain or river-bank, sometimes called the women's coffee-house. Children indulge in numerous 'gang' activities, and it is noticeable that the growing popularity of soccer football throughout most of southern Europe derives considerable strength in some towns from the ease with which gangs of children can practise the game in roads and alleys.

It has sometimes been said that persons reared in these conditions find it very difficult to settle happily in places where settlement is more dispersed or where they may be expected to pioneer lonely wastes in empty lands. The Marchese Testaferrata Olivier, for example, when discussing Maltese migration to Cyprus in 1878-80, asserted that the venture would fail unless enough Maltese were settled in one spot to recreate the close social conditions of their villages of origin.[9] Certainly the story of Maltese emigration during the nineteenth and early twentieth centuries supports this view: Maltese settlements in British Guiana, Grenada, North Africa, and Australia showed that Maltese labourers and artisans preferred to work in close proximity—frequently crowded into small huts and cottages—and in areas not too remote from market-towns.[10]

Another important force keeping southern European migrants together is their desire to be in close touch with persons from the same town, village, or group of villages and hamlets. This desire, it seems, springs in part from the way in which the close communal life of nuclear settlement often fosters dependence on familiar friends and faces, on habitual activities pursued in company with fellow-villagers and townsfolk, on social customs and traditions peculiar to that particular town or district.[11] The

[9] T. Olivier, *Report on Lands in Cyprus for a Maltese Settlement, 1879.*
[10] C. A. Price, *Malta and the Maltese.*
[11] This work makes no attempt to distinguish primary-group and secondary-group relationships, or to show the influence of such relationships on settlement abroad. This would require detailed field-work beyond the scope of the general survey contemplated here.

fact that so many villages and towns of southern Europe have
their own patron saints and own special days of festival and re-
joicing; the fact that in all the dialects of Spanish and Italian
the words *paisano* and *paesano* have much less the force of a
rustic labourer, or a small rural landholder, and much more the
force of a fellow-townsman or person from the same small
district of origin; the way in which, before World War II,
numerous Italians would say 'sono Molfettesi' or 'sono Milanesi'
in tones that showed they felt that in their commune rather than
in their nation-state lay the real object of their loyalty, their true
patria;[12] the fact that so many southern Europeans abroad were
prepared to help their village friends come to join them: these
are but a few of the symptoms of this dependence on local customs and traditions.

This dependence, of course, is not entirely the product of the
close communal life of compact settlement: difficulties of communication over broken rugged country;[13] the lack, until recently, of the radio and cinema and forms of entertainment other
than local gossip, games or dances; the survival of marked local
dialects; the existence of strong district and regional governments; the strength of family ties and relationships which often
reinforce district loyalties and bounds: these and numerous other
forces have all played an important part.

From all these factors, however, a somewhat new issue emerges.
The basic geographic and social factors—rugged terrain, subdivision of holdings, garden cultivation, disease, piracy and war
—have manifested themselves in much the same way in nearly
all our districts of origin. But the more purely cultural and
political matters involve a variety of local customs and traditions
that make it necessary to consider the numerous districts of
origin much more as separate entities. To avoid too much fragmentation and to preserve some general coherence, these are
examined to see how certain general characteristics and institutions—the family, religion, race, language, nationalism, and the
like—have manifested themselves in different ways in particular
localities.

[12] Cf. R.N.G.H.S., *Italy*, vol. II, p. 273; Foerster, *Italian Emigration*, p.
432.

[13] In the late nineteenth century it was an eight-day journey from the
Valtellina to Milan, the regional capital—see Foerster, op. cit., p. 431.

RACE

The first of these general factors is race, or physical type.[14] Here there are two major difficulties. On the one hand is the difficulty of obtaining agreement about the physical characteristics of any of the so-called basic racial types; on the other hand is the very great complexity resulting from the fact that southern Europe has been subjected to mass invasions for many thousands of years. As a result, many varieties of the Mediterranean, Alpine, and Nordic races are now so intermingled that it is highly doubtful whether safe generalizations can be made about any country or major region, let alone assertions—such as so many Australians make—that migrants from northern Italy and Yugoslavia are mostly tall fair Nordics and Slavs while those from southern Italy, Greece and Spain are nearly all short dark persons of Mediterranean-African origin.

It is, perhaps, worth examining these matters more closely, and the several illustrations of racial intermixture that emerge have important implications, both racially and culturally. First, the invasion of northern Italy by various Germanic tribes after the break-up of the Roman Empire did not everywhere drive out the existing Italian inhabitants, with the result that in parts of the north many of the original characteristics still predominate. Second, after the end of the Roman Empire both southern Italy and Spain received considerable numbers of Nordic invaders: in Spain the Vandals and Visigoths occupied Catalonia and later established control over most of the peninsula; in southern Italy and Sicily bands of Lombard warriors, and later Norman adventurers, wrestled for supremacy with native Italians, Greek colonists, and Saracen invaders. These Nordic warriors, though never numerically predominant, have left their mark on the physical characteristics of many of the population. Third, from the eighth century A.D. onwards numerous Moslems

---

[14] The usage here follows that of Aleš Hrdlička: 'One of the plainest facts regarding man is that he differs, physically as well as otherwise. . . . In every human community, however, from the larger family groups or "lines" onward, there are evidences of the formation of *strains*, the individuals of which approach or resemble each other in pigmentation, stature, build, and more or less even in physiognomy. The larger the human group the more such strains there usually are, and the more some of these tend to become *established*, both somatologically and territorially. Such strains now form *types*, which, if allowed further to develop and multiply and segregate, begin to assume the status of *races*; which, with time, develop again their own strains and types and perhaps races' (E. V. Cowdry (ed.), *Human Biology and Racial Welfare*, Chapter VII; original italics).

E

of Arab or mixed Arab-Berber origin—Saracens as Christendom
came to know them—spread westward and northward into Spain,
Malta, Sicily, South Italy, and Provence. The first three countries they held for several centuries, leaving an impression deeper
than that left by the Moslem Turks in more recent times on
Greece, Yugoslavia, and Bulgaria—despite the survival of a few
pockets of Turkish peoples in eastern Macedonia, north-eastern
Greece and southern Bulgaria. Fourth, from the end of the fifth
century A.D. various Slav peoples, expanding southward from
their home in north-eastern Europe, began to penetrate what
are now the lands of Friuli, Dalmatia, Albania, and Greece.
Although they did not conquer the main cities, or the mountain
fastnesses where the old Illyrian stock of Albania survived practically untouched, they occupied the open country to such an
extent that in the eighth century the southern Balkans, including western Greece and the Peloponnesus, were known by the
general name of 'Sclavinia'. Finally, in the fourteenth and fifteenth centuries, under the pressure of economic troubles and
Turkish invasion, numerous Albanians began to leave their
homeland and settle in Macedonia, Greece, and Italy: substantial colonies are still recognizable, not only in the disputed
territory of Epirus in northern Greece, but in certain districts
north of Athens and Corinth, in the eastern peninsulas of the
Peloponnesus, in the Aegean islands of Evvoia and Andros, and
in various districts of Sicily, and parts of southern Italy. Some
of these places have given migrants to Australia.[15]

Clearly, these and similar movements make it very difficult to
generalize about racial composition and physical characteristics:
the most that can be done is to examine particular districts of
origin to see what physical characteristics are, in practice, dom-

____

[15] It is unnecessary here to enter the battle between those who follow
J. P. Fallermeyer in declaring that the Slav and Albanian immigrations were
on such a large scale that the modern Greeks have 'not a single drop of
Greek blood in their veins', and those who assert that the modern Greek is
a pure descendant of the classical Hellenes: place-names and local customs
make it plain that both Slavs and Albanians have made a considerable contribution to the population of many districts in modern Greece—see
R.N.G.H.S., *Greece*, vol. I, Chapters 6 and 11, *Albania*, pp. 131, 182, and
W. Miller, *Greece*. Likewise it is unnecessary to enter the controversy between
persons who follow Freeman in describing Dalmatia as a 'Slavonic land with
an Italian fringe' and persons who claim Dalmatia was never Italian but
Illyrian, Greek, and Slav—e.g. L. Voinovich *Dalmatia and the Yugoslav
Movement*. Here it is relevant simply to note that the Italianate appearance
of many Dalmatian cities conceals the fact that ethnically and culturally the
modern Dalmatians are unquestionably Slavs.

inant in any one of them and then to see to what extent these characteristics prevail amongst persons migrating from the district to Australia. Migrants are not necessarily typical of the areas from which they come and it is the migrants with which the Australian people are confronted. Appendix 5 gives information on three of the main physical characteristics for more than 1,600 male migrants from sixteen principal areas or origin: height, colour of hair, and colour of eyes.[16] These characteristics raise several interesting points. The first concerns the Asiago Plateau of Vicenza in the Venetian Alps (the Seven Communes), where certain Nordic tribes, having driven out the original inhabitants, kept themselves relatively free from intermixture and until quite recently maintained a Germanic language and social organization. Here alone, with an average height of nearly 5'8½", with nearly two-thirds of the total with blue, grey, or hazel eyes, and only one-quarter or so having really dark hair, does a migrant group approach the tall, blonde, blue-eyed stereotype of a north Italian which so many Australians have in mind. The effect of this Nordic influence is also visible in the Vicenza foothills below the plateau: here the Nordic strain has intermixed with other types to produce a migrant group averaging some 5'8" in height, with just over half the total having light-coloured eyes, and one-fifth having light-coloured hair. Both these groups are significantly different from migrants from the Treviso foothills a few miles away, where no German tribes monopolized nearby plateaux; these, like northern Italians from the Valtellina and the Monferrato, average an inch less in height and have an appreciably lower proportion of fair-haired, light-eyed persons in the total.

Somewhat similar in colour of eye and hair to these darker Italians from Treviso, the Valtellina, and Monferrato, but at least an inch taller, are the predominantly Slav migrants from central Dalmatia. Very like these are the northern Italians from Friuli, which the Slavs invaded after the collapse of the Roman Empire. The Slav-speaking Macedonians from the district around Florina are somewhat shorter and considerably darker, as are migrants from the nearby Albanian district of Korçë; even so, these people are as tall as the average Englishman.

The migrants approximating most nearly to the Australian stereotype of the short, dark, southern European are those from Reggio Calabria. They average 5'5" in height, and some 80 per

16 Appendix 5 is based on information in the naturalization records.

cent have dark hair and dark or brown eyes. Persons from the
nearby province of Catania, and perhaps those from the Molfetta district in Apulia, are substantially taller, and have appreciably lighter hair and eyes, than the Calabrians. Lipari islanders, however, like migrants from the Greek islands of Kythera,
Ithaca, and Kastellorizo, are less easy to place: they are quite as
dark as the Calabrians but are an inch or so taller—about the
same height, in fact, as the average Welshman.

From these figures, then, it appears that migrants from our
districts of origin in southern Italy and Greece are, on average,
definitely darker than those from northern Italy, Yugoslavia, and
Albania but that many of these southern Italians and Greeks
are quite as tall as some of the northerners. Even so there are
sufficient numbers of short dark northerners to make even this
generalization dangerous for practical purposes. In 1947 in
Ingham, Queensland, for instance, there were about 500 adult
males of Italian origin, three-quarters of whom derived from
the Monferrato, the Valtellina, and the Venetian foothills and
about one-quarter from Catania in Sicily: on the basis of the
regional distribution of physical characteristics this meant that
of the dark-haired dark-eyed Italian males of less than 5'6"
settled in Ingham at that time some two-thirds came from northern Italy and the remaining third from the south. Likewise in
1947 in Griffith, N.S.W., there were about 1,000 adult males of
Italian origin, about two-thirds of whom came from the Venetian foothills and a little less than one-third from the southern
regions of Abruzzi, Calabria, and Sicily; this meant that just
over half the short dark Italians in Griffith at the time came
from northern Italy.[17] As there are many other places in Australia where northern Italians exceed southerners, these two examples are not at all untypical.

The point of these figures in relation to widespread Australian
attitudes is best illustrated by an actual incident in a country
town in New South Wales. One afternoon a local school-teacher
held forth about the low intelligence of the 'short dark southern
Italians' and their general undesirability as immigrants. That
evening some eighteen adult Italians attended an English class
and the same teacher was invited to assess, from the look of the
pupils and their performance in class, exactly how many were
from the north and how many from the south. The teacher there-

---

[17] Recent heavy immigration to Griffith from southern Italy will by now
have tipped the balance the other way.

upon stated that he thought the seventeen dark persons were from the south and the one brown-haired person was from the north. Each pupil then gave his village and region of origin: the seventeen darkish persons were from the Venetian foothills in north Italy; the one brown-haired person came from Abruzzi in the south.

Thomas Arthur Ferry, Commissioner appointed in 1925 to inquire into the effects of alien immigration into Queensland, thought in the same slipshod way. Despite statistics produced by the Italian Consul, Mr Commissioner Ferry preferred evidence which fitted in better with his own impressions: 'another Italian witness considered that for every one that comes from Northern Italy two come from Sicily, and judging by the appearance of the new arrivals this estimate is fairly correct'.[18] According to the naturalization statistics, of the Italians arriving in Queensland during the 1920s only 36 per cent came from Sicily and the south, some 5 per cent from the centre, and the remaining 59 per cent from the north. Such wishful thinking and prejudiced opinions are unlikely to reach other than erroneous and unfortunate conclusions. In other words, with all the physical types involved, and with all the racial intermixture that has occurred, it is almost impossible to deduce place of origin from physical characteristics.

One of the main outcomes of this racial intermixture has been a corresponding mixture of languages and dialects, since many of the local dialects spoken by our principal migrant groups directly result from invasion and conquest. Local dialects, however, present certain difficulties and before tackling them it may be as well to survey the linguistic field as a whole.[19]

LANGUAGE AND DIALECT

Broadly speaking, southern Europe is divided into three main language groups: the Latin or Romance group dominates in

18 'Ferry Report', p. 42 (A 28, p. 16).

19 The word 'dialect' has several connotations. This work follows the usage of that group of comparative philologists who think of dialects as closely-related languages stemming from the same source—e.g. Dutch, German, and Danish are dialects of the Teutonic language. Thus this study treats Basque as a separate language from Spanish, and Greek as separate from Albanian, but regards as 'dialects' all regional and district variations of one language, whether they are great or small, whether they cross political boundaries or not. It uses the term 'local dialect' to denote the particular tongue of any one district and the term 'regional dialect' to denote the general pattern of local dialects in any one region.

Portugal, Spain, France, and Italy; the Slav group prevails in Yugoslavia, Bulgaria, and northern Macedonia; the Greek group dominates in the Greek mainland and islands and in the islands of Tenedos, Imbros, and Cyprus. In addition there are three much smaller but important language groups: Basque, an ancient language apparently unconnected with any other tongue in Europe, is spoken by some 500,000 persons in the western Pyrenees of France and Spain; Albanian is the last survivor of ancient Illyrian—a language spoken quite widely over south-eastern Europe in classical days—and is now confined to Albania and one or two districts beyond; Maltese, apparently a mixture of ancient Phoenician and more recent Arabic, is the Semitic tongue of the 300,000 or so inhabitants of the Maltese archipelago. Finally, in the Alps, on the southern borders of the great Teutonic language group, about one-third of Venetia Tridentina are German-speaking Tyroleans closely related to the German-speaking peoples of Austria and Switzerland.

When we examine this broad scene in detail, however, we find it much more complex. In the first place, invasion and migration have produced numerous foreign-language pockets within the one dominant grouping, and many of our districts of origin have been affected. Varieties of Greek, for instance, are still spoken by persons of Greek descent in the Korçë and Gjinokastër districts of Albania and in the Bova district of Reggio Calabria. Again, varieties of Albanian are still spoken by descendants of Albanian settlers in the Greek islands of Evvoia and Andros and in parts of northern Apulia, Calabria, and Sicily. And, in the Vicenza plateau of the Veneto, survivors of invading German tribes maintained a Germanic tongue until well into the twentieth century.

In other districts of origin, settlement and conquest resulted in the grafting on to the existing language of many new words and idioms. Consequently there are often marked differences in the dialects of neighbouring regions that have experienced somewhat different histories of conquest and invasion. The long Venetian occupation of the Ionian islands and Crete has left on the prevailing Greek a legacy of Italian words and phrases, and the Cretan dialect also contains relics of the Saracen occupation of the ninth century A.D. Likewise the Saracen invasions have left many traces in the dialects of southern Spain, Sicily, Calabria, and the Lipari islands. Modern Bulgarian, in its turn, contains numerous traces of Albanian and Turkish.

Even more important than the effects of war and conquest

have been the historical processes whereby a fairly coherent language, such as classical Latin or early Slavonic, breaks up in the course of time into different dialects in different regions. Sometimes these dialects move quite widely apart and then develop their own district variations or local dialects. The Latin group, so far as our districts of origin are concerned, has split into a number of large divisions: the Castilian Spanish of central and southern Spain; the Catalan of Valencia, Barcelona and the south-western corner of Mediterranean France; the Gallo-Italian of north-western Italy (which includes both the Valtellina and the Monferrato and also, for certain curious reasons, various places north and west of Mount Etna in Sicily);[20] the soft-sounding Venetian of the Veneto; the Rhaetian tongue of northern Friuli and south-eastern Switzerland; the central Italian dialects of Tuscany, Umbria, and Rome; the southern Italian dialects of Apulia, Calabria, Sicily, and the Lipari islands. Each of these major dialect divisions has in turn developed marked local variations; hence the difference between the local dialects of Valencia and Barcelona in coastal Spain, of the Valtellina and the Monferrato in north-western Italy, or of Molfetta, Reggio Calabria, and north-eastern Messina in southern Italy. There are even minor differences between districts as close to one another as the eastern and western slopes of the Aspromonte range in Calabria.

Much the same has happened with the South Slavonic language group, which has split into several major divisions, and these again into lesser dialects. This has resulted in our South Slav districts of origin differing in speech quite markedly from one another: the Medjumurje speaks, or used to speak, the Kajkavian dialect of Serbo-Croat, interlarded with numerous Hungarian and German words; the central Dalmatian islands and Split, together with a small section of the northern coast round Rijecka, use the Čakavian dialect of Serbo-Croat; the bulk of the Dalmatian coast uses certain varieties of the Štokavian dialect of Serbo-Croat; the Tirnova district of north Bulgaria uses a variety of Bulgarian; the Macedo-Slavs of the Florina

---

[20] The Gallo-Italian areas of Sicily appear to be survivals from north Italian garrisons brought in by the Normans as an insurance against Saracen rebellion—see Nunzio Prestianni, *L'Economia Agraria della Sicilia*, p. 34. Australia has received a few migrants from these places, notably from S. Fratello in north-western Messina and from Randazzo and Maletto in northern Catania. In some places the Gallo-Italian dialects have almost disappeared but they were still in use at the time migrants left there some decades ago.

district of Macedonia have a dialect transitional between Bulgarian and Serbo-Croat.

Greek has split up less than the Romance and southern Slav language groups, largely because the Byzantine Empire maintained political unity in the east very much longer than did the Roman Empire of the west. Even so, differences have emerged in the course of time. The handful of migrants Australia has received from the Tzakonian dialect area of the eastern Peloponnesus spoke on arrival a variety of ancient Doric Greek, while Kastellorizan and Rhodian Greeks spoke somewhat differently from migrants from the nearby island of Astypalaia, which was depopulated by plague in the fifteenth century and resettled by colonists from the northern Cyclades.

Even the smaller language divisions have their own local variations. There is a marked difference between many of the local dialects of the Basque country in Spain, and also between the speech of those inhabiting the main island of Malta and its smaller neighbour Gozo. Albanian also has developed pronounced dialect distinctions, notably between the 'Geg' speech of the north and the 'Tosk' speech of the south: Australia's Albanian migrants are nearly all from the Tosk-speaking areas of Korçë and Gjinokastër.

These minor differences in dialect do not normally produce conditions of mutual incomprehensibility: Maltese can understand Gozitans, Calabrians can understand most Sicilians, Dalmatians from the islands of Vis and Korčula can usually understand persons from the mainland villages near by. Major differences of dialect, however, have much more the force of distinct languages. A Reggio Calabrian or Sicilian cannot normally understand the Gallo-Italian dialect of the Valtellina, nor can Rhaetian-speaking Friulani understand the Gallo-Italian of the Monferrato. When, therefore, migrants from these areas settle in the same place in Australia they communicate either in English or in another tongue known to both. This is why, when a man from Friuli meets a girl from the Monferrato in Queensland, both have to brush up their standard Italian or English before marrying and starting a home.[21]

Major differences in dialect that are backed by strong regional loyalties are often more important as isolating factors than the

21 Standard, or official Italian, derives principally from the dialect of Florence in Tuscany. Though it now differs in several respects from the dialect spoken by educated families in Florence, it is closer to that than to any of the other historic dialects of Italy.

small islands of some entirely different language that result from war and conquest. Whereas the German-speaking peoples of the Vicenza plateau early learnt to speak Venetian for a second language, or the Greek and Albanian colonists of Calabria learnt Calabrian, it is only comparatively recently that many Catalans have begun to learn official Castilian Spanish as their second language, or many Calabrians and Sicilians have begun to learn standard Italian as theirs. Much, of course, depends on the ability of central governments to override regional loyalties and to compel people to attend schools where they can learn to speak, read, and write the official language of the country concerned. The countries of southern Europe have only lately developed policies of compulsory education, and as recently as 1930, well after the peak of pre-war migration to Australia, the proportions of illiterate persons in the total population were approximately: Spain 53 per cent, Italy 21 per cent, Greece 41 per cent, Yugoslavia 44 per cent. The proportions were much higher in rural districts than in the cities, and also much higher in some regions than in others—5 per cent in the regions containing the Monferrato and the Valtellina compared with more than 40 per cent in Calabria and Sicily, 5 per cent in Slovenia compared with 60 per cent or more in Dalmatia and Yugoslav Macedonia, less than 35 per cent in Athens and Evvoia compared with 40-50 per cent in Ithaca, Kythera and the northern parts of Greek Macedonia. Illiteracy has usually been much higher amongst women than men—24 per cent of Greek men compared with 58 per cent of Greek women, or 33 per cent of men in Yugoslavia compared with 56 per cent of women. These figures of illiteracy are most important, because Australia drew so many of its pre-war migrants from districts and classes where illiteracy was relatively high.[22]

Many illiterate persons have learnt to speak, as distinct from learning to read and write, the official language of their Folk or country as a second language while serving in the armed forces or working as sailors, petty traders, or as seasonal labourers in different parts of the country. It is only in recent years, however, that their number has become appreciable. In any case these influences affected the men rather than the women, who remained much more dependent on local dialect; and it is the

[22] For these statistics see the censuses for Spain 1930, Italy 1931, Greece 1928, Yugoslavia 1931, and the volumes of annual statistics produced by those countries. The standard of literacy amongst post-war migrants seems much improved.

language of the womenfolk that normally determines the language spoken in the home, both in Europe and in settlements overseas.

In sum, then, it appears that many southern European migrants to Australia—especially those from southern Italy and Sicily, from Dalmatia and Macedonia, from the Greek countryside and islands—have been largely illiterate and very dependent on local dialect. Where these local dialects represent wide linguistic differences—as between Calabrian and Sicilian on the one hand and the Gallo-Italian dialects of the Monferrato and Valtellina on the other—migrants find much difficulty in understanding each other in settlements abroad. Furthermore, even when migrants are able to speak a common official tongue they tend to speak it as a second language—for business purposes, not for the more intimate aspects of social life: relaxation in the home, joking and laughing over games and supper, or discussing the selection of a bride whom the eldest son can bring to live with the rest of the family. This holds, too, for the inhabitants of small foreign-language islands, and even for the population of districts whose dialects are basically not far apart but which have peculiar words and phrases arising from different local histories —as with the local dialects of Crete, Ithaca, and Kastellorizo or of the Dalmatian coast and islands.

The existence of strong local and regional dialects, then, even when they do not involve complete incomprehensibility between migrants settled in the same place abroad, does act as a powerful force in keeping together persons who have come from the same district or region of origin. An understanding of the dialect problem is thus essential to any real understanding of the way migrants act when settling abroad, more particularly of the way in which they so often form settlement groups and blocs. It certainly throws yet further doubt on the wisdom of treating migrants in terms of broad national or ethnic divisions.

FAMILY AND FAMILY STRUCTURE

Equally important in relation to group settlement abroad is the family. Its importance springs from the fact that, taken by and large, the family ties that existed in our districts of origin in pre-war years—and that to a great extent still exist— were not only very strong but tended to operate on a village or district basis, and as a result tended to reinforce village or district loyalties overseas. It is true, of course, that family patterns did vary considerably from area to area. In most parts of Greece,

Sicily, Calabria, the Monferrato, and to some extent the Valtellina and the larger urban centres, each married couple and their single children (the nuclear family) tended to establish themselves independently of their relatives, in small cottages, houses, or flats of one, two or three rooms; in this tendency to establish independent households they approximate more closely to the Australian pattern than do many other southern Europeans. In parts of Dalmatia, the Friuli, the Venetian foothills, and elsewhere there was a greater tendency to adopt an extended family system—for married sons and their dependants to live in the parental home, either sharing the general facilities or partitioning the home into semi-independent flats. In parts of Bulgaria, Serbia, and Albania this tendency sometimes went even further. The Serb *zadruga* (large family farm), for example, might contain twenty or more married couples and their dependants, all related to each other by male descent or adoption and all sharing the property and its work; though the members might all live together in one large house they more usually cooked and ate in one central dwelling and slept in small huts scattered about the yard and garden.[23] Migrants from extended family homes have had to choose between conforming to the nuclear family system prevalent in Australia and attempting to recreate in Australia the system in which they were reared in Europe.

Another important difference between our particular districts of origin lies in the degree to which the women of a family were permitted to pursue social and business activities outside the home. In many districts of Greece, southern Italy, and southern Spain there was a general opinion that a man and woman left alone together would inevitably make love.[24] Consequently unmarried girls were not allowed out unless strictly chaperoned, nor might an unaccompanied married woman walk or talk with any man not her husband; in like manner women were permitted to do certain jobs on the family property but were not allowed, unless well chaperoned, to find employment in farms, shops, or factories belonging to other people.[25] In parts of northern Italy and Catalonia this strict attitude had been progressively relaxed: unmarried girls could be alone with boy-friends during the day

[23] R. Trouton, *Peasant Renaissance in Yugoslavia 1900-1950*, pp. 27-9.
[24] Cf. J. S. McDonald, 'Italy's Rural Social Structure and Emigration', and authorities quoted in *Occidente*, XII (1956), esp. pp. 446-8.
[25] Bagnara Calabra just north of Reggio, is one exception: here the women run contraband and act as mobile fish-vendors; they have a relatively high social status.

and wives might dance, talk, and walk with men other than their husbands;[26] furthermore, the women of these districts could find work outside the family home and property—as agricultural workers, or factory hands, or shop assistants, though parents still tended to dislike their daughters taking jobs in cafés and other places where they might make undesirable male acquaintances. In most of our Albanian and South Slav districts, as well as in certain areas of North Italy such as Friuli, men tended to keep a strict eye on their womenfolk's social activities but had few worries about the proper form of female employment since the women were fully occupied with numerous tasks on the family farms—a custom deriving from the centuries of guerrilla fighting against the Turks or from the ancient tradition of seasonal migration, when many men spent whole seasons away from home and left the bulk of the farming to the women.

Another difference between the various districts of origin has been the age of marriage and size of family. Girls in Calabria and Sicily have married two years younger than girls in North Italy—the average age of marriage for single girls in Calabria rising from 19 or so at the turn of the century to 22 in the late 1930s, whilst over the same period the average age in the Monferrato, the Veneto, and the Valtellina rose from approximately 21 to 24. Partly as a consequence, families have been larger in Calabria and Sicily than in the northern districts, a fact which is reflected in the crude birth rates: in the 1930s, for example, the birth rate in the northern districts averaged about 20 per thousand whereas in southern districts it averaged about 30 per thousand; even here, however, there were local variations, Reggio Calabria having a higher birth rate than the Messinian and Catanian provinces of Sicily and the Veneto and the Valtellina having a higher birth rate than the Monferrato. Similar differences existed in Spain in the same period: the birth rate in the Catalonian and Basque provinces has long been lower than that of the Spanish average—19·5 and 19·5 compared with 28. Likewise in the mid-thirties the birth rate in Slovenia and the Medjumurje (24 per thousand) had for some time been lower than those of Dalmatia (34) and Yugoslav Macedonia (36). The differences between the various districts of Greece are more difficult to determine, but the national average was some 28 per thousand in the early thirties. It is interesting to contrast all these rates with those that prevailed in Australia during the same period—

26 J. S. McDonald, 'Rural Social Structure and Emigration'.

17 per thousand—and those that have prevailed since 1945—22 or so per thousand.

In sum, before World War II considerable differences appeared to have existed in the average size of family in all the districts of origin. In some places married couples had become accustomed to having families very little larger than most Australians: in others, the tendency was to have families considerably larger. It is worth noting, however, that in nearly all these districts the size of family had been falling since the 1880s—the most conspicuous exception being Malta, which from 1880 to 1940 maintained the relatively high birth rate of 33 and more per thousand.[27]

So far we have been considering the differences between the family habits of our main districts of origin, but strong similarities existed too. In the first place, no matter whether the family were organized on the nuclear or extended system, the social conventions of nearly all the districts of origin gave great authority to the head of the family household. It was he who pronounced upon the arrangements for work and leisure, controlled the earnings and expenditure of all members of the home, was responsible for good behaviour and discipline, represented the household in its relations with outsiders, acted as the final arbiter in arranging the children's marriages, and so on. Usually this authority was exercised only after consultation with other members of the family; in the Basque lands, for instance, the head of the house normally tempered his almost dictatorial powers by

[27] Two warnings are necessary here. (1) Size of family does not necessarily increase as age of female marriage decreases, particularly in places where birth-control is practised or where seasonal or long-term migration separates husbands and wives. From the data available, in the years under review migration seems to have affected all our districts of origin and the areas with higher ages of marriage—the larger towns and parts of northern Italy and Catalonia—seem to have been the only areas where birth-control was practised at all frequently. Consequently, it seems fairly safe to assume that a lower age of marriage results in larger families. (2) Crude birth rates, as used in the text, reflect other things than size of family, notably the proportion of married women of child-bearing age in the total population and the proportion of each married cohort to the total of women of child-bearing age. Speaking generally, mortality seems to have been higher in those areas showing the higher crude birth rates, and this partially explains the difference between the crude birth rates of our various districts of origin. But a variety of other material suggests that social customs also exerted some influence and that, over a long period, most areas of southern Europe showing high crude birth rates have also shown relatively large family size. Consequently the crude birth rates may be used as a convenient, though rough, measure of long-term trends in size of family.

consulting the family, and even the servants, on matters affecting the home as a whole; likewise in the Serb *zadruga* the patriarch customarily consulted with the elder men about the management of the family property.

In most districts this consultation was limited to the menfolk; women occupied a definitely subordinate position except in washing, cooking, sewing, and other matters considered to be purely of female concern. This was true even of those Catalan and northern Italian districts where women had been attaining greater freedom to pursue social and business activities outside the home—even then the tradition persisted that women were subordinate creatures whose primary duty was to minister to the needs of their menfolk. Not that this tradition necessarily involved women in great hardship: even in Albania, where they had fewer rights and privileges than in most other places, women were normally much respected in the home and were unofficially consulted on all manner of problems, more especially those relating to the upbringing and marriage of the children. To this extent the system reflected the view that the menfolk in general, and the head of the home in particular, received authority as a trust: their rights and privileges presupposed the clear duty of ministering to the welfare and happiness of their dependants.[28] Though in practice this system often gave wives and children much freedom, it differs greatly from the Australian system, where the state is responsible for much of the life of dependants and where the equal position of women is more clearly recognized by law and custom. Migrants from such areas, it seems, have often found it difficult to adapt themselves to the Australian pattern.

The second similarity between the main areas of origin relates to the wider family group—first cousins, second cousins, grand-uncles, grand-nephews, and all the rest of the blood relatives, both husband's and wife's. In most districts the links between the wider kinship grouping were relatively strong. Probably they were strongest in the wild regions of northern Albania where the wider kinship group survived from classical days as a highly organized tribe or clan, with elaborate codes to govern behaviour and disputes between members of the clan as well as between members of different clans. Though by the nineteenth

---

28 The principal exception to this generalization lay in the Basque lands, where a girl could become head of the household and exercise all the authority attached thereto. Her husband would have no more importance than any other male member of the home.

century this organized tribal system had largely broken down in the Korçë and Gjinokastër districts of southern Albania, the inhabitants there still cherished their tribal status and allegiance, despite numerous differences in religion, language, and economic standing. The majority of South Slav areas also maintained a relatively strong kinship system, finding it most advantageous in the troubled centuries of Turkish occupation and threat; if disaster overtook one village most of its inhabitants found help and temporary security with relatives established elsewhere.[29] Even in areas such as Catania, Messina, and Reggio Calabria— where the small nuclear family system generally prevailed—the wider kinship group still retained some significance.

For the story of migration and settlement abroad the most important consequence of these wider kinship ties is the convention that the more prosperous members of a family have a duty to assist their poorer relatives. One successful settler from the Veneto somewhat ruefully expounded the workings of this convention when he described what he intended to be a long visit to his town of birth: every relative in the town, both close and remote, descended upon their 'wealthy' relation with prayers for assistance of every conceivable kind; he cut short his visit 'before becoming completely bankrupt' and spent the rest of his trip elsewhere in Italy. Actually this is a somewhat extreme case. Far more often a successful settler in Australia has felt some prickings of family conscience and has assisted his relatives to this country by paying for their passages and guaranteeing their accommodation and employment. It is true that the Australian sponsor often derived some advantage—a cheap farm labourer or shop assistant—but a feeling of family duty seems also to have been involved. At all events, this system of sponsoring relatives has been one of the major forces in determining the rate and character of migration from southern Europe to Australia.

It should be noted here that blood relationship was not the only factor involved in this kind of migration. In most districts of origin, but more particularly those where the Orthodox faith prevailed, the relationship of godfatherhood was almost as strong as that of kinship. In ordinary life the godfather or godmother played an important social role, which settlers abroad quickly endeavoured to recreate by obtaining a close friend or fellow-townsman to act as godparent to their Australian-born children. Furthermore, in the absence of natural parents a godfather could

29 Trouton, *Peasant Renaissance in Yugoslavia*, p. 26.

assume direction of a child's life, and it was this which enabled so many Greek *padrones* (employers) in the United States at the turn of the century to bring out young Greek lads as cheap labourers; a Greek shoe-cleaning *padrone* or flowershop proprietor would return to his native village, stand as godfather to a number of boys, and take them back to America to work as low-paid shoe-blacks or shop assistants until they saved enough to set up on their own.[30] To some extent, it seems, this system has operated with southern European migration to Australia.

This emphasis on the wider family and godparental relationships has meant that in all districts of origin family festivals are really important. Baptisms, weddings, and burials are outstanding social occasions, usually organized with elaborate ritual and at comparatively great expense. To them come all those relatives and friends who can, and great efforts are made to attend. Furthermore, such functions are useful occasions for introducing to each other the younger members of the kinship group, and for enabling older people to discuss future activities, plan marriages, consider emigration, and so on. Amongst settlers overseas such functions greatly assist in keeping together migrants who, though related to each other, have settled some distance apart in their new country; migrants from the Greek island of Kythera, for example, have tended to disperse throughout the country towns of New South Wales and southern Queensland, but many of them make an effort to get to Sydney for special family functions.

This example of the Kytheran Greeks brings us back to the original question: to what extent do family ties and loyalties operate over a wide geographical area—and therefore independently of local custom and convention—and to what extent do they tend to reinforce local bonds and loyalties? So far as the districts of origin in Europe are concerned (the Australian situation will be examined more closely later), there had been some migration to the larger cities by the turn of the century—numbers of Kytherans and Ithacans, for instance, had by then migrated to Athens, Constantinople or Smyrna—and though the migrants usually kept in touch with their families, they were also exposed to influences and customs quite unlike those of their native district. For the most part, however, the greater portion of each family tended to stay in the home village, town, or district, reinforcing their ties with neighbouring families by

[30] See Fairchild, *Greek Immigration to the United States*, pp. 172-88; U.S.A., *Report of the Immigration Commission*, 1907-10, vol. 1.

intermarriage, godparental relationships, and so on. To this extent family ties tended to strengthen village and district customs and have been of considerable importance abroad.

RELIGION AND ANTI-CLERICALISM

This discussion of godparents, baptisms, and weddings leads on to the next major social force—religion. Here again the story is somewhat complicated and requires elaboration. Apart from a handful of Protestant Christians and Jews, the southern European districts of origin have been divided among the three great religions of Islam, Orthodoxy and Roman Catholicism. Table III shows Australia's pre-war immigrants, on the assumption that migrants from any one district were drawn in equal proportions from the religions existing in that district.[31]

TABLE III

RELIGIONS OF PRE-WAR IMMIGRANTS—ESTIMATES

Origin	Number	Roman Catholic %	Orthodox %	Moslem %	Other %
Spanish, French, etc. ..	1,500	95	..	..	5
Italian	33,700	98	..	..	2
Maltese	3,300	97	..	..	3
Slovene	240	95	..	..	5
Croat*	5,020	99	..	..	1
Serb†	340	..	88	12	..
Macedonian	1,900	..	95	5	..
Bulgarian	550	..	94	3	3
Albanian	1,400	3	42	54	1
Greek	12,500	1	98	0·5	0·5
TOTAL	60,450	71	25	2	2

* Includes northern, central, and some southern Dalmatians.
† Includes Orthodox from southern Dalmatia.

The first point to note about Table III is that the small proportion of Moslem migrants greatly understates the real influence Islam has had on southern Europe. At various times between the eighth and the seventeenth centuries fervent Moslem invaders occupied most of Spain, Sicily, Calabria, the islands of the eastern Mediterranean, and nearly all the Balkan lands except

[31] We cannot test this, since no statistics exist for the religions of immigrants. Nor can we use the cross-classifications of religion by birthplace which exist in the 1954 census tables, because these include post-war migrants and because such figures reflect religious changes which have occurred after years of residence in Australia.

Slovenia and northern Dalmatia. These periods have left few Mohammedan adherents behind them—except in central and southern Yugoslavia (25 per cent), Bulgaria (14 per cent) and Albania (67 per cent), and even here the proportions are somewhat lower in the districts from which Australia's Yugoslav, Bulgarian, and Albanian migrants have come. But the invasions have left many traces on the life and customs of the people: on their physical characteristics, their languages and dialects, their dress and diet,[32] and, it is said, on social customs such as that which keeps the womenfolk in parts of Sicily in a state of recluse.

More important still has been the fierce hostility the Moslem conquest often aroused amongst the Christian population, and the modes of behaviour and thought through which this hostility found expression. In practice, of course, there was much peaceable co-existence between Christian and Moslem—particularly in places such as Albania where tribal loyalties remained so strong that they tended to override the fact that some members of the tribe were Christian and some Moslem. But hostility was often very near the surface. Indeed, in some places people at times saw life as nothing but a ceaseless crusade against Islam, a war to the death between the Cross and the Crescent, an undying ideological conflict between the white knights of Christendom and the black Satanic forces of the Moslem infidels. The Maltese provide a good example of this. Not only does the theme enter into island lore—the stories of Christian maidens abducted to Moslem harems in Barbary or the triumphant preservation of the Gospel throughout the Saracen occupation—but it also feeds on great historic dramas such as the bitter defence of the Grand Harbour Fortresses against the Moslem forces of Suleiman the Magnificent in 1565. Small wonder that in more recent times these feelings have flared into open hostility, as they did in Tunis in 1843-4 when a Maltese settler was found guilty of murder by a Moslem court acting with British sanction: 'Maltese Brethren, the Mohammedans, enemies of the Cross, must not steep their sacrilegious hands in the blood of Christians. No, never! Long live the True Faith.'[33] Similar episodes abound in the histories of Spain, Sicily, Serbia, and Greece. For many southern Europeans,

[32] The traditional dress for men in Central Albania, for example, includes wide trousers on the Turkish pattern. Likewise the faldetta, the traditional head-dress of the Maltese women which has fallen markedly from favour since the war, is usually attributed to the period of the Saracen occupation.
[33] C. A. Price, *Malta and the Maltese*, p. 55.

in short, their religion is not just a positive way of life; it is the antithesis of a particular evil force.

Islam has not, of course, monopolized Satanic forces in the religious eyes of southern Europe: the conflict between Catholic and Orthodox has at times been just as bitter. This was so in Kastellorizo and other Dodecanese islands in the 1920s and 1930s when the Italian administration tried to prohibit Orthodox festivals and ceremonies and replace them with Catholic rites. Even more bitter has been the long-drawn-out conflict in Serbo-Croat lands, through which passes the dividing line between Catholic west and Orthodox east. Internecine war has often broken out between Catholic Croats and Orthodox Serbs, engendering a hostility which migrants have sometimes carried with them to Australia. (The great majority of Australia's pre-war migrants from Serbo-Croat districts were Catholic Croats from the Medjumurje and central Dalmatia, but a number were Serbs from the mixed areas of Dubrovnik and Kotor in southern Dalmatia and from Bosnia, Herzegovina, Serbia, and Montenegro—see Table II.)

The second point to notice in relation to Table III is that the division of migrants into Roman Catholics, Orthodox, and Moslems has concealed the existence of two other important systems of belief. The first covers various rationalist creeds such as rationalism proper, agnosticism, atheism, anarchism, or Communism, and may loosely be described as based on the belief that reason is more important than revelation and that highly organized dogmatic churches are an insult to man's intelligence and a barrier to social progress. In Catholic Europe many rationalists, for purely conventional and social reasons, describe themselves at census time as Catholic and permit their families to be baptized and wedded in church. But, in essence, they are opposed to organized ecclesiastical policy and make up a substantial part of the 'anti-clerical' movements of southern Europe. Unfortunately, this conventional description of themselves as Catholics prevents any assessment of their numerical strength. Clearly they are quite strong in certain places and amongst certain classes, especially in the industrial areas of Catalonia and northern Italy and amongst the professional classes of the larger cities; they have also been growing in strength in Valetta and amongst a number of those involved in the Peasant Party of Croatia.[34] On the whole, however, they have been less

[34] Hugh Seton-Watson, *Eastern Europe between the Wars*, pp. 260 ff.

numerous amongst the peasant classes from which the majority
of Australia's pre-war migrants came.

Probably more important in Catholic peasant areas is the
second set of beliefs concealed by official statistics—the system, or
lack of it, we may describe as paganism. The term is appropriate
here since it comes from the same root-word as 'peasant'—from
pagus, the rural district attached to an *oppidum* or town—and
refers essentially to the cult of local rural deities and powers.
The survival of such cults in areas which have been subject to
Christian teaching for a thousand years or more may at first
seem strange. It is very understandable, however, when we remember that an influential strand of Catholic thought has felt
it inadvisable to sweep away older beliefs in a violent endeavour
to introduce the sublimist forms of Christian life and thought in
one short missionary campaign: rather is it 'the way of religion
to lead the things which are lower to the things which are higher
through the things which are intermediate, for according to the
law of the universe all things are not reduced to order equally
and immediately'.[35] Hence the advice of Pope Gregory the Great
to Saint Augustine that the pagan shrines and ceremonies of
Anglo-Saxon England should not be destroyed but transformed
into places and occasions for Christian worship. But sometimes
the programme of leading the things which are lower to the
things which are higher bogs down and remains indefinitely in
a quagmire of mixed Christian and pagan beliefs. This has
happened in a number of districts of origin and is well illustrated by religious life in Calabria and other parts of southern
Italy in the early twentieth century.

Norman Douglas, in his penetrating and well-documented
book, *Old Calabria,* sums up the situation very clearly, making
the same points as those made by other writers and illustrating
these with some vivid examples drawn from his own observa-
tions.[36] At first the ancient district gods received Christian baptism—by taking Christian names or becoming identified with
local holy men and martyrs—yet retained their ancient shrines
in caves and hill-tops and kept their ancient wonder-working
powers; these 'man-saints' did wondrous deeds in defending their
particular communes against African intruders, against the
jealous attacks of neighbouring communes, and even—as in the

---

[35] From the Bull *Unam Sanctam* of Pope Boniface VIII.
[36] See esp. Chapter XXXI; see also L. F. Pisani, *The Italian in America,*
p. 166; C. Barbagallo, *La Questione Meridionale,* p. 274; *Encyclopaedia
Italiana* (1949), articles on Calabria, Folklore, etc.

case of Saint Januarius of Naples—against the might of volcanic eruption. Later on the power and vigour of these male saints were sapped by the spread of the cult of the Madonna, a cult which the Vatican encouraged as an instrument of policy against Byzantine survivals in the south but which local semi-pagans readily adapted in their own fashion: amoeba-like, for their benefit, the Madonna split herself into numerous forms to take over the particularist functions of many male saints. In this the

> decentralizing spirit of South Italy was too strong for her. She had to conform to the old custom of geographical specialization. In all save in name she doffed her essential character of Mother of God, and became a local demi-god; an accessible wonder-worker attached to some particular district. An inhabitant of village A would stand a poor chance of his prayers being heard by the Madonna of village B; if you have a headache, it is no use applying to the *Madonna of the Hens*, who deals with diseases of women; you will find your-self in a pretty fix if you expect financial assistance from the Madonna of Village C: she is a weather specialist. In short, these hundreds of Madonnas have taken up the qualities of the saints they supplanted. They can often outdo them; and this is yet another reason for their success.[37]

On the other hand, woe betide any Madonna or saint who failed to protect the district when the locals have persistently made the proper offerings of candles, processions, and the like. During the Vesuvius eruption of 1906, for instance, countless statues of Madonnas and saints were tossed into ditches for not protecting their worshippers, for failing to keep their share of the bargain.

In the same way as the Madonna and saints took over the wonder-working functions of the ancient local deities, so did the Madonna adapt herself to other local views and customs. One reason for her popularity was the strength of those pastoral institutions in which the Mother plays so conspicuous a role. 'This accounts for the fact that their Trinity is not ours; it consists of the Mother, the Father (Saint Joseph), and the Child—with Saint Anne looming in the background. The Creator of all things and the Holy Ghost have evaporated; they are too intangible and non-human.'[38] For the same reason there are, in the south, only three human aspects of the life of Christ: the *bambino* cult, which not only appeals to the people's love of babyhood but also carried on the old traditions of the *Lar Familiaris* and of Horus; next, the youthful Jesus; and lastly

[37] Douglas, op. cit., p. 260.
[38] Ibid.

the Crucified—that grim and gloomy image of suffering so strongly fostered by the Spaniards. The adult Jesus—the teacher, the Word of God—is practically unknown, while the maxims of the Sermon on the Mount are so repugnant to the south Italian as to be almost incomprehensible. The local codes and customs still prevail: family honour and personal pride are still much stronger than the Beatitudes.[39]

What is true of Calabria is not necessarily true of other Catholic areas of origin. Indeed the Italians themselves admit the pagan characteristics of Calabrian religion when they say '*i Calabresi non sono Cristiani*' ('the Calabrians are not really Christians'). Nevertheless there are districts other than Calabria where paganism still survives. The Basques have a simple piety and dignity in their faith, but the cult of images is strong in Spain farther to the south. Likewise there are many areas where a former local deity survives in the shape of a local patron saint who looks after the well-being of the district and whose annual day is an occasion for special holiday and festivals.

An important consequence of these pagan survivals and local religious festivals is that they provide yet another force in knitting together the inhabitants of any one locality in Europe. On the other hand they are not always easy to transplant abroad. A fairly large group settlement can celebrate its traditional festivals and hence maintain this bond amongst themselves—a number of Italian settlements have already done this in Australia.[40] But hill-top shrines where one entreats divers works of wonder are more difficult to move. Nor do these semi-pagan cults, with their absence of any systematic Christian code of conduct, fit easily into the more rigorous requirements of the Irish Catholicism prevalent in Australia. As a result many migrants have felt themselves landed in an alien religious world and have taken advantage of the much greater religious freedom existing in Australia to join their rationalist compatriots in deserting the church altogether, or at least reducing their religious observances to family occasions such as baptisms, weddings, and burials. This has happened with many Italian and Dalmatian settlers in Australia.

With Orthodox migrants the position has been somewhat different. In certain places there has been a similar emphasis on local shrines and wonders, and similar festivals to celebrate

39 Ibid., p. 258. There are signs that the church may have been successful in making some impact lately.
40 E.g. the Molfettese Italians at Port Pirie, see pp. 237-8 below.

days dedicated to local patron saints; and there has also been much rationalist free-thinking, especially in larger cities such as Athens.[41] But in other respects there have been vast differences between the Catholic and Orthodox worlds. The most important is the fact that the Orthodox faith, unlike Catholicism, has not normally striven to impose one hierarchy and administration on all believers: rather has it tended to promote the principle of autocephalous (self-governing) ethnic churches, each with its own independent hierarchy and administration. As a result, the four ancient and independent Patriarchates of Constantinople, Antioch, Alexandria, and Jerusalem have been joined by a number of self-governing ethnic churches, each headed by its own Patriarch, Exarch, or Metropolitan: Albanian, Bulgarian, Cretan,[42] Cypriot, Rumanian, Russian, Serbian, Ukrainian and so forth. These bodies, which together make up the 'Holy Orthodox Catholic Apostolic Eastern Church', all accept the findings of the first seven general councils of the Christian church, are all in communion with one another, and all reject the doctrine of Papal supremacy.[43] They do not, however, all use the same language in their liturgical services: some use the vernacular; others, the old Greek *koine* (that form of Greek in vogue in the east in the first few centuries of Christian history); others, the 'Old Slavonic' rite, which is essentially a translation of the Greek rite made by Saints Cyril and Methodius in the ninth century A.D. as part of their work in converting the eastern Slavs.[44] These

41 The Australian-Greek paper, *Hellenic Herald*, has sometimes shown signs of rationalist anti-clericalism.

42 The Cretan church, in the period in which we are interested, was not completely autocephalous since the Patriarch of Constantinople appointed the Cretan Metropolitan. But the Metropolitan and his seven bishops ran the island's ecclesiastical affairs.

43 The Orthodox churches hold that the church of Rome was the fifth ancient and independent Patriarchate but that the emergence of the doctrine that the Bishops of Rome are Vicars of Christ, with the *plenitudino potestatis*, has effectively obscured this.

44 In the Roman Catholic world there are also liturgical differences, most conspicuously in Central and Eastern Europe, in the Levant, and in the Greek and Albanian areas of South Italy and Sicily, where the Vatican has accepted the submission of former Orthodox communities but has not compelled them to surrender their Greek or Old Slavonic rites, nor to abandon their married clergy. These Uniat churches, as they are called, are not self-governing in the Orthodox sense but come under the hierarchical administration of the Vatican. There were very few Uniats amongst Australia's pre-war immigrants but an appreciable number have come since the war, particularly from the Polish Ukraine. These Ukrainian Uniats now have their own Australian bishops.

semi-archaic languages are not, of course, used for preaching and for other activities where the modern idiom is more appropriate.

This principle of self-governing ethnic churches has meant that very often an Orthodox church has become involved in some vital ethnic struggle, very often the life-battle of a Folk to shake itself free from alien domination and establish independence or autonomy. The church in Greece, for instance, was primarily responsible for keeping alive the Greek traditions and culture during the centuries of Turkish rule, and it was the local priests who were largely responsible for arousing that patriotic fervour for a reborn Hellas which started off the Greek War of Independence. The Serbian and Bulgarian churches did much the same for the cause of Serbian and Bulgarian independence during the eighteenth and nineteenth centuries.

An interesting result of this identification of church and Folk has been that no matter how indifferent their religious beliefs may be, and no matter how annoyed they may become at the conservative social policies pursued by ecclesiastical leaders, most persons of Orthodox background retain a deep affection for an institution which has played so prominent a part in furthering Folk-nationalist interests. As one historian commented on the fierce opposition of the Serbs during the twenties and thirties to the Concordat with the Vatican so ardently desired by the Catholic Croats: 'the Orthodox Church, which normally plays little part in politics but comes to the front when the nation is in danger, commands a profound loyalty. An attack on the Church is felt by the Serbs, probably the least religious people in Eastern Europe, as an attack on the whole nation.'[45]

It is obvious that this discussion of orthodoxy and nationalism has been considering forces which tend to operate against the trend to regional and district separateness. Many Greeks, for instance, would deny that there are any significant differences in the local customs, dialects, and loyalties of the various Greek districts of origin. A Greek, they would argue, is first and foremost a Greek and only secondarily a Kytheran, Ithacan, or Kastellorizan; for the Greek church, by preserving the Hellenic language and culture through centuries of persecution and conflict, laid the foundations for that fervent Greek patriotism that has completely overridden all petty distinctions of territorial origin. Just how true this is is debatable, particularly amongst Greek settlements abroad. Certainly the Greek church abroad has at times exercised a strong unifying influence, and wherever

45 Hugh Seton-Watson, *Eastern Europe*, p. 235.

there are enough persons of Greek origin they have usually co-operated, no matter what their particular place of origin, in forming a 'Greek Community' whose primary task is to found a local church.[46] But it is not always true that in practice this unifying tendency has overridden all local distinctions (see pp. 242-8), particularly when a church serves migrants other than Greeks, such as those Macedo-Slavs, Albanians, and Syrians brought up according to the Greek rite. Much the same considerations apply to those Bulgarians, Serbs, and other peoples brought up according to the Old Slavonic rite. Taken by and large, however, it does seem true that the various Orthodox churches abroad—because of their much greater identification with Folk-nationalist aspirations in Europe—have played a greater part than the Catholic church in welding migrants into communities which have strong Folk loyalties, as distinct from regional or district loyalties.

FOLK-NATIONALISM, STATE-NATIONALISM: REGIONAL AND DISTRICT LOYALTIES

The connexion between religious and Folk-nationalist aspirations leads naturally to a consideration of the effects of nationalist loyalties on the principal districts of origin and to the power of central governments to override those forces making for local autonomy. The distinction was drawn earlier (see p. 5) between Folk and the modern nation and between Folk-nationalism (the endeavours of a Folk to achieve or retain political independence or autonomy) and state-nationalism—the process whereby an artificial nation-state such as Yugoslavia intentionally or unintentionally uses political unity to foster loyalty to the political unit as a whole. Let us first consider the relationship between the Folk and local areas such as the district or region. This is simple where the Folk occupies little more territory than a region—as with the Maltese, Basques, Slovenes, or Macedo-Slavs—for here regional loyalties tend to coincide with Folk loyalties. Where the Folk occupies a wide geographical area, however, as with the Greeks, there can be much conflict between Folk and regional forces, let alone between Folk and district forces.

District loyalties, based as they are on propinquity, mutual intelligibility, speed of communication, common political his-

---

[46] The Greek churches abroad normally come under the direct control of the Patriarch of Constantinople, not under the control of the self-governing churches of Greece, Cyprus, Crete, etc.

tory, and so on, arise spontaneously with very little effort. Regional loyalties also, for much the same reasons, frequently develop without much effort, especially where a region has had a prolonged history as one administrative or feudal unit. But Folk loyalties, particularly when the Folk is widely dispersed, usually require something more positive. Some historians find this positive cohesive force in a written Folk-national literature, claiming that 'nationalism is an intellectual concept, impossible without literacy. The man who cannot read and write speaks a "dialect"; this becomes the "national language" only on the printed page.'[47] There is much truth in this contention, as evidence the difference between Spain and Italy. Spanish 'state-nationalism' has failed to prevent the Basque and Catalan peoples persisting in attempts to gain autonomy and independence, partly because there appeared in the nineteenth century a Basque and Catalan literature and press sufficiently strong to offer an alternative to Castilian literature and learning. In Italy the regional dialects and cultures failed to develop literatures sufficiently viable to resist the impact of official Italian; partly as a result the various Italian regions have never developed an effective Folk-nationalist spirit. Likewise in France, the medieval Provençal literature was too remote from everyday life to provide a modern vehicle for the vague stirrings of Provençal autonomy.

The contention that Folk-nationalism requires a written literature, however, ignores the fact that a literature only becomes necessary for the preservation of a Folk when literacy is widespread and education is general; a written language confined to a few 'literati' has little relevance for an unlettered peasantry, but when numerous peasant children are taught to read and write then a language can only flourish if it is itself the language taught in school. Several important consequences flow from this. First, in conditions of widespread illiteracy such as prevailed in many districts of origin during the years in which we are interested (p. 57 above), other important forces than a Folk-nationalist literature may be at work. Besides the oral teaching of nationalistic parish priests, there has been the potent force of those many ballads and epics that have been passed down the generations by family storytellers or travelling bards and poets: the Nemanjid cycle, which chronicles the mighty deeds of Serbia's medieval princes; the Kosovo cycle, which sets forth the tragic struggles of

47 A. J. P. Taylor, *The Hapsburg Monarchy*, p. 30.

the South Slav peoples to defend themselves against the on-coming Turks;[48] the story of Skanderburg, that extraordinary warrior who successfully defeated all Turkish attempts to con-trol Albania in the mid-fifteenth century—these and other national epics have been as effective as any written national literature in Europe and have been carried abroad by emigrants, there to pass on by word of mouth to the first and second gen-erations born abroad.

Second, there may well be great differences in the sentiments of succeeding generations. This is not so apparent with Slovenia, Croatia, or Serbia, where the various languages attained literacy and official status before the creation of Yugoslavia. But in Italy the case has been very different; only in recent years has the spread of general education enabled standard Italian to exploit the failure of the regional dialects to obtain official literary status. As a result, peasant farmers who were young in Reggio Calabria, Catania, or the Veneto between 1890 and 1920 had only a vague sense of loyalty to the Italian Folk superimposed on their well-developed regional loyalties and sentiments; where-as young persons in the same areas since World War II often have a much more strongly developed feeling of loyalty to the Italian fatherland, and find it much easier to take an interest in the societies and papers organized on the basis of the Italian Folk. These differences are clearly reflected abroad and, when added to differences arising from changes in the customs and standards of living in Italy itself, go far to explain why there is often great diversity, even conflict, in the opinions and senti-ments of the pre-war and post-war generations of migrants.

A third consequence of this situation is the cultural rift that has so often appeared between educated and illiterate families. In part this reflects class distinctions that have prevailed over much of Europe, especially over those parts of Calabria, Sicily, and Dalmatia that for long maintained large aristocratic estates and all the associated class distinctions. But in part this rift re-flects a genuine difference of sentiment towards the culture and literature of the country in question. In Serbia, Bulgaria, Greece, or any other country where the Folk-nationalistic sentiments of the peasantry coincided with those of the educated classes— largely because the Turkish overlords had long since eliminated the local gentry, so forcing the peasantry themselves to provide

48 'Kosovo' is still held as a national day amongst the Serbs of California, and is one of the great festivals that helps keep the Serb people of California together.

the commercial and professional classes—this particular conflict did not develop. In Spain, Italy, and the old Austro-Hungarian Empire, however, there often appeared a conflict between the educated classes conversant with, say, Florentine Italian, the writings of Dante and Machiavelli, or the nationalist literature of Mazzini or Gioberti, and the illiterate peasantry who possessed little more than their district and regional loyalties.[49] This conflict has often appeared abroad, and it is one of the main tasks of any detailed inquiry into migrant settlement to discover how far the peasantry tended to form communities based on district or regional ties and how much, or little, interest they took in the Folk-nationalist societies and papers founded by the minority of their educated compatriots

It is true of course, that Folk self-consciousness has sometimes been increased by the mere fact of emigration. An illiterate peasant abroad has often become much more aware of his own Folk, largely 'in consequence of the feeling of the striking difference between his speech, his customs, his conceptions, from those of the people who surround him'.[50] This in turn has reacted upon relatives and friends still in Europe—as one Albanian said: 'I had never realized I was an Albanian until my brother came from America in 1909. He belonged to an Albanian Society over there.'[51] Indeed, this heightened awareness of Folk, both amongst those migrating and those remaining, together with the funds collected by Folk-nationalist societies in the outer world, played no small part in building up the nationalist movements of Europe during the nineteenth and early twentieth centuries. But this situation has not greatly affected the clash between regional and Folk loyalty amongst people such as the Italians. Just as being flung against persons of a different country has heightened the Folk-nationalist sentiments of many migrants, so being flung against compatriots of another dialect, culture, and system of beliefs has sometimes heightened awareness of regional differences. It is very easy for a Sicilian living in a predominantly Venetian community abroad to feel he is a being quite apart and to repeat the old saying that in the nineteenth century Italy

49 Many of the peasantry took part in Garibaldi's campaigns to unify Italy, but these activities were short-lived outbursts of nationalist ardour, quite different from the long-term nationalist activities of the intelligentsia.

50 A. Giller, letter to *Gazeta Polska* of Chicago, 1879, quoted R. E. Park and H. A. Miller, *Old World Traits Transplanted*, p. 135.

51 Manas Laukas, 'Life History' (MS.), quoted Park and Miller, op. cit., p. 146.

was united but not unified. This indeed has happened in Australia and this factor, also, the investigator of settlement abroad must endeavour to examine.

The general conclusion of this discussion on Folk-nationalism, then, is that with peoples who have had a long Folk-nationalist tradition, and have reinforced that tradition with literature and education, these traditions will act strongly against the forces working for district and regional separateness. This applies particularly to the Basques, Catalans, the South Slav peoples, the Greeks, Albanians, and Maltese. With the Italians, however, the failure of the regions to develop strong written dialects in self-protection against standard Italian has produced a marked difference between the various generations of migrants: on the older, illiterate peasant migrants the forces of Italian Folk-nationalism act rather feebly against district and regional forces; on the younger generation they sit more heavily and may well prove to act as strongly against district and regional forces as in the case of other southern Europeans.

So much for the relations between district, region and Folk. What of the relations between Folk and state in those countries that embrace more than one Folk? Or, putting the question in terms of emotions and aspirations, what of the relationship between Folk-nationalism and state-nationalism? Here we are not primarily concerned with political units, such as Greece or Italy, that consist almost entirely of one Folk but have small minorities of other Folk in border provinces—Macedo-Slavs and Albanians in northern Greece and Tyrolean Germans in northern Italy. Countries such as these, often frightened that they may lose their border provinces to neighbouring powers, have frequently tried to consolidate their position either by insisting that all citizens adopt the language and culture of the predominant Folk or by asserting that the minority Folk does not really exist, and that those citizens who have unfortunately come under alien influences must be speedily reconverted. Hence the numerous stringent campaigns of Hellenizing and Italianizing border minorities and the resultant bitterness amongst minority peoples affected. This bitterness had been of very great importance abroad—especially in determining relationships between Greeks and Macedo-Slavs. It is, however, less a problem of relationship between Folk-nationalism and state-nationalism than the identification of state-nationalism with the Folk-nationalism of the predominant Folk and the attempted elimination of all other Folk-nationalism.

The situation has been somewhat different in countries such as Spain, where border minorities have been less important than major Folk differences within the well-established boundaries of an ancient political entity. By the time migrants from Spain began coming to Australia the Castilian ethnic culture had succeeded in dominating two-thirds of the state and may well have eliminated all other cultures had not the Basque and Catalan peoples produced a lively literature of their own and made strenuous efforts to resist Castilian literature, culture, central administration, and economic discrimination. Had the Castilian Spaniards succeeded without fuss Spain would have become very like France and Italy: countries with marked regional differences but, except perhaps for the Sardinians, with no people so definitely distinguishable from the majority that they could be described as a separate Folk. In practice, if not in policy, Spain has fluctuated, rather like Great Britain, between a one-Folk state similar to Greece and a union of Folk on the lines of modern Yugoslavia, where Folk-nationalism operates in terms of federation and state-nationalism is left by itself to keep, or attempt to keep, the state together as an effective political unity.

The disentangling of the history of all these ethnic and political fluctuations is unnecessary here; what matter are the attitudes and characteristics of migrants coming to Australia. The position of the Spanish is somewhat obscure, since the number of migrants has been so few that the small Basque and Catalan settlements have never had much opportunity for showing whether they were governed primarily by Folk- or state-nationalist considerations. What little is known of Basque settlers in northern Queensland and of Catalan settlers in Melbourne suggests that loyalty to Spain and consciousness of having much in common with other Spaniards have been much less important than district, regional, and Folk loyalties on the one hand and a general identification, at any rate so far as the Catalans are concerned, with the larger Latin ethnic grouping on the other.

The position of the South Slavs is much clearer, though here again it is necessary to be somewhat arbitrary about the complexities of ethnico-political relationships. Folk-nationalism has always been strong in Yugoslavia—so much so that the greatest internal threat to the unity of the country since its beginning in 1918 came from the violent reaction of many Croats against Serb attempts to run inter-war Yugoslavia as a Serb-dominated state. The central government at Belgrade was therefore regarded with grave suspicion by a great many Croats, and the development of a Yugoslav nationalist spirit greatly impeded thereby. Indeed, it can be argued that state-nationalism was strongest in the days of the Hapsburg Empire—when the Yugoslav state existed only as a dream—and in the early twenties, when elation and goodwill at the success of their joint efforts to overthrow the Hapsburgs were still very strong.

All this emerges very clearly in the history of the South Slavs abroad. Slavonic—later Yugoslav—societies, for example, were often at their zenith between 1870 and 1930 and then declined before the separate Serb and Croat societies that with fierce ardour espoused the cause of their Folk home in Europe. This trend became even stronger with the bitter clashes between various Croat and Serb forces during World War II, and it was only with Marshal Tito's successful resistance to Russia that Yugoslav state-nationalism obviously became as powerful as the existing Folk-nationalist forces. These more recent fluctuations have also been important abroad, especially in the relationship between members of the old Slavonic societies and those intransigent and bitter Folk-nationalists who left Europe as displaced persons.

POLITICS, ADMINISTRATION, LAW AND ORDER

The sentiments and loyalties that lie behind Folk-nationalism and state-nationalism do not necessarily march with political and administrative realities. A strong state-nationalist spirit does not necessarily imply a strong central government. Nor does a strong Folk spirit imply strong Folk government or autonomous administration. Nor, indeed, do strong regional loyalties and sentiments necessarily imply the existence of strong regional governments. As a result, it is quite possible for national or regional loyalties to exist side by side with conditions of administrative incompetence or anarchy in which local units such as the village, district, or family provide the only effective forces of law and order. To some extent this was the situation in Sicily and Calabria under the Bourbon princes, who provided southern Italy and Sicily with such venal and incompetent government that they became a byword throughout the western world. This 'negation of God erected into a system of government'[52] left marks upon southern Italian administration long after the unification of Italy in 1860; indeed, right up till the decades which saw the beginnings of migration to Australia. In conditions where many acts of vio-

[52] A phrase coined by W. E. Gladstone when discussing the iniquities of the Neapolitan régime.

lence passed unheeded by the authorities, where many judges
were venal, where the innocent were imprisoned five years or
more in awaiting trial, where the brutal and corrupt police
released ne'er-do-wells and terrorized the neighbourhood, it is
small wonder that people took justice in their own hands, practised vendettas, glorified bandits, and told children that police-
men should be shot on sight.

In areas where incompetent administrators represented foreign
conquerors such as the Ottoman Turks the situation was often
worse. During the eighteenth and nineteenth centuries the Ottoman Empire grew steadily weaker and the rapacity, corruption,
and arbitrary behaviour of its local officials correspondingly
worse. Not unnaturally the natives avoided contact with Turkish
authorities as much as possible. The periodic struggles for
liberation produced an even greater break-down of organized
administration and left the people no alternative but their own
resources. In Macedonian and Serb districts the *zadruga* often
administered its own justice and maintained its own code of
morality and order. In most Albanian districts, where the tribal
system has remained strongly entrenched, the tribe or clan was
responsible for keeping order among its members and for controlling relations with other tribes—usually on the lines of the
code of Lek Dukagjin, a fifteenth-century Albanian chieftain
whose somewhat grim ordinances were designed to check crime
by prescribing specific punishments, to permit fine and house-
burning as humaner alternatives to death, and to enable a blood-
feud (the normal method of revenging murder) to terminate if
the elders of both tribes were prepared to meet in council and
lay down conditions for a settlement.

The general effect of these conditions in southern Italy and
the Balkans was that homicide, assault, wilful personal injury,
rape, and abduction remained relatively frequent—in the early
years of the twentieth century the rate for such acts of violence
was three times as high in Calabria and Sicily as in the northern
regions of Italy.[53] To some extent these tendencies have been
carried overseas to countries of settlement, since migrants find
it difficult to realize overnight that they have landed in countries
where the governments and police forces are relatively efficient
and incorrupt—hence the great outcry in the United States during the early years of the twentieth century at the high crime

---

[53] *Statistica Guidizaria Penale* 1905-6, quoted by the U.S.A. Immigration
Commission, 1907-10 *Reports*, vol. 4, pp. 196 ff.

rate amongst migrants from southern Europe.[54] Taken by and large, however, these crimes of violence were confined to members of the same ethnic group and tended to diminish when settlers realized the efficiency of governments abroad.[55]

At this point it would be appropriate to extend the survey of administration and justice into the workings of the various political systems and the policies and ideologies of the various political parties. Unfortunately it is not always easy to discover reliable information about political affiliations in such small areas as our particular districts of origin. Nor is it possible to obtain documentary information about the political opinions of migrants coming to Australia before 1939. Even detailed inquiries in the field produce deceptive results—not solely because they are often unrepresentative but also because migrants have not always been willing to make their true opinions plain.

There is, however, one general point worth making. The vast majority of Australia's pre-war migrants were rural and urban labourers or artisans and it seems that a very great number were less interested in politics than in establishing themselves in their new country. Indeed, there is evidence to suggest that in many places the more politically conscious peasants and labourers tended to stay in Europe in order to take part in political activities; the less politically conscious were inclined to leave their native land and settle overseas.[56]

Those peasant migrants who were clearly influenced by the Peasant and Agrarian Parties of the decades just before and just after World War I are obvious exceptions to this. And here a word of warning is necessary. Some think that all peasant peoples are backward superstitious folk to whom Socialism or Communism represents a fierce attack on traditional religious beliefs and on ancient notions concerning the private ownership of land. In practice, the Peasant Parties of pre-war Europe were usually anti-clerical and very often highly sympathetic to Communist Russia—especially in those South Slav countries which had received support from Russia in their struggles for independence.[57] To some extent this explains why so many pre-war migrants from the Roman Catholic areas of central Dalmatia became sympathetic to the Communist movement in Australia

54 U.S.A. Immigration Commission, 1907-10, loc. cit.; Foerster, *Italian Emigration in our Time*, pp. 404 ff.
55 See p. 307 below.
56 Cf. McDonald, 'Italy's Rural Social Structure'.
57 Hugh Seton-Watson, *Eastern Europe between the Wars*, esp. pp. 261-4.

G

and were able to found many local societies on this basis.[58] Many
other Dalmatians, of course, remained loyal to the social teaching of the Roman church, and only a close examination of each
group will reveal the strength of each ideology, and also the
number of those who have remained indifferent both to the
church and to Communism. Much the same holds for other peasant migrants, both Catholic and Orthodox.

[58] See p. 241 below.

CHAPTER IV

MIGRATION TO AUSTRALIA

The sails were fill'd, and fair the light winds blew,
As glad to waft him from his native home;
And fast the white rocks faded from his view,
And soon were lost in circumambient foam:
And then, it may be, of his wish to roam
Repented he, but in his bosom slept
The silent thought, nor from his lips did come
One word of wail, whilst others sate and wept,
And to the reckless gales unmanly moaning kept.

Childe Harold's Pilgrimage, I, 12

THERE are those who leave their native land in the spirit of high adventure, or aglow with joy at escape from domestic scenes too narrow and too confined; there are others who leave with a shadow on their souls, the unspoken fear of permanent separation from the home that gave them birth. Those who have themselves experienced emigration and have later written about it, as well as those who have watched and described the process from close at hand, have often dwelt on this moment of parting, so poignant for those who stay behind as well as for those who leave. Some have described incidents where the pain of separation became too great, as when a father on the dock of a migrant vessel leaving Valetta for Australia could no longer bear the sight of his wife and children weeping on the quay below and rushed ashore just as the gangways were being withdrawn. Others have dwelt on the nostalgia that, from the moment of departure, grows steadily and inexorably until it forces the immigrant away from the new land back to the country of his birth. Indeed, some observers have made this nostalgia the central theme of their examination, as did Fortunato Mizzi in Valetta in the 1880s when he opposed organized Maltese emigration to Australia on the grounds that such schemes meant 'eternal separation' from the beloved Maltese archipelago—*il fior del mondo*—and cut clean across the traditional Maltese system of settling in Mediterranean countries sufficiently close to Malta to enable frequent and easy re-migration.[1] Whether such

[1] See Mizzi's newspaper *Malta*, Valetta, 28, 30 Nov. 1883, 14 July 1884.

observers were justified in making nostalgia the central theme of their analysis is, of course, another matter: a high re-migration rate may not represent a permanent movement home but a purely temporary movement undertaken by male migrants in order to sell property, choose brides, collect families, or visit relatives and friends.[2]

Other writers have emphasized quite different themes of the migration story. Some have concentrated on the difference between the eighteenth and nineteenth centuries—'free periods' when restrictions on both immigration and emigration were few and ineffective—and the twentieth century, a controlled period with well-policed quota laws and strongly enforced restrictions on emigration that have markedly affected the course of world migration. Other observers have been more interested in contrasting the power of economic forces such as wage and price levels with that of non-economic forces such as language, religion, and family structure (the opinion that economic forces normally dominate the process of emigration and settlement has recently been challenged). Yet other writers have highlighted the causes of migration and have spent much time speculating on whether forces which 'push' migrants away from their place of birth—overpopulation, poverty, political upheaval, religious persecution—are more or less important than forces which 'pull' migrants to the place of settlement—booms, high wages, unoccupied areas, the lure of distant lands, or the wish to be with friends happily settled far away.

One aspect of the migration story has not, perhaps, received all the attention it merits: the mechanics of migration and the different settlement patterns that result from different modes of venturing abroad. Admittedly, many writers have described organized colonization—schemes sponsored and controlled by government and public companies. Indeed, in the activities of such bodies lie the exciting and often romantic origins of Europe's settlement of the Americas and Australasia and her occupation, influential even though temporary, of much of Africa and Asia. Certainly this mode of migration, and all the resulting patterns of land settlement and colonial administration and politics, have received close attention.

Private ventures by individuals and small groups of friends, however, or the quiet success of a pioneer and the unspectacular

2 The movement back to a country of origin, here called 're-migration', is a complex movement; for the distinction between 're-migration', 'return movement' and 'second-time migration', see Appendix 2:4.

arrival of one relative and friend after another to join him—
often without assistance from any government or company—
have stirred only slight ripples on the waters of historical writing. Yet these smaller enterprises, too, have their glamour and
excitement, and the migrant communities and settlements spring-
ing from them have an appeal distinctively their own. Numbers
of writers, it is true, have touched upon them, but only a few
have explored their fascinating intricacies in any detail. Yet these
quieter events have been of paramount importance in the story
of southern European settlement in Australia and are intimately
linked with the phenomenon known as 'chain migration'. Much
of what follows, therefore, will relate to the small-scale movements of friends and relatives and to the mechanics of chain
migration.

This does not mean that the mechanics of migration is the
only factor needing examination. On the contrary, all the themes
just mentioned—nostalgia and re-migration, government pro-
hibitions and controls, 'push' forces and 'pull' forces, the relative strength of economic and non-economic factors—all enter
the story of privately arranged migration and settlement and
must all be considered in turn. At this point there is no need to
dwell on the question whether economic forces have completely
overshadowed cultural forces such as language, religion, and
family structure. The whole trend of this book, to say nothing
of the detail set out in the previous chapter, makes it plain that
in our view cultural forces are every bit as important as economic. In this sense the book itself is a discussion of the question
and further reference is redundant.

It is necessary, however, to dwell for a moment on the contrast
between the so-called free period of the nineteenth century and
restricted period of the twentieth, since there are certain miscon-
ceptions about the importance of governmental controls that it
would be as well to clarify before describing the process of
migration.

GOVERNMENT CONTROL OF MIGRATION

In practice, controls were imposed by the countries of origin
and Australia, but the former were relatively unimportant and
can be discussed quite quickly. The Italian government was one
that tried to control and supervise the process of emigration,
notably in its efforts since the 1870s to control the employment
of children abroad, supervise conditions of employment, discourage emigration to countries where unemployment or social up-

heaval were prevalent, and supervise conditions on transoceanic ships. But such controls had little effect on the long-term volume of emigration to Australia. The only noticeably effective restrictions were those which various belligerent countries in Europe placed on the emigration of men of military age during the later years of World War I and those promulgated in 1927 by the Fascist government of Italy in its efforts to build up the Italian population of Europe and Africa—neither set of restrictions lasted very long: the former until the end of the war, and the latter until 1930 when the depression forced the Fascist government to let Italian unemployed seek occupations abroad.[3] There were other controls placed on emigration—restrictions on the number of passports issued for Australia during the 1920s and 1930s, for example—but these were usually the result of direct requests by Australia, or at least of negotiations between Australia and the countries concerned, and are better considered as part of Australia's restrictive immigration policy.

This policy goes back to the years before Federation when the governments of the various colonies enacted their own legislation prohibiting or controlling the entry of Asiatics and of persons unsuitable for reasons of health or morality. Indeed, the first Commonwealth Immigration Act of 1901 did little more than sum up these colonial Acts and regulations. These measures, however, had very little effect on immigration from southern Europe, especially as diseases such as malaria, which were widespread throughout the Mediterranean (pp. 44-5 above), were not considered a bar to immigration. Altogether, less than a hundred southern Europeans seem to have been denied entrance for reasons of health or morality before World War I.[4]

Later Acts and regulations of the Federal government extended the categories of those prohibited but, despite protests against the arrival of Maltese and others who allegedly imperilled 'Australian civilization' by their low living standards and the safety of Australian workers by their ignorance of English when engaged in hazardous occupations such as blasting,[5]

[3] For a full treatment of Italy's emigration policy towards Australia, see McDonald, Migration from Italy.

[4] Commonwealth of Australia, Parliamentary Papers (henceforth Com. Parl. Pap.): 'Returns of persons denied entry to the Commonwealth'.

[5] Questions in Senate and House of Representatives on 17 Aug. 1912, 24 Sept. 1912, 2 Oct. 1912; letter from Federated Mining Employees' Association of Australia Mt Lyell branch, to Minister of External Affairs, 14 Aug. 1912 (Commonwealth Archives Office—henceforward C.A.O. C.P. 235) 12/18479.

these had little application to southern European immigrants until 1916. In that year, however, the government prohibited the entry of all Maltese and Greeks—except close dependent relatives of those already settled in Australia—apparently because the arrival of several hundred Greeks and Maltese on the eve of the government's referendum for conscription for military service overseas produced an immediate outcry that the government intended to replace Australian conscripts by cheap southern European labour.[6] After strong representations the restrictions were lifted in 1920, though Australia insisted that Malta limit the number of passports issued for Australia to 260 per annum, the average intake of the years 1912-14.[7] In 1923, after representations by the British government that this Australian quota was not only contributing to Malta's overpopulation difficulties but was aiding anti-British feeling in Malta itself,[8] the Australian government agreed to raise the limit to a maximum of twenty new settlers per month per each port of disembarkation—a measure calculated to give a maximum intake of about 1,200 per annum—provided that illiterate Maltese were sponsored by relatives in Australia.[9]

In retrospect, these war-time and immediate post-war restrictions seem relatively unimportant. First, transport difficulties and conscription in Europe reduced the immigration of southern European groups to practically nothing during the later war years. Secondly, not only was the prohibition relaxed for numbers of Greeks already on the way but immigration from Greek islands such as Ithaca and Kastellorizo actually fell away after the restrictions were lifted in 1920. Finally, the small rise in

6 Prime Minister to Premier of N.S.W., 6 May 1920 (C.A.O. C.P. 235 20/5870); Malta's *Report on Emigration 1922-3*.

7 *Report on Emigration 1922-3*, p. 7; memo by Dept of External Affairs, 19 Apr. 1917 (C.A.O. C.P. 235 17/18651).

8 Quotas are fixed limits placed on the number of any one nationality, occupation, or class that may leave or enter a country in a given period of time. They may be incorporated in a statute—as in the U.S.A.—or fixed under some general statutory power enabling the executive to control immigration by whatever administrative devices it thinks best. The statutory quota has the advantage of publicity and the disadvantage of rigidity: the administrative quotas are much more flexible but they sometimes lack much publicity. Quotas imposed by Australia have always been administrative, and their existence has not always been realized.

9 Prime Minister to Premier of S.A., 19 Aug. 1925 (C.A.O. C.P. 235 25/22679); Malta Government Notice on Emigration to Australia, 10 Jan. 1924; *Report on Emigration 1924-5*, p. xxvii.

Maltese immigration after the quota was raised in 1923—from about 200 to 360 per annum—suggests that the annual quota of 260 imposed on Maltese immigration between 1920 and 1923 affected relatively few persons, no more than 500. These ups and downs in migration appear in Table IV, which sets out the significant trends in the immigration of new adult male settlers from 1908 to 1940.[10]

The next restrictions on southern European immigration were those of 1924, when the government, in effect, extended its limit of 1,200 new settlers per annum, and its linguistic restrictions, from the Maltese to other immigrant peoples. During 1923-4, largely as a result of unemployment amongst friendless Italians arriving in the previous two years, the government passed an Amending Immigration Act prohibiting the entry of any alien likely to become a charge on the public funds through insufficiency of means.[11] At first it did not use these powers as it had already reached agreement with Italy that passports would be refused to persons likely to become a public burden. But late in 1924, as a result of unemployment amongst groups of Albanians, Greeks, and Yugoslavs, who had recently arrived with very little money and with insufficient English to obtain jobs easily, the government decided to prohibit the entry of any alien not possessing a written guarantee from some sponsor in Australia or £40 of his own. These measures were accompanied by requests to the governments of the various countries of origin, and to the British consuls therein, that they discourage persons with inadequate English, refrain from issuing passports and visas to persons lacking the required money or guarantee, and limit the number of new passports and visas issued each year to approximately 1,200 each for Albanians, Greeks, and Yugoslavs, and to a number for the Italians that could be easily absorbed into the Australian economy—in practice, about 5,000 per

10 Statistics of newly-arrived adult settlers, when obtainable, are preferable to statistics of total immigration. For meaning of the term 'settler' see Appendixes 1:3, 2:2-3.

11 A clause in the 1901 Act prohibited the entry of persons likely to become a charge on public funds, but its interpretation was doubtful. The government could have applied the dictation test and deported pauper migrants who failed it; but the government was somewhat averse to applying this test to European immigrants after they had already entered Australia and preferred to have a clause specifically prohibiting the entry of Europeans who might become paupers. See Senator Pearce's speech, 12 July 1923, Commonwealth of Australia, *Parliamentary Debates* (henceforward Com. *Parl. Deb.*), CIII, 1030-1.

INDEX OF ANNUAL AVERAGE IMMIGRATION OF ADULT
MALE SETTLERS 1908-39
(Period 1924 = Index of 100)

District	Date of First Arrival									
	1908-14	1917-19	1920-21	1922-24	1925-27	1928	1929-30	1931-34	1935-36	1937-39
Total	40	4	24	100	129	69	25	5	8	32
Veneto	10	..	10	100	211	78	28	7	3	23
Valtellina	48	..	27	100	71	34	19	3	2	17
Monferrato	15	..	7	100	58	26	13	4	2	6
Apuan Alps	39	..	..	100	289	56	17	14	17	11
Abruzzi	7	..	..	100	714	285	110	17	36	71
Molfetta	65	..	155	100	225	125	40	..	5	75
R. Calabria	1	..	..	100	184	55	33	11	9	68
Lipari	14	..	54	100	86	14	..	3	15	3
Salina	108	..	153	100	131	8	23	..	8	15
Messina	29	..	53	100	173	153	30	3	10	31
Nth Catania	13	..	51	100	78	28	28	5	3	9
Ithaca	77	9	2	100	38	23	8	4	12	27
Kythera	77	4	31	100	34	38	3	1	12	53
Kastellorizo	48	30	6	100	31	35	10	1	10	17
Lesbos	5	..	..	100	65	30	..	..	5	35
Athens	60	6	10	100	60	20	45	..	10	25
Medjumurje	..	..	..	100	2,800	2,400	100	100	200	700
Dalmatia	37	2	4	100	190	75	10	2	7	29
S.W. Macedonia	3	4	..	100	139	119	47	1	10	59
S.E. Albania	2	..	..	100	177	1,062	269	4	61	400
Malta*	71	..	71†	100†	104	51	28	9	18	?
Spain*	?	?	?	100	182	289	132	58	53	61

Source: Appendix 1: 17.

* Male arrival statistics, as no date of first arrival available.
† Periods run 1920-22 and 1923-24, to show influence of quota.

annum.[12] All these events, together with the fear that the new United States restrictions on immigration would divert hordes of southern Europeans to Australia, led the government to pass in 1925 an Immigration Act enabling it specifically to prohibit the entry of aliens of any nationality, race, class, or occupation; but this legislation, coming after all the excitement was over, remained virtually inoperative.

These restrictions of 1924, drastic though they may seem, in practice had little depressive effect upon southern European immigration, and so contrast markedly with the American restrictions of 1924; whereas the United States laws of 1917-24 reduced total Italian immigration to less than 40,000 from the 215,000 per annum that had prevailed in the first decade of the century, the Australian restrictions of 1924 were followed by an increase in total Italian immigration—from approximately 3,200 to 6,000 per annum. And, so far as new adult male immigrants are concerned, the naturalization records suggest that immigration from most districts increased after the restrictions came into force, the exceptions being various Greek islands, Catania, the Monferrato, the Valtellina, and the island of Lipari (see Table IV), and there are special reasons why these districts of origin had passed their migration peak by 1925.

Moreover, although the 1924 restrictions were followed by an increase in immigration from most districts of origin, this increase did not often reach the quota limit of 1,200 new settlers per annum, even though in practice these limits were

[12] Letters from the Prime Minister to State Premiers and from Secretary for Home and Territories to foreign consuls—Dec. 1924 to May 1925 (C.A.O. C.P. 235 25/21985); also P.M.'s speeches to House of Representatives, 25 June 1925 (Com. *Parl. Deb.*, cx, 457-8), and M. Charlton, 23 Feb. 1928 (ibid., cxvii, 3346 ff.). The visa arrangement did not apply to Maltese, who were British nationals, or to Italian nationals, who by an agreement like those with north European countries needed no visa to enter Australia. No limit was suggested for Spaniards or Portuguese, since their immigration was a mere trickle and showed no signs of increasing, or for Bulgarians, who still came under the five-year ban imposed on the immigration of ex-enemy subjects by the Immigration Act of 1920. The Maltese arrangement of 1923 remained untouched by the 1924 agreements.

At this time, then, Australia administered its quota system by asking the governments and consuls in Europe to limit the number of passports and visas. After 1931-2 this was no longer necessary as Australia adopted the landing permit system whereby aliens seeking entry had to possess a landing permit, normally issued beforehand by the government department responsible for immigration and sent to the intending migrant. After 1931-2, therefore, Australia could administer a quota system simply by controlling the number of landing permits issued.

not rigidly enforced either by the British consuls or the Australian officials, who sometimes offset a surplus in one period against a deficiency in another. Indeed, the Yugoslavs, with about 1,100 immigrants for the period 1925-7, were the only people to press against the limits; others—Greeks about 700, Albanians about 100, and Maltese about 300 per annum—were well below it.[13]

The Labour opposition were quick to notice that immigration fell well below quota limits and between 1924 and 1929 frequently attacked the government, on the grounds that the quotas were much too high, that the sponsorship system was too liberal, and that the whole procedure failed to prevent appreciable numbers of southern Europeans coming to Australia and competing for jobs with unemployed Australians.[14] The Bruce-Page government, however, refused to impose further restrictions until mid-1928; then increasing unemployment moved them to ask the consuls and governments concerned to halve the 1,200 quota on Albanians, Greeks, and Yugoslavs; for the same reason they accepted with pleasure the Fascist government's new policy of stopping the emigration of all Italians except close dependent relatives (an estimated maximum of 3,000 Italian immigrants each year, including women and children).[15] The Labour Party, however, were quite unappeased by these measures, and when they took office late in 1929 immediately halved the quotas again and then, towards the end of 1930, completely prohibited the entry of all southern Europeans except close dependent relatives of persons already settled in Australia or persons with considerable financial resources of their own.[16] This, in effect, meant abandoning the quota system altogether and relying entirely on other kinds of restriction; it also meant moving away from agreement with Italy, which was by 1930 relaxing its 1927 restrictions on emigration. The Lyons government, which succeeded the Labour

13 These figures are below the figures of annual arrivals because, referring only to newly-arrived adult males, they exclude persons re-entering Australia after a visit back to Europe, wives and children coming to join their husbands and fathers, etc.

14 E.g. debates in House of Representatives, 29 Sept. 1927 and 23 Feb. 1928.

15 S. M. Bruce (Prime Minister) to House of Representatives, 12 June 1928, Com. *Parl. Deb.*, cxix, 5912-3.

16 A. Blakeley (Minister for Home Affairs) to House of Representatives, 10 Dec. 1930, Com. *Parl. Deb.*, cxxvii, 1227; *Commonwealth Year Book* 1931, p. 678 (ii).

government early in 1932, in effect continued this policy until
1936, though it did agree in 1934 to define the financial resources
required by an independent settler as £500. The fall in the
immigration of new adult settlers associated with all these
measures, though not necessarily caused by them, is clearly
visible in Table IV. In absolute numbers it meant that the
immigration of new adult settlers, for the years 1931-4, fell to
something like 250 Italians per annum, 125 Greeks, 100 Yugoslavs, 20 Albanians, and 50 Maltese. Table IV also shows the
fall in Italian immigration associated with the Italian government's restrictions enforced between 1928 and 1930.

In 1936 the Lyons government decided that economic conditions had improved sufficiently for them to relax the restrictions
on southern European immigration by reducing the £500 for
independent settlers to £200 and by permitting those already
in Australia to sponsor not only close dependent relatives but
also adult workers who had £50 of their own and intended
to enter occupations where vacancies existed.[17] The government,
however, did not overtly reimpose any quotas,[18] apparently
because it felt that the modified restrictions would be adequate
to keep the immigration of new adult settlers down to manage-
able numbers—in practice about 3,000 Italians per annum for
the period 1937-9, 900 Greeks, 400 Yugoslavs, 100 Albanians, and
100 Maltese. These numbers represent a considerable rise from
the immigration of the depression years, the extent of which is
set out in Table IV.

On the surface these restrictions of the late twenties and
thirties seem most important: when they came into force
immigration appeared to fall rapidly and when they were
relaxed immigration appeared to rise at once. It is very doubtful,
however, if they were as influential as they seem. Indeed, there
is much to be said for the opinion that the restrictions usually
followed migration trends already determined by other forces.
Thus the fall in immigration during 1929-30, which followed
the quota reductions of 1928-9, went far below the reduced quota
levels. Newly-arrived adult male Greeks and Yugoslavs totalled
only about one-third the quota, and even if we add in all the
non-quota persons—settlers returning to Australia after visits to
Europe, dependent children, and so on—the numbers of Greeks

[17] Paterson (Minister for the Interior) to House of Representatives, 5 May
1936, Com. *Parl. Deb.*, CL, 1246; *Commonwealth Year Book*, 1936, p. 454.
[18] J. McEwen (Minister for the Interior) to House of Representatives, 5
Oct. 1938, Com. *Parl Deb.*, CLVII, 437.

and Yugoslavs still reached only two-thirds or so of the quota limit. Quite clearly factors other than reduced quotas were involved.

It could, with some truth, be argued that what pulled immigration down during these years were the non-quota restrictions (the guarantee by an Australian resident or the £40 landing money); that during depression days far fewer Australian residents could guarantee immigrants a job and far fewer immigrants would have possessed £40; that this being so the restrictive policy was still controlling the migration process. But we must remember that in 1929-30 European migrants were finding Australia economically so unattractive that they were leaving the country in large numbers—far more, in fact, were leaving than were arriving. Table V shows this clearly, even though, by including dependent children coming out to join their fathers in Australia in the total of arrivals, the figures make the surplus of departures over arrivals seem less than in fact it was.

TABLE V

MIGRATION 1929-30

Nationality	Males			Females	
	Arrivals	Departures	A/D*	Arrivals	Departures
Italian	2,804	3,856	72·7	1,367	432
Yugoslav	504	947	53·2	260	98
Greek	497	873	56·9	215	118
Maltese	201	457	44·0	68	20
Spanish	99	105	94·3	47	28

* Arrivals as proportion of departures.

This high departure rate makes it clear that during 1929-30 Australia was not at all attractive to new settlers and that, so far from government restrictions causing a fall in immigration, it is much more likely that many potential immigrants refused to make the long and expensive journey to Australia, even before the heavy restrictions initiated by the Labour government at the end of 1930. Quite apart from this high departure rate, however, there is the plain fact that the distance and expense of travelling to Australia threw the main burden of financing migration on to those already successfully established in Australia and that they, restrictions or no restrictions, were in times of severe depression usually quite unwilling to bring out

impoverished friends and relatives for whom they would have
great difficulty in finding employment. They might be willing
to bring out their womenfolk and families, but that was all
(see pp. 122, 189 below and Table V for excess of female arrivals
over departure in the depression).

The only time administrative restrictions may well have
played an important part in keeping immigration down was
the period 1935-6, just before the government eased restrictions
on independent settlers. The sudden jump in the number of
independent settlers arriving from most districts of origin after
the relaxation of controls—see Table IV—suggests that a number
of potential emigrants in Europe and sponsors in Australia
were awaiting an opportunity to renew migration. But this
was only a short period and the point cannot be pressed too
far: the slight rise in emigration from many districts when the
controls were still in force in 1935-6 shows that, even under the
heavy burden of £500 landing money, migration could get
under way when persons in Europe and Australia were economically placed to start it off again. On the whole, then, it seems
that for the late twenties and thirties, as for the earlier twenties,
Australia's restrictive policy did not decisively determine the
trend of migration, the increase or decrease in which was due
primarily to forces other than administrative policy.

One important question still remains. The imposition of
controls by Australia might not have caused increased or
decreased migration at any particular time, but it might nevertheless have acted as a heavy drag at times of increasing inflow.
Did the restrictions of the mid-twenties and mid-thirties have
such an effect? Would southern European immigration during
the years 1925-7 and 1935-9 have soared much higher than in
fact it did? Would the fears of those who framed the policy of
1924-5—that the United States restrictions would divert thousands of poverty-stricken Europeans to Australia—have been
realized had not restrictions been enforced?

In discussing these questions we must first note that the
restrictions did not necessarily act as a drag upon the increase
in immigration of southern Europeans who had no resources
when they arrived and no settled job arranged for them in
Australia. The histories of various settlers in Australia show
quite clearly that the 1924 clause requiring £40 landing money
or a sponsor in Australia did not prevent a person already in
the country, anxious for the companionship of friends and
relatives, from nominating some poverty-stricken friend even

though he himself might be engaged only in temporary work such as timber-cutting or seasonal fruit-picking and was quite unable to give a firm guarantee of employment.[19] This, of course, happened mainly during periods of relative prosperity when the chances of finding another temporary job were good, both for sponsor and nominee; but it shows how slight was the control over destitute persons who had some sort of contact with persons already in Australia. Even the 1936 provision— that nominees must have £50 of their own—led to much the same situation in that a sponsor with a good but temporary job could find £50 to remit to Europe for the use of an intending emigrant. Still less, of course, did the regulations hold up the migration of persons sponsored by those with settled jobs and economically capable of helping the immigrant considerably on arrival.

From this it is possible to argue that the effect of the restrictions was not to interfere with migration from districts of origin already well represented in Australia—for which there were plenty of sponsors available—but to act as a heavy drag on emigration from districts not well represented in Australia when the restrictions came into force, thereby accentuating and perpetuating the restricted territorial origins of Australia's southern European population that resulted in the great majority of settlers coming from relatively few districts of origin (see p. 13 above). There is some truth in this, and it may be that the 'cluster' picture of southern European settlement in Australia would not be quite so sharp had the restrictive policy never existed.

The importance of this can, however, be exaggerated. In the first place the argument assumes that relatively few districts of origin were represented in Australia when the restrictions came into being. This is not so. Though the great majority of Australia's pre-war southern Europeans came from relatively few districts of origin, the remainder came from a very wide scatter of districts all over southern Europe. But for various reasons these numerous towns and villages did not take advantage of the existence of representatives in Australia. Thus, of forty Greek

19 Interviews and documentary material from field-work among Yugoslavs at one time working in bush areas of N.S.W. and timber areas of W.A.; also with various Italians and Yugoslavs in Murray-Murrumbidgee Irrigation districts. See also McDonald, Migration from Italy, and M. Charlton (Leader of the Labour Opposition) in the Federal Parliament, 1 July 1925, Com. Parl. Deb., cx, 564-5.

islands that sent migrants to Australia only thirteen became
major districts of origin—yet the other twenty-seven all had representatives in Australia by 1924 and could have increased their
numbers under the sponsorship system. In fact, except perhaps
for Kasos in the Dodecanese, the rate of immigration from all
twenty-seven islands slowed up considerably after 1924; as indeed it did from major isles of origin such as Kythera, Ithaca,
Kastellorizo and Lesbos, all of which had hundreds of representatives in Australia by 1924—see Table IV. Quite clearly other
factors than Australian restrictive practices were at work in slowing down the rate of immigration increase and in controlling the
territorial origins of Greek settlement in Australia. Again, to
take an illustration from southern Italy, there were well over
fifty villages and towns of origin for pre-war immigrants from
the region of Campania (Naples), nearly all of which had representatives in Australia by 1925. Yet none of these places, except
Naples itself, ever developed into a really important district of
origin. The same phenomenon appears when we examine migration from, say, northern Italy or Yugoslavia.

In the second place, the existence of restrictions did not stop
quite rapid increases from some districts of origin poorly represented in Australia before 1925. Over 120 villages and towns of
south-east Albania were represented in Australia before 1940,
but apparently less than one-third of these had representatives
in Australia by 1924. The great increase in Albanian emigration
occurred in the period 1925-8—see Table IV—and case histories
suggest that this increase arose partly from the entry into Australia about 1925-6 of various Albanians who had returned to
Albania after earning good money in the United States, become
tired of life in their villages of origin, and used their savings
to produce the £40 necessary to enter Australia when they found
the United States closed to them after 1924. In the later twenties
and thirties, these then proceeded to nominate their friends and
relatives. Emigration from the villages of the Abruzzi-Molise
region of Italy suggests much the same thing. Indeed, it is significant that the districts of origin to recover most rapidly from
the depression were those in Abruzzi, Reggio Calabria, the
Medjumurje, south-east Albania, and south-west Macedonia,
which had been the latest to enter the immigration process—
see Table IV. In short, though the restrictions did to some extent slow down the rate of immigration increase, they certainly
did not prevent a fairly rapid increase in immigration from districts of origin poorly represented in Australia before 1925.

Again, then, forces other than government policy seem to have been predominant in the migration process and in controlling the territoral origins of Australia's southern European settlers. Certainly it seems most unlikely that Australia's restrictive policy converted into a modest stream what otherwise would have become a mighty flood.

The conclusion that in the decades before 1940 government restriction had relatively little influence on the course of migration may seem strange to persons familiar with the complex and effective system of controls enforced by the United States government since 1924 and by the Australian government since 1946. The sharp drop in Italian and Greek migration to Australia after 1956, for instance, occurred primarily because the Australian government decided to restrict severely the practice of southern European settlers in Australia sponsoring numerous relatives and friends from Europe, and refused to accept nominations from almost any sponsor except a child, husband or parent of those desiring to emigrate.[20] But this post-war system has operated in circumstances where there are not only great numbers involved but where Australia has maintained prosperous and peaceful conditions for a relatively long period. The pre-war decades were here very different.

Those familiar with post-war conditions might also feel that government policy has influenced migration very substantially, not only through negative measures such as restrictions, but also through positive measures such as the appointment of Australian representatives abroad whose task it is to select suitable immigrants and arrange for their free or assisted passage to Australia. But here again conditions before World War II were very different in that the various Australian governments almost invariably confined their assisted passage schemes to persons from the United Kingdom. This matter of assisted passages is of great importance and needs elaboration.

The long sea distance from Europe to Australia and the relatively large costs of the passages have tended to act as a dam against the great flood of immigrants received by countries much closer to Europe, more especially by the United States in the early twentieth century when total immigration several times

---

[20] In the two years 1957-8 (the first two-year period after the new restrictions started to affect migration substantially) the net number of permanent arrivals from Italy, Greece, Cyprus, and Malta fell from 41,000 per annum to 19,000 per annum, and their proportion of total immigration from 47% to 27%.

H

exceeded one million persons a year. The expense of travel to Australia has been such that, apart from sailors, the only ones who could afford their own tickets have been businessmen, migrants who had once gone to the Americas and there saved enough to move on to Australia, soldiers receiving accumulated pay on discharge from the army after World War I, and peasants able and willing to sell enough land to cover their expenses.[21] For the majority, however, migration to Australia has been virtually impossible without assistance from someone in Australia. The first source of assistance has been governmental, notably the 1891 venture of the Queensland government which was anxious to replace Kanaka labour in the sugar plantations and brought out 335 agricultural labourers from North Italy. Likewise, after World War I, the Federal government occasionally gave assistance to Maltese wives and children anxious to join their husbands and fathers in Australia.[22] These measures, however, were exceptional and, for southern European migration in general, the state and federal governments gave virtually no assistance until after World War II.

British-Australian employers anxious to obtain southern European labour for their own special projects have also been a source of assistance, one early example being the sugar planters who brought seventy Maltese agricultural labourers out to Queensland in 1883 to replace Kanaka labour. The venture proved a complete failure, however, primarily because the Maltese so disliked being paid at Kanaka rates, well below those paid to other Europeans in Queensland, that they drifted away from the plantations to Brisbane and Sydney.[23] Subsequently other Australian employers brought out a few skilled or unskilled persons from southern Europe, but this practice, it seems, did not become common, and it played a minor role during the years under review.[24]

The third kind of assistance was that given by relatives and

---

[21] Some peasants from the Medjumurje, after the peace treaties following 1918, found some of their property on one side of the River Mur in Yugoslavia and some on the other in Hungary. Though most hung on grimly to their ancestral plots, a few sold their Hungarian property and bought tickets to Australia (interviews with Medjumurje Croats in Australia).

[22] See Malta Govt Reports on Emigration—Supplementary Report for 1920 and Annual Report for 1926-7.

[23] C. A. Price, *Malta and the Maltese*, pp. 178 ff.

[24] Cf. 'Report of the Royal Commission on the Immigration of Non-British Labour', W.A. *Votes and Proceedings of the Parliament*, 1904, vol. 2, Paper A7, pp. 7-8.

friends already successfully established in Australia who could afford to help with passage expenses. This practice, arising essentially from the southern European's sense of loyalty to family and friends (see pp. 62-3 above), became very common. In a sample survey of Italian families from the Veneto, for example, for every adult male who came to Australia between 1910 and 1930 under his own resources there were at least two who had come with the help of family and friends; in the 1930s the proportion of those assisted became still higher. Indeed, despite the large-scale governmental assistance given to southern Europeans since 1947—the Federal government had assisted some 115,000 by June 1962—the practice is still widespread: of the 270,000 or so southern Europeans who came to live in Australia in the period 1945-60, and received no public help, a considerable proportion were persons assisted by relatives and friends already in the country.[25]

The position with re-migration to the country of origin has been somewhat different, since persons wishing to return to Europe have generally needed no assistance. The fact that for over a century the level of real wages has been much higher in Australia than in the Mediterranean has meant that a person quite unable to save money for his passage to Australia could save his return fare relatively quickly. Thus, when the first Maltese and Italians came to Queensland in the eighteen-seventies and eighties, they found that whereas a labourer's wage at home averaged 1s. 3d. or so a day, in Queensland it averaged 8s. or more a day; by living at the same standard to which they were accustomed—and this cost them about 2s. 6d. per day at Queensland prices—they could save at least 5s. per day towards their return fare of £16.[26] This wage-cost differential between the Australian and Mediterranean worlds explains why, in the half-

[25] There is little documentary evidence on assistance given by friends in Australia; the matter can only be assessed in the light of interviews with immigrants themselves. Many persons interviewing immigrants have noted it, e.g. A. H. Martin, tide-surveyor at Fremantle at the turn of the century (evidence to Royal Commission on Immigration of Non-British Labour in W.A., 1904); Ferry ('Ferry Report', p. 49; A28, p. 23); Hempel, Italians in Queensland, p. 80. I have noticed the phenomenon in several Italian, Greek, and Yugoslav communities in Australia, as have Bromley and McDonald, op. cit. For an important American reference see U.S.A. Immigration Commission, 1907-10 Reports, 4, p. 61.

[26] See F. S. Decesare, Reports upon the Suitability of the British Colonies in Australasia as a field of Maltese emigration; also C. A. Price, Malta and the Maltese, p. 178.

century or more before 1940, anything up to 50 per cent of
southern Europeans migrating to Australia were able to make
short trips home to see their families, marry their fiancées,
settle their inheritance, and so on, or else return home permanently or migrate to another country.[27] Governmental authorities
had almost nothing to do with this process of re-migration,
unless the few southern Europeans deported by the Australian
government count as persons receiving public assistance to return
home.

It seems clear, then, that in the century before 1940 governmental control over the course of both migration and re-
migration—either negatively, as restrictions, or positively, in
assisted passages—was relatively unimportant. Southern European
migrants, in short, were primarily influenced by their own
desires and financial capacities or by those of their relatives.

THE PROCESS OF MIGRATION

Any worth-while discusssion of the process of migration must
early make reference to migration statistics, since these are not
only our main source of information but are often difficult to
interpret. Census figures, for example, even when they show
birthplace cross-tabulated by duration of residence in Australia,
can be deceptive if used as an index of immigration and settlement—primarily because of the anomalies concerning members
of a Folk born outside Folk territory, changing political boundaries, and the custom of counting some dependencies as part
of the European power concerned (see pp. 6, 12 above). Other
difficulties arise because census tables do not record persons
who migrate to Australia but die before census day; nor do
they distinguish between persons who come to settle and persons
who stay only a short time before going back to Europe or on
to another country. It is possible to make due allowances for
these anomalies, however, and to use the results with some
confidence.

Annual migration statistics can also be deceptive. Statistics
of arrivals and departures by nationality, such as Australia has
possessed since 1914, do not indicate whether an Italian, say,
has entered Australia to settle indefinitely or merely to pay a
short visit; nor whether an Italian leaving Australia is a visitor
returning home, a person who had intended to settle in Australia
but is either being irresistibly drawn back to Italy or on to

[27] For more precise statistics, see Appendix 2:4-12.

New Zealand or America by a spirit of restless wandering, or a settler making a temporary trip back to Italy to see his family.[28]

Settlers making trips home to Europe can make a considerable difference to the real numbers of persons entering or leaving a country; if many migrants are saving quickly and making temporary visits home to their families they will swell both the number of departures and the number of arrivals, and consequently may falsify the appearance of the migration process. One way to tackle this problem is to discover how many migrants, later well settled in Australia, made trips to and from Europe and elsewhere after their original migration. The information available here, though slender, gives a general picture for the Italians, Greeks, and Yugoslavs during the years 1922-40. W. D. Borrie was able to use an analysis of Italian males entering Queensland between 1927 and 1943, which showed that about one-third returned to Italy three to six years after arrival and that approximately three-quarters of these later came back to Australia.[29] This fits very well with information from the naturalization records which suggest that, between 1924 and 1946, of those Italian men who had been resident in Queensland for ten years or more when naturalized some 30 per cent had made one or more trips back to Europe. The figure for Italian men in Australia as a whole was somewhat smaller—about 23 per cent—while those for Greeks and Yugoslavs were 14 per cent and 12·5 per cent. The proportion making trips to other countries was much smaller, no more than 3 per cent.

Using these proportions as a guide it is possible roughly to reassess the migration statistics by eliminating the double-counting of those visiting Europe or elsewhere. This procedure, which is set out in Appendix 2, suggests that the true number of southern European men coming to Australia was up to one-fifth less than the figures of total arrivals. It also reduces the number and proportion of immigrants who later left Australia and did not return. Even so the numbers here are still relatively high: between 1922 and 1940 about 30 per cent of

---

[28] For detailed discussion of migration statistics, for definition of the terms 'permanent', 'long-term', 'temporary', and 'short-term', and for reasons why historical demographers should prefer statistics based on results rather than 'intention', see Appendix 2. Since May 1962 the Commonwealth Bureau of Census and Statistics has been publishing more detailed statistics; these solve, for the years 1959 onwards, some of the problems posed above.

[29] *Italians and Germans in Australia*, p. 76.

Italian, 37 per cent of Greek, and 45 per cent of Yugoslav adult male immigrants later left Australia and did not return; the proportions before 1920 seem even higher.

Why should the number of southern European men leaving Australia have been so great, especially in these earlier years? The answer lies partly in the force of nostalgia and partly in the fact that economic difficulties in Australia, especially during the depressions of the 1890s and 1930s, caused numbers of migrants to leave, many of whom did not then return when conditions revived. But the answer lies also in the attractive power of other countries of settlement: some of the Dalmatian settlers at Kaitaia and other districts in northern New Zealand came to Australia for a few years before settling in New Zealand; some of the older Dalmatians in California worked for a few years in the gold-fields of Western Australia before joining their relatives in America; similarly, some of the Ithacan Greeks who came to Melbourne between 1890 and 1928 seem to have returned home and then migrated again to the Ithacan colonies in South Africa.[30]

The answer lies also in the fact that many migrants had no intention of leaving Europe forever but came to Australia for all manner of short-term reasons. Some left their country to avoid short-lived persecution or danger, like one Albanian who became involved in a mountain family blood-feud, was nearly shot on his wedding day, fled with his bride to a nearby city, was found again by his enemies so departed with all speed overseas and did not return until the feud came to an end some years later. Others came to earn money with which they could return home to improve their family properties (see p. 31). Still others came from regions where short-term migration had been practised for centuries: peasant labourers from the Alps of Venetia or Lombardy who emigrated regularly for summer work in the Danubian valley and then re-migrated home for the winter; fur-traders and cutters from Kastoria who often made long journeys through Russia and Asia Minor, always to come back to their little lake-side city in the mountains of Macedonia; Greek traders from islands such as Kythera or Kastellorizo who made periodic trips to Constantinople, Cairo, or Smyrna and might stay there for some years before returning home. Persons such as these found it quite easy to contemplate extending their

[30] From interviews with Dalmatian and Ithacan families in Australia and California.

travels to Australasia, make some money over a few years, and return home.[31]

Slightly different from this kind of temporary migrant were those who came to spend ten or twenty years in Australia, make their fortunes, and then return home to live as wealthy and respected elders in their native villages. Ithacan Greeks have done this to such an extent that the resplendent white houses of returned migrants are a conspicuous feature of many Ithacan villages. Other southern European villages reveal the same phenomenon, though in most regions the establishments of the 'Americani'—those who had made their money in America— were far more numerous and well-known than those of the 'Australiani'.[32]

Without considerably more field-work in Europe, America, and Australasia it is impossible to estimate how many migrants leaving Australia belonged to the different categories outlined above.[33] This in turn makes it impossible to answer the question posed at the beginning of the chapter: whether those persons were right who suggested that many southern Europeans so loved their homeland, and would be so homesick for it when overseas, that for this reason alone southern European migration to Australia was doomed, if not to complete failure, then to very great wastage. The size of southern European communities abroad indicates that the theme of nostalgia has been considerably exaggerated. Nevertheless, whatever the reasons, before 1940 wastage undoubtedly occurred and re-migration remained at a comparatively high level: between 1921 and 1940 approximately one-third of the southern European men migrating to Australia left again and did not come back; if we add those who re-migrated home for temporary visits before finally settling in Australia, the number leaving Australia was about half the

31 The above illustrations come from my own field-work amongst southern Europeans in America and Australia. Many other writers have noticed the same things, e.g. Foerster, *The Italian Emigration of our Times*, pp. 22 ff., R.N.G.H.S., *Greece*, vol. I, 1944, p. 340; J. Hempel, *Italians in Queensland*, p. 10.

32 For Ithaca see R.N.G.H.S., *Greece*, vol. I, p. 339. There are numerous references to migrants returned from America, e.g. R.N.G.H.S., op. cit., p. 340; Emily Balch *Our Slavic Fellow Citizens*, pp. 181 ff., Foerster, op. cit., pp. 456 ff.; S. Pribichevich, *Living Space*, p. 270.

33 We can get some information from statistics of migrants by last and future place of permanent residence; but it is not consistent for all countries and fails to distinguish between those migrating for the first time and those migrating for the second or third time.

number entering. For the years before 1921 the proportions seem even higher.

Two things make this phenomenon easier to understand: first, many of these men from the Mediterranean were young and unmarried and, second, many of those who were already married when they first arrived in Australia left their wives and families behind in Europe. The position, of course, varied considerably from group to group,[34] but the general situation is clear. Before 1921 about two-thirds of southern European men first entering Australia were single men under twenty-five, and, though thereafter the proportion fell, it was still not much below 50 per cent at the outbreak of World War II. Furthermore, of those already married on arrival less than 10 per cent brought their families with them. This helps explain why, despite the later arrival of many women and children to join their menfolk, the number of southern European women in Australia during this period was much less than the number of men; at the 1911 census there were only 20 females for every 100 males and, though the number increased thereafter, at the 1933 census there were still only 30 females for every 100 males.[35]

The migration of these years, then, more especially of the earlier years, was largely a wandering of young men with no established homes in Australia, their eyes constantly turned towards their families in Europe or relatives settling in other countries, and of the right age and capacity to save passage costs away from Australia comparatively quickly. Some of them, indeed, became footloose wanderers, ranging the world for many years until they finally made a permanent home for themselves, either in their native village or in some distant land overseas. One Macedonian family in New South Wales, for instance, is descended from a native of a little mountain village near Florina who fled with his uncle to Constantinople when his parents were killed by roaming bands of guerrillas in 1898; in 1904, after a short visit to his old home, he emigrated to the Middle West of the United States and after three years came back to Macedonia to marry and build a house; in 1909

[34] See Appendixes 8-21: 'Arrival, Single at', 'Marital Status at Naturalization, Married Abroad'.

[35] The annual migration statistics for these years contain no information concerning nationality by age or marital status and if they did, to be relevant, they would have to distinguish first-time migrants from second- and third-time migrants. The information above concerning age and marital status comes from the naturalization records. For more detailed information re the various areas of origin see Appendixes 8-21.

he emigrated to Detroit, came back to Greece for the Balkan Wars in 1911, returned to America by himself in 1919 and thence back to Macedonia when his family fell sick in 1923; in 1924 he came to cut timber in the southern tablelands of New South Wales, returned to Macedonia during the depression, and came back to New South Wales in 1937; in 1938 he brought his family out to join him and thenceforward made his permanent home in Australia. An Italian example is that of a prominent fruit-farmer on the Murrumbidgee who was born in 1881 in a mountain township in Reggio Calabria. In 1896, when still a lad, he emigrated to the United States and after ten years there moved on to Canada; he returned to Italy to take part in World War I but went back to Canada soon after his marriage in 1919; he returned to Italy in 1924 and in 1925 decided to try his luck in Australia; he finally established himself in the Murrumbidgee Irrigation Area and brought his family out to join him in 1929. The movement of Dalmatian men about the Pacific from 1850 onwards is another example of this large-scale wandering: as sailors or as miners, timber-cutters, fishermen and restaurant-keepers they moved between Australia, New Zealand, Chile, Peru, California, and Alaska, some settling in one place and some in another; as a result, many Dalmatians in Australia have distant relatives in other parts of the Pacific. The movement of Ithacan and Kytheran Greeks between the United States, Egypt, South Africa, and Australia is yet another example.

This kind of wandering migration explains why an appreciable number of immigrants to Australia did not arrive green from their homes in southern Europe but already had experience of life in other countries. Aware that the customs of the Mediterranean did not prevail throughout the world, experienced in adapting themselves to new conditions, often fluent enough in English to find jobs without help, possessing sufficient savings to buy their own tickets to Australia, these men played no small part in establishing southern European settlements in Australia and in encouraging others to join them. They were not, of course, the only pioneers—quite a number of southern European settlements, especially those northern Queensland settlements stemming from Italian pioneers from the Monferrato, were founded by persons who had never before ventured from their own district but who successfully adapted themselves to Australian conditions. Nevertheless, these second- and third-time migrants from other countries were of considerable importance in many parts of Australia. They were, it seems, rarely in a numerical majority, and over the whole period 1890-1940 probably made up no more than 15 per cent of total immigration. Their number, furthermore, varied considerably from group to group and from time to time, as Table VI shows.

TABLE VI

PROPORTIONS OF MALE SETTLERS WHO HAD LIVED IN OTHER COUNTRIES

(%)

Selected Places of Origin	Arrivals			
	before 1920	1920-29	1930-39	Total
Greece:				
Ithaca	9·4	4·7	..	7·4
Kythera	13·2	9·0	5·9	11·1
Kastellorizo	21·5	20·8	10·5	20·6
Rhodes	12·5	8·4	33·3	10·3
Samos	29·3	25·0	..	27·0
Lesbos	40·0	22·6	..	21·3
Cyclades	50·0	13·8	..	36·4
Peloponnesus	29·1	10·1	23·5	16·3
Mainland Greece	35·9	52·5	8·3	40·5
Total Greece	22·2	19·3	6·8	19·7
Italy:				
Valtellina	5·7	4·5	..	4·8
Veneto	1·6	2·7	..	2·4
Reggio Calabria	45·0	6·0	1·8	5·7
North Catania	2·9	2·4	4·8	2·7
Lipari Isles	2·7	3·3	..	2·8
Total Italy	4·6	3·5	1·1	3·6
South Slav:				
Vis isle	4·1	..	..	2·8
Hvar isle	37·5	2·9	..	13·2
Korčula isle	26·7	2·1	..	6·9
Dalmatia	19·4	2·4	1·4	7·7
N.W. Macedonia	..	8·0	2·9	6·8
Bulgaria	9·9	4·3	2·5	6·5
S.E. Albania	..	5·4	1·1	3·8
Total South Slavs	17·9	4·2	1·6	6·6
TOTAL SOUTHERN EUROPE*	12·49	6·42	2·47	7·9

Source: Estimates based on information in the naturalization records. Interviews with some old settlers who had not shown residence in other countries on their applications for naturalization suggest that some forgot to fill in this item; the true proportion is almost certainly higher, perhaps half as much again.

* Excluding Spain, Portugal, Southern France and Malta.

This table gives further evidence of the difficulty of generalizing in terms of national origin and of how necessary it is to examine particular districts and regions. Though persons with experience of other countries were relatively fewer amongst Italian immigrants as a whole than amongst Greeks and South Slavs, they were relatively numerous amongst immigrants from Reggio Calabria; indeed nearly half the total of Reggio Calabrians settling in Australia before 1920 had lived in other countries, mainly the United States, the Argentine and Brazil. Even adjacent areas behaved quite differently in this respect: the relatively large number of Cycladian Greeks who had been elsewhere had lived mainly in Egypt and the United Kingdom, whereas those from the nearby island of Kythera had lived in the United States, South America, South Africa, Egypt, Russia and France; numbers of migrants from the Alpine areas of Lombardy and Venetia had tried their luck in the United States, the Argentine, Brazil, New Zealand, and France, whereas those from the Monferrato hills on the other side of the River Po had almost always come direct from the Monferrato to Australia.

In one respect, however, most districts of origin can be treated alike—for nearly all groups it is true to say that migrants with experience of other countries were at their greatest importance in the years before World War I. Thereafter—despite a number who had once been to the United States, failed to get back there after the quota laws of 1922-4, and so turned to Australia instead—their relative strength steadily decreased until during the 1930s they made up a very small fraction of total immigration (see Table VI). In other words the 1920s, and still more the 1930s, showed a marked increase in the proportion of persons coming direct from the Mediterranean to Australia. This, to a very great extent, reflects the fact that most of the southern Europeans we are considering had relatives and acquaintances sufficiently well established to attract people direct from Europe. And here we have reached a position where we can delve more deeply into the phenomenon of chain migration—that phenomenon already described as one of the most intriguing and influential forces in migration history.

CHAIN MIGRATION

The term 'chain migration' reaches back to the late nineteenth and early twentieth centuries when hundreds of thousands of migrants were entering the United States each year. Officials watching this great movement speedily became aware that one of the major factors involved was the letter to the home-folks written by an enthusiastic settler and containing glowing descriptions of wages and conditions in the New World.

> That letter [said the U.S. Commissioner-General for Immigration in 1907] is read by or to every inhabitant of the village, or perhaps even passed on to neighbouring hamlets. Others are thus induced to migrate—selling their belongings, mortgaging their property, almost enslaving themselves to procure the amount of the passage. They come, find employment at what seems to them to be fabulous wages, then write letters home; and so the process goes on and on. . . . These letters constitute the most extensive method of advertising that can be imagined; almost innumerable 'endless chains' are thus daily being forged link by link.[36]

The Commissioner-General also mentioned the influence of the occasional visit home, for direct personal communication by a successful settler overseas on visit to his home town operated in precisely the same way as a letter.[37] Indeed, with semi-literate peasant peoples intimate direct conversation and visible signs of success in the form of gold watches or brand-new clothes and shoes have had even more spectacular effects than letters from abroad. A case in point is Angelo Bassani, who came from the little town of Rocca d'Arsie in the Venetian Alps and settled as an oyster saloon proprietor in Port Pirie, South Australia, at the turn of the century; about 1908 he returned home for a short visit, scattered gold sovereigns about the village inn, and so bedazzled all who saw him that twenty or so young men arranged to join him in Port Pirie. Later on some of these persuaded others to join them; the 'endless chain' here was forged by letter and visit together.[38]

In the pages that follow there will be frequent mention of 'chain migration', and it will be as well to assess its influence at once. Letters and visits from friends and relatives abroad are merely one phase of the process by which a country of settlement makes its circumstances known to people living in Europe. There are many other means. In the story of migration to America itinerant ticket agents, appointed by large shipping companies to tour Europe and eulogize the New World, were

[36] Report of Commissioner-General, 1907, p. 60. See also Fairchild, *Greek Immigration to the United States*, pp. 88, 119, M. L. Hansen, *The Atlantic Migration*, W. I. Thomas and F. Znaniecki, *The Polish Peasant in Europe and America*.

[37] See also U.S.A. Immigration Commission, 1907-10 *Reports*, vol. 4, p. 58.
[38] See Bromley, The Italians of Port Pirie, p. 29.

common and influential; so were agents of American businessmen looking for European labour. Books and newspapers were
also important. Nevertheless, the influence of relatives and
friends was clearly paramount, as evidence the years 1908-10
when questions at ports of arrival revealed that 79 per cent
of immigrants were entering the United States to join relatives
and 15 per cent to join friends, leaving only 6 per cent entering
otherwise.

In the history of migration from the Mediterranean to
Australia the activities of shipping agents and others have been
much less important than in the United States, and there can
be little doubt that letters and visits from abroad accounted
for the very great majority of new immigrants during the years
1890-1940. Precise figures are lacking here, because it is only
since 1924, when Australia introduced the system of a written
guarantee by someone living in the country (see p. 88 above),
that suitable records have been available and because these
records have rarely been analysed.[39] An estimate based on the
naturalization records, however, suggests that over the whole
period 1890-1940 only 7 per cent or so of southern European
settlers came to Australia outside the chain process.[40]

There is another, somewhat different, way of using the term
chain migration. R. A. Lochore, in his book *From Europe to
New Zealand*, follows those who use the term to denote migration along a 'migration chain', that is an 'established route
along which migrants continue to move over a period of many
years from a European peasant community to a modified peasant
community in the new land' (p. 24). He gives as illustration a

39 McDonald (Migration from Italy, pp. 264, 431) analysed some of the
sponsorship records for the early 1950s. His remarks on the difficulties of
this kind of source material are relevant here, though his conclusions relate
to a later period than ours.

40 For this estimate see Appendix 3:25,26. In field-work I have come across
cases of migrants who tried to enter the U.S.A. about 1924, were prevented
by the quota laws, and accepted the advice of passport officers and travel
agencies to try Australia instead. Clearly these were outside the chain
migration system but were only of importance about 1924-5. I have also
found instances (especially amongst discharged servicemen of the early
twenties with sufficient deferred pay to purchase tickets and with a desire
to travel born of life in the forces) of immigrants with no relatives or close
friends in Australia but who heard about Australia from letters received by
neighbours. These men, though they sometimes settled independently of an
ethnic group, were inspired by the chain letter system and come within the
general category of chain migration (interviews with Croatians at Mildura
and Berri, Italians at Griffith, Dalmatians in Sydney and Perth, Greeks in
Sydney, Melbourne, and Canberra).

fisherman from the island of Stromboli who came to New Zealand about 1890, returned home for a visit and persuaded his brother and later a cousin to join him; these then persuaded other Strombolesi to emigrate and so 'year after year people continued to move along the migration chain, until they built up what was virtually an Italian village in New Zealand'. Later, other Strombolesi started migration chains to one or two other places in New Zealand, so that this one place of origin in southern Europe gradually built up two or three Italian villages abroad.

There is, of course, a very clear connexion between Lochore's usage of 'chain migration' and that of earlier American writers—in particular both stress the dominant influence of letters, visits, and encouragement from abroad. But Lochore's usage is much narrower in that it virtually confines itself to the process whereby a particular village or town in Europe sends numerous of its sons and daughters to build up counterparts of itself overseas; a process we may designate as migration from a major village of origin to village concentrations abroad. This kind of migration has been most important—the naturalization records suggest that nearly one-half of Australia's pre-war southern European population came from some major village of origin and settled in village concentrations in Australia, these settlements being either solitary affairs or else associated with concentrations from other places.[41]

The other half, however, did not migrate in this way. Sometimes only a few migrants came from one particular village and formed no more than a small group, eight or ten families perhaps; a process we may call migration from minor village of origin to small village concentration abroad. In other cases persons from one village, inspired and helped by fellow-villagers abroad, decided to try their luck in Australia but did not all stay in the principal village settlements; rather, they tended to separate soon after arrival in Australia, move to other localities and there join migrants from other villages or towns in the same European district, region, or Folk territory of origin. This process we may term migration from a major or minor village of origin to several district, regional, or Folk concentrations abroad. In yet other cases news of a successful settler spread to nearby towns and villages, but only a few villages responded by sending forth enough migrants to form village

41 See p. 112 below and Appendix 3:24-30.

groups abroad; the majority sent only a few families each and
these then associated with each other, or with migrants from
the same region or Folk, to form settlements where village
connexions were far less important than the fact that they all
came from the same district, region, or Folk. This process was
visible in the early stages of Albanian settlement at Shepparton,
Victoria, or at Moora, Western Australia, and may be termed
migration from unproductive villages in major and minor
districts of origin to district, regional, or Folk concentrations
abroad.

Another kind of migration is that of family migration when
members of the family concerned are scattered over a considerable area of Europe yet maintain close contact with each other.
When one of the family successfully settles abroad he may
encourage several of his relatives to come and join him, so
building up a family group that is not associated with any
particular place of origin.[42] This kind of emigration has been
more common amongst Jewish families from northern and eastern
Europe than amongst southern Europeans; but it has appeared
occasionally amongst the latter, especially where business
activities or seasonal migration have resulted in some scattering
of the original family. There is, for example, one Italian family
at Griffith whose members came from several villages in different
parts of Verona province, and there are Greek families in
Sydney and Melbourne whose members came from an island,
Athens, Constantinople, Smyrna, and occasionally Egypt. This
process we may term migration by a scattered family to a
family group abroad.

Quite apart from these different kinds of emigration—all of
which are outside Lochore's definition and all of which result
in group settlement abroad—the Lochore usage does not allow
for emigration produced by the activities outlined in the 1907
Report of the American Commissioner-General but which do
not result in group settlement abroad. For example, some
village may send forth a young man whose letters, visits, or
offers of help encourage others to come to Australia; but these,
after an initial period of settling down with their sponsor's help,
find jobs and homes too far removed to form an effective group
settlement. They may then encourage others to come who,
after a time, may settle independently. In short, though migra-

42 On the part family ties play in village or district migration see pp. 62-5
above; this kind of localized family migration is included under village or
district migration and group settlement.

tion may continue for some considerable time, it here does not result in any form of group settlement abroad and may be termed migration from major village or district of origin to dispersed settlement abroad.

Though these other forms of migration are not as common as that outlined by Lochore, they are nevertheless an important element in the migration story; it therefore seems better to include them all in the general term chain migration. An estimate of their relative importance is set out in Table VII.[43]

TABLE VII

TYPE OF CHAIN MIGRATION

	%
1. Major village to village concentrations	46·3
2. Minor villages to small village concentrations	8·4
3. Major or minor village to several district, regional, or Folk concentrations	20·4
4. Unproductive villages in major or minor district of origin to several district, regional, or Folk concentrations	9·7
5. Scattered family to family group	0·5
6. Major, minor, and unproductive villages in important districts of origin to dispersed settlement	7·9
7. Migration outside the chain process	6·8
8. Total southern European settler immigration	100·0

These different kinds of chain migration, their relationship to each other, and the way in which one kind occasionally turns into another are extremely important, but a full understanding of them depends on describing the chain process in sufficient detail to make the basic issues plain. These issues emerge most clearly from a brief description of the first two types of chain migration set out in Table VII.

These chain processes usually start when some wanderer from the old world alights in a particular place abroad and sets himself up successfully as a market-gardener, fruit-seller, restaurant-keeper, fisherman, or in some other business where hard work rather than much capital enables a newcomer to find secure foothold. Then, feeling alone in a strange world, mindful of his poorer relatives at home, remembering the friends with whom he marched in the village fiesta or drank and chatted in the local inn, anxious to hear again the cadenced sounds of

[43] For the full table of these statistics and their source, see Appendix 3:14-24, 29-30.

his native dialect, he writes home to his family suggesting that
one of his brothers, cousins, or friends, come out to join him—
often adding the inducement of help with passage expenses. Or
he may write to relatives and friends in America, South Africa,
or New Zealand, speak glowingly of his circumstances, and
persuade them to take ship to Australia as soon as they can.
Over the following years a number of young men from that
village, or from nearby villages to which the news spreads, move
out to join the successful pioneer, frequently receiving his help
with jobs and accommodation; the job will usually be in the
same mine, industry or farming area as his and may sometimes
be partnership or engagement in his own business; the accommodation will normally be close to his and may often be a bunk
or mattress in his own crowded bedroom or shed. In this way
there gradually builds up a group of compatriots, closely connected through employment and place of living, sharing a
common background of dialect, customs, and outlook, and
feeling these ties reinforced as together they face an alien world.
Some may marry British-Australian girls and make contacts
outside the group, but others will have few contacts other than
their compatriots.

The next stage emerges when those more securely established
feel able to bring out their wives and children or, if they have
not married British-Australian girls, to re-migrate home and
choose brides to bring back with them. With the coming of
women and children the group at once takes on more permanent
characteristics. Rough temporary accommodation gives place to
the sharing of houses, or even separate homes. Jobs originally
sought for quick earnings give place to jobs offering greater
security and independence; and here the peasant love of self-
sufficiency appears in the purchase of farms, market-gardens,
cafés, houses or fishing boats.[44] All this time, too, traditional
ceremonies and social occasions become more numerous—
especially baptisms, weddings, and funerals—and the customs
and values of the old country become more strongly entrenched;
so strongly, in fact, that those men who have married British-
Australian girls may feel that they and their children are
becoming increasingly estranged from a hardening core in the
ethnic group. Furthermore, greater attention is given to education and religion; it is at this time that moves to form an
Orthodox community, or obtain a Catholic priest who speaks

[44] For good examples of improvement in housing and jobs see Bromley,
Italians of Port Pirie, pp. 68 ff.

I

their own tongue, become important and that efforts are made to start afternoon schools where Australian-born children can learn the language and history of their region or country of origin. In short, a group of unattached men becomes transformed into a more or less complete and self-sufficient community, recreating to a very considerable extent the customs and habits of the particular district of origin in Europe.

Once this community life becomes well known in Europe a change may occur in the character of the migration. Older people may migrate, as when a well-established settler brings out his aged parents knowing that they will have plenty of people to talk to in their own language and plenty of social occasions to make life interesting. Some families in Europe, who once were fearful of letting their young sons and well-guarded daughters go to the rough conditions of antipodean life, now change their minds since they feel their children will be well looked after by aunts and cousins already there. Men with less enterprise than the first generation of pioneers decide that life in Australia may not be such a fearful risk after all, and migrate in ever-increasing numbers. The whole process of migration, in fact, expands and quickens until a time may come when there are more villagers in Australia than in Europe.

At times, indeed, a village in Europe may be half empty and many of those left behind seek every chance to evacuate their decaying and uninteresting abode. The Macedonian village of Antarktikon, for instance, in the hills near Florina, has lost so many by emigration to Toronto that the inhabitants now total only a few hundred and many houses are standing empty; there are about two thousand persons of Antarktikon origin in Toronto itself and many of those left in Macedonia are making efforts to join them.[45] One or two individuals have said the same thing about the town of Cavaso del Tomba in the Venetian foothills; the number of persons from Cavaso at Griffith, New South Wales, is now about a thousand, about one-third the number in Cavaso itself, and there are suggestions that some of those left behind are finding the life of the town increasingly slow and uninteresting. The same kind of thing may happen with families. There are two much intermarried families from Plati, in the hill-country of Reggio Calabria, which can trace

[45] From information obtained in Toronto in 1958. Many of these emigrants think of themselves as Slav rather than Greek and call their village by its Slav name, Zheleva: see p. 317 below.

their origin back to one peasant farmer born about 1800; in 1955, of the forty-two great-grandchildren, ten were in the United States, one in Sydney, one in Broken Hill, two in Adelaide, twenty-six in Griffith, and the last two left in Italy were making arrangements to move to Griffith to be with the bulk of their kinsfolk.

It is at this point that chain migration is every bit as strong as those schemes of family migration organized by governments. The emigration fever it generates, indeed, has occasionally depopulated whole areas. Large-scale emigration to the Americas between 1871 and 1911, for instance, reduced the population of numerous places, including many districts of Basilicata and Abruzzi in southern Italy, several islands and districts in Dalmatia, and parts of Epirus and the Peloponnesus in Greece; in some cases the population declined to such an extent that cultivated land was either converted to pasture or abandoned altogether, intensive cultivation such as viticulture was given up or converted to something requiring less labour, and villages were left empty or half-filled.[46] Large-scale emigration to the Americas also contributed to the depopulation of many Alpine districts of Italy, though here falling birth rates and migration within Italy to growing industrial cities—itself a form of chain migration since it often worked in the same way as the process outlined above—also had some influence.

Emigration to Australia has been less important in relation to population decline than emigration to America, except in those relatively restricted areas which produced numerous settlers for Australia (see Table II). In Alpine regions this means the Venetian foothills and the Bergamasque Alpine valleys, notably the Valtellina, where migration to Australia between 1880 and 1930 was such that, allowing for children born in Australia, it has deprived the Valtellina of some 15,000 souls in a total of little more than 100,000.[47] Migration to Australia from the Lipari islands has contributed to the decline

[46] See Foerster, *The Italian Emigration of our Times*, pp. 449 ff.; Emily Balch, *Our Slavic Fellow Citizens*, p. 200; I.L.O. *Labour Problems in Greece*, p. 57, etc.

[47] Exact estimates are not possible because it is not possible to determine accurately the number of children born in Australia to parents of Valtellina origin (see Appendix 4:8); nor is there any certainty that parents having six children, say, in Australia would have had six children had they stayed in Italy, especially as birth rates in the area had been declining for some time. This rough estimate does, however, give some idea of the magnitude of the movement.

of population there from some 22,000 in 1881 to 15,000 or so in 1951—there are about 7,000 persons of Lipari origin now in Australia. It has also contributed to population decline in various Greek islands, notably Kythera and Ithaca, where by 1940 the total of inhabitants had fallen to about two-thirds of the number there in the 1860s and the amount of land under cultivation to nearly half.[48]

Chain Migration and Causes of Emigration

Chain migration, whether to foreign countries such as America and Australia or to other places within the country of origin, has not been the only reason for large-scale emigration and declining population. Another important reason has been the rapid disappearance of traditional resources: phylloxera laid waste great areas of vines in many districts of Dalmatia towards the end of the nineteenth century, just when commercial treaties with Italy exposed Dalmatian wine to the competition of Italian wine throughout the Austro-Hungarian empire; at the same time a series of bad fishing seasons and the growing competition of foreign steamships drastically affected those Dalmatians partly or wholly connected with sailing vessels. As a result many people from island and coastal areas dependent on a combination of intensive viticulture and small sailing ship fishing and commerce preferred to emigrate to America and Australia rather than endure severe poverty at home.[49] A similar situation prevailed in the Ionian islands and other parts of Greece in the early twentieth century: phylloxera had destroyed many French vineyards in the 1860s and 1870s and Greek peasants took advantage of the resulting shortage and high price of wine to pull down olive groves and plant vines; when French vignerons found a phylloxera-resistant stock at the end of the century French wine again dominated the market and many Greek peasants found themselves in severe difficulties.

Political upheaval has been an even more potent force in producing population decrease, since it can cause large-scale refugee movements overnight. Most of Australia's Greek families

[48] These estimates allow for anomalies such as the unreliability of early censuses and the present problems of area and administrative division—e.g. whether neighbouring islets are included or not. For agricultural decline in the Ionian isles see N. J. Polyzos, *Essai sur l'emigration grecque*, p. 64.

[49] Emily Balch, op. cit., pp. 194 ff.; interviews with Dalmatians in California and Australia.

from Smyrna, and other towns in Asia Minor, came after the fighting of 1921-2 when the Turks defeated the Greek army of invasion and then retaliated by exterminating or putting to flight Greek families who had been settled in Asia Minor for many generations. The island of Kastellorizo is another example. Here the Greek population fell from some 10,000 in 1908 to 2,000 or so in 1917, primarily because the Turkish government imposed severe restrictions on the islanders' commercial activities in 1908 and followed this up by shelling the town from the mainland during the war in 1916; during these years numerous Kastellorizans moved to America, Egypt, and eventually Australia, and when less troublous conditions prevailed they were too well settled to return.[50] Occasionally violent natural upheaval has driven people abroad in much the same way as political disturbance: many southern Italians, for instance, emigrated to America and Australasia after the great earthquake and volcanic eruptions of 1911; likewise, after several local earthquakes, there have been temporary upswings in the number of Greeks leaving Ithaca for South Africa and Australia.

For the most part, however, neither disappearance of traditional resources nor political and natural upheaval have been sufficiently severe in the Mediterranean to depopulate whole districts in one fell swoop: rather have they exerted a slower, steadier pressure, thereby encouraging families in Europe to listen to the news of successful compatriots overseas and to heed the requests of friends and relatives abroad to come and join them. Pressures of this kind, in fact, tend to speed up the process of chain migration and to hasten the time when prosperous friends and large ethnic communities abroad continue to draw people overseas, even when local resources have recovered and political pressure ceased. Dalmatian sailors and traders, for instance, had been conscious of steamship competition for several decades and had been drifting overseas piecemeal for some time before phylloxera and fishing famine put yet more families in difficulties towards the end of the century; the success of these settlers abroad then acted as a precipitant in encouraging later migrants to make up their minds about when they should leave and where they should go. Likewise the periodic earthquakes and eruptions or the prolonged persistence of malaria (see pp. 44-5 above) only occasionally acted as over-

---

[50] Agapitidis, *The Population of the Dodecanese Islands*; interviews with Kastellorizans in Australia.

whelming forces of expulsion; normally they inspired semi-permanent fear and irritation which encouraged families to join their friends overseas. The same may be said of guerrilla warfare and insurrection in the Albanian and Macedonian districts of origin, and of banditry and anarchy in Calabria and Sicily. Indeed, this is partly true even of Kastellorizo. The first Kastellorizan seems to have arrived in Australia in the 1880s, and by 1908, when Turkish pressure became really unpleasant, a small but steady stream of migrants had been coming to Australia for nearly twenty years; events between 1908 and 1916 caused the number leaving to rise steeply, but emigration continued even after conditions had settled down in the early 1920s and gradually reduced the population from 2,700 in 1922 to 660 in 1947; there are now several thousand persons of Kastellorizan origin in Australia and others in the Americas.

The same assessment may well be made of the still popular opinion that emigration from the Mediterranean has arisen primarily because of the expulsive force of overpopulation, and of the poverty that derives from it, particularly in rural areas such as those which before 1940 gave Australia over three-quarters of her southern European settlers. During the nineteenth and early twentieth centuries, it is held, with the improvement in medical and health measures fewer people died, and the geographically restricted habitation districts became too full to support everyone;[51] many of them emigrated, and in places the population eventually declined until there was enough land and employment to support those who remained. To some extent this is true. Death rates certainly did decline much more rapidly than birth rates in many parts of Europe, as is clear not only from published statistics but also from family histories; the records of one Calabrian family, for instance, show that of twenty persons born in the 1870s and 1880s some eight died while young, whereas of the forty-five persons born in the next generation only one died young.[52] This increase of population

[51] For habitation districts see p. 26 above.

[52] The crude death rate in most southern European districts of origin fell from about 30 per thousand in the 1860s to 20 or less in the late 1930s: Piedmont 14, Lombardy 13, Veneto 12, Calabria 15, Sicily 15, Greece 15, central Dalmatia and southern Albania about 17, Malta 20. Over the same period birth rates dropped much less, except in northern Italy—from 35 per thousand or so in the 1860s to 16 in Piedmont, 21 in Lombardy, 24 in the Veneto, 30 in Calabria, 27 in Sicily, 33 in Malta, 34 in Dalmatia—see also p. 60 above.

did cause considerable pressure on land and other local resources, and it was largely responsible for the poor diet and housing and for the minute subdivision and fragmentation of properties mentioned earlier (see pp. 27-8 above). Though it is usually impossible to obtain reliable statistics of population density—since administrative divisions in southern Europe often include large areas of unusable mountain and rock—in many peasant districts, such as coastal Messina, Catania, and Calabria and in parts of Malta and Gozo, population density seems to have exceeded 1,000 persons per square mile. Moreover, this population pressure did give rise to emigration, as evidence the statements of many southern Europeans in America and Australasia that while one brother stayed at home to work the family farm or business the other four or five brothers settled overseas.

But overpopulation as the explanation of emigration, though useful in some ways, has definite limitations. First, there is the problem of deciding the optimum population for any given area in order to obtain a standard to assess the extent of overpopulation. Many methods have been suggested, but all run up against the difficulty of finding a measuring rod suitable for all the diverse areas existing.[53] Second, the view that overpopulation in Europe is essentially the product of falling death rates during the late nineteenth and early twentieth centuries ignores the fact that some districts have had high population densities for centuries and that families had been moving from these districts for generations: the Greek settlements in Rumania, the Ukraine, and Egypt, for example, date back at least to the eighteenth century and sometimes much earlier; Albanian settlers, especially Albanian Moslems, had for long been scattered throughout the old Ottoman Empire; Italians had been moving to Greece, Tunis, Algeria, and Egypt since the early nineteenth century and had been migrating for the season into central Europe for much longer—movements, which, incidentally, make it necessary to use considerable care

[53] Moore (*Economic Demography of Eastern and Southern Europe*) has an interesting discussion of this difficulty: the measure he uses, though one of the least unsatisfactory available, is still open to the objection that it fails to distinguish adequately between various kinds of production, especially where there is a good deal of peasant self-sufficiency. His statistics are very useful when dealing with large regions but less useful when considering our districts here.

when referring to southern Europeans as 'new immigrants'.[54] Third, the overpopulation theory does not explain why emigration has sometimes continued long after the population has reached a point where there is enough land and employment to maintain families at a standard formerly enjoyed only by the more prosperous, nor why land should be abandoned and villages deserted, nor why a whole great family should leave its ancestral home and settle abroad. Furthermore, the overpopulation-poverty theory fails to explain why emigration has sometimes risen in conditions of local prosperity and fallen in conditions of local depression, as happened in Malta when emigration reached an all-time record during the great wave of prosperity caused by the Crimean War in 1855 and fell away sharply during the depressed conditions of 1857-8.[55] In other words, overpopulation and poverty may have exerted a slow, steady pressure for emigration, but the actual precipitation of dissatisfaction into definite decision to emigrate seems usually to have come from the influence of persons settled abroad.

What actually precipitates a person's decision to emigrate is not merely the presence of friends abroad and the existence of ethnic communities and institutions capable of providing families with some semblance of European life, however, though they are important elements. The friends and relatives, through their visits and letters, are the agents by which a country of high living standards and peaceful political circumstances makes those conditions known to people in Europe. In themselves these conditions are a strong attractive force—or, in times of economic and political upset, a strong repellent force—and often quite override any other considerations. Several American writers have pointed this out in connexion with European migration to America before the quota laws,[56] more particularly the way in which both immigration and re-migration rose and fell with booms and depressions in the United States rather than with events in Europe. Much the same thing happened with migration to Australia. The steep fall in the immigration of adult males from all the main districts of origin during the early 1930s (see Table IV) to less than one-tenth the total

54 The term 'new immigration' was evolved in the United States, and can equally well be used in Australia, to distinguish immigrant peoples from southern and eastern Europe—important from the 1880s onwards—from the predominantly north-western European migrations of earlier times.

55 C. A. Price, *Malta and the Maltese*, pp. 107, 114, 223. For other drawbacks to the overpopulation theory see J. S. McDonald, Migration from Italy.

56 Notably Harry Jerome, *Migration and Business Cycles*.

prevailing between 1925 and 1928 shows the effect on migration of severe depression in Australia. Table VIII shows the same kind of fall in relation to the depression in Australia during the early 1890s.

TABLE VIII

INDEX OF ANNUAL AVERAGE IMMIGRATION OF ADULT MALE SETTLERS 1888-99

(Period 1888-91 = Index of 100)

Place of Origin	Date of First Arrival		
	1888-91	*1892-95*	*1896-99*
Kythera	100	60	340
Ithaca	100	72	530
Kastellorizo	100	10	300
Samos	100	100	500
Cyclades	100	20	40
Evvoia	100	10	10
Peloponnesus	100	25	175
Athens	100	125	325
Dalmatian islands	100	80	290
Dubrovnik-Kotor	100	10	150
Trieste	100	45	78
Monferrato	100	21	44
Valtellina	100	54	120
Veneto	100	55	30
Basilicata	100	30	30
Lipari isles	100	61	180
Total	100	53	123

Source: Naturalization records.

Chain migration is, then, very sensitive to booms and depressions in the country of settlement—as is inevitable when persons abroad may have to finance their friends' passages and find them accommodation and employment. Some writers have praised chain migration for this sensitivity, arguing that the system is essentially self-regulating: when conditions in America or Australasia are prosperous, and the country can absorb more labour, then chain migration imports workers; when conditions are depressed chain migration ceases and the country is not burdened with newcomers competing for scarce employment.[57] This is very largely true, if unemployment difficulties are aggravated more by fresh supplies of labour than by policies and events which lead to the reduction of employment available, or if a praise-

[57] Lochore, *From Europe to New Zealand*, p. 25.

worthy system of immigration brings people to a country when
conditions are good, even though they arrive shortly before the
boom bursts. In any case, these remarks apply only to adult males.

The third stage of chain migration—the bringing out of fiancées,
wives, and children—has often continued through a depression:
those southern European settlers who have been diligently
saving during prosperity have frequently taken advantage of
a depression to buy bankrupt farms and businesses and still
have enough left to bring out their families; this reunion they
desire, not just for personal reasons, but also because wife
and children can help with the farm or business and so reduce
wage expenses and promote self-sufficiency. During the depression
years 1929-33, for instance, whereas the number of southern
European male settlers entering Australia fell to 10 per cent of
the 1925-8 figure, the number of females entering dropped only
to 85 per cent or so; furthermore, whereas the total number
of males entering Australia during the period was very much less
than the number leaving Australia, the total number of females
entering Australia remained nearly three times as great as the
number leaving.[58]

This kind of migration is also very sensitive to political
disturbances in countries of settlement; Italian emigration to
and re-migration from various South American countries or
Maltese movement to and from North African states have
varied sharply with political conditions in those areas of settlement. Migration to the United States or Australia has not
been affected in this way since political conditions in these
countries have remained relatively stable.

All these factors—economic, social, and political—indicate the
answer to the question posed earlier concerning the relative
importance of forces 'pushing' persons from their homeland
and of forces 'pulling' persons to their new land of settlement.
Clearly, except for occasional circumstances where political or
natural disaster forced people to flee from their homeland, 'pull'
forces within the countries of settlement have been more
important than 'push' forces in southern Europe; the latter

[58] See Table V and Australian annual migration statistics. There are no
statistics for women comparable with those of male settlers as constructed
from the naturalization records (see p. 88n.); therefore figures of total
arrivals and departures must be used, even though they contain temporary
visitors, women returning after a visit to their home country, etc. For Greek,
Italian, Maltese, Spanish, and Yugoslav females the relevant totals are:
1925-8, arrivals 3,795, departures 1,039; 1929-30, arrivals 1,957, departures
696; 1931-3, arrivals 2,012, departures 612.

may have exercised a steady pressure for emigration but the decisive forces controlling the directions and occasions for emigration came from abroad.[59]

These forces involve a high degree of relativity—that is to say that migration chains have grown stronger or weaker because persons in Europe, through the medium of their friends and contacts, could in their own minds relate conditions in Europe to conditions abroad. Without this possibility for comparison, there would have been no chain migration; no matter how poverty-stricken people may have been in Calabria, for example, they did not emigrate until they knew there was somewhere better to go.[60] This goes far to explain why, in its early stages, migration from southern Europe to Australia was largely from coastal cities—in the nineteenth century the inhabitants of coastal towns had far more opportunity to hear about conditions overseas than had anyone else, except perhaps inhabitants of large inland cities which for long had had commercial connexions with the outer world. Table IX shows this trend more clearly; it also shows that, between 1850 and 1940, the proportion of settlers from coastal areas was always high—never less than 40 per cent—but that between 1850 and 1870 it was over 80 per cent of the total. A few of these early settlers came from small coastal towns, notably from the ancient trading ports Dubrovnik and Split in central Dalmatia, which in 1850 were relatively small, having either declined from their former greatness or not yet expanded to meet the demands of the nineteenth century. A greater number came from the islands; some were from active little ports on various Aegean islands, the Cycladian islands of Syros and Andros, and Ionian islands such as Ithaca; others were villagers from Evvoia and Kythera, from the Dalmatian isles of Brač, Hvar, Vis and Korčula, from the Maltese archipelago and from the Lipari islands of Salina and Lipari. The greatest number, however, came from larger sea-ports such as Barcelona, Marseilles, Genoa, Leghorn, Naples, Messina, Venice, Trieste, and Athens.[61] This confirms information from interviews and other sources that many of the first settlers were sailors, either on small French,

59 For an interesting assessment of 'push' and 'pull' factors, see William Peterson, *Planned Migration*, p. 64.

60 This point has been well made on European migration to America by, e.g., Fairchild in *Greek Immigration to the United States* and Foerster, in *The Italian Emigration of our Times*.

61 Larger sea-ports are those which had a population of at least 10,000 by 1840 or thereabouts.

Italian, Dalmatian, and Greek vessels or, more commonly, on a
British vessel that had been calling at various ports in the
Mediterranean some time before coming to Australia. It is
noticeable that nearly all of the relatively small number from
inland districts came from large towns such as Milan and Turin,
which had a long tradition of international commerce behind
them, or else from areas such as the Valtellina, where some
families had a long history of seasonal migration and by 1860
had been putting forth exploratory fingers towards the New
World.

TABLE IX

ADULT MALE SETTLERS 1850-1930
(%)

Zone of Origin	Periods of Arrival					
	1850-69	1870-96	1897-1906	1907-16	1917-29	1930-39
Coastal:						
Cities	47·0	17·7	14·8	7·7	7·3	3·7
Small towns and villages.. ..	8·0	4·8	6·4	12·9	11·8	19·0
Islands	26·0	32·4	42·5	46·6	24·5	20·9
Total	81·0	54·9	63·7	67·2	43·6	43·6
Inland:						
Cities	9·0	10·0	10·4	5·1	2·2	2·9
Small towns and villages.. ..	10·0	35·1	25·9	27·7	54·2	53·5
Total	19·0	45·1	36·3	32·8	56·4	56·4
TOTAL ..	100·0	100·0	100·0	100·0	100·0	100·0

Source: Naturalization records.

The next period in Table IX, 1870-96, shows the rapid decline
in importance of migrants from the larger coastal ports. Though
their number increased at least fourfold, their relative strength
dwindled before the great upsurge of migrants from peasant
areas well inland; those from the Alpine valleys of Lombardy
and the Monferrato of Piedmont were most numerous, but a
few pioneers came from other inland regions such as the Alpine
mountains and foothills inland from Venice, the Apuan Alps
behind Leghorn in Tuscany, the mountainous areas inland from
Naples, the limestone valleys of the Peloponnesus north of
Kythera, and the mountain valleys of central Bulgaria. Immigration from the islands also increased, especially from Ithaca,
Kythera, the Lipari islands, and the Dalmatian isles; it was during this period, too, that migrants made their appearance from

Kastellorizo and other Greek Dodecanese islands then controlled by the Turks. At the same time a number of pioneers came to Australia from southern Italian coastal towns such as Molfetta in Bari and Reggio in Calabria and from coastal villages in north-eastern Sicily and central Dalmatia. Quite evidently, information had seeped back from the more active commercial towns to districts farther away from the main lines of communication with the outer world.[62]

In subsequent years, many of the migration chains started by these early pioneers developed quite quickly. Others made their first appearance. Settlers from the hill country of Reggio Calabria appeared towards the end of the century, while migrants from the mountain villages near Korçë in Albania and Florina in Macedonia came shortly before World War I. The solid little group from the Medjumurje, now concentrated in the irrigation belt between Mildura in Victoria and Berri in South Australia, sent its first representatives soon after the war. By the mid-1920s migration chains from all the main districts of origin had either been established or else had been working for several decades—the pattern of southern European settlement, in short, was becoming clearly visible.

These first representatives, the first links in the chains that after them became so important, emigrated to Australia for all manner of reasons. Their followers, the great majority, migrated because they felt the pressure of poverty or political disturbance and thought they would be better off with their friends overseas, or else they came to be with their relations in a prosperous ethnic community abroad. But these pioneers came for somewhat different reasons. Some were sailors who left ship in Sydney or Melbourne before or during the gold-rushes of the 1850s; others were sailors who suffered shipwreck in the Pacific and worked their way to Brisbane or Sydney in small boats; yet others were sons of sailors who had returned home and excited their children with tales of the southern seas, as had some of the early sailors from Pelješac and other places in Dalmatia.[63] Some were discharged soldiers restless from the

[62] For details of each district of origin by period of arrival see Appendixes 8-21: 'Arrival, % in Periods'.

[63] These and later details concerning pioneer settlers come from interviews with pioneers or their descendants, death registration certificates, naturalization records, street directories, etc.; also from works such as the July-August 1957 issue of *Krikos*, a Greek review published in London. In almost every case it has been possible to check interview material against documentary.

wars, as were several Spartan Greeks in New South Wales, Medjumurje farmers at Berri and Mildura, and Venetian horticulturalists at Griffith; others came to avoid military call-up, notably a number of Dalmatians who came of age when their country was still part of Austro-Hungary and who refused to serve in the armies of their alien conquerors; yet others were Ionian island Greeks who met and liked Australian soldiers in South Africa during the Boer War of 1899-1901 and so decided to come to Australia. Some were labourers from Malta and the Monferrato who accepted contract labour on the Queensland sugar plantations in the 1880s and 1890s: others were farmers, from the Monferrato, Veneto, Friuli and other regions in northern Italy, who took part in the ill-fated attempt of the Marquis de Ray to found a colony in the New Hebrides in 1877-9, were brought semi-starved to Sydney in 1881, and eventually took up land in the Richmond River district of New South Wales, there establishing a settlement known as 'New Italy'.[64] Some were wandering musicians sent out in the 1860s and 1870s from Viggiano in Basilicata (southern Italy), as part of a general system whereby that town trained youthful street musicians and sent them all over the world to earn money for their families; others were Greeks who found their traditional fields of settlement in Rumania, Bulgaria, and Russia becoming increasingly unpleasant in the early twentieth century when the governments of those countries imposed restrictions on immigrant activities; yet others were Albanians, Macedonians, and Italians who had wanted to settle in the United States after World War I and found their way blocked by the quota laws of 1922-4. Others, as already noted, were wanderers planting roots in Australia after years of roaming round the world, or refugees from earthquake, feuding, and war.

So we could go on and on. Indeed, the founding migrants' reasons for coming are almost as numerous as the founders themselves, and anyone wishing to understand the history of any immigrant group or chain must be prepared to trace the story back to the original pioneer and his particular reasons for coming to Australia. Tracing these stories back, however, raises problems other than causes of emigration.

[64] Places of origin of these 'New Italy' settlers from the naturalization records. 'New Italy' is, for the most part, in the Shire of Woodburn. For details see F. C. Clifford, *New Italy—a Brief Sketch of a New and Thriving Colony*; J. H. Niau, *The Phantom Paradise—The Story of the Expedition of the Marquis de Ray*.

Chain Pioneers—Fact and Fancy

The first problem arises from a propensity inherent in all human societies—to clothe one's forebears in shining robes and their deeds in clouds of glory. In part this arises from accident or slips of memory; in part, from certain tendencies noticed by those who have studied the way in which myths and legends grow and work. First, there is the tendency for great deeds to outlive the name of the doers, so that some spectacular action may be attributed to several heroes, as the horseman's leap over Bodrugan Head in Cornwall is told variously of Sir Bors, Sir Tristam, and Henry of Bodrugan. This tendency, allied with the desire of many persons to attach to themselves a notable pedigree, is probably the reason why a number of southern European families tell precisely the same spectacular story about their pioneer ancestors. Various Lipari islanders in Sydney, for instance, trace their community back to a seaman who fell from the mast of a sailing ship in Sydney harbour, broke his leg, came ashore to hospital, had not recovered by the time his ship sailed, and eventually made good in Australia;[65] Lipari islanders of Wellington, New Zealand, too, trace their community back to a seaman from Stromboli isle who was put ashore in Wellington with a leg broken on board and eventually remained in New Zealand.

The second tendency is for particular ethnic groups to highlight the importance of their contribution to the life of their new country. Often this highlighting is an understandable and salutary reaction against the attitude of older immigrant peoples who underestimate, or ignore altogether, the positive contributions of later arrivals; the spate of historical writing by persons of Pennsylvania-German descent, for example, very largely represents the reaction of a pioneer people that feels its role in opening up the backwoods of eastern America and in winning the War of Independence has often been ignored by writers of New England or Virginian origin. Equally often, however, the highlighting is an exaggeration, or even an invention, of some ethnic historians who either exaggerate the importance of their own pioneer families or else wrongly attach some of their pioneers to some great historic figure in the new country. This is much more obvious in North America where ethnic historical societies are much older and more numerous than in Australia;

65 Story told to J. S. McDonald when working with Lipari islanders in Sydney, 1955-8.

but the tendency is apparent even amongst the relatively young southern European communities of Australia. For example, the story in the *Australian Encyclopaedia*—that Greek settlers first came to Australia in the 1830s from the Ionian islands to tend the experimental vines established on the Camden estates of the Macarthur family—may have originated as a slip of the pen; but it is the beginnings of a myth which ministers to the self-esteem of a number of Ionian island families in Australia.[66]

The third tendency is that of all peoples to twist and turn events, and to build fanciful and colourful legends upon some slender foundation of fact in the lives of their ancestors. Amongst some members of a Greek community in Australia, for instance, there is a story that the brothers who started off their particular migration chain came to Victoria in the 1860s, suffered shipwreck in a colossal storm in Port Phillip Bay, and swam spectacularly ashore amidst the wreckage. The facts seem to be that the brothers first arrived in Melbourne during the 1880s and because of an outbreak of smallpox had to go to quarantine.[67]

Now Malinowski and other anthropologists suggest that myths and legends are not just idle tales to make pleasant hearing around the camp-fire or to fill in gaps in knowledge of events; rather are they hard-working beliefs doing yeoman service in maintaining communal life.[68] The detailed workings of ethnic communal life are beyond the scope of this inquiry; but it is relevant here to suggest some of the functions of ethnic group legends and some of the reasons why pioneer careers become coloured and exaggerated. It is beyond dispute that, apart from a few musicians, scientists, and professional men, the great majority of southern Europeans who came to Australia entered occupations not highly regarded by most native Australians. Some then did very well economically, and finished their lives as great landowners or city magnates. Furthermore, most of them came to join relatives and friends and often received much financial help when establishing themselves in cafés, market-gardens, fishing boats, farms, and so forth. The twisting

---

[66] Malcolm Ellis, the biographer of John Macarthur, tells me he can find no record of any Greek vinedressers amongst the Macarthur papers. There is possibly confusion here with some German vinedressers James and William Macarthur brought out to Sydney about 1839.

[67] Interviews in Sydney and Melbourne.

[68] B. Malinowski, 'Myth in Primitive Psychology', in W. R. Dawson (ed.), *The Frazer Lectures 1922-1932*.

process (as seen in the tales of shipwreck and of the fall from the mast) may very well be the early stages of a legend-building process that fulfils at least two functions: first, it impresses upon those newer members of the community receiving help from older arrivals that they should not grumble if they work long hours and in hard conditions; second, it shows British-Australians that despite great disadvantages, and despite lowly and little regarded occupations, many southern Europeans have made good and become men of great importance. So there emerges the legendary and stereotyped figure of a southern European pioneer: someone who enters Australia with nothing —preferably by accident or in colourful circumstances such as shipwreck—but who rises by skill and hard work to a position of wealth and eminence.

It is much too early to pronounce definitely upon the strength and nature of these twisting tendencies and ethnic legends— but they should be watched for by all persons endeavouring to unravel the story of those pioneer settlers who gave rise to large migration chains.

Chain Pioneers—Success and Failure

The second problem concerning chain pioneers arises from the fact that not all early settlers began migration chains, and that many gave rise to short-lived movements which rapidly petered out. At Griffith, in the Murrumbidgee Irrigation Area of New South Wales, for instance, there were in June 1954 some 4,200 persons of Italian origin, 60 per cent of whom derived from thirteen small towns or villages, most of the remainder coming either from nearby villages or else from townships well represented elsewhere in Australia.[69] A few, however, were descended from settlers who had been amongst the first Italians in the area but who did little more than bring out their wives, children, and one or two friends. One settler from a small village in the Monferrato in Piedmont was working on the Burrinjuck dam and irrigation scheme as early as 1913 and later took up a horticultural farm near Griffith; the chain he started, however, consisted only of his wife and one fellow-villager who came with his sister to Griffith about 1932. In the late 1930s other families of Monferrato origin came to the area, many of them from Piedmontese settlements in northern

[69] Based on documents and field surveys during 1954-5, part of which is reported in C. A. Price, The Italian Population at Griffith.

K

Queensland, but these derived from other Monferrato villages and towns and seem to have been part of a noticeable move from the semi-tropical sugar areas to the more temperate climate of central New South Wales rather than the results of chain migration stemming from the original Monferrato family in Griffith. The reason for this lack of chain development lies, it seems, in the fact that the original settler was a somewhat cantankerous soul, often at loggerheads with his neighbours and with government officials, and not the kind of person to attract other families from Italy; furthermore, his one fellow-townsman married a girl from a Calabrian family in Griffith and found himself drawn into relationships with other places than his home-town.

In contrast to this is another source of northern Italian migration to Griffith, the two adjacent townships of Cavaso and Possagno in the Alpine foothills of Treviso province in the Veneto. These small towns are only a couple of miles apart and their chain movement started with a half-dozen men from each town who came to work in the Broken Hill mines in about 1913. Most of them returned to join the Italian armies in the later years of the war, but two stayed in Australia (one having brought his wife out to join him in 1914) and in 1917 followed a few other Venetians who had moved to the Murrumbidgee Irrigation Area as construction and agricultural labourers. These two remained in touch with their former mining comrades who, when they left the Italian army, came out to join the two pioneers at Griffith. The process of helping friends and relatives then accelerated until by mid-1954, despite the interruption of depression and war, there were in the Griffith region 261 men who had come out as adult labourers, 177 women who had come out as wives, fiancées, or housekeeping sisters, 142 second-generation persons who had been born in Italy and emigrated as small children with their mothers, 400 second-generation persons born in Australia and some 53 children of the third generation; in all 1,000 or so souls of Cavaso-Possagno origin.[70]

A similar contrast exists in Griffith with migrants from southern Italy. A settler from one small village in Messina, Sicily, arrived in Australia in 1906 and, after working in various places, settled in Griffith in the early 1920s; in 1926 he was

[70] In migration literature there are conflicting uses of the word 'generation'. For the usage adopted in this work see Appendix 4:3-6.

killed in an accident before any chain movement got under
way. (The few other settlers of Messina origin who later came
to Griffith derived from other places in Messina and had, it
seems, no connexion with that particular settler or town.) The
other extreme is represented by the small town of Plati in the
mountainous country just north of the Aspromonte in Reggio
Calabria. One or two Plati men, who had previously been to
Canada and the United States, decided to try their luck in
Australia in 1923-4 and on arrival in Sydney were told by the
Italian consul that opportunities for work existed in the Murrumbidgee Irrigation Area. They, with a few other Calabrians,
came to Griffith in 1924-5, obtained jobs as agricultural labourers, and communicated with their friends and relatives at
home. By mid-1954 there were some 160 men who had come
as adult labourers, 120 wives and sisters, 140 persons who had
come out as children, 170 persons born in Australia, and 15
grandchildren of the third generation; in all some 600 souls
of Plati origin.

A typical Greek contrast is that between one of the thirteen
Greek islands that became major districts of origin before
1940 and one of the thirty or so islands that gave pioneers to
Australia in the nineteenth century but that did not become
important in the chain migration process. The first known
settler from Psara, a small island in the Aegean Sea near Chios,
was shipwrecked near Australia whilst sailing on a Greek ship
from New Zealand to Europe, apparently some time in the
1860s or 1870s. He reached Sydney, joined forces with some of
the Kytheran Greeks there and, it seems, became completely
absorbed with his Kytheran and British friends; few of his
friends and relatives came out to join him and by 1940 there
were only a handful of Psaran Greeks in Australia. The opposite case is that of the Ionian island of Ithaca. One of the first
Ithacans in Australia, a member of the Lekatsas (Lucas) family
now so strong in Melbourne, came to Australia gold-mining in
the 1850s and on his return home several years later spoke
so well of Australia that during the 1870s and 1880s a number
of his nephews and their friends engaged themselves as sailors
on vessels bound for Oceania. They succeeded in establishing
themselves in oyster saloons and cafés, persuaded numerous
friends to join them, and founded the flourishing Ithacan
communities of Melbourne, Sydney, and Newcastle; by 1940, it
seems, there were more than 3,000 persons of Ithacan descent in

Australia, of whom at least 1,000 were of the second or third generation.[71]

These illustrations of the differences between successful chains and potentially successful chain movements that came to nothing could be continued almost indefinitely. The reasons for the differences, however, are worth further consideration. In part, the answer lies in the fact migration from some districts was already directed towards another part of the world, so that the pioneer representative in Australia, though he might attract a few close friends and relatives, could not change the main current. The number of Greek settlers who came from the Dodecanese islands of Kalymnos and Kasos, for instance, remained small partly because the first settlers came to Australia in the late 1880s when migration had already started to France, Greece, Africa, and America (including the large-scale movement from Kalymnos to the sponge fisheries of Tarpon Springs, Florida). Likewise, immigrants who came to Australia in the 1860s and 1870s from the Konavali district in southern Dalmatia had to compete with migration streams already flowing to Louisiana, California, and South America; by 1940 the number of Konavali families in just the one small district of Santa Cruz, California, greatly exceeded the number of Konavali families in Australia as a whole, and there were many other families elsewhere in America.[72]

This did not always happen, however; numerous districts of origin were able to maintain migration chains simultaneously to several parts of the world, the towns and villages on the central Dalmatian island of Hvar, for example, providing California with 10 per cent or more of its considerable Dalmatian population there before 1914, yet over the same period giving Australia an appreciable number of settler families.[73] All this suggests that the answer lies very largely in the careers and characters of the early settlers themselves. As the cases of individual pioneers outlined previously indicate, when the original settler was difficult or self-centred, or suffered unex-

[71] Estimates based on the marriage and child data in the naturalization records, interviews, and statistics of births by birthplace of parents.

[72] Based on the author's field-work in Santa Cruz in 1958-9. The naturalization records suggest that by 1940 there were in Australia less than ten families from the Konavali and no more than thirty families from Kalymnos or Kasos.

[73] From Australian naturalization records, naturalization and marriage records in Santa Cruz and Oakland, and John V. Tadich, 'Reminiscences' in V. Meler (ed.), *Slavonic Pioneers of California*.

pected accident, chain migration might not get under way. On other occasions migration did not develop because the pioneer proved to be restless and unreliable, always flitting from 'big chance' to 'big chance' and never establishing himself securely enough to entice relatives abroad; or he succumbed to the difficulties of immigrant life by taking to alcohol, or even attempting suicide.[74] At other times the pioneer married a British-Australian girl or a girl from another European district and gradually lost contact with his family in Europe. Though this did not always happen—many of the early Kytherans and Ithacans in Australia married British-Australian girls yet still brought out numerous friends and relatives from home—it happened sufficiently often to explain the failure of some early settlers to initiate chain migration.[75]

In this sense chain migration, as indeed all migration, has an accidental quality that is not always at once apparent. It is not enough simply to describe the conditions of poverty prevailing in Europe and to compare them with the high living standards of the new world. The middle term, the way in which information about the new world presents itself to the old, is a necessary stage in the progression, and here personal idiosyncrasies and all manner of accidents and incidents are relevant and influential. The southern European population of pre-1940 Australia was the product not just of distress in southern Europe and prosperity in Australia but of the careers of those individuals who first arrived. To a very great extent their characters and personalities created the pattern of immigration and settlement.

The general picture seems clear. Of the several thousand southern European towns and villages that sent settlers to Australia between 1850 and 1940 only 15 per cent gave rise to large migration chains and another 25 per cent to small migration chains: the remaining 60 per cent provided only the original pioneer and perhaps his wife, children and one or two friends.[76]

74 I have seen several decrepit farms and bankrupt businesses arising from incompetence, restlessness, and alcoholism. Where these represent the career of only one of a number of settlers the chain process has suffered little; where the person concerned was one of the few representatives of his district of origin in Australia, the chain movement has been hit hard.

75 Similar instances are given by McDonald, Migration from Italy, and Bromley, Italians of Port Pirie.

76 For the individual village and town a 'large' migration chain means that twenty or more of its adult males settled in Australia and became naturalized; a 'small' migration chain refers to more than five but less than twenty. See Appendix 3:3-6.

It is necessary here to recall that some unimportant villages of origin were located in the same district; in themselves they were relatively unproductive, but when taken together they produced at least one small district migration chain (see p. 110). Similarly a number of towns and villages producing no more than small chains could, when located close enough, be treated as the source of one large district migration chain.[77] This last is particularly noticeable with islands. The dozen or so villages on the central Dalmatian island of Hvar gave Australia an average of fifteen or so families each and these, when totalled, make a not inconsiderable migration; the same may be said of the villages covering the thirty-mile stretch from Vathia to Styra in the south of the Greek island of Evvoia. The same thing occurred in some mainland areas. Only half a dozen of the hundred-odd villages in the mountainous country around Korçë in south-east Albania gave rise to respectably large migration chains; yet taken together as one district of origin they gave Australia well over a thousand male settlers and a number of wives and children as well.

Even when this kind of district migration is added to migration from districts where numerous major villages of origin sent forth great numbers of settlers to Australia, districts producing large migration chains appear to have made up very much less than half the 400 or so districts of origin—perhaps 33 per cent in all. In fact, a very important element of migration from southern Europe to Australia before 1940 seems to have been that of a pioneer from one village influencing no more than one or two fellow-villagers—producing, therefore, no migration chain—or else influencing one or two families in the townships round about—so causing a small district chain.

'Important element' in this context refers to numbers of townships and districts, not to numbers of migrants. The pattern of settlement (see p. 112), as distinct from the pattern of emigration, was dominated by the great swarms of emigrants coming from the relatively few important villages and districts: nearly two-thirds of the total number of southern European settlers in Australia before 1940 derived from major villages of origin and over 80 per cent from major districts of origin, the most spectacular example of the latter being from the three small islands of Ithaca, Kythera, and Kastellorizo, which between them

[77] For districts, as distinct from individual villages, a 'large' migration chain refers to 101 or more naturalized settlers and a 'small' chain to something between 21 and 100. See Appendix 3:3-6.

provided Australia with nearly half of its pre-war Greek population—43 per cent or more.[78]

Varieties of Chain Migration

In the light of this discussion we can now elaborate the somewhat simplified outline of chain migration given earlier (pp. 112-14). This elaboration appears most clearly in tabular form.

I A pioneer influencing almost no one in his own village or in the surrounding district.

II A pioneer influencing a few persons
  (a) in his own village—small village chain
  (b) in nearby villages—small district chain.

III Pioneers and later settlers influencing numerous persons
  (a) in one village—large village chain
  (b) in other villages and towns—large district chain.

IV Large-scale emigration from both villages in particular and the district in general—this may produce an absolute decline in the area's total population.

It is at once apparent that there need be no hard and fast line between these different types of chain migration. Sometimes, of course, the distinction is very clear, especially between II(a) and II(b), or between III(a) and III(b). Thus in the early twentieth century a few settlers from Poggioreale, an inland town of Trapani province, Sicily, started off a small village chain which, during the 1920s, became quite a large movement. But at no time did this emigration have more than the scantiest effect on the district round about or on the province as a whole. In some other places, however, as with emigration from the Makarska district of central Dalmatia, the village and district movements have been very closely connected.

Emigration from Makarska also illustrates another connexion between the various types of chain migration tabulated above—the fact that each type can be one phase in a single process of development and can pass almost imperceptibly into the next. Settlement from the district began with the arrival in the 1860s of one or two pioneers from Makarska town; for many years, however, there was little further development—phase I. Then, shortly before the depression of the 1890s, a few more settlers from Makarska town and one or two persons from nearby villages arrived—phase II(a) and (b). During the depres-

[78] For the complete figures and their derivation see Appendix 3 and Table II.

sion immigration slowed down, but quickened again during
the early twentieth century until by the outbreak of World
War I there were well over twenty settlers each from Makarska,
Podgora, Zaostrog, and Vrgorac, and a sprinkling of settlers
from at least another fifteen towns and villages in the same
area—phase III(a) and (b). After a short cessation during the
war migration again increased, until by the onset of the great
depression in 1929 at least twenty towns and villages had large
chains at work and another twenty had small chains; the
effect on the total population of the district, in fact, was
appreciable—phase IV.

When examining these various phases some scholars have
tried to work out a regular time sequence; one authority, for
instance, when speaking of various Italian chains in northern
Queensland, has concluded that 'chain migration reaches a peak
approximately 10-20 years after the arrival of a sufficiently large
group'.[79] An examination of many different migration chains
suggests that this kind of generalization is somewhat risky.
Depression, war, or change of government policy, to say nothing
of quirks of character displayed by potential sponsors in Australia, have all combined to make the chain process a highly
erratic thing the normal duration of which it is almost impossible to assess. The Makarska illustration, for instance, shows
that a single chain migration, while varying considerably in
response to boom and depression and to peace and war, may
last for at least seventy years; indeed, there is evidence to
suggest that if the Yugoslav government lifted its barriers
against emigration many persons in the Makarska district would
come to join their relatives in Australia.[80] In that event the
chain process would have lasted for more than a century. With
the Ionian islands of Ithaca and Kythera the chain process
has already lasted a century or so, the earthquakes in Ithaca
in the 1950s giving migration from that island yet another push
towards Australia.

One of the most potent factors to affect the chain sequence
in recent years has been the unusually long period of prosperity
prevailing in Australia since 1945. This, together with the
complete change in government policy that enables some
southern Europeans sponsored by friends and relatives in Australia to obtain public assistance with passage costs, has recently
converted many inactive places into very active areas of origin.

[79] Hempel, *Italians in Queensland*, p. 82.
[80] Interviews with Dalmatian families in Australia.

Before 1940 the New South Wales settlement of Griffith experienced heavy immigration from the foothill villages of Treviso province in the Veneto but relatively little from villages such as Paese and Riese further out on the plain towards Treviso city; these villages of the plain, in fact, were an excellent example of a wide scatter of townships providing Australia with one or two settlers each. After 1947, however, immigration from these villages increased quite rapidly—in 1954 a number of them each had between six and twelve representatives in Griffith and many more were arranging passages. Similarly, the villages of the Sulmona limestone basin in Abruzzi had only a score of representatives in Griffith between them in 1940; by 1954 they had well over a hundred and were sending many more.

There is another change in the pattern of chain migration for which post-war conditions are partly responsible. From time to time the Australian government has restricted the immigration of all but wives, children, and certain close relatives of southern European settlers already in Australia—and has virtually confined assistance with passage costs to certain wives and families.[81] These have encouraged a chain migration process that starts with the arrival of an adult male who later brings out his wife or fiancée, then his parents or parents-in-law, then brothers and sisters, and finally—if he is able—remoter relatives and friends. Though this sometimes happened before the war, it was not nearly so common as the sequence outlined earlier: settlers who persuaded first their male friends and relatives to join them and only later brought out their wives, parents, and children.

This increase in what might be termed the 'women and children first' system has not been caused by post-war conditions alone: there were signs of it for some years before the war. One fairly reliable measure of this change is the steady decline in the interval between the arrival of the male settler and the arrival of his wife, or between his arrival as a single man and his marriage to a girl from the same region—whether that marriage took place in Australia, by proxy, or on a short visit home to Europe. For southern Europeans as a whole the average interval of time was $13 \cdot 3$ years for the decades before 1907, $11 \cdot 2$ years for the decade 1907-16, $8 \cdot 2$ years for the decade 1920-9, and $5 \cdot 9$ years for the period 1930-9. The earlier periods, with the

81 The restrictions have varied from time to time since 1947—see McDonald, Migration from Italy.

relatively long average intervals of 13·3 and 11·2 years, gave settlers plenty of time to persuade their male relatives and friends to join them before their womenfolk appeared on the scene: the 1930s, with an average interval of less than 6 years, gave many settlers little time to sponsor male friends before they set about the business of bringing out wives, fiancées, and children.[82]

Several reasons exist for this gradual shortening of the interval between arrival of male settlers and their families: changing social values and marriage patterns in the countries of origin; the fact that, for most areas of origin, emigration to Australia gradually passed its experimental pioneering stage and became a recognized mode of settling permanently overseas rather than a way of obtaining quick money before returning home; the building up of stable ethnic communities in Australia capable of attracting complete families relatively early in the migration process; the effects of the great depression of the early 1930s, whereby many southern Europeans in Australia could raise enough money to bring out wives and children but not enough to help other relatives with passage costs, jobs, accommodation, and so forth.[83]

These reasons, however, were not equally relevant for all migration chains; nor, indeed, did all migration chains show this gradual shortening of the interval between arrival of menfolk and arrival of women and children. The detailed statistics set out in Appendixes 8-21 suggest that there was considerable variation between different areas of origin and that these variations frequently cut across national groupings. Once again, therefore, we must take care to examine each area of origin on its own merits and refrain from lumping it indiscriminately into a general national category.

[82] See Appendix 6 for detailed figures. Another index of this change is the increase in the proportion bringing wives and children either at the same time or within the first year of settlement; statistics are less reliable here, but suggest that during the 1920s some 6% brought families in the first year whereas during the 1930s some 22·4% did so. Hempel, *Italians in Queensland*, p. 80, suggests that the women and children first system was the normal system even in pre-war decades. The evidence presented above, and in the next chapter, suggests that this did not become common until the 1930s.

[83] For reasons explained earlier, government policy does not seem to have had much effect before 1947. Restrictions imposed on the sponsorship of all but close dependent relatives lasted only from 1930 to 1936 (pp. 91-2), when economic conditions restricted migration more effectively than governmental controls (pp. 92-3).

At this point we have gone as far as possible in describing the different kinds of chain migration, in so far as this means a description of emigration from diverse places of origin to the continent of Australia. The next step is to describe the pattern of settlement in Australia itself, the way in which these numerous streams of migrants came to terms with their new country.

CHAPTER V

SETTLEMENT IN AUSTRALIA

Between the banks which bear the vine,
And hills all rich with blossom'd trees,
And fields which promise corn and wine,
And scatter'd cities crowning these,
Whose far white walls along them shine,
Have strew'd a scene, which I should see
With double joy wert *thou* with me.
And peasant girls, with deep blue eyes,
And hands which offer early flowers,
Walk smiling o'er this paradise.

Childe Harold's Pilgrimage, III, 64

LITERARY and descriptive writings rarely distinguish sharply between the places where men live and the occupations they pursue. And rightly so; for literature records the scientific truth that geographers stress: the impossibility of separating the activities of man from his natural surroundings, and the risk of examining man's mode of living without constant reference to his place of settlement. Yet books on immigration frequently draw just such a distinction; at best they devote separate chapters to the two topics. Sometimes this arises from the fact that it is often easier to write of the two things separately—here constant cross-reference can guard the work against misleading separation. But it also arises from the fact that much migration literature deals with European immigrants in the industrial cities of the United States of America; and here, if anywhere, it is assumed, one can safely concentrate on conditions at the factory bench or mining pit-head and take it for granted that such conditions vary little from place to place.

With southern European migration to Australia it is most important to keep these topics closely entwined. In the first place, the majority of older southern European settlements are closely related to particular kinds of occupation: the Piedmontese and Sicilian settlements in the sugar-cane areas of northern Queensland, for instance, the Molfettese fishing communities at Fremantle and Port Pirie, or the Albanian horticultural settlements at Shepparton; so closely related, indeed, that even separate chapters become somewhat misleading. In the second place, it is often difficult to tell whether migrants went to a particular place in Australia because they wished to take the kind of jobs offering there, or whether they took certain jobs because they wished to settle in that particular place. Sometimes it is easy to answer this question. Those persons from northern Italy and Dalmatia who went to Kalgoorlie and Broken Hill in the 1890s did so not because they particularly wanted to settle there but because the mines offered favourable openings for unskilled labour: conversely, many Italians from the Veneto and Calabria at Griffith practised horticulture, shoe-making, blacksmithing, building, and so on, not because they were particularly wedded to those occupations but because they wanted to be with their friends and relatives at Griffith and there found those occupations open to them; so also with some of the Piedmontese and Catanian settlers in northern Queensland. But no one can say for certain whether most of the Kytheran restaurant-keepers in Sydney at the turn of the century went there because they wanted to run restaurants or because they wished to be with Kytheran friends in Sydney. And there are numerous other examples of this kind. For reasons such as these it is much better to treat place of settlement and occupation together in one chapter.

Before embarking on a detailed analysis of this intricate topic, however, one more point is needed by way of introduction. The great importance of the village, district, and region, both in terms of the European background and of the process of chain migration have already been stressed; for general discussion it is often convenient, and enlightening, to talk about characteristics common to southern Europeans as a whole, but for more detailed work it is necessary to dig deep, through the general categories of Italian, Greek, or Yugoslav, and examine the smaller units underneath. Precisely the same thing holds with the pattern of settlement in Australia. It is convenient, therefore, to survey those problems common to all southern Europeans in Australia and then look much more closely at the activities of migration chains from particular villages and districts of origin.

PEASANT BACKGROUND AND OCCUPATIONS

The first general problem concerns peasant origins and ambitions. Over three-quarters of Australia's southern European population between 1890 and 1940 came from small coastal or inland towns and villages inhabited by peasant families whose main activity lay in cultivating land that over the generations had been repeatedly subdivided; furthermore, these people normally strove for family self-sufficiency and for an independent estate that could be handed down through the family from generation to generation (see Chapter II).

The ambitions of temporary migrants—those intending to earn money quickly and return home—centred on the family holding in Europe. Those who came to settle permanently, however, or those who came intending to stay temporarily but changed their minds after some time in Australia, frequently expressed this traditional desire for peasant independence as a 'craving for an independent successful business', to quote the words of one Dalmatian settler in New South Wales, that could then be handed on to their children in Australia. (The point also appears in the remark of one old Macedonian (S. Pantos) who refused large sums of money for a small market-garden he had acquired in a residential area of Queanbeyan after years of work in the Captain's Flat mine. 'No, I will not sell; after years of working for other people I have at last got a place that really belongs to me and my family and here I am going to stay.')

For these men the chief question was 'What can we best do to achieve this independence?' and their answer lay in the connexion between the particular experience they brought with them and the particular openings offering to them in Australia when they arrived. So far as European experience is concerned these young peasant men were very adaptable. They had come from families who usually engaged in the 'garden cultivation' of cereals, vegetables, fruit-trees, and vines, not infrequently combined with the rearing of poultry, pigs, and sheep, occasional herding, fishing and seafaring, and considerable experience in local marketing and trade. In a sense then they came as Jacks-of-all-trades, able to specialize, with little further experience, in mixed farming, market-gardening, horticulture and other kinds of special crop farming, vine growing, poultry farming, pig raising, dairy work, fishing, and small-scale bargaining and commerce. Furthermore, those who had come from areas such as Friuli, where there had been a long tradition of alternating farming activities in the summer with carpentry, terrazzo-work, and other skilled crafts during the winter, could find employment as artisans and work up to a small business in one of the skilled trades. Over all this was a tradition of hard sustained labour for long hours in conditions that were frequently most uncomfortable; and, of course, an intimate acquaintance with the spade, the pick, and the axe (see Chapter II).

For many immigrants, choice of any one of these possible occupations, and the place at which they could pursue it, was not a matter of great moment: they simply came to join a friend or relative in Australia and followed his example in taking a job. For the first generation of settlers, however, on whom later developments very largely rested, the choice was much more complex. In any event, before they could advance far along any one of the possible avenues to independence they needed some nodding acquaintance with Australian economic conditions and customs. This involved a preliminary period as relatively unskilled labourers and assistants, as agricultural labourers, as fruit-pickers, as cleaners or carriers in fish and vegetable markets, as assistants to small shopkeepers, as waiters and second cooks. At times, in order to save money to rent or purchase a farm or business, some of them found it easier to take relatively unskilled but moderately well-paid jobs at which they had little special training: cutting pit-props or sleepers, clearing bush or cutting trees, load-carrying, carrying and digging on irrigation areas.

A number of immigrants remained in these industries, advancing from unskilled labourers to miners, timber contractors, carriers, or builders. They paved the way for their friends who came later—hence the relatively old Italian and South Slav communities in the eastern gold-mines of Western Australia, in the silver-lead mines at Broken Hill, in the timber-cutting districts of southern New South Wales or south-west Western Australia, in the smelters of Port Pirie. Even here, however, when conditions became difficult or better opportunities offered elsewhere, many settlers moved away to places where they could follow occupations more in line with their peasant background and ambitions: Venetian immigrants moved from the mines of Broken Hill to the horticultural blocks of the Murrumbidgee Irrigation Area from 1915 onwards; Dalmatians, from the gold-fields of Western Australia to the market-gardening and flower-growing areas around Perth from 1912 onwards; the Greeks of Evvoia, Symi, and Rhodes, from Port Pirie and Broken Hill to the fishing grounds of the west coast of South Australia in the 1920s; and, more recently, the Macedonian eucalyptus-cutters from the southern tablelands of New South Wales to the market-gardens, greengrocery shops and restaurants of Canberra.

The result of all these activities during the decades before 1940 was a wide scattering of southern Europeans throughout the continent: at the 1947 census there were southern European-born men in 84 per cent of the 1,000-odd local government areas into which the country was then divided, the most noticeable gaps being in the western areas of Queensland and New South Wales and certain mixed farming areas of Tasmania.[1] But this wide geographical scattering was accompanied by a marked concentration in the kind of occupations outlined above. This is shown plainly in Table X, especially in the last two columns, which contrast the occupations of southern European settlers during the thirties and forties with those of the Australian population as a whole. The concentration of southern European men in agriculture and small catering businesses is particularly noticeable, while their entry into mining, timber-work, and fishing, though not as conspicuous, was still significantly greater than that of the general Australian adult-male population.

Table X also provides a contrast between the periods 1904-29 and 1930-45. The fall during the thirties and forties in the population of southern Europeans engaged in mining, timber-work, and general labouring is partly explained by the tendency mentioned, for many to leave these occupations for independent businesses, notably farming. There was also a most interesting decline in the proportion of those engaged in small catering businesses, largely because a number of important groups involved in this kind of activity—Ionian islanders from Kythera and Ithaca, for instance, or Lipari islanders from Salina—had received well over half their immigrant members before World War I and by the twenties and thirties were obtaining relatively few new recruits from Europe (see Tables IV and V, also Appendixes 8-21: 'Arrival', '% in periods').

[1] This survey deals only with persons arriving by 1940; it must, however, draw on the 1947 census because that gives very relevant details of the numbers, occupations, and living places of these pre-war settlers before the great wave of post-war immigration in many places submerged them. Further, it is important to separate adult immigrants or settlers (I's) from those second-generation children born abroad and brought to Australia when infants (IIa's)—see Appendix 4:3-12—because the IIa's often behave far more like their second-generation brothers and sisters born in Australia (IIb's) than like their parents. Census statistics do not separate IIa's from I's, but include them all in the general category of foreign-born. Consequently, the following census information concerning southern European settlers living in certain places and engaged in certain occupations is distorted through inclusion of some of the second-generation, fortunately only slightly, because the proportion of IIa males is fairly low for most groups—7 per cent on average.

TABLE X

OCCUPATIONS OF SOUTHERN EUROPEAN SETTLERS IN AUSTRALIA 1904-46*

Occupations	Southern Europeans			Australians
	Total 1904-46	1904-29	1930-46	Males in work-force 1947
Farmers:				
Sugar, fruit, market-gardens, other intensive	17·9	..	..	..
Other	3·4	..	..	..
Total	21·3	16·3	25·2	11·0
Agricultural Labourers	11·0	10·0	11·8	5·0
Total Agriculture	32·3	26·3	37·0	16·0
Catering:				
Restaurants, fruit-shops, etc. ..	20·9	24·3	18·2	1·5
Assistants (waiters, cooks, etc.) ..	8·3	8·9	7·8	2·5
Total Catering	29·2	33·2	26·0	4·0
Professions and Business	1·5	1·9	1·2	4·1
Craftsmen	3·5	2·4	4·5	20·1
Miners	7·3	9·1	5·9	2·0
Timber-workers	5·0	5·2	4·8	1·0
Seamen	0·8	0·8	0·8	0·4
Fishermen	2·0	2·2	1·8	0·4
Labourers and Operatives	15·9	17·3	14·8	27·2
Other	2·5	1·6	3·2	24·8
TOTAL	100·0	100·0	100·0	100·0
TOTAL No.	22,261	9,807	12,454	2,479,269

* Based on naturalization records and so excluding those not qualified for naturalization. The figures therefore represent those persons resident in Australia for some years—the average is just under 12—so that we are dealing with the settler element rather than with temporary immigrants. Consequently these statistics cannot be compared with census statistics of occupations by European birthplace, since census statistics combine permanent and temporary immigrants (see also Appendix 7:1).

From this brief outline of southern European occupations and places of settlement there emerge a few perhaps unexpected gaps, both in occupations and in distribution throughout Australia. It is understandable that first-generation southern Europeans should not be numerous in the professions, in large-scale business enterprises, or in skilled trades for which they had no previous training. But on the surface at least it may seem odd that very few southern Europeans arriving in Australia before 1940 occupied themselves with grazing sheep or beef-cattle. This is clear from two things: first, the almost complete absence in the naturalization records of any reference to sheep or beef-cattle graziers; and, second, from the fact that a great many local government areas where southern Europeans were either completely absent or very thinly scattered were those areas where pastoral activities prevailed—the western pastoral areas of New South Wales, the northern regions of Western and South Australia, or the western divisions of Queensland. In 1947, for example, in the north-west, far west and south-west

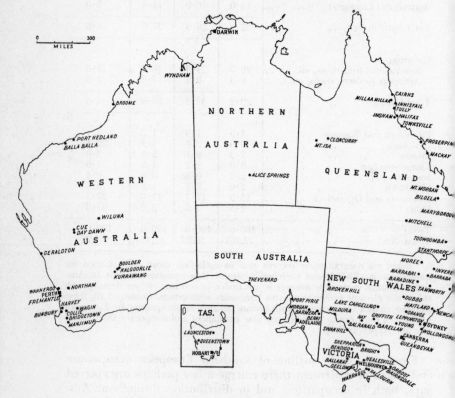

FIG. 3—Australia, showing selected places of settlement of southern Europeans.

statistical divisions of Queensland there were some thirty men of southern European birth scattered about in seven local government areas—mainly small groups of Greek restaurant-keepers and North Italian miners—but none at all in the remaining thirteen. In the upper north division of South Australia there were, at the 1947 census, some five local government areas primarily concerned with grazing. One of these contained a solitary person of Italian birth, the remainder, no one of southern European birth.[2]

This avoidance of sheep and beef-cattle grazing may seem to run against the tendency of southern Europeans to enter occupations of which they had possessed some previous experience (see p. 29): it does not, however, run against their desire for independent establishment. By the time they began to enter Australia in any numbers, towards the end of the nineteenth century, most of the good pastoral land of Australia was already occupied, and grazing properties required much capital to buy and maintain. Southern Europeans, it seems, quickly realized that, no matter how thrifty they were, and no matter how long they stayed as station-hands learning the ropes, they were unlikely to obtain their own property and that they would achieve independence far more surely and quickly elsewhere. Besides, station life, with its great distances and long periods of loneliness, was a far cry from the crowded noisy conditions from which most of them derived: market-gardening, horticulture, sugar-farming—these made possible a way of life much more akin to the compact sort of settlement in which they had grown up. Furthermore, when a few of them ventured forth to stake their hands and fortunes on grazing they sometimes came to grief. One Venetian, for instance, who had made some money from a combination of building and horticulture, invested much

2 There are occasional references to 'station hands', but there is no sign that many 'station hands' ever obtained their own properties. The naturalization records are here better than census figures as no census before 1954 cross-classifies birthplace by grazing occupation. The 1954 census is deceptive, partly because it includes in 'grazing' all persons associated with the industry —clerks, managers, post-diggers—and partly because by 1954 a number of southern Europeans had been assisted to Australia and went to pastoral areas. Even so, the proportion engaged in the whole pastoral industry in 1954 was only 1 per cent of the total number of southern European men in the work-force. Also, census statistics include amongst the foreign-born those second-generation persons born abroad (the IIa's), whose occupational pattern is more like the rest of the second-generation than like their first-generation parents and who are not here under discussion—see Appendix 4:3-12.

capital in a sheep station in the 1930s, ran into a series of droughts and bad prices, and finally had to give up his station and return to building. This failure made a deep impression on the southern Europeans in that part of New South Wales, confirming many of them in their impression that they had far better remain in small-scale farming where, if things went wrong, they could at least keep themselves and their families by raising vegetables, poultry, pigs, and fruit for their own consumption.[3]

The second unexpected gap in the distribution of Australia's southern European population between 1890 and 1940 lies in the cereal-sheep zone—the term here denoting those parts of Australia primarily devoted to the mixed farming of wheat and barley in conjunction with wool-sheep or fat lambs. Though most of them had come from a mixed farming background in Europe, there were relatively few southern Europeans in the cereal-sheep zone of Australia, and the majority of these did not engage in mixed farming of this kind; either they controlled restaurants and fruit-shops or else occupied themselves in market-gardening, horticulture, timber-cutting, or charcoal-burning near the country towns. In the three western slopes divisions of New South Wales in 1947, for example, there were, outside the incorporated towns, a mere 150 southern European born men in thirty-eight local government areas, only half a dozen or so of whom were cereal-sheep farmers. Similarly in the rural areas of the Wimmera division of Victoria there were only thirty men of southern European birth, less than ten of whom were engaged in farming or agricultural labour. The figures for cereal-sheep areas elsewhere in Victoria tell much the same story, as do those of South Australia and the Darling Downs of Queensland.[4]

[3] From interviews with North Italians in N.S.W. The Medjumurje Slavs on the lower Murray River also gave fear of losing capital in the risky venture of sheep-grazing as one of their main reasons for staying in the safe and well-understood field of horticultural farming (interviews, 1955). Some Australian-born persons of southern European parentage have become graziers, as is clear from interviews and marriage records. Their total is, however, unknown, because there is no census information concerning persons of foreign parentage (cf. pp. 190-1).

[4] These and subsequent statements on occupations are from the 1947 census tables (birthplace by local government area), supported by information on occupations in the naturalization records, 1930-47. The farmers mentioned above may not have been cereal-sheep farmers but orchardists or market-gardeners—they simply returned their occupation as 'farmers'.

In Western Australia the story is somewhat different, for here southern Europeans of all kinds—Greeks, Macedonians, Albanians, Bulgarians, Dalmatian Yugoslavs, North Italians, Calabrians, and Sicilians—moved into the cereal-sheep belt in appreciable numbers. Certainly many of these were engaged in country restaurants, fruit-shops, orchards and market-gardens, while others, as late as 1935-46, were still timber-cutters and clearing contractors or miners and prospectors in the various gold-bearing deposits scattered throughout the country, but more than a third, it seems, had their own farms while others worked as agricultural labourers on the farms of their compatriots or of British-Australians.[5]

The reasons for this difference between the cereal-sheep regions of Western Australia and other states are many and complex. Here it is sufficient to note that whereas comparatively close settlement in Queensland, New South Wales, Victoria, and South Australia occurred in the second half of the nineteenth century, before southern Europeans came to Australia in number, in Western Australia it did not take place until the twentieth century, when considerable numbers of North Italians, Dalmatians, Bulgarians, and Greeks were working in various mines and timber areas; these were in a more favourable position to take up cereal-sheep land than their compatriots interstate.

This point, however, cannot be pressed too far. Southern Europeans have clearly shown that when they are intent on purchasing properties they can bide their time, saving capital meanwhile, and then buy out other Australian farmers who

5 At the 1947 census there were 782 males of southern European birth (I's and IIa's) in 35 cereal-sheep local government areas, to which should be added 200 or more IIb's, and all the womenfolk. The naturalization records for the years 1930-46 suggest the occupational distribution of the I's was: farmers 36·0%, agricultural labourers 14·7%, timber-cutters and contractors 14·6%, carriers 2·6%, railway workers 1·3%, miners 10·5%, market-gardeners 5·5%, restaurant-keepers and fruit-shop proprietors 8·3%, station hands 2·6%, others 3·9%. The 35 L.G.A.s concerned were: Northampton, Upper Chapman, Mullewa, Geraldton-Greenough, Irwin, Mingenew, Morowa, Three Springs, Carramah, Perenjori, Dalwillinu, Mt Marshall, Moore, Victoria Plains, Goomalling, Nungarin, Westonia, Yilgairn, Merredin, Kellerberrin, Cunderdin, Northam, Bruce Rock, Narambeen, Kondinin, Corrigin, Brookton, Pingelly, Narrogin, Wickepin, Kulin, Lake Grace, Katanning, Broomehill. In the four other main cereal-sheep L.G.A.s (Koorda, Wyalkatchem, Wagin, and Dumbleyong) there were virtually no southern Europeans, because these areas were settled in the 1890s before southern Europeans were numerous.

have been getting into difficulties or have had their fill of rural life. This accounts for the rapid increase in the number of farms owned by southern Europeans in the sugar districts of Queensland, in the horticultural regions of New South Wales, Victoria, and South Australia, or in the market-garden areas around various large towns; there can be little doubt that had they strongly desired to adopt mixed farming in the cereal-sheep belt they could have done so, especially during the great depression when numerous small farmers faced bankruptcy and trouble.

The fact remains, however, that before 1940 southern European settlers in Australia tended to take to the large holdings and extensive farming methods prevalent in most cereal-sheep areas far less than to the smaller holdings and more intensive methods involved in horticulture, market-gardening, sugar-cane growing, or tobacco-farming. This is true even of Western Australia. The three local government areas of Manjimup (tobacco and timber), Harvey (potatoes, orchards, and timber) and Waneroo (market-gardening) in 1947 contained more men of southern European birth between them than all the cereal-sheep areas together.[6] It is more noticeable still elsewhere: in the sugar and tobacco regions of northern Queensland; in the sugar, tobacco, and cotton district near Biloela in central Queensland; in the orchard and tobacco district centred on Stanthorpe in southern Queensland; in the banana-growing areas around Lismore and Mullumbimby in northern New South Wales; in the orchard districts near Bright and Myrtleford in north-eastern Victoria; in the horticultural sections of the irrigated zones of New South Wales, Victoria, and South Australia. The best-known of all these places are probably the sugar-cane districts of northern Queensland where Piedmontese and Sicilian Italians, together with Maltese,

[6] Similarly, the seven intensively-farmed L.G.A.s of the south-west (Upper Blackwood, Drakesbrook, Harvey, Manjimup, Bridgetown, Balingup, and Preston) and the similar L.G.A.s near Perth (Waneroo, Swan, Mundaring, Fremantle, Gosnells, and Armadale-Kelmscott) in 1947 contained three times as many men of southern European birth as all the cereal-sheep areas together. The argument that intensive farming encouraged smaller holdings and a larger total population, so that the proportion of southern Europeans to total population was no higher than in the cereal-sheep areas, is here not valid: southern European born males made up less than 3% of the total population in the cereal-sheep areas compared with 9% in intensive areas. The intensive area with the highest proportion of southern European born males in 1947 was Waneroo, 36·7%, or nearly 50% when an estimated total of IIb's is included.

Spaniards, Greeks, Dalmatian Yugoslavs, and Albanians settled in strength from the late nineteenth century onwards; in 1947 the Cairns statistical division alone contained over 6,000 persons of southern European birth—three-quarters of them Italian— and probably well over 3,000 children born in Australia; in all, more than one-quarter of the total population. In some sub-divisions of these sugar areas, of course, southern Europeans made up well over half the total population.[7] When to these areas are added the market-gardening and poultry-farming districts around the various cities and country towns, some five-sixths of the southern European farming population seem to have been engaged in intensive farming of one kind or another (Table X shows 17·9 per cent in intensive farming to 3·4 per cent in other farming).

'Other farming', which engages the remaining one-sixth, includes a category not yet mentioned: dairy-farmers. Their exact number is difficult to estimate since much dairying took place in combination with other kinds of farming and the person concerned frequently described himself simply as 'farmer' or 'mixed farmer'. Clearly, taking Australia as a whole, southern Europeans engaged in dairying, or in mixed dairying and other farming, were not very numerous, but there is evidence to suggest that in one or two places they became quite strong. In the dairying regions of East Gippsland, in Victoria, for instance, near Bairnsdale, Mossiface, and Orbost, and again in those of West Gippsland near Loch, Moe, and Warragul, there were by the 1930s a number of Macedonian, North Italian, Apulian (South Italy), Sicilian, and Albanian farmers, some of whom described themselves as dairy-farmers or dairy-managers. Others described themselves as market-gardeners while the remainder, it seems, included a number of settlers who were combining dairying with various kinds of intensive cultivation. In this sense it is difficult to assess dairying adequately; that is, to decide when it belongs to large-scale extensive farming and when to small-scale intensive farming. Table X includes it with extensive farming but it is clear that some dairy-farmers should be counted as small holders, so raising still higher the proportion of southern Europeans engaged in small-scale intensive farming.

The third somewhat unexpected gap in the distribution of southern Europeans in Australia before 1940 is in Tasmania. Here, at the 1947 census, the southern Europeans made up only

7 See Borrie, *Italians and Germans in Australia*, pp. 91-5; J. M. Bertei, Innisfail, Ch. 5; A. Grenfell Price, *White Settlers in the Tropics*, pp. 72-3.

1 in every 2,000 persons (0·05 per cent) whereas they were more than ten times as strong for Australia as a whole (0·77 per cent). Their absence from the pastoral areas of the island accords with their behaviour elsewhere, but their absence from the horticultural, market-gardening, and dairying areas is as difficult to explain as it is conspicuous.[8] This cannot be attributed to Tasmania's relatively wet cold climate, primarily because many southern Europeans, especially those from more mountainous regions, were accustomed to greater wetness and cold than prevail in Tasmania; furthermore, many southern Europeans have shown themselves ready to live in Canadian and other new world climates more severe than that of Australia's southernmost state. Probably the relatively static economic conditions of pre-war Tasmania were more influential—a suggestion confirmed by the fact that as the island has shared in Australia's rapid economic development since the war so has she shared in the rapid expansion of her southern European population. (There were twelve times as many southern European born persons in Tasmania at the 1954 census as at the 1947.)

The exact reasons for southern European failure to enter Tasmanian farming in the years 1890-1940, however, are beside the main point here: that one-third or so of southern European settlers in Australia engaged in some kind of farming activity, that this proportion rose as the years passed by, and that over five-sixths of those concerned adopted some kind of intensive farming. Clearly we are here witnessing something more than the efforts of a peasant people to achieve the peasant goal of independence—we are witnessing the tendency of persons reared in the tradition of small-scale garden cultivation to re-establish that tradition in Australia. In Australia the old Italian proverb has also held: 'The plough has a colter of iron but the spade has an edge of gold.'

At this point we may well ask why this peasant garden tradition asserted itself so much more strongly in Australia than in most parts of the United States. At times the techniques of garden agriculture were manifest there, especially in the work of those labourers wielding the pick and shovel on railway track building or mining. But vast numbers of migrants surrendered

---

[8] The naturalization records show no market-gardeners at all, while they, with the 1947 census tables, suggest that the 26 L.G.A.s most concerned with dairying and intensive cultivation contained only 20 or so southern European settlers, of whom some were timber-workers and general labourers.

all connexion with previous experience when they entered foundaries, engineering works, textile factories, meat-processing works, and so forth. Though precise statistics are lacking, it appears that well under 20 per cent of southern Europeans in the United States were engaged in agricultural activity by 1920 and that half or more were employed in manufacturing and mining.[9] (It is convenient to relate the United States census of 1920 to the Australian census of 1947; both come at the end of a great migration episode, just before a new episode is ushered in.)

The answer to this question is highly complex. Several points, however, may be emphasized. First, North America received its southern and eastern European immigrants at a time when the homestead movement westward was losing impetus and when heavy industry, railway building, and mining were expanding rapidly; indeed, some immigration to America arose directly from the efforts of American industrial and commercial companies to recruit cheap labour from Europe by sending their own agents on tour of European villages and by giving various privileges to the Europeans already in America who could persuade numbers of their compatriots to emigrate. The huge immigrant concentrations so formed rapidly developed social institutions and customs that proved most attractive to new arrivals and exercised a strong brake on moves to abandon city life for rural activities: the southern European population of central Chicago, for instance, numbered some 50,000 by 1920; in Manhattan borough, New York, it totalled well over 200,000; while (to take a city with a total population smaller than that of Sydney or Melbourne) in San Francisco it totalled some 30,000. In general, it seems that over 80 per cent of the southern European born population of the United States were living in urban areas by 1920. In this sense southern and eastern European migration to North America was very largely a rural-to-urban movement of the same kind as that taking place within Europe itself—from the Alpine valleys to the industries of Milan and Turin, for instance.

Southern European migration to Australia was not as markedly rural-to-urban as that to the United States; by 1921, indeed, only just over half the total of southern European born persons (57·4 per cent) were living in urban areas, and this proportion was maintained throughout the following decades; in 1947 it

9 U.S. censuses of 1910 and 1920; *Reports of the Immigration Commission,* 1907-10.

was still 55·7 per cent.[10] The explanation for this contrast lies partly in the fact that, though as in the United States the homestead movement outback was slackening when southern Europeans began to arrive in numbers, other parts of rural Australia offered more inducement than their American counterpart—more especially the plantation areas of northern Australia where there was no native-born Negro population to compete with white labourers.[11] But the explanation lies also in the fact that in Australia secondary industry, though expanding, did not grow at the same rate as in North America and did not encourage the development of great urban concentrations of European migrants. Moreover, assisted passage schemes, being normally confined to persons from the British Isles, tended to bring British rather than southern European immigrants to Australian industry. Some concentrations did develop in one or two places. By 1947 in central Sydney there were over 1,000 persons of Italian birth, well over 1,000 Greeks, and several hundred Maltese and South Slavs, while the eastern part of the city of Melbourne (Carlton), together with the adjacent areas of Richmond, Collingwood, Fitzroy, and Brunswick, contained nearly 3,000 persons born in Italy, 1,000 born in Greece, and several hundred Maltese and South Slavs.[12] Lesser concentrations existed in parts of central Brisbane, Adelaide, and Perth, in the mining towns of Boulder-Kalgoorlie and Broken Hill, and in the industrial-fishing town of Port Pirie.

Compared with the United States, these are small concentrations indeed. Nevertheless they are important: first, because they

[10] Urban areas here refer to the classifications, used in the censuses of Australia, of 'metropolitan' and 'urban-provincial'. Exact comparison with the U.S.A. census of 1920 is not possible, as the U.S.A. defined urban areas as all incorporated towns of and above 2,500 persons—plus similar unincorporated townships in certain New England States—whereas Australia defined urban-provincial areas more or less as all incorporated townships, some of which were of less than 2,500 persons. This discrepancy only serves to highlight the contrast between the two countries, since a 2,500 division between rural and urban would have increased the proportion of southern Europeans living in rural areas of Australia.

[11] In the 1890s Kanaka labourers (Pacific islanders) were being expelled from northern Queensland under the dictates of the White Australia Policy, and planters were forced to look to southern Europeans for an alternative labour force; these later bought their own farms.

[12] Census of Australia 1947: central Sydney consists of the local government areas of Glebe, Paddington, Redfern, and Sydney—the last including Pyrmont, Chippendale, East Sydney, Woolloomooloo, Kings Cross and Darlinghurst. These, with other L.G.A.s, were all combined into the L.G.A. of Sydney before the 1954 census.

were often large enough to provide ethnic churches, societies, or other institutions encouraging a strong ethnic group life; second, because they tended to act as nuclei around which much of the heavy post-war immigration has settled; and finally, because they serve to highlight the fact that in other Australian commercial and industrial cities the southern European population remained very small. Greater Newcastle, the principal mining and industrial area of New South Wales outside Sydney, contained only 200-odd southern Europeans by 1947, most of them Greek restaurant-keepers, while Geelong, Ballarat, and Bendigo, the principal towns of Victoria outside the metropolitan area of Melbourne, had together attracted only 300 or so. The remaining mining towns of Australia also contained very few: the Yallourn brown coal areas in Victoria and the coal areas of Greater Wollongong, New South Wales, each contained between two and three hundred, while the copper, lead, and iron mines at Mount Morgan and Cloncurry never attracted more than a handful.[13] In sum, it is clear that southern Europeans did settle in many commercial, industrial, and mining towns, but in small groups rather than in the large numbers associated with southern European settlement in many American cities; furthermore, that what urban concentrations did exist were most noticeable in the heart of the metropolitan cities, particularly Sydney and Melbourne.

The occupations pursued by southern European settlers in these inner metropolitan concentrations present a relatively uniform pattern. A minute fraction (2·4 per cent or so) were either professional men—teachers, priests, musicians, viticultural scientists, and doctors—or else were engaged in commerce—importers, dealers, merchants, brokers, and salesmen. A slightly larger number were fishermen and seamen (5·1 per cent), though naturally most of these lived in Brisbane, Sydney, and Melbourne where the city centre was relatively close to fishing wharves and mooring stations. A fifth or so were unskilled labourers employed on roads, wharves, and buildings, or else as porters, night-watchmen, window-cleaners, or liftmen. Another fifth were engaged in the skilled trades, ranging from ancient crafts such as tailoring, shoemaking, terrazzo- and marble-work, blacksmithing, or hairdressing, to more modern activities such as photography, printing, and motor engineering. Much the largest number, however, were

13 The naturalization records show that movement of southern Europeans in and out of Mt Morgan, Cloncurry and Mt Isa between census years was very slight; in 1947 these places contained fewer than 6 between them.

persons connected with small catering businesses: wine saloon-keepers, oyster-bar proprietors, fishmongers, restaurant-keepers, fruiterers, confectioners, ice-cream vendors, florists, hotel proprietors, cooks, waiters, barmen, or shop assistants. In inner Sydney and Melbourne the proportion in catering businesses declined somewhat in the 1930s and 1940s, whereas it rose in the skilled trades; even so, small catering businesses still accounted for nearly half the southern European population during these later decades (see Appendix 7:4).

There are many reasons for this gravitation into small catering businesses, but most are linked with the traditional peasant desire for independence and with the anxiety, evidenced by many new settlers all over the world, to establish themselves in positions of security and proprietorship. For this the small catering businesses were ideally suited. They required little capital to start; and here it is noticeable that many prosperous fruiterers, fish-shop proprietors, ice-cream manufacturers and chocolate manufacturers started life in Australia as fruit-barrow boys, itinerant fish sellers, ice-cream cartmen and sweets pedlars. They were convenient in that a number of men in partnership, or later a complete family group, could live above or behind the shop premises, so reducing accommodation expenses. They were less subject to trade union and legislative restrictions on shopping hours than most retail businesses, thus enabling new settlers to work long hours without falling foul of the law. They fitted in well with the peasant tradition of family labour—the wife and children could help in the kitchen or behind the counter, thereby reducing labour costs very substantially. They required little knowledge of English, save in the man in charge; and he could manage with relatively few commercial words and a basic knowledge of the currency. They were not, of course, the only kind of small business that promised relatively rapid independence. Fishing, commerce and some of the skilled trades—tailoring, cabinet-making, shoemaking, hairdressing, or terrazzo-paving—offered similar opportunities. The evidence here is not sufficiently precise to permit any statement concerning the number of those who had already achieved independence by the time they applied for naturalization, but it is significant that settlers in occupations offering independence made up well over half of the total southern European population in these inner city areas and that this proportion fell very little with the passage of time (see Appendix 7:4).

Inner cities, however, are not necessarily representative of a whole metropolitan area. Only about half of the southern European settler population in the metropolitan areas of Australia (59·4 per cent in 1947) have lived in the central city and adjacent suburbs; the remainder have been distributed through the residential and industrial suburbs and in the market-gardening and horticultural zones included within the metropolitan boundaries. In practice, it seems, these suburban southern Europeans followed much the same occupations as those in the inner cities, except, of course, for the considerable number of market-gardeners and horticulturalists. This quite substantial number of 'metropolitan farmers' must be remembered in any discussion of the so-called tendency of southern Europeans to gravitate to metropolitan towns, especially as it is often taken for granted that a person living in a metropolitan zone must have an urban occupation and residence. Indeed, assuming from the evidence of the naturalization records that 20 per cent of the southern European metropolitan population of 1947 were actually small-scale farmers and excluding them from the metropolitan population on the grounds that they were not typically urban, the proportion of southern European born persons living in metropolitan areas falls from 42·1 per cent of the total to 33·7 per cent.[14]

These small-scale farmers, living just inside or just outside the metropolitan boundary, formed more conspicuous concentrations than any other metropolitan settlers except those in the inner city. In Melbourne, for instance, the most noticeable concentration outside the inner area was at Werribee; in Adelaide it was the local government areas of Woodville and West Torrens, especially near Lockleys and Fulham. In Perth there were two concentrations, one to the south around Spearwood and the other to the north from Osborne Park to Herne Hill. In Sydney also there were two principal concentrations, one in the western areas —Blacktown, Holroyd, Fairfield, Cabramatta, and Nepean—and the other to the north around Brookvale and Warriewood. In areas such as these substantial numbers of North Italians, Calabrians, Sicilians, Dalmatian Yugoslavs, Bulgarians, Macedonians, Maltese, and occasional groups of Greek islanders were settled in market-gardening, poultry-farming, pig-farming, horticulture,

14 This point also applies to the United States, where the high urban concentration of southern Europeans must be interpreted in the light of these urban farmers. This does not, of course, weaken the point made previously about large concentrations of southern Europeans, since nearly all the figures quoted referred to the inner cities.

viticulture, and commercial flower-growing.[15] (Brisbane and Hobart, containing relatively few southern European farmers, followed a somewhat different pattern.)

Elsewhere in the metropolitan areas southern Europeans tended to be distributed in fairly small groups, near enough to the inner city to take advantage of ethnic societies and churches, but not part of a solid residential concentration. Here again the majority were in small catering businesses. Indeed, it appears that about a third of all southern European settlers who were engaged in catering lived and worked in these suburban zones, the other two-thirds being distributed fairly evenly between the inner cities and the non-metropolitan cities, townships, and villages. Professional and commercial men, craftsmen, and unskilled labourers were distributed in much the same way.[16]

This brief word on caterers, labourers, and craftsmen completes our survey of those general categories, characteristics, and problems relevant to the settlement pattern of Australia's southern European population as a whole. It is now possible to move much closer to this broad and sweeping picture, to examine in detail the highly variegated and distinctive mosaic stones that together make up the colour and line of the total settlement pattern, by examining the numerous little migration chains—village

[15] The 1947 census tables do not give Albanians, Bulgarians, Portuguese or Spaniards; therefore the totals of persons of southern European birth in these areas are approximate only, viz.: Werribee 580; Woodville-West Torrens 670; Fremantle R.D. (Spearwood, etc.) 440; Perth-Swan R.D.s (Osborne Park-Herne Hill) 1,530; Cabramatta-Blacktown-Holroyd-Fairfield-Nepean 1,800; Warringah (Warriewood, etc.) 400. To these, of course, should be added children born in Australia.

[16] The metropolitan proportion was, according to the naturalization records: caterers 64·3%; craftsmen 71·3%; unskilled labourers (excluding agricultural labourers) 63·9%; professional and businessmen 75·8%; farmers 24·3%. Though the census birthplace categories are not very satisfactory, the following figures, corrected to show Newcastle as a metropolitan area, show the complete distribution of the main groupings of southern European settlers.

Grouping	Migratory	Rural	Provincial	Metro-politan	Inner City and Suburbs	Inner City
Italians ..	0·2	51·6	5·2	43·0	23·2	7·4
Greeks ..	0·5	24·3	18·2	57·0	43·9	28·5
Maltese ..	1·2	31·4	5·4	62·0	35·4	26·7
Yugoslavs ..	0·3	54·5	7·2	38·0	16·4	8·6
Total	0·3	44·2	8·5	47·0	28·1	13·8

and district—and the very diverse ways in which members of these chains selected certain places to live in and occupations to follow.

MIGRATION CHAINS AND THE SETTLEMENT PATTERN

This approach might well be challenged, on the grounds that, no matter how important details of village, district and regional units may be to any understanding of the European background, nor how influential they are in the process of chain migration, they are far less relevant to the story of settlement itself, and that general statements about southern Europeans as such, or at most about broad Folk groupings, are quite adequate here. Thus, of the Greeks, it is said that they nearly all abandon their agricultural and seafaring background and enter the catering trades as soon as they arrive in the new world: they have done so in the United States,[17] they have done so in Canada,[18] and, as such documents as the Ferry Report of 1925 show,[19] they have done so in Australia.

The real problem then, according to this argument, is not to examine the behaviour of small group after small group but to explain why Greeks generally have entered catering businesses in much greater strength than other southern Europeans. Is it that they are 'natural-born cooks', as one American writer suggests, and therefore favour the restaurant business or confectionery-making?[20] Or is it that Turkish laws forbade the ownership of land by Christians, so that Greeks who left Greece proper over several centuries to settle in Constantinople, Smyrna, or Alexandria tended to enter small urban businesses rather than agriculture, so establishing a migration tradition that was subsequently carried to the outer world by Greek migrants in the nineteenth and twentieth centuries? Or is it simply, as one writer suggests, that poor agricultural lands have forced the Greeks into commercial activities, that they have a seafaring tradition dating back to the Odyssey, that by now 'the Greek aptitude for commerce is proverbial',[21] and that this has led them into occupations such as catering rather than agriculture or the crafts?

17 Fairchild, *Greek Immigration to the United States.*

18 G. D. Vlassis, *The Greeks in Canada.* My own field-work in Toronto in 1958 shows that over two-thirds of Greeks settling in Toronto, 1926-50, entered the catering trades.

19 'Ferry Report', p. 12; see also Appendixes 8-21 for the ratio of Greeks entering the catering trade to other southern Europeans.

20 Fairchild, op. cit., p. 171.

21 B. Sweet-Escott, *Greece: A Political and Economic Survey 1939-53,* p. 10.

The problem is not, however, as simple as it may seem. Other Mediterranean peoples have a seafaring and commercial tradition dating back over many centuries; have established colonies in Constantinople, Smyrna and Alexandria and were affected by Ottoman laws of property; have been hailed as natural-born cooks. There is, indeed, almost certainly something in the Greek character and tradition that, when away from Hellas itself, turns naturally to commercial activities—of which catering is almost the easiest for newly-arrived settlers with little either of capital or of fluency in the language. But the phenomenon owes as much, if not more, to other factors. In the first place we must make sure that what may on the surface appear to be the workings of some national characteristic is not, in fact, simply the effects of chain migration. The strong tendency for those coming out with the aid of friends and relatives to adopt the same occupations as their sponsors can mean that a few large migration chains dominate the settlement pattern of a whole nationality. This to some extent happened with Greek settlers in Australia— migrants from Ithaca, Kythera, Kastellorizo and the Peloponnesus made up more than half the number of Greek settlers before 1940 and their high concentration in the catering trades— an average of 84 per cent—did much to lift the whole Greek average above the southern European average of 29 per cent (Appendix 7:5).

There are other considerations, too. There is the very important fact that most Greeks were loyal sons of the Greek Orthodox Church and, other things being equal, preferred to settle where there were enough fellow-Greeks to form an Orthodox community or to justify the visits of an Orthodox priest. As a result, there was a tendency for Greek immigrants to seek out older established Greek settlers and for new chain pioneers to see quickly the success that members of older Greek groups were achieving in the catering business. Indeed, the information often reached the immigrant before he left home. News of a Kytheran Greek successfully establishing himself in the fish restaurant business in the 1870s apparently spread through the Ionian islands, those parts of the Peloponnesus adjacent to Kythera, and to commercial ports such as Athens, Constantinople and Smyrna, with which some Kytheran small shipowners were accustomed to trade; some later pioneers from other parts of Greece were, it seems, already aware of Kytheran success in catering when they arrived.

Even with these forces acting for uniform behaviour, the fact

remains that not all Greek groups concentrated in catering businesses. Well over half the total of settlers from the Dodecanese
island of Symi, for instance, took up fishing in Australia,[22] and
the majority of settlers from Evvoia island became farmers,
labourers, and fishermen. Nor is it true that Greeks have been
the only southern Europeans to enter the catering trades in
strength. Italians from the Lipari islands, for example, concentrated more strongly in catering than any Greeks save those
from Kythera, Ithaca, and Levkas; and many Albanian settlers
were also concentrated in the catering trades.

Apart from all this the detailed statistics reveal considerable
variation amongst the Greek catering groups themselves. In the
United States some Greek groups became involved in the manu-
facture of chocolate and confectionery or in running flower-
shops; in fact, the statistics available suggest that many more
Greek settlers became engaged in these activities than in the
restaurant business.[23] In Toronto, Peloponnesian Greeks had
considerable interest in the flower business, in tobacco processing,
and in general commerce, whereas the Macedonian Greeks were
much more highly concentrated in the restaurant business or, if
from the Macedonian town of Kastoria, in the fur trade. In Australia there was also much variation. Most Kytheran Greeks were
in the fish and general restaurant business, whereas a much
higher proportion of Ithacan Greeks established themselves in
confectionery and fruit-shops. To these occupational differences
must be added pronounced differences in the way the various
Greek catering groups settled into the places of their choice:
three-quarters of the total of Ithacan caterers settled in metropolitan areas, particularly Melbourne, whereas only one-third
of Kytheran caterers did so, the rest dispersing through the
country towns of southern Queensland, New South Wales, and
northern Victoria; indeed, by 1947, a very large number of the
country restaurants of New South Wales were in Kytheran hands.
There are numerous other examples (see Appendix 19).

From all this it is clear that Greeks cannot be treated as a
single national grouping: only a detailed examination of each
migration chain will reveal the story of Greek settlement in Australia in its true perspective. This applies even more strongly
to other southern Europeans, among whom there is no strongly
marked tendency for any one Folk to concentrate in any one
place or occupation. In short, there is no way of avoiding a close

---

22 For these and subsequent statistics see Appendixes 8-21 'Occupations'.
23 Fairchild, op. cit., pp. 165 ff.

M

examination of the mosaic stones of the settlement pattern—the dozens and dozens of individual migration chains, both large and small.

A close examination of these smaller migration units reveals the very great differences between them, even though many originated in the same part of the Mediterranean. In Sicily, for instance, the three main areas of origin were all in the north-east corner of the island: the Mount Etna area covering northern Catania and south-east Messina; the north and north-east coasts of Messina; and the Lipari islands, themselves part of Messina province for purposes of administration. Yet there are great differences among settlers from these three areas (see Appendixes 14, 15). Nearly 90 per cent of migrants from the Mount Etna area settled in northern Queensland as farmers and agricultural labourers; those from northern Messina settled principally in Western Australia and Queensland, dividing themselves almost equally between catering, farming, and other activities such as mining, timber-cutting, unskilled labouring and fishing; while over three-quarters of the Lipari islanders settled in Sydney and Melbourne, mainly as fruiterers.

The same kind of contrast existed between migration chains from the two adjacent areas of Korçë and Gjinokastër in southern Albania: migrants from the Korçë area tended to concentrate in agriculture and unskilled labouring in Western Australia, Victoria, and Queensland, whereas the majority of those from Gjinokastër entered small catering businesses in Perth, Melbourne, and Sydney (Appendix 21). Likewise migrants from the foothills of Treviso province, in the Veneto of northern Italy, settled predominantly as farmers and agricultural labourers in rural South Australia, New South Wales, and Queensland, whereas those from similar country thirty miles away in Vicenza province gravitated far more often to the mines and farms of Victoria (Appendix 10).

Nearby islands, too, often displayed similar contrasts. The difference between the Ionian islands of Ithaca and Kythera has already been mentioned. The Greek Dodecanese islands are another example. Two-thirds of the total of settlers from Kastellorizo island settled in metropolitan cities, principally Perth and Sydney, where they busied themselves with restaurants, fish-shops, general labouring, and the occasional pig-farm. Conversely, the majority of migrants from Rhodes settled in Queensland, Victoria, and South Australia, many in catering but at least a quarter as farmers in places such as the cotton-growing district centred on Biloela, central Queensland. Quite different again were settlers from the nearby island of Symi, over half of whom became fishermen in Sydney and in the small town of Thevenard on the Great Australian Bight (Appendix 19).

These areas of origin, both mainland and island, though geographically very close, are quite distinct. The contrast between the various migration chains becomes still more striking when illustrated by neighbouring villages in the same district. On the east coast of the Greek island of Evvoia, for instance, there are two villages only two miles or so apart, Androniacos and Kimi. Before 1940 the majority of settlers from Androniacos had settled in Broken Hill—some as caterers but more as miners—while a number of others had settled as fruit- and vine-growers in Mildura, Victoria. A few persons from Kimi also settled as horticulturalists at Mildura and caterers at Broken Hill but the majority settled first as labourers at Port Pirie and then as fishermen on the Australian Bight or as horticulturalists in the Murray River irrigation settlements of South Australia.[24]

An interesting Yugoslav example comes from the Dalmatian island of Korčula. About half the total of migrants from the little town of Korčula, at the eastern end of the island, settled in Western Australia, the majority as miners in the eastern gold-fields; the remainder settled in New South Wales and Queensland, most as market-gardeners, poultry-farmers, and craftsmen in Sydney but a few as farmers in northern Queensland. On the other hand, nearly all persons (90 per cent) from the nearby township of Račišće settled in Western Australia, many as miners and timber-cutters in the eastern gold-fields and the rest as timber-workers and farmers in the south-western districts or in the market-gardening areas near Perth (Appendix 18).

Several striking contrasts come from northern Italy. The town

[24] With villages of origin we are sometimes considering numbers so small that statistical tests show no significant difference between one group and another at the 5% level, even when the proportions are widely different. This does not matter since here we are not concerned with the *tendency* of migrants from one particular place to behave differently from migrants from another place (this would need rigorous use of significance tests since it involves treating the migrant groups in Australia as samples of the total number of persons in the world born in those places). Rather are we concerned to note that, when examining naturalization records at a sample ratio of 1/1 or 1/2, we discern marked differences between the actual behaviour of migrant groups in Australia and that these differences can often be directly related to the careers of pioneer settlers and the Australian conditions in which they found themselves.

of Albosaggia in the Valtellina, for instance, sent less than one-fifth of its Australian emigrants to settle in Western Australia, the great majority settling as farmers and labourers in the Upper Murray regions of Victoria and in the Cairns district of north Queensland. The town of Montagna, however, four miles away on the opposite side of the river, sent four-fifths of its settlers to Western Australia, principally as miners, timber-workers, and farmers (Appendix 9). A typical southern Italian contrast is that between two nearby villages on the northern slopes of the Aspromonte in Calabria. Two-thirds of those who came from Delianuova settled as market-gardeners, labourers, craftsmen, and fruiterers in the metropolitan areas of Perth, Melbourne, and Sydney and most of the remainder as farmers and labourers in the south-western districts of Western Australia. Of settlers from Scido, four or five miles to the east, less than half settled in metropolitan areas and only a few in rural Western Australia; the rest became farmers in northern Victoria and New South Wales (Appendix 13).

Contrasts such as these (see Appendixes 8-21) may be drawn from districts all over southern Europe. Why should this be so, especially with villages cheek by jowl in the same district? The answer lies partly in the processes of chain migration described earlier and in the accidental way in which many chain founders established themselves in Australia (see p. 133 above). Australian conditions at the time the new migrant arrived, employment opportunities near his port of arrival, accidental meetings and occurrences during his first few months of work: all these worked together to determine that the career of a particular pioneer, and the chain subsequently founded on him, should differ quite substantially from that of a pioneer from another village or district. Indeed, in some cases, a single village of origin produced several pioneer settlers and migration chains, all somewhat different in character and history.

Accident and Incident in Settlement History

This accidental motif in migration history is worth pursuing for a moment since much of the history of southern European settlement is explicable in these terms. Take, for instance, the interesting group of settlers from the Medjumurje, that triangle of country in north-west Croatia between the Rivers Mur and Drava. Late in 1924 five men from the village of Kotoriba were arranging to emigrate to the United States—where two of them

222

had been earlier—when they suddenly found that the quota laws had come into operation and stopped their entry.[25] Having made all arrangements to leave home, and in no mood to settle again to the humdrum round of village life, they consulted the travel agent in Zagreb who said he could book passages on a ship leaving in three days' time from Genoa, for Australia. Hurriedly scraping together all their savings and borrowing from relatives they managed to raise the extra passage cost, caught the boat, and arrived in Perth in December.

On arrival there they wondered whether they should disembark, but finally decided they had enough money to go farther east. When they arrived in Adelaide, however, they apparently concluded that their cash resources were getting so low they ought to disembark. That night, which happened to be Christmas Eve, they spent on the hospitable floor of the local police station—being unable to find alternative accommodation—and next day found lodgings in a boarding-house in Hindley Street run by a Maltese. There they met a Dalmatian settler on holiday from the mines at Broken Hill and were very pleased to discover that the two dialects were sufficiently similar to permit easy conversation. The Dalmatian, indeed, was so taken with the youngest member of the party that he wanted to take him back to Broken Hill. The party, however, refused to divide and, as the miner apparently did not feel able to find jobs for all five in Broken Hill, he told them that some Dalmatian migrants were finding work on the irrigation areas on the Murray River.

Soon after this the five friends caught a train to Morgan, wandered across country to the irrigation district at Berri, and eventually found a Dalmatian timber-contractor who was under contract to supply wood for the Berri steam pump. He lent them a tent and supplies and took one of them on as a full-time woodcutter. The others managed to find jobs on various fruit farms and soon afterwards were able to borrow a disused house and obtain an almost unbroken sequence of agricultural jobs.

In mid-1925, after several months at Berri, they began writing home to friends in Kotoriba and the news spread rapidly to the nearby villages of Dubrava, Vidovech, Gorican and others; by late 1925 and early 1926 many more migrants were on their way to join the five pioneers. Subsequently these settlers began to purchase their own farms and to spread along the river as far as Mildura. In 1947 there were nearly 200 men, 100 women, and

25 The five men were John and Frank Vidovich, their nephew Andy Matotek, and two friends, Steve Siladi and George Soko.

numerous children born in Australia, most of them settled on their own properties. A few of these Medjumurje settlers have moved away to Melbourne and elsewhere but the great majority are still on the Murray between Barmera and Mildura where, in fact, they make up practically the whole Yugoslav population of pre-war origin. The quite accidental decision to disembark at Adelaide and the accidental meeting with a Dalmatian who knew that there were jobs available on the Murray have resulted in one of the most interesting and homogeneous group settlements in Australia.[26]

Another interesting and important illustration of the accidental character of southern European settlement comes from the Kytheran Greek community in Sydney and its extensions in rural New South Wales. This community apparently began when Jack Melitas, who had come to Australia during the gold-rushes, returned to Kythera and spread the news about Australia. In the early seventies one, Athanasios Comino, worked his way out on a sailing ship and became an unskilled labourer in Sydney. Then, so the story goes, he was joined by John Theodore of Psara and the two found work in the old Balmain colliery. Some time later Comino fell sick and the doctors told him he had been affected by colliery work, would have to leave his job, and should find himself some light occupation. One day, while still without work, he was walking down Oxford Street, Sydney, saw a fish-shop owned by a Welshman, remembered that the doctors said he could eat fish, so went in for a meal. While there he saw that the Welshman did no more than drop fish into boiling fat, fork it out after a few minutes, slap it on to a plate or some paper, and hand it to the customer. After some time watching this Comino began to think that here was an occupation requiring little experience or hard labour, just the solution for his own problem. At all events he and Theodore decided to try it, rented some premises, and opened a small fish-shop at 36 Oxford Street, some time in 1878.

At first they met certain difficulties arising from their ignorance of the language and of the finer points of frying fish. For instance, one day a man came in and asked for fried oysters and they had not the remotest idea whether such a dish should be fried in or out of the shell; on this occasion they put the complete shell into the fat. Despite these early difficulties they kept

[26] Personal information from interviews with Andy Matotek and seven others at Berri and Mildura in December 1955; statistical details from naturalization and census records.

at it, began to sell coffee as well as fish, and later became interested in the actual supplies of oysters and fish. Eventually Comino went north to the Hawkesbury River to take up oyster allotments and supervise oyster-gathering, while Theodore kept the shop in Sydney going. They both made a good deal of money, Comino later becoming known as the 'Oyster King'.[27]

During the eighties Comino began to bring his brothers out to join him. One brother joined him in running the oyster-beds while two others stayed in Sydney and opened more oyster-bars and fish restaurants. News of these successful pioneers spread rapidly through the hamlets of Kythera and this, together with a steady stream of Comino friends and relatives, substantially increased the number of Kytheran Greeks in New South Wales. By 1911 there were, apart from a score or so of women and fifty children, some 400 persons of Kytheran birth in the state, about 70 per cent of whom were either controlling or working in oyster-bars, fish-shops and restaurants.

Not all, however, were in inner Sydney. By the turn of the century many newcomers found the inner city somewhat overcrowded with oyster-bars and fish restaurants and, with the assistance of friends already established, began to move into the suburbs of Sydney and into the country towns of New South Wales and southern Queensland. They were primarily concerned with opening more fish-shops and restaurants, but occasionally a Kytheran settler set himself up as a grocer, greengrocer or fruiterer, often in conjunction with a restaurant—about 15 per cent in all. By 1911 slightly over half the Kytheran population were in country towns and villages and the rest in Sydney itself.[28]

By 1947 the Kytheran population of New South Wales totalled somewhere between 2,000 and 3,000, of whom half or more were adult male settlers and the remainder wives and children born in Greece or second- and third-generation persons born in Australia.[29] By this time, too, more had moved into non-metropolitan

27 Personal details from interviews with John Raftopoulos and others in Sydney, April 1956, and from death certificates and Sydney street directories; statistical details from naturalization and census records. The Welsh fishmonger in Oxford Street was presumably J. Hughes at 131—he ran a fish shop all through the seventies.
28 From the 1911 census birthplace statistics taken in conjunction with birthplace and occupational data in the naturalization records; see also Appendix 19.
29 Excluding wives of non-Kytheran origin and counting children of mixed marriages as half each. Information from the 1947 census, naturalization records, and marriage records of the Orthodox community in Sydney.

areas, leaving less than one-third in Sydney itself. The occupational pattern, however, remained the same: 70 per cent in restaurants and fish-shops (the old name, oyster-bar or oyster-saloon had now almost completely vanished), and another 20 per cent in retail businesses such as groceries, confectioneries, and fruit-shops. The career of Athanasios Comino and his accidental entry into the fish restaurant business has produced no insignificant harvest.

It would be quite wrong to overemphasize this accidental element in settlement history, just as wrong as to ignore it altogether. Historical characteristics and traditions have played some part, as we have seen with Greek caterers. Likewise booms and depressions, availability of jobs, government regulations, and peasant love of independence, have been most influential in determining the spread of southern Europeans throughout the country. But these have controlled the general outline, not the detailed pattern; they decided that there should be southern Europeans in certain places and jobs at certain times but not the particular kind of southern European that arrived and the particular kind of community or group that appeared. In this, as in most history, there is a subtle balance between general controls and particular events, between the grand historical force and the individual will and career.

This subtle balance, this phenomenon of large-scale forces working themselves out through the sparkling diversity of individual careers and particular migrant groups, emerges more clearly in a detailed examination of chain settlement. The first step in such an examination is to divide the process of settlement into several stages. First, there is the pioneering stage, the arrival of one or two chain founders and their life in Australia before they persuaded any substantial numbers of persons to join them. The second stage covers the arrival of numerous friends and compatriots, few of whom had womenfolk with them and most of whom were ready to move with great rapidity from one part of Australia to another in search of jobs. In the third stage the women and children arrive and normal family life begins, and—for the most part—movement about Australia slows down. The fourth stage covers the later years of settlement, including the behaviour of the second generation reared and educated in Australia.

Two points must be noted here. First, these stages are phases in the process of chain settlement in Australia, not phases in the process of chain emigration from Europe. The latter relate

to the way news of successful settlers abroad affected people
still in Europe and brought about marked changes in the
character of emigration from the various districts and regions
of origin. These phases are by no means identical with the
stages of settlement, though they are, of course, very closely
connected.

The second point is that the length of each stage of settlement
varied considerably from chain to chain. Sometimes the pioneer
period was quite prolonged (Appendix 3:12). Andreas Lekatsas
of Ithaca, for instance, who came to Australia in the 1850s,
did not start any chain process worth speaking of until he
returned home twenty years or so later and encouraged a small
band of men to settle in Victoria in the 1870s and 1880s. Likewise the pioneering career of Nick Anticovich from Pelješac
peninsula, who arrived in New South Wales in the 1850s, lasted
about thirty years; his later life, from the 1880s onwards, belongs
to the second stage of settlement since he encouraged and helped
numerous young Dalmatian immigrants, especially those from
Pelješac. In other cases there was very little time lag between
the arrival of the first pioneers and the coming of their friends
and compatriots: the five pioneer Medjumurje Croats at Berri
and Mildura had been here less than a year when their first
friends and compatriots arrived. This means that the second
stage virtually began with the coming of the pioneers. The
same kind of variation is visible with the second and third
stages.

Stages in Chain Settlement—I

So much has already been said that there is no need to add
anything here about the first pioneers beyond the fact that
their careers were of paramount importance; on their success
or failure hung the fate of migration from their particular
village or district of origin.

Stages in Chain Settlement—II

The most obvious feature of this phase of settlement is the
mobility of new arrivals. Sometimes this arose because the
pioneer himself was engaged in a mobile occupation—construction work, timber-cutting, prospecting or fruit-picking—and
those compatriots who joined him moved with him in his
peregrinations. At other times the pioneer stayed put, but some
of his compatriots, having stayed with him for a time, went off

singly or in groups in response to employment opportunities elsewhere; these then gave rise to further complicated movements of groups and individuals—some of which will emerge more clearly later.

The whole scene, indeed, is one of extreme complexity and very rapid change and movement—factors inherent in the early stages of chain migration when many southern Europeans came to Australia as young men anxious to make money quickly, seldom with a clear-cut intention of staying, bringing few womenfolk with them, and quite ready to pack up to move on to some other place in Australia, to return to Europe, or to join a relative in California, New Zealand, South Africa, or elsewhere (pp. 102-7 above). In this sense a high rate of movement about Australia is simply part of the general tendency to wander about the world at large. A model career (based on documents and life histories of numerous Dalmatian migrants) could well be a young man from, say, Korčula, who arrived in Western Australia in the 1890s and joined a group of fellow-islanders in exploiting the new discoveries in the eastern gold-fields; after a few years moving from field to field there he might go on to join the colony of Korčula gum-diggers in the northern island of New Zealand; some years later he might return to Sydney as a general labourer and then go north to join a group of compatriots cutting cane near Townsville; finally, after hearing from a cousin in San Francisco, he might set off for North America, perhaps spending some time en route in one of the Dalmatian colonies in Chile, and eventually settle permanently in California. This kind of migrant career reveals the great disadvantages of treating overseas migration as a completely separate topic from internal migration—a matter of analytical importance that will receive more attention later.

Persons moving about the world were not the only ones to cover great distances in their travels: some of those who stayed within the continent of Australia also had quite astonishing careers. A typical mining case is that of an immigrant from Vrgorac in Dalmatia. He arrived in Perth in 1910, spent some five years in Wiluna, four years in Yundaga, the next four in Kurrawang, then two in Southern Cross, another two at Lakeside, two years at Kalgoorlie just before the great depression, then one year at Comet Vale, another year at Niagara, and finally back to Kalgoorlie in 1932—in all well over 5,000 miles.

Some men in the catering business also moved a good deal.

One young Greek from Androniacos in Evvoia island arrived in Sydney in 1924 and stayed there for two years, apparently as an assistant cook or waiter in a restaurant. In 1926 he moved to Hay for a year, then Lake Cargelligo for six months, then to Barraba for six months, then to Barellan for another six months. He then moved to Moree where he gave himself a breathing-space for two years and then a still longer breathing-space when he moved to Inverell for four years. Eventually, about 1937, he went to Mitchell in Queensland but after twelve months moved down to Balranald in the Riverina of New South Wales. After a year there he moved north again to Grenfell, at which point we lose track of him. Needless to say he was not married. Altogether his known travels covered some 5,000 miles.

These two cases have been of men who remained in the same occupation most of the time they were travelling. Others changed their occupation with great frequency. One young man from the Monferrato landed in Sydney and after several months of general labouring moved up to Babinda in northern Queensland, as an agricultural worker. After a year he abandoned agricultural labour and moved to Cairns, but after a lapse of twelve months or so returned to agricultural work at Proserpine. A few months later he found a suitable farm near Eton, Mackay, purchased it and settled down. Another case is that of a pioneer from Hvar island in Dalmatia who arrived in Brisbane in 1884, moved to Sydney for three years, then to Melbourne for four years, then to Bendigo for two years, then back to Queensland about 1894. In Queensland he stayed for one year at Bundaberg, then tried Townsville for four years, and eventually settled down near Pioneer, Mackay, about 1899. This sturdy soul apparently tried his hand at all manner of jobs during his 3,500 miles of travel and in 1924, at the age of 70, was still doing some general labouring.

For much of the time, then, this relatively high mobility represented the efforts of immigrants who had not yet settled into one definite occupation to find remunerative jobs wherever they were offering. In his early years of settlement a migrant might be one year carrying loads in the smelters of Port Pirie, next year cutting timber for the railways, two or three years later digging drains in Melbourne, soon afterwards helping in a fish or vegetable market, and only after a number of years in Australia might he rent a restaurant or farm and settle down more or less permanently. As a consequence, those southern European migrants who were still in the early stages of chain migration were a highly mobile labour force, turning their hands to almost any unskilled work as opportunity offered. To some extent southern Europeans who have arrived in Australia since 1947 have acted in the same way: they provide, it seems, at any rate in their first few years, a labour-force that is more willing to undertake hard jobs in hard conditions, and that moves much more easily in response to changes in the employment situation, than the native Australian population. It was, of course, precisely the same in other countries of immigration, such as the United States. In this way unattached immigrant men, without homes and families, have played an important part in the labour-force of all countries of immigration.

A good illustration of this relatively high immigrant mobility is provided by southern European movement in and out of the mining city of Broken Hill. Southern Europeans have never made up a large proportion of Broken Hill's total labour-force,[30] but Greeks, Macedonians, Bulgarians, Dalmatians, and North Italians have been there in appreciable numbers since the 1890s and have been a very mobile element of the working population. The naturalization records suggest that over the whole period 1892-1921 between one-third and one-half of the southern European section of the work-force entered or left Broken Hill each year—and this is almost certainly a considerable understatement.[31] These are only average figures and in years of labour strikes or of sudden changes in employment policy the rate of movement was naturally much higher. During the strike year of 1892, for instance, over four-fifths of the southern European population of Broken Hill moved to or from the town. The year 1924 was another year of heavy movement, primarily because many immigrants came direct to Broken Hill from the Mediterranean.[32]

[30] Because so many Greeks, Macedonians and Bulgarians were included with the Turkish population before the 1921 census, and so many Yugoslavs with the Austrian, exact figures are not available. Estimates suggest the southern European men made up roughly the following proportions of the working population: 1891—1·1%, 1901—1·2%, 1911—1·3%, 1921—1·6%.

[31] The complete annual figures are: 1892-1901—arrivals 23·4%, departures 16·3%, total 39·7%; 1902-11—arrivals 26·9%, departures 8·0%, total 34·9%; 1912-21—arrivals 26·3%, departures 22·8%, total 49·1%. Naturalization records understate the true rate of movement; see Appendix 3:8-13 for details and for method of calculation.

[32] 1892: 38·5% entered, 46·7% left; 1924: 71·4% entered, 17·8% left.

Another illustration comes from Bridgetown, a timber, farming and market-gardening area in the south-west of Western Australia. Various groups of southern Europeans—more particularly Macedonians, Dalmatians, northern Italians from the Valtellina, and southern Italians from Reggio Calabria—had started moving into Bridgetown before World War I and by 1947 made up some 10 per cent of the male working population. In the late thirties and forties, when migrants began to take up farms in considerable numbers, movement to and from the area slowed down quite noticeably, but over the period 1912-31, when the various chains were still in their early stages, well over half the southern European working population moved in and out of the area each year.[33]

The statistics for the southern European population within Australia as a whole are not as impressive as those for Broken Hill and Bridgetown. The first reason is that when discussing Broken Hill or Bridgetown, or any other place in Australia, we are concerned with the flow of southern Europeans in and out of that place, and must therefore take account of all new arrivals, whether they came from a town in the same state, from another state, or direct from overseas. For Australia as a whole, however, we are more concerned with the movement of southern Europeans about the continent than with arrivals direct from overseas, the exclusion of whom lowers the annual rate of movement considerably. The second reason is that many immigrants stayed in one metropolitan area and, though they often moved a great deal within that area, are not recorded as having changed their town or city of residence.

Despite all this, mobility for many immigrant groups was high. Between 1896 and 1919, which covered the early years of chain migration from Kythera and Levkas in the Ionian islands and from Hvar, Makarska and Vrgorac in Dalmatia, well over one-tenth of the immigrant population from those places moved each year to another state or to another town in the same state. So also did immigrants from Friuli, Catania, the Korçë area of Albania, the north-western parts of Greek Macedonia, and from various parts of central Dalmatia during the period 1920-8, which were the early years of chain migration from those areas. Immigrants from places such as Ithaca and the Lipari islands showed a lower rate of movement, primarily

[33] Naturalization records give the following annual figures: 1912-21—33·3% entered and 18·5% left, 51·8% in all; 1922-31—38·7% entered and 22·6% left, 61·3% in all.

because they tended to move about within the one metropolitan area.[34]

During the years 1880-1919 an average of at least one-tenth of the southern European population of Australia moved each year to another state or to another part of the same state. Between 1920 and 1928 some of the older chains were settling into stability, but they were more than outweighed by the large number of new chains and the annual rate of movement, if anything, rose a little.[35]

So far, mobility during the early stages of chain settlement has been discussed from the standpoint of Australia as a whole, or of particular places in Australia. It must also be examined from the standpoint of the migration chains themselves. Here the picture is most intricate. Some groups formed early in the chain process maintained much of their coherence because members moved together from place to place. Others maintained a central core from which individual migrants split off every now and again, moving to other places. Yet others split up completely during the process of movement, into a number of smaller groups around whom new large-scale groups sometimes formed when migrants came direct from Europe to join friends and relatives in Australia. Frequently these splinter groups or individuals rejoined each other in a new place of settlement, usually when one of the original band successfully established himself in a new place and informed his former comrades of his good fortune. This phenomenon may be termed 'secondary chain migration', since it involves precisely the same kind of forces as in primary chain migration, the only difference being that it operates inside the country of settlement. The new groups so formed may be termed 'secondary group settlements'; they have been an important element in the history of immigration, not only to Australia but to other countries as well (see pp. 182, 233 below).

[34] The naturalization records, which tend to underestimate annual movement (see Appendix 3), give the following statistics of annual movement within Australia (the statistics in parentheses combine movement within Australia with new arrivals, so giving some comparison with statistics from Broken Hill and Bridgetown quoted earlier): 1896-1919: Kythera 9·7% (18·9); Levkas 11·5% (21·8); Hvar 13·1% (20·8); Makarska and Vrgorac 11·2% (20·2); Ithaca 6·6% (14·8); Lipari islands 3·3% (9·0). 1920-28: Friuli 14·8% (37·5); Catania 10·1% (26·2); Korçë 20·6% (58·8); Macedonia 15·2% (40·6); central Dalmatia, various, 13·0% (29·6).

[35] The naturalization records, underestimating as they do, show 7·2% (14·7) for 1896-1919 and 10·0% (24·1) for 1920-8.

Many migration chains show signs of all these activities, and it is often exceedingly difficult to reconstruct the precise history of the original group of settlers. Moreover the naturalization records do not cover every immigrant, so that the careers of some pioneers have gone unrecorded.[36] Nevertheless it is possible to assess the history of many chains in general terms. A relatively simple case is that of the village of Račišće, on the Dalmatian island of Korčula, from which settlers came to the gold-fields of Boulder-Kalgoorlie in the 1890s and there some of them stayed. Others, however, moved backwards and forwards between Boulder, Kurrawang, and other mining towns in the eastern gold-fields. A smaller group of Račišće folk moved to Melbourne just before World War I. Some of these also were restless, including one who left Melbourne in 1914, spent a year at Broken Hill, then a year at Port Pirie, and returned to Melbourne in 1916. Another Račišće migrant left the Boulder group for Perth in 1907, moved on to Cairns in Queensland about 1912, joined the Melbourne colony in 1914, and after a few years moved a few miles south to Portarlington. There were, of course, other Račišće settlers outside the records available; nevertheless it is plain that by 1917 there were at least two main groups of Račišće folk in Australia—one in Boulder-Kalgoorlie and one in Melbourne—with individuals scattered here and there. During this phase of immigration about 60 per cent of Račičše immigrants were single men, 30 per cent were married but had left their wives in Europe, and the remaining 10 per cent had wives with them.

Another fairly simple illustration is that of Rakvicke, near Korçë, Albania, a village that sent most of its pioneers to Australia in the mid-1920s and was still in the early stages of chain migration by the mid-1930s. A number of immigrants came to Lilydale, east of Melbourne, in 1927, moved together to Shepparton in 1930, then to Swan Hill in 1935, then back to Shepparton, and finally on to Emerald in the Dandenong hills near Melbourne. Others came to Warragul, in western Gippsland, in the late 1920s and then divided, some moving to Traralgon, others to Maryborough, and others to Emerald. Another lot came to Kinglake in 1927, moved to Healesville in 1930, and then joined their fellow-villagers at Emerald in 1934.

---

[36] Roughly speaking there are records for every second pioneer. For the whole period 1890-1940 there are records for about two-thirds of European settlers but the proportion is somewhat lower for the first three decades of this period (see Appendix 1).

By 1940, then, there was apparently a secondary settlement of Rakvicke folk in the Dandenong hills near Emerald and a number of scattered families elsewhere. During these years of high mobility about two-thirds of the men concerned were single, a quarter or so were married but had left their wives in Albania, and the remainder had either married in Australia or brought their wives out from Albania to join them.

A much more complex example of movement during the early years of settlement is that of immigrants from Kastellorizo, the one town on the minute Dodecanese island of the same name. The first known Kastellorizan pioneer (Athanasios August) fled from his island home after attacking some hated Turkish officials, came to Australia as a seaman in the mid-eighties, worked for a while in several states, and returned to Kastellorizo about 1896. In 1898 he came back to Australia with a friend, this time to Perth, and soon afterwards the two pioneers began to encourage others to join them. By the outbreak of World War I there were close on a hundred Kastellorizan men in Perth itself, mainly engaged in general labour, fruit-shops and restaurants. From this central core some had moved off to other places in small groups of three or four, and occasionally a score or so. The principal settlements in Western Australia were at Northam, some fifty miles north-east of Perth; at Wagin, Collie, and Murray in the south and south-west; at Cue, Day-Dawn, and Kalgoorlie in the northern and eastern gold-fields; and at Balla Balla, Port Hedland, and Broome on the north-west coast; here immigrants busied themselves at general labouring, timber-cutting, mining, fishing, coastal sailing, and the catering trades. Other Kastellorizans had moved farther east to Port Pirie and Adelaide in South Australia, to Broken Hill and Sydney in New South Wales, while a few had settled in Brisbane and Melbourne; the main occupations here were general labouring, mining, unskilled labouring in fish and vegetable markets, and assisting in fruit-shops and restaurants.

Then, just before World War I, the Federal government introduced its new programme of development for the Northern Territory, notably the extension of railways south from Darwin and a contract with the British firm of Vesteys involving the construction of a large meat-processing factory and the enlargement of the Darwin wharves. One or two Kastellorizans apparently moved up from the relatively close ports of Balla Balla, Port Hedland and Broome and became involved in the early stages of this programme. When construction work got well under way in 1915-17 many other Kastellorizans from Perth, Port Pirie, and elsewhere came to join them. Furthermore, many islanders fleeing from the Turkish commercial restrictions and the bombardment of their homes (see p. 117) heard about developments in the Territory and came direct to join their friends in Darwin. By 1917 there were two hundred or so Kastellorizans in the Territory, most of them employed as labourers on the railways and as building labourers at the new meat-works and wharves; a few, however, were occupied in carpentering, wharf-labouring and catering.

By 1918-19 the volume of work in Darwin was decreasing rapidly and many islanders decided to move on. Nearly half went back down the west coast. Many of these stopped at Wyndham, where a new meat-works under construction offered the same kind of employment as at Darwin, but a few went on to join the little colonies of Kastellorizans at Port Hedland and Balla Balla. Others joined the small group of Kastellorizans who were establishing themselves as fishermen, market-gardeners, fruiterers and restaurant-keepers at Geraldton, a coastal town on the northern edge of Western Australia's agricultural belt. Yet others drifted right back to Perth to join their former comrades there and elsewhere in the south.

Of the Kastellorizans left in Darwin a few moved direct to Adelaide, Melbourne and Sydney. The majority, however, moved east from Darwin into northern Queensland in 1918-19. Here they split into three major groups—at Townsville, Ingham, and Innisfail—finding employment as bush-clearers, sugar-cane cutters, labourers in the sugar refineries and on the Queensland railways, carpenters and blacksmiths with various construction firms, or as cooks, restaurant-keepers, and fruiterers. Some of those migrants then decided that the actual farming of sugar, on the lines laid down by North Italians from the Monferrato, held the greatest chances of profit making; accordingly some pooled their savings to raise the deposit for a sugar farm, at this time somewhere about £300 for a £3,000 farm. A few others combined to buy dairy-farms serving the butter factory at Millaa Millaa, in the back country from Innisfail.

These northern Queensland Kastellorizans at first did so well that many others followed them a year or so later, in 1920-1, particularly from Perth and Sydney, and also from Broken Hill where the little colony of Kastellorizans practically disappeared. Even more came from Wyndham, where construction

N

work was now slackening, thus re-uniting men who had been comrades together in Darwin two years before. Others of the Wyndham group preferred to seek their fortunes with those Kastellorizans settled in Perth and Sydney. The relatively large secondary group settlement at Darwin, therefore, had dwindled to quite a small number by 1921 and the majority of its former members were following each other about the country to group settlements in northern Queensland, Sydney, and Perth.

From 1923 onwards some of the northern Queensland settlers came south, especially those who were engaged in seasonal cane-cutting and desired some city life in the off season. A number obtained jobs in the catering establishments of their fellow-islanders and abandoned their Queensland connections; a few, however, maintained the custom of going north for the cane-cutting season right up to the 1950s. Of those who did come south a few joined the Kastellorizan colony in Brisbane but the majority joined those settled in Sydney. Indeed, it is from 1923 onwards that the Sydney colony began to grow very rapidly and to attract large numbers of Kastellorizans direct from the Mediterranean.

Meanwhile those Kastellorizans who had stayed in Western Australia had also moved about considerably. The Geraldton group remained comparatively stable, but those in the mining towns and in the agricultural and timber districts of the south-west were very restless. By 1923 there was a small colony left in Boulder-Kalgoorlie but very few elsewhere in the gold-fields; likewise in the south-west most immigrants, after following each other from township to township, had either moved back to Perth or else had concentrated at Bunbury, the principal coastal town in the south-west. Some of the Bunbury settlers, indeed, had managed to attract a few friends from northern Queensland. The main occupations, both at Bunbury and Perth, were connected with the catering trades, but a few islanders were still engaged as general labourers, fishermen and the like.

By 1923, then, when the second stage of Kastellorizan settlement came to an end, the original group of settlers in Perth had grown, split, rejoined, and re-split into quite a number of secondary group settlements. Apart from the Perth colony, still the most important in the country, the largest settlement was in Sydney. There were, however, other important ones in northern Queensland, Brisbane, Melbourne, Adelaide, and Port Pirie, and a few smaller ones at places such as Boulder-Kalgoorlie,

Geraldton, and Bunbury. The Darwin colony too, still survived, but with greatly reduced numbers.[37]

At this time Kastellorizans still engaged in a number of different occupations—in farming, carpentering, fishing, and general labouring. There was, however, a clear tendency, especially in the capital cities, for later-comers to follow the example of those early settlers who had established themselves successfully in the catering trades.[38]

During these years of relatively high mobility the proportion of Kastellorizans who had wives with them was somewhat higher than usual in the early stages of chain settlement, because many women had left the island during the troubles with Turkey and come with their husbands to Egypt and then to Australia. Even so, the number of single men, together with those who had left their wives in Kastellorizo or Egypt, made up well over two-thirds of the total. Before 1914, when Turkish pressure was not quite so severe, men with wives in Australia were less than 10 per cent of the total.

This description of Kastellorizan settlement from 1898 to 1923 has brought us to the end of the second phase of chain settlement and to the beginning of the third. These dates are, of course, simply convenient marking stones; they do not necessarily represent the abrupt end of one migration process and the sudden beginning of another, though with some migration chains this did happen, especially when the outbreak of a war or the onset of a depression brought rapid changes. It is usually, however, quite impossible to draw hard and fast distinctions between the various stages: one tends to merge into the next so gradually that it is very difficult to give a precise date to the moment of transition. Furthermore, it is often possible to discern several intermediate steps between the principal stages. With this caveat it is now possible to pass on to the next and in some senses the most interesting phase of all since it covers the transformation of an unstable band of men into a fully-fledged and colourful ethnic community.

[37] Exact figures are impossible here. The naturalization records show about 120 Kastellorizan men in Perth in 1923 and 100 in Sydney. These figures must be multiplied at least by two to obtain a reasonable estimate of the total number of adult males.

[38] Information on the early years of Kastellorizan settlement comes from naturalization records, census tables, and from interviews with Kastellorizans in Sydney in March 1956, more particularly Dr K. K. Barris and Mr L. Leondis.

Stages in Chain Settlement—III

The most important and definitive feature of this third stage of chain settlement is that unattached men who had come to Australia during the first and second stages gradually gathered families around them: if married before arrival, by bringing out their families from Europe; if single on arrival, by marrying a British-Australian girl or a girl of their own ethnic stock and setting up home in Australia. Not that all these early settlers married. Quite a number became confirmed bachelors, wandering from place to place and occupation to occupation until the end of their days.[39] Nevertheless, though the position varied considerably from group to group, there was a distinct tendency for early arrivals to set up homes and achieve a normal family life.[40]

A second feature of this stage of settlement was a change in the occupations followed by most early arrivals. The movement of Macedonians, Albanians, and Italians from timber and bush clearing in the back country of New South Wales and Western Australia to small-scale farms nearer the centres of settlement; the movement of Molfettese Italians and Evvoian and Dodecanese Greeks away from unskilled labour in Port Pirie to deep-sea fishing in the Southern Ocean; the gradual settling of Kastellorizan Greeks into farms and catering establishments in northern Queensland, Sydney, and Perth: these are all illustrations of a settling-down process that usually took place towards the end of the second phase of settlement or at the beginning of the third. During the third phase proper these early settlers used their small-scale farms or catering establishments as the foundations on which they strove to build independent and prosperous careers.

---

[39] The naturalization records show that, of persons who had come out as unmarried adult settlers and had been in Australia over twenty years when naturalized, some 38% of the Kytherans and 39% of the Ithacans remained unmarried. Some of these had been in the country well over thirty years, had wandered from place to place, but apparently never had the desire or opportunity to settle down to married life.

[40] Exact figures are difficult to obtain but the naturalization records suggest that, in the first ten years of the third stage, the proportion of unattached men amongst those who had migrated during the second stage fell quite noticeably for most groups. The following are examples: Vis isle, 90%-36%; Račišće village (Korčula isle), 90%-60%; Korčula isle, 94%-72%; Kythera isle, 90%-70%; Ithaca isle, 89%-63%; Kastellorizo isle, 69%-40%; Brescia province, 88%-62%; North Catania, 72%-39%; Lipari archipelago, 81%-36%; Macedonia, 92%-57%. Interview material and census records tell the same story.

This settling into permanent occupations is obviously very closely connected with the increase in the number of women and children. Normally an immigrant postponed bringing his family to Australia, or postponed marriage, until he had settled into some permanent job and could offer his family security and independence, although sometimes an immigrant brought his wife and family to Australia while he was still an unskilled labourer with indefinite future prospects; the arrival of his family then spurred him on to finding a job with better possibilities. Whichever way round it happened, the effect was the same—the settling of southern Europeans into their permanent occupations usually went hand in hand with the development of family life.[41]

This change in the way of life of early settlers noticeably affected the activities of many new arrivals. During the early phases of chain settlement new arrivals joining compatriots abroad tended to adopt the same habits of moving from place to place and job to job: during the third phase, when joining friends and relatives well established in Australia, new arrivals tended to stay in the place where their fellows had established themselves. (This was so even though later immigrants continued to arrive predominantly as unattached men and could have moved about Australia as easily as their predecessors.) As a result the pattern of settlement—both of earlier settlers and later arrivals—became much more fixed and rigid. This emerges very clearly from statistics of mobility, which show that most groups moved about Australia very much less during the third stage than the second.[42]

It is important to notice here that what movement did occur during this third phase of settlement was often of a different kind from the earlier. Instead of being the peregrinations of a highly mobile body of men trying job after job in place after place, it quite frequently indicated the decision of well-

41 Where these two developments do not coincide—when, for example, families increased substantially but the occupational pattern remained very much as in earlier years—then the increase of families is taken to be the more important factor in determining the advent of the second stage of settlement; as with the Dalmatian groups of W.A. described below (p. 184).

42 About 6·3% of the Ithacan immigrants moved to another place in Australia each year during the second stage but only 3·2% each year during the third. For other groups the percentages are: Kastellorizo, 11·5-4·7; Akrata, 18·3-13·5; Macedonia, 10·7-7·5; Korçë (Albania), 20·6-10·8; Monferrato, 14·7-4·8; Brescia, 6·3-5·0; Treviso, 6·2-1·9; Vicenza, 6·0-4·0; Reggio Calabria, 6·0-1·9; Catania, 8·3-6·3 (from naturalization records; see Appendix 3:13).

established settlers to abandon their particular farm or business and move to establishments in more congenial surroundings, in more profitable areas, or nearer friends and compatriots. Thus during the thirties and forties a dozen or so Italians from the Veneto, who had settled as sugar-cane farmers in northern Queensland, sold out their properties in Queensland and bought horticultural farms in the Murrumbidgee Irrigation Area of New South Wales, partly because they wished to join the large number of friends and relatives settled there and partly because they were finding the heat and humidity of the sugar areas increasingly unpleasant.[43] Another example is the movement of those Bulgarians, Dalmatians, and Albanians, who had become well established as miners at Broken Hill, but left there in the late twenties and early thirties for the market-gardening and poultry-farming areas of outer Sydney. Here again the reasons were mixed: difficulties arising from the depression, fear of contracting lung diseases in the mines, anxiety to obtain something that offered greater security in their old age than did mining, and a desire to join their one or two compatriots who had opened up successful farms between 1928 and 1931 in the outer Sydney area.[44]

Secondary chain movements, such as these, and the secondary group settlements so formed are an important element in this stage of chain settlement. They may be found all over the world, one example being those market-gardening settlements in New Jersey, U.S.A., that came into being in the 1930s when several members of Ukrainian groups in nearby towns decided to abandon their well-established jobs in factories and invest their savings in farming.[45] Other examples come from the old Norwegian settlements of Illinois, Wisconsin, and Iowa.[46]

A similar kind of movement during this phase of settlement arose when persons owning a successful catering business sold out and bought a similar business elsewhere. Many Ithacan restaurant and hotel proprietors, for instance, left Boulder-Kalgoorlie in Western Australia between 1916 and 1919 and moved to Melbourne where they had numerous friends and relatives, their main reasons being the strong anti-Greek feeling in Boulder-Kalgoorlie at the pro-German policy of King Con-

[43] C. A. Price, Italian Population of Griffith, Table I.
[44] From naturalization records and interviews with Albanian and Dalmatian farmers in N.S.W. in 1956.
[45] W. Halich, Ukrainians in the United States, p. 49.
[46] T. C. Blegen, Norwegian Migration to America, vol. II, pp. 36, 489.

stantine and the riots that broke out in 1919 against all southern Europeans in the area; on this occasion much Italian, Greek, and Dalmatian property was destroyed and many were either driven from town or decided to remove themselves.[47]

Other caterers moved during the third stage of settlement, not to avoid trouble but because better opportunities beckoned elsewhere. Kytheran Greeks, indeed, became abnormally prone to do this. As they spread over rural New South Wales and southern Queensland opening restaurants, fruit-shops and small mixed businesses, they developed what might almost be called a 'system of business promotion', a procedure whereby many newcomers started as assistant cooks, waiters and counter-boys in an established restaurant or shop, then moved on after a few years to their own little business in some other town, then gradually passed on from town to town, each time obtaining a larger and more prosperous business; finally many of them moved back to Sydney as men of means and substance. One Kytheran, from the little village of Milopotamos, came to New South Wales early in the century to join his three cousins in Sydney. After a while there he took over a small restaurant in Tamworth and there stayed for nearly two years. He then moved to a larger restaurant in Maitland for eighteen months, on to Narrabri for three years, and thence to Wauchope for five years. He then moved back to Sydney and invested his savings in various city hotels. During the depression his Sydney investments deteriorated badly so he moved out to the country again, to a small town near Kempsey, and did not return to Sydney until he had again achieved some measure of prosperity. Throughout this ascent from larger establishment to larger establishment he usually sold out to a Kytheran slightly behind him on the ladder of progress and bought from a compatriot somewhat further advanced.[48] So many of them became involved in this kind of activity that the rate of Kytheran movement about Australia became considerably higher during the third stage of settlement than the first.[49] Even so, this high rate of mobility, this advance—often with family and children—from one secure foothold to another, was very different from the

[47] Naturalization records and interviews with Ithacans in Melbourne in Sept. 1957; see also pp. 208-9 below.

[48] From interviews with the settler concerned in Sydney in 1956.

[49] Naturalization records suggest that Kytheran movement in the second stage (1880-1914 approximately) was $8 \cdot 1\%$ per annum and in the third stage (1920-28), $12 \cdot 3\%$.

earlier movement of unattached propertyless men from cleaning fish in the fish-market, to washing dishes in a restaurant, to becoming an assistant cook in a hotel, and so forth.

One or two groups maintained through much of the third stage of settlement the same kind of movement about Australia as in earlier years, sometimes actually increasing their rate of mobility. Some Dalmatian groups, who had started coming to the Western Australian mining areas in the 1890s, maintained their practice of moving about from mine to mine even after they brought some of their womenfolk to join them. Furthermore, though a number of them had taken up small-scale farming as early as 1910, many did not leave the mines for agriculture until the late twenties and early thirties, that is, until well into the third stage of settlement; and even then, especially during the depression years, some of these moved several times about the timber and farming districts before finally finding some permanent vineyard, farm, or market-garden. The many later immigrants, most of whom came to join their compatriots during the early 1920s, adopted the same way of life and it was not until the mid-thirties that these Dalmatian groups became relatively fixed and stationary.[50] When these chains are considered in conjunction with those Dalmatian chains that did not start until after World War I, and were consequently still in the first stage of high mobility during the twenties, the great restlessness of the Dalmatian population is evident during these years, especially in Western Australia.[51] In short, during the 1920s, a great many Dalmatian chains, old and new, were still fulfilling the southern European role of providing Australia with a small but relatively mobile labour-force willing to move wherever economic circumstances dictated.

These Dalmatians, however, and one or two other immigrant groups, were somewhat exceptional. The general trend during the third phase of settlement was for immigrant groups to become firmly established and settled—to abandon their first role of a mobile labour-force and to take up their next, that of providing Australia with small-scale farms and catering estab-

[50] Annual movement about Western Australia for islanders from Korčula was, according to the naturalization records: 1901-19, 3·6%; 1920-8, 10·4%; 1929-34, 19·5%; 1935-9, 4·1%. For Vis islanders the figures were 4·7%, 5·3%, 3·2%, 2·9%.

[51] For Australia as a whole the mobility statistics for immigrant groups of central Dalmatian origin were, according to the naturalization records: 1896-1919, 11·2% per annum; 1920-8, 15·0%; 1929-33, 5·9%; 1934-9, 6·3%.

lishments, with deep-sea fishing fleets, and with skilled crafts such as terrazzo-paving.

This change of role during the third phase of chain settlement, this settling down into conditions of stability, is interestingly manifested in the occupational structure of immigrant groups. For earlier arrivals it usually meant a concentration in the principal occupations of their choice and a marked increase in the proportion of persons controlling their own businesses. Less than one-tenth of the Venetian farming groups at Griffith, N.S.W., for example, controlled the farms on which they worked during the second stage of settlement in the 1920s. Of the same generation of immigrants, over two-thirds controlled their own farms during the third stage in the thirties and early forties (see Appendix 7:6).

This settling down process, moreover, frequently led a number of early arrivals to enter the skilled trades, partly because the coming of women and children both enlarged and consolidated various group settlements and thereby increased the demand for ethnic group craftsmen: shoemakers, tailors, hairdressers, watch-repairers, blacksmiths, mechanics, and the like. These did not become a very large element in most group settlements but they were usually noticeable and important (see Appendix 7:6).

All these activities of the early immigrants greatly affected those arriving during the third phase of settlement. In the first place, new arrivals tended to enter the same occupations, very often as unskilled assistants in the restaurants, workshops and farms controlled by their predecessors. Second, those already established could give their greener friends so much valuable advice and guidance, and often lend them so much capital, that later arrivals were able to achieve independence relatively quickly (see Appendix 7:6).

Assistance by earlier arrivals, though very useful in the long run, undoubtedly had its price, and most newcomers found themselves working very long hours and in very hard conditions. One young Ithacan arriving in Melbourne in 1909, for example, entered his cousin's restaurant and found himself waiting, cleaning, and washing for 2s. 6d. a week plus keep. Another young Greek from Sparta, who landed in Sydney about 1912, was put to work cleaning fish in the fish-market from 6 a.m. to 11 p.m. for 7s. 6d. a week; his accommodation consisted of a mattress on the floor of an upstairs room in a Kytheran-owned fish-shop—a privilege he shared with nine others.[52] Agricultural and unskilled labourers working on farms owned by their compatriots experienced similar conditions, except that in outback areas they frequently lived crammed up in tents and sheds.[53]

These working conditions at times resembled those prevalent during the great influx of European immigrants to North America at the turn of the century; conditions which produced such an outcry that eventually measures were taken to control them.[54] But they did not always indicate deliberate exploitation by avaricious settlers seeking cheap labour. Low pay and long hours frequently represented an agreement whereby an established settler regained the money he had advanced towards his friend's fare to Australia. Nor did such conditions prevent newcomers from achieving independence relatively quickly, in their turn to act in precisely the same way towards friends and compatriots fresh from Europe. Furthermore, these wages, hours, and living quarters were no worse than those to which both employer and employee had been reared from infancy in Europe; indeed, many immigrants often preferred to retain their style of living—at any rate the crowded quarters—and there are several cases on record where a number of new arrivals were offered quite roomy accommodation but eventually crowded together in a small wooden shack on the grounds that it was more companionable and more like home.[55]

There is one more important consideration here: the fact that the established settlers, who had themselves experienced similar conditions during first phase of settlement, often continued to live in much the same circumstances as their employees. With the advent of wives and children primitive tents and sheds gave way to houses and rooms but the settler, forcing himself and his family to work for very long hours and spend very little on anything except necessities, frequently confined his family to the use of one or two rooms and let the

---

[52] From interviews with the two settlers in question in Sydney, April 1956; see also 'Ferry Report', p. 38 (A28, p. 12).

[53] Interviews and 'Ferry Report', p. 39 (A28, p. 13).

[54] See, e.g., Peter Roberts, *The New Immigration*; M. R. Davie, *World Immigration; Reports of the Immigration Commission* 1907-10.

[55] There was one case in Canberra as recently as 1954. Maltese have chosen similarly elsewhere in the world, judging by their activities in British Guiana in the 1830s (C. A. Price, *Malta and the Maltese*, p. 78). For conditions in Europe see p. 46 above.

remainder to unattached young men in need of accommodation. Family-home-cum-boarding-houses such as these existed in many parts of the capital cities and country towns.[56] One old settler, looking back on this period of his life, remarked, 'Now I am a gentleman but once I was a slave.'[57]

Relatively hard working and living conditions continued for some time, then, both for earlier arrivals and more recent immigrants. These, together with other aspects of the third stage of chain settlement—the coming of families and the settling into permanent occupations and homes—are well illustrated by a group of central Dalmatians now established as market-gardeners and poultry-farmers between Fairfield and Leppington in the outer western districts of Sydney. Settlement here began about 1930 with the appearance of two young migrants from Brijesta village on Pelješac peninsula.[58] They had arrived in Australia during the 1920s, that is, during the second stage of migration from that village to Australia. During this early period one of them, Tony Perish, moved about the back country of New South Wales as a timber-cutter, then joined some friends gum-digging in New Zealand, returned to Sydney as a building labourer about 1928, and then went bush-clearing with other Dalmatians in the Barradine district. In 1930 he moved to Leppington and bought a poultry run, at that time no more than some land, a few fowls, and a hut. He slowly enlarged his run and his hut until he felt able to bring out his wife in 1931, his sisters in 1934, and eventually his brother-in-law and cousin in 1938.

Meantime George Sartara, who had joined Tony Perish and the rest bush-clearing at Barradine and had then moved on to Dubbo, Young, and other country towns of New South Wales, came to Sydney for a visit in 1930. There he found a family boarding-house run by a Dalmatian from Brač island who provided—according to the numbers of persons requiring it—

---

56 Some of these—for example those in George Street, Sydney, and Lygon Street, Carlton, Melbourne—emerge from naturalization records, especially when a dozen or so men all give the same address in the same few months. Information of others comes from interviews and from documents such as the 'Ferry Report'. Sometimes the family provided meals; sometimes they charged upwards of 1s. a day for a bunk or mattress and expected lodgers to go out for meals.

57 Interview with Philip Varvaregos in Melbourne, Sept. 1957.

58 There are records of a few South Dalmatian farmers (from Kotor) in the Canley Vale area as early as 1906 but they seem to have had little connexion with the central Dalmatian group under discussion.

more or less crowded accommodation for Bulgarians, Serbs, Croats, Slovenes, and occasional other immigrants. Living in this house was an older migrant from Zaostrog, a mainland town some twenty-five miles north of Brijesta. He had made several trips to Canada and the United States but had finally settled as a labourer in Sydney and had brought his daughter out to join him in 1929. At this time she was working as a cook and cleaner in a Czech restaurant for twenty-seven shillings a week, from which she had to support her father when he was out of work.

In 1931 she and George Sartara married and decided to invest their savings in a small farm, preferably somewhere near the district where Tony Perish was building up his poultry run. At first they tried a small market-gardening farm near Rooty Hill, some fifteen miles north of Leppington, but after struggling hard with bad drainage and salting up of the soil, and wearying of eking out an existence by picking mushrooms and peddling them from house to house, they sold out in 1933 and moved south to a farm on much better soil at Cabramatta. When things improved he brought out his two brothers-in-law and then four other families, either friends or relatives. These all worked and lived on his farm for twelve months or so after arriving, and then received his help in obtaining their own little farms in the same area.

The success of Perish and Sartara quickly attracted other Dalmatians, not only bush-clearers and timber-workers from the outback but miners from Broken Hill who were threatened with lung trouble or looking about for some security. By the mid-thirties quite a large secondary group settlement had grown up in this outer western district, many of whom had families with them and were sponsoring friends and relatives direct from Europe.[59]

This description of the third stage of Dalmatian group settlement reminds us of the impossibility of fixing any precise length of time for the second and third stages and for the period of transition from the one to the other. At Griffith, in the Murrumbidgee Irrigation Area, those northern Italians who came from southern Belluno in the Veneto between 1920 and 1925 were well into the third stage by 1927; here the second phase lasted only five years or so. With southern Italians from

[59] Personal details from interviews, *Napredak*, street directories, etc.; statistical details from naturalization records.

Molfetta at Port Pirie about ten years elapsed between the arrival of the first main body of settlers at the turn of the century and the establishment of the relatively stable fishing community there about 1910-11. With other groups—Kastellorizan Greeks or Dalmatians from Vis island, for example—twenty years or more elapsed between the arrival of the first main group and the establishment of settled community life.

Variation in the number of years taken by different migrant groups to pass from one stage to the next, plus the fact that some migration chains started much earlier than others, means that at any given moment Australia contained migration chains in every stage of development. As a result, relating the development of chain settlement as a whole to the general conditions prevailing in Australia, or elsewhere, in any particular year is a complicated matter. The depression of the 1930s, and the economic revival following it, for example, affected the various sou'thern European chains in many different ways. Some of those chains that had entered their third stage well before World War I simply ceased all activity during the depression and for all practical purposes failed to revive thereafter; less than 5 per cent of settlers from Vis isle, Dalmatia, for example, came to Australia in the late 1930s, and these few arrived eight years after the last previous recorded immigrants from Vis landed in 1928 (see Appendix 18). Other chain movements, which had begun at the same time as that from Vis but whose third stage continued vigorously until the late 1920s, declined somewhat less during the depression and returned to life more strongly after it, primarily because they bore more immigrants to Australia during the late twenties and these were ready to sponsor wives and fiancées during the depression and friends and relatives after it. The island of Kythera and the Tirnova district of Bulgaria are examples (see Appendixes 19, 16).

Sponsoring of womenfolk during the depression and of friends after it was still stronger amongst those chains (among which Reggio Calabria was conspicuous—see Appendix 13) that had not started active life until the early 1920s but had developed very quickly by 1928. The most interesting effects of the depression, however, manifested themselves amongst those chains, from the Korçë districts of Albania, for example, that did not start active life until 1927-8 and were thus just beginning their first stage in 1929. The story here is complex. First, the economic upheaval did not have the same depressing effects on the immigration of new settlers as on other chains—the records suggest that only two depression years failed to produce any new settlers from Korçë. Second, the sponsorship of male compatriots during the later thirties was very much stronger here than with most other groups, showing that the first generation of immigrants were still in the stage of wanting their male friends and relatives. Third, many Korçë settlers had not reached the point of bringing out their womenfolk when World War II suddenly arrived and prevented them doing so. Consequently the third stage of settlement was forcibly postponed for several years, numerous Korçë settlers impatiently seeing the war through in Australia while their families and fiancées remained in the turmoil of Balkan warfare; furthermore, many of them had to continue waiting impatiently during the post-war period because the communist government of Albania imposed so many restrictions on emigration. Since migration from Korçë has made up the great bulk of immigration from Albania, it is not surprising that the number of Albanian women has been relatively lower than that of any other southern European people in Australia.[60]

Stages in Chain Settlement—IV

The definitive feature of the fourth stage of settlement is the growing to maturity of the second generation, both those who migrated as infants with their mothers and their younger brothers, sisters and cousins born in the new land (see Appendix 4:3). Their entry to the ranks of the adult community, their acceptance of the responsibility for ordering their own lives, their capacity to marry and set up their own homes, all brought about profound changes in the pattern of many southern European settlements abroad.

Unfortunately, on this particular subject Australian material is very defective. The United States has included in its censuses ever since 1870 a question concerning parents' place of birth as well as a question concerning the person's own place of birth; consequently her scholars have been able to assess the numbers, occupations, and geographical location of both the first and second generation of immigrant peoples. Canada, since 1871, has obtained much the same kind of information from its census

---

[60] The sex ratio for Albanians in 1947 was 9·8 females for every 100 males and 16·0 in 1954. In 1947 Malta was next lowest with 31·0. During the late twenties and thirties about one-third of Albanians arrived married and of these two-thirds still had their wives in Albania when naturalized, on average ten years later. Of those arriving single less than one-tenth had married when naturalized, on average ten years later.

questions concerning ethnic origin. When such material is allied
to information about 'mother tongue', the language commonly
used in the home, it is clear that both Canada and the United
States have for many years been in a very strong position to assess
the contribution of both immigrants and their children to the
life and growth of the country in general, and of various districts and occupations in particular.[61]

Australia has no comparable information. Some idea of the
numbers of Australian-born children is possible from the statistics of infants born each year in Australia to foreign-born parents; but this enables a rough estimate only,[62] and in any case
gives information for broad national groupings in the country
as a whole, not for any particular place of settlement or particular area of origin. Indeed, this work has had to rely on special
surveys for its assessment of the numbers of Australian-born
persons of the second generation: the estimate used earlier in
connexion with persons of southern European origin in various
areas of Western Australia—that the Australian-born made up
between one-third and one-half the total—was based on the fact
that this was the proportion revealed by a special survey of the
southern European population at Griffith, a settlement of much
the same age and character as those in Western Australia.[63]

Quite apart from mere numbers there is the problem of what
second-generation persons do when reaching maturity, where
they live, and what occupations they follow. Here the published
statistics of births to foreign-born parents are quite useless and
again special surveys are necessary. Consequently this section
on the fourth stage of settlement has less general statistical back-
ing than the earlier sections and leans more heavily on special
inquiries. This qualification applies, of course, only to the activities of the second generation; the history of first-generation
settlers during this period has the same documentary support
as had the earlier periods.

During the fourth stage of settlement, movement about Australia by those who had arrived some time earlier continued to

61 See, e.g., N. Carpenter, *Immigrants and their Children*; Hutchinson,
Immigrants and their Children 1850-1950; W. B. Hurd, *Racial Origins and
Nativity of the Canadian People*, and authorities there cited.

62 'Rough', since there are no comparable statistics for emigrants and
deaths and thus there is no way of telling how many Australian-born
children of foreign parentage have died or left the country—see Appendix
4:8.

63 See p. 149n., above; C. A. Price, *Italian Population of Griffith*.

decline. Partly they were getting older and less inclined to move; partly they had so improved their farms and businesses that many became decreasingly ready to sell out and move elsewhere; partly their children, now reaching adulthood, were forming strong friendships and interests in one locality and did not relish the thought of being whisked away elsewhere at the whim of their parents. Some families did move: a few more moved from sugar farms in northern Queensland to less humid regions farther south; others, whose children were entering the professions elsewhere, retired to a home nearer their children. But the general trend was for somewhat increased stability.

As in the third stage, this further quiescence on the part of older settlers affected new arrivals, and the total mobility rate for many groups declined still further. Even the restless Kytheran café-keepers seemed to have slowed down the speed at which they moved from place to place, while those Dalmatian groups that had maintained their early rate of mobility during the third stage sank into conditions of comparative stability.[64]

There were, however, some groups that did not follow this pattern. Some chains, during the fourth stage of settlement, were affected by a great upsurge of migration from Europe, at times so great that the traditional places of settlement became saturated and many newcomers found themselves seeking jobs elsewhere. This seems to have happened to a number of the older Monferrato chains that had borne agricultural labourers to northern Queensland as early as the 1890s and were entering their fourth stage of settlement in the 1920s. There are signs that it may also be happening in the post-war period in districts such as the Murrumbidgee Irrigation Area, as well as to groups that were not well represented before World War II but have experienced heavy immigration since 1949—chains from Lesbos, Cyprus, and parts of Calabria, for instance.[65]

Other Italian chains, which had reached their fourth stage just before the outbreak of war in 1939, were affected by the internment policy of the Australian government; many immigrants, especially in Queensland, were sent to various camps

[64] About 12·3% of the immigrant Kytheran population moved to another place in Australia each year during the third stage and 10·5% during the fourth; for Korčula the figures were 8·5%-3·8%; for Vis, 5·0%-2·8%.

[65] No evidence exists for the M.I.A. and these chain groups apart from interviews and personal observation. The naturalization records give some evidence for the Monferrato chains of northern Queensland: annual mobility in the early period 14·7%; third period (1902-14) 4·8%; fourth period (1920s) 7·9%.

elsewhere in Australia, thereby artificially raising their rate of mobility.

The general problem of mobility in the fourth stage of settle-ment is rendered still more complicated by the activities of the second generation. In migration history these have sometimes become most important, as in the western movement of the American frontier. The Australian evidence is too slight to per-mit any general statement but it is plain that in a number of groups the second generation has moved away from traditional rural areas of settlement—as, for example, those Italians who have moved from the sugar areas to the larger coastal cities of Queensland. In other cases—for instance a number of Greek farmers—the second generation has moved away from the inner cities to the outer suburbs.

This movement by persons of the second generation to some extent reflects the fact that they did not always enter the same occupation as their parents. There have been periods in the history of settlement where children have followed the occupa-tions of their parents generation after generation, as in a num-ber of the old German settlements of Pennsylvania and South Australia. Here the traditional peasant ideal of sons following the father in maintaining, improving, and extending the family heritage has been clearly visible. These, however, were relatively old rural communities established before the advent of modern transport, communication, and all the other apparatus of twen-tieth-century mechanization made farming people so much more aware of other kinds of life. Modern conditions have now affected many of these older rural communities and, *a fortiori*, the southern European rural settlements of Australia, all but a few of which were founded relatively recently and have seen the growing to maturity of the second generation only in the last twenty-five years or so.[66] The Venetian settlements at Griffith show this very clearly: whereas less than one-tenth of the first generation were engaged in occupations other than farming, about one-quarter of the second generation were engaged in non-farming activities such as mechanical and electrical engin-eering, carpentering, catering, clerical work, and the professions;

[66] A notable exception is the Old Order Amish, an extreme wing of the German-Swiss Mennonite church in America. They have maintained a closely-knit rural community that discourages intermixture with outsiders and refuses to have dealings with such devil-inspired contraptions as domes-tic electricity, telephones, or motor cars. There is a considerable literature on this sect.

O

and this excluded those second-generation persons who had moved away from Griffith to enter industry, commerce, and the professions.[67]

A somewhat different example is that provided by second-generation Greeks in New South Wales. Whereas 10 per cent or less of first-generation settlers entered the skilled trades, the higher branches of business, and the professions, very nearly half the second generation have done so.[68] It is interesting to note that the various Greek groups centred on Toronto in Canada have acted in much the same way as those centred on Sydney in New South Wales; here well under one-quarter of the first generation entered the skilled trades, professions, and higher branches of commerce, whereas three-quarters of the second generation have done so.[69]

At times this shift in the occupational pattern represents a sharp rift between the two generations. Some older immigrants, who had toiled away for the better part of their lives to found a farm or business that could be handed down to sons and grandsons, occasionally became bitterly disappointed when their sons decided to abandon farming or business and become wage-earners, albeit skilled ones, in some factory or shop. This disappointment was all the more bitter if the second generation established independent homes in remote suburbs or towns when the parents had expected them to follow the traditional custom of bringing wives to live in the family home, of maintaining close family relationships, and of looking after their parents in their old age. One dismayed Greek restaurant-keeper when speaking of his sons, all of whom had been in the family business but had left home to take wage-earning jobs and create their own homes in the distant suburbs, asserted that the effort had not been worth it and that he and his wife would never have slaved the way they did if they had realized there would be no one to

[67] See Appendix 7:6, last column. Though no precise figures are available, the general evidence suggests that much the same thing happened with the Italian communities in northern Queensland—see Borrie, *Italians and Germans in Australia*, pp. 101, 107-8.

[68] See Appendix 7:10, columns A and 2nd generation. We are not here comparing the second generation with first-generation arrivals of the fourth stage (column B) but with first-generation arrivals of stages two and three (i.e. their parents).

[69] From occupational information on the marriage records of the Greek community of Toronto, analysed by the author in Toronto in the summer of 1958.

carry on the business and look after them in their old age.[70]

At other times, however, the occupational pattern of the second generation represents either an agreement or a deliberate policy on the part of the first generation that some of their children should enter occupations that complement and reinforce their own. Amongst Venetian horticultural farmers at Griffith it has sometimes happened that one son has stayed on the family farm while another has become a mechanical or electrical engineer and opened a garage or workshop 'that could service modern farm machinery and equipment. On other occasions an immigrant family has encouraged one or more of its sons to launch himself on a career carrying relatively high social status. One Calabrian farming family, for instance, having enlarged its original holding to establish four sons as farmers, has been making efforts to set up the fifth son as a lawyer. Moreover, a number of caterers, who looked on their restaurants as a way of achieving rapid independence and wealth rather than as the beginning of a family inheritance, have been content to assist their sons into commerce or the professions and then sell up their restaurants and retire to live with one of the children. The number of Ithacan restaurants on lower Swanston Street, Melbourne, for instance, has decreased very rapidly in recent years, largely for this reason.

This entry of some second-generation persons into higher occupations, and the retirement of the older folk, is all part of a general easing of life on the part of the older established families, parents as well as children. Not that they abandoned work altogether and simply rested on their laurels. Far from it. But in many ways life became much more comfortable and much less a concentration on naught but building up a business and making money. Long working hours for the whole family, skimping and saving on all but sheer necessities, crowded living quarters: these could not be maintained by second-generation persons in the professions or other occupations requiring a certain elegance of living and a certain amount of contact with society as a whole; or, indeed, by any second-generation family, including those engaged in farming or catering, who wished to take part in general social activities and public life. In any case, with the successful establishment of their children, whether in

[70] A very good general description of this situation is in Asen Balikci's Remarques sur la Structure du Groupe Ethnique Bulgare et Macedonien de Toronto, pp. 87-8 and p. 24, n. 19. I also came across a few cases amongst Peloponnesian and Athenian Greeks when working in Toronto in 1958.

the family business or farm or in some other occupation, many
first-generation settlers felt the time had come to relax their
efforts, to reap the reward for their years of concentrated toil,
to live 'like gentlemen rather than like slaves', and to demonstrate to the Australians around them that southern Europeans
did not always have to 'live on the smell of an oily rag' but
were as capable as anyone else of living in conditions of solid
decency.

The fourth stage of settlement, then, saw the more successful
business families moving into good city or suburban homes and
the more successful farming families transforming their little
wooden or iron farmhouses into much larger and more comfortable residences of brick, stone, or fibro—homes containing
modern plumbing, showers, refrigeration, furniture, radiograms,
TV sets, and even an occasional pianoforte and bookcase. One
has only to visit Kytheran, Kastellorizan, Ithacan, or other
homes in Sydney, Melbourne, and Canberra; or Dalmatian,
Bulgarian, and Albanian homes in the market-gardening and
horticultural areas of Osborne Park, Fulham, Cabramatta, and
Leppington; or Croatian, Calabrian and Venetian farmhouses
in the horticultural districts of Berri, Mildura, and Griffith, to
see that many southern European settlers of the first generation
have thus transformed their earlier conditions of life and are
now living in circumstances equal or superior to some of their
British-Australian neighbours.[71]

Easier living conditions for older settlers and their families,
and the entry of some second-generation persons into higher
status occupations, had one curious but important result. New
arrivals during the second and third stages of settlement usually
found their predecessors pursuing much the same occupations,
and living in much the same conditions of hardship, as they
themselves were expected and ready to adopt; the expectation
on the part of older settlers that newcomers should 'rough it'
as they themselves had done, and were still doing, therefore
aroused little hostility (see pp. 185-6 above). (Occasionally some
very early pioneer had built up a flourishing business and comfortable home by the second stage; but newcomers realized he

---

[71] In a survey covering 30 Italian and 30 British-Australian randomly
selected farmhouses at Griffith in 1954, 26 Italian and 22 British-Australian
homes rated 'good' or 'fair' and 4 Italian and 8 British-Australian homes rated
'poor' or 'bad' (C. A. Price, Italian Population of Griffith, p. 33). This difference is not statistically significant in showing that Italian houses were
better than British-Australian but it is significant in showing that they were
no worse.

was somewhat exceptional and tended to revere him for his help
and for his example of what they themselves might one day be—
as the central Dalmatians of New South Wales between 1900
and 1930 tended to revere the Cunich family, the 'cherry kings'
at Orange and Young, N.S.W.) During the fourth stage, however, new arrivals found a great many of their forerunners, together with their children, living in conditions of relative prosperity; yet they, as newcomers, were still expected by older
families to rough it as folk had in earlier years. An older settler
who brought his nephews to Australia during this period not
unnaturally might feel that they should work for as relatively
low a wage and long a day as he had done; they too would
eventually repay their passage money, pile up their own savings,
establish their own business, and earn a less austere existence;
the fact that he had one son helping him run the farm or business from his own comfortable home, and another son happily
established as a physician or solicitor or land-agent, had nothing
to do with the matter. On their side the nephews saw only that
their uncle was expecting them to work long hours labouring
on his farm, or washing dishes in his café kitchen, for a wage
less than they could earn elsewhere, while their cousins were
living in far more comfortable circumstances than they themselves were experiencing.

This kind of situation, not unnaturally, sometimes generated
much friction between early arrivals and newcomers—hostility
that became all the more bitter if conditions of life had eased in
the country of origin in the interval between the migration of
the uncle and nephews. The old man thought his nephews had
come with ideas far above themselves and were soft, lazy, and
ungrateful; the nephews thought their uncle a hard and grasping old exploiter who was quite behind the times in his failure
to see that radios, films, and motor-cars were all part of a young
man's rights and privileges.

This general situation has been very noticeable in Australia
since World War II, primarily because so many southern European chains were still in the third stage during the 1930s and
were only just getting into the fourth stage when they found
themselves confronted by the possibilities of large-scale immigration in the post-war years (see pp. 136-7 above). It crops up time
and time again in the interviews,[72] and its prevalence can be

[72] Bromley and McDonald (op. cit.) have also accumulated evidence of
this. Balikci (op. cit.) has set forth some interesting cases of tension amongst
the Macedonians of Toronto.

assessed by comparing the occupational pattern of newcomers during the fourth stage with that of older settlers and their second-generation children. At Griffith, for instance, nearly 90 per cent of those who had arrived during the post-war years of the fourth stage were working during their first few years as agricultural labourers, general labourers and catering assistants (mainly as agricultural labourers on the farms of older settlers) —a marked contrast with the low proportion of agricultural labourers amongst older settlers and their children (see Appendix 7:6, Pt B). A very similar situation existed in the Macedonian-Greek community in Toronto, where over half those arriving during the post-war years of the fourth stage started as dish-washers, cooks, and waiters, mainly in the restaurants of older compatriots.[73]

One can, of course, easily exaggerate the friction involved and assume that no group has been able to solve the problem without strain. One can also assume that the problem is a lasting one whereas it frequently solves itself in a few years; especially when new arrivals learn English and do not feel so dependent on their older-established friends and relatives, and when, after a period as labourers and assistants, these young newcomers obtain enough capital from their relatives to set up on their own. This apparently happened quite quickly with fourth-stage arrivals from Kythera and Akrata between 1948 and 1955; these were relatively few compared with the powerful Kytheran and Akratan communities already established in New South Wales and after a comparatively short time many of them received help from their wealthy compatriots and started business on their own (see Appendix 7:10).

The situation was more difficult when the number of fourth-stage arrivals became very large in relation to the number of those already established, as with islanders from Symi and Lesbos. Here older settlers had not the resources to help the majority of newcomers towards anything but the cheaper unskilled jobs; which partly explains why the proportion of catering assistants and labourers amongst fourth-stage arrivals from Symi and Lesbos was relatively high, even after several years' residence in Australia. This, however, cannot be the whole explanation, since a relatively high proportion of fourth-stage arrivals from Kastellorizo were still catering assistants after several years in Australia; yet the number of fourth-stage arrivals

[73] From occupational information on the marriage records of the Greek Orthodox community of Toronto.

was small compared with the number of Kastellorizans already established in New South Wales (see Appendix 7:10).

At this point it becomes plain that relationships between earlier and later settlers cannot be explained simply in terms of numbers, occupations, and period of arrival. All sorts of other factors enter, some of which have been mentioned already: social status, changing social conditions in the country of origin between arrival of earlier and later settlers, family relationships, and so on. Likewise the discussion on differences between first and second generations touched on matters that go beyond an analysis of occupations and place of settlement, notably the way the second generation often adopted the customs and outlook of their Australian contemporaries. It is now time to consider these other matters more closely, more especially the way settlers and their families tackled the problem of assimilating themselves to the social conditions around them.

CHAPTER VI

ETHNIC GROUPS AND ASSIMILATION

Here woman's voice is never heard: apart
And scarce permitted, guarded, veil'd, to move,
She yields to one her person and her heart,
Tamed to her cage, nor feels a wish to rove:
For, not unhappy in her master's love,
And joyful in a mother's gentlest cares,
Blest cares! all other feelings far above!
Herself more sweetly rears the babe she bears.

Childe Harold's Pilgrimage, II, 61

BYRON's reference to life in an Albanian home appropriately introduces a discussion of the assimilation of southern European settlers in Australia. In the first place, it highlights one of the most profound differences between life in Australia and life in the Mediterranean. Though the family customs of early nineteenth-century Albania were more extreme than those prevailing in most parts of southern Europe, they sprang from the same general habit of life and point to the area where, by and large, southern Europeans have experienced greatest difficulty in adapting themselves to Australian ways. In the second place, assimilation normally takes place most quickly where there is intermarriage between immigrant and native stock; yet it is because southern Europeans have endeavoured to maintain their ancient family customs that intermarriage has often been resisted and assimilation slowed down. Before taking the matter further, however, it will be as well to explain what is meant by the term 'assimilation'.

ASSIMILATION

Definition

In the study of migration problems the term 'assimilation' has often aroused considerable argument.[1] Some social scientists are dubious of the word because users do not always make clear whether they mean the term to cover the whole long process whereby immigrant groups gradually lose their ethnic charac-

[1] See *Cultural Assimilation of Immigrants*; Borrie, *The Cultural Integration of Immigrants*, Chapter IV; Arthur Lermer, *The Evolution of Canadian Policy towards Cultural Pluralism*.

teristics and become indistinguishable from the rest of society or whether they mean it to describe simply the final state of invisibility. Others are worried because some use the term without any reference to a final condition of invisibility but speak as if assimilation is complete when immigrants have done no more than become happily incorporated into the economic system of the country, or when immigrant and native stock have adapted themselves to each other sufficiently well to maintain political and social cohesion but otherwise retain their ethnic identity.

As a result, some social scientists have decided to adopt a fuller terminology: 'absorption' to denote the incorporation of immigrants into the economic life of the country; 'accommodation' to denote a condition where immigrant and native stock tolerate each other to the extent that they can, for the time being at any rate, live together in the same country; 'integration' to denote the process whereby two or more ethnic groups adapt themselves so well that they can accept and value each other's contribution to their common political and social life; 'acculturation' to denote the intermixture of languages, dress, diet, sport, and other cultural characteristics of two or more different peoples; 'amalgamation' to denote the intermarriage of different physical strains and the consequent blending of biological characteristics. The term 'assimilation' may, however, be used to cover not only all these processes—from the immigrant's very first attempt to adjust himself to his new land onwards—but also a stage beyond any of them: a final stage when the immigrant stock not only becomes indistinguishable from native stock in terms of culture and physique but feels itself, and is felt by others, to be quite indistinguishable. This terminology, though open to some criticism, does greatly clarify discussion and is used here.

The argument about 'assimilation' does not, however, stop here. Some writers have used the term with biological overtones to suggest that the population of the receiving country (the body) takes in new immigrants (the food) and assimilates (digests) them so thoroughly that they bear no trace of their old world culture and customs.[2] This biological analogy has greatly irritated some of those who belonged to, or sympathized with, immigrant groups desirous of preserving their ancestral customs and values; it has particularly irritated many Canadians, who live in a country where official policy affirms

2 See H. P. Fairchild, *Immigration*, pp. 396 ff. Borrie ably discusses this point in *The Cultural Integration of Immigrants*.

the equal status of at least two cultures and where the term
assimilation is often taken to mean the desire of one historic
culture to dominate all others.[3] Consequently, many people
prefer to think in terms of integration rather than assimilation,
and to envisage a state of 'cultural pluralism', that is a state
where various ethnic groups are integrated into a polity but
maintain their separate ethnic cultures indefinitely.[4]

In a sense this particular attack on the concept of assimilation has arisen because the biological analogy has often been
misinterpreted; misinterpreted because those defending or
attacking it have not always understood the nature of the receiving society. That which does the digesting is not a mono-
lithic static body of older inhabitants intent upon forcing newcomers into complete uniformity but an ever-changing society
of diverse groups and associations; for this constantly changing
society immigrant persons and groups are only one element in
the digestive process and may at times be assimilated more easily
to modern trends in a society than some of the native stock—
as evidence the difficulty of the mid-twentieth-century United
States in assimilating some of the hill-billy groups of Ken-
tucky and Tennessee. Indeed, it is sometimes the advent of large
numbers of immigrants, with novel but attractive characteristics
quickly commanding widespread support, that hastens the pro-

[3] For some Canadian views see Watson Kirconnell, preface to *Canadian
Overtones*; Lermer, op. cit.

[4] Some writers admit that the term 'cultural pluralism' literally refers
to any type of cultural diversity within a given area, i.e. to cultural distinctions arising from differences of religion, rural-urban status, occupation, and
standard of living as well as those arising from differences of racial and
ethnic history. But, they continue, because the term has been used mainly
by students of immigrant and ethnic groups it is advisable to restrict it to
racial and ethnic matters (e.g. Clyde V. Kiser, 'Cultural Pluralism', in
Annals of the American Academy of Political and Social Science, CCLXII
(1949)). Such a restriction often leads to ambiguity. For instance, the Old
Order Amish came to America as part of the seventeenth- and eighteenth-
century waves of German-Swiss migration but developed increasingly rigid
views and steadily cut themselves off, not only from colonists of other stock,
but from their German and Swiss compatriots. It is nonsensical to leave
them out of any discussion of cultural pluralism; yet they are a distinct
cultural group less because of their descent or language than because of their
religion. And if we must consider the Old Order Amish when discussing cultural pluralism, why not the Mormons and similar sects? Similarly with
ethnic groups that pursue a particular occupation and have remained
distinct primarily because of economic specialization. In short, it is much
more sensible to use the term cultural pluralism in the wider sense—as, in
fact, a number of social anthropologists do—to include all forms of marked
cultural diversity.

cess of social change and makes more difficult the assimilation of conservative native groups to new conditions. The recent extension in some of the Australian states of drinking hours in public houses, the introduction of improved hotel amenities for evening entertainment, the easing of laws concerning the taking of wine with meals, despite the fierce resistance of British-Australian temperance groups, is partly due to the arrival of immigrants from countries with more liberal drinking customs; here it is the native temperance groups that are finding assimilation difficult, not the immigrants.

From this standpoint, assimilation does not imply a one-sided process in which immigrants do all the adjustment and the native stock none. It certainly does, however, imply a process whereby immigrant families may become virtually indistinguishable from any other family. Cultural pluralism will remain—as it necessarily will, to express all the different social and religious groups in a society—but there is no need to assume that it will always involve permanently surviving immigrant groups who intermarry little with others and maintain, generation after generation, a distinctive way of life. Whether some groups survive or not, there can be no doubt that intermarriage, internal migration, and similar forces have in the past sometimes broken up immigrant groups so thoroughly that the term assimilation is far more apt than the word integration to describe the final outcome. This work, then, uses both the terms integration and assimilation—the former to describe a stage of mutual appreciation and acceptance along the road to complete assimilation.

Australian Official Attitudes

The term assimilation is especially relevant to a discussion of European settlers in Australia. The large-scale immigration of the post-war period has confronted Australia with many non-British immigrants and has led a number of British-Australians to contemplate the possibility that immigrant groups and cultures will survive in an integrated society for many generations. But in earlier years, when non-British settlers were relatively few, public opinion—in so far as it considered the matter at all —did not contemplate any other outcome than complete assimilation; furthermore, it contemplated nothing but fairly rapid assimilation. This may be seen in documents already quoted (see Chapter I) and in numerous press reports, articles, and letters.

Common Australian attitudes are best summarized in the

official reports and speeches associated with the Commission to inquire into alien labour in North Queensland in 1924 and the Commonwealth Amending Immigration Act of 1925; 'best', because the reports and speeches sprang from persons holding responsible positions in political life and crystallize in relatively temperate language the feelings of many British-Australians in the same way that the documents and speeches associated with the Congressional Acts of 1921-3 crystallized the opinions of many native-born citizens of the United States.

The Queensland story goes back some way—back at least as far as the arrival of various Maltese and North Italians in the 1880s. Feelings oscillated with changes in economic and social conditions, but during the early 1920s a great many southern European migration chains became very active and brought many thousands to the state, from Malta, the Monferrato in northern Italy, Catania in Sicily, various Greek islands such as Kastellorizo, and various places such as Korčula on the central Dalmatian coast.[5] Despite a slight fall in the price of sugar, conditions at the time were relatively good and prevented any violent opposition on the grounds that new arrivals were clearly depriving British-Australians of employment or were accepting wages below award rates on any significant scale. Nevertheless, the heavy influx caused much criticism—especially from trade union organizations annoyed at the way many southern Europeans took no notice of regulations concerning limited hours of work, from various Labour organizations frightened that employers might persuade new arrivals to accept low wages and eventually force British-Australian labourers out of work, from Returned Soldiers' and similar societies afraid that the 'British' stock would be swamped by non-British aliens, and from many persons aghast at the standards of housing that southern European settlers were prepared to endure in their first and second stages of settlement.

As a result of all this feeling the Queensland Labour government decided to appoint a Royal Commissioner, Thomas Arthur Ferry, a member of the Chief Secretary's Department in Brisbane. With tremendous energy Ferry rushed about North Queensland, visiting southern European farms, bush-camps, restaurants, and clubs, and brought in a lively but somewhat

---

[5] The net immigration of southern Europeans to Queensland was about 5,000 between 1922 and 1925. See Borrie, *Italians and Germans in Australia* (especially on British-Australian attitudes to Italians in Queensland from 1890 to 1954), and Commonwealth immigration statistics.

superficial report that strongly criticized all southern Europeans except those from the Monferrato Hills in Piedmont and the Bergamasque Alps in Lombardy.

> It is worth noting [he wrote] that these latter hailed originally from the cool mountains of Piedmont and Lombardy and are much superior to the Southern Italians and the Mediterranean races generally. . . . Unfortunately the majority of the new arrivals in Queensland appear to be from the South, many of them being Sicilians. . . . The Southern Italian is more inclined to form groups and less likely to be assimilated into the population of the State.[6]

The Greek settlers—at that time mainly from Kythera, Kastellorizo, Lesbos, Chios, and Athens—Ferry dismissed in a few short words after visiting a few restaurants, clubs, and bush-clearing camps: 'socially and economically this type of immigrant is a menace to the community in which he settles, and it would be for the benefit of the State if his entrance were altogether prohibited'.[7] The Maltese he let off fairly lightly, saying they were 'hard-working and honest but mostly uneducated, and their standard of living is inferior to that of the British or Italian'.[8] Albanians and others he dismissed in a few passing remarks, criticizing the deplorable living conditions in bush-clearing camps (p. 39).

Clearly running through Ferry's mind, then, was a strong distaste and distrust for all southern Europeans except those from the mountains and the hills of northern Italy. Understanding little of the European background or migration history, he failed to see that the Mediterranean immigrants he so criticized were nearly all in the first and most impoverished stage of settlement whereas the North Italians he so praised were amongst the oldest established of Queensland's southern Europeans, were well into their third and fourth stages of settlement, and relatively far advanced along the road to prosperity.[9] Furthermore, with strong views about 'racial' superiority and inferiority, he tended to attribute characteristics he did not like to southerners, greatly exaggerated the number of southern Italians entering the state (see p. 53 above), wrongly gave the impression that southerners were more disposed to form groups (see pp. 250-1 below), and completely failed to mention that some of the older Catalan Spanish families, who had been in Queensland almost as long as the

6 'Ferry Report', pp. 36, 42 (A28, pp. 10, 16).

7 Ibid., p. 38 (A28, p. 12).

8 Ibid., p. 36 (A28, p. 10).

9 See Appendixes 8-21: 'Arrival, % in Periods'; also Borrie, *Italians and Germans in Australia*, p. 112.

North Italians and lived and behaved in much the same way, were from the same coastal conditions and of the same sort of mixture of ethnic stocks as the southern Italians and Greeks he so despised.[10] Despite all this, Ferry's views were widely accepted and became quite influential.

Partly as a result of this unrest in Queensland, and partly through fear that the United States quota laws would divert hordes of southern Europeans to Australia, the Federal coalition government decided to introduce an Amending Immigration Act in mid-1925. Though in fact it already had nearly all the powers it required and the Act had very little effect on the course of immigration (p. 90 above), the government pushed the legislation through against the cries of the Labour opposition that the Bill was merely a cunning way of empowering the government to deport British trade unionists whose radical sympathies displeased it. The interesting thing from our point of view, however, is not the motives of the government in introducing the Bill, or of the opposition in contesting it, but the fact that both government and opposition made liberal use of Ferry's report and agreed on the need for slowing down the entry of immigrants who did not rapidly become assimilated. So S. M. Bruce, the Prime Minister, stated in his opening speech that one reason for the Bill was to give the government power to exclude those 'deemed unlikely to be readily assimilated or to assume the duties and responsibilities of Australian citizenship, within a reasonable time after their entry'.[11]

For his part the second Labour speaker, Arthur Blakeley, asserted that he had

> seen Jugo-Slavs, Maltese, Greeks, Italians—both southern and northern—Turks, Sicilians and Syrians. Where they have been assimilated and have adopted the customs, traditions, ideals, and standards of this country, they have made extremely good citizens, and many of them have married and are rearing Australian families. In those cases they have not congregated in communities of their own. [But] I object to any system, such as is in operation in Australia to-day, that allows large numbers of people to come into this country who cannot be assimilated, and who will take positions which, at present, are held by Australians. . . . In 1907 the more thoughtful Americans realized that if that wholesale influx of Jugo-Slavs, Maltese, Italians, Greeks, Austrians, and Syrians continued, America would cease to have a homogeneous population, and would be merely a conglomeration of many peoples. . . . Each race [there] congregated

---

10 Information on Spaniards from naturalization records; see also speech by J. E. Fenton in Federal Parliament 1925 (Com. *Parl. Deb.*, cx, 586).

11 25 June 1925, Com. *Parl. Deb.*, cx, 459.

in communities, which became foreign settlements upon American soil. [Those] people were not becoming assimilated with the people of the United States, and they never could become Americans until they had learned the language and developed a sense of responsibility. . . .[12]

Through the whole debate and legislation, and all the public statements associated with them, ran the supposition that though northern Italians were better than anyone else, it was generally true that southern Europeans should not enter Australia in large numbers and those that did enter should permit themselves to become rapidly assimilated, the inferences being that in its early stages assimilation involved the speedy learning of English, the rapid adoption of Australian economic and living standards, and a steadfast refusal to form any kind of ethnic group or association, and that in its later stages it involved intermarriage with British-Australian stock and the disappearance of southern Europeans as separate ethnic groups and families.

Local Australian Attitudes

From the southern Europeans' point of view, however, what mattered was less the official attitude than the behaviour and opinion of British-Australians in the particular places they happened to settle. This varied considerably according to the locality and the year, and a general work such as this cannot possibly deal with every situation.[13] In some places British-Australians were comparatively favourable or indifferent, especially where numbers were small and intermarriage occurred. In other places feeling at times became most hostile. The adjacent towns of Boulder and Kalgoorlie in the gold-fields of Western Australia provide good examples, and events there are worth examining in some detail since they reveal the main issues very clearly.

Friction between British-Australians and southern Europeans arose before the turn of the century when many Italians from the Bergamasque Alps of Lombardy and Slavs from central Dalmatia entered the district soon after the discovery of gold in 1894, either as miners or as timber-cutters providing wood for pit-props or furnaces; they were accompanied by a number of Ithacan, Kastellorizan, and other Greeks, of whom some mined or cut timber but others followed a few Italians and Slavs in opening restaurants, hotels, and clubs. Before long British-Australian workers became very incensed at alleged agreements

12 1 July 1925, Com. *Parl. Deb.*, cx, 575.
13 A useful general survey of British-Australian attitudes to Italian immigrants is in Borrie, *Italians and Germans in Australia*.

whereby employers brought southern Europeans to Australia under contract to work at less than standard wages; they were also very disgusted at the insanitary habits of southern Europeans in the mines and the difference between southern European and British-Australian ways of life in the area, and fearful of the dangers arising from southern European carelessness with explosives arising from their ignorance of English. Two Commissions were appointed to investigate the charges:[14] both, in essence, upheld all charges except that of contract labour; the rapid influx of southern Europeans, they concluded, was due not to the nefarious activities of employers but to the system of chain migration.[15]

Conditions fluctuated in subsequent years, though the government imposed regulations that permitted only those with some knowledge of English to work in the mines. Then in 1912, after considerable unrest amongst British-Australian miners, the state government introduced legislation to abolish the contract system of mining, a system that allegedly enabled groups of southern Europeans to operate diggings or cut timber at a price that gave them less per hour than the normal wage. The Bill also contained a proposal to compel mine employers to limit their alien employees to 10 per cent of their work-force, its purpose being to raise the proportion of British-Australian employees and also force aliens to become naturalized, cease evading the provisions concerning the learning of English, and take up the duties of full citizenship. The Bill passed all stages in the lower house but was rejected in the Legislative Council.[16]

In 1915 British-Australians gained a signal victory when the government required all miners to join the Miners' Union and abide by wage agreements. This did not, however, prevent a great outburst of xenophobia in 1916 against the Dalmatians—who though mostly anti-Hapsburg were subjects of Austria-Hungary and technically enemy aliens—and against the Greeks,

---

[14] On 'Foreign Contract Labour in Western Australia' (Com. Parl. Pap. 1901-2, vol. 2, pp. 871-926) and on the Immigration of Non-British Labour (in W.A.): W.A. V. & P., 1904, vol. II (A7, pp. 1-102); also Borrie, Italians and Germans in Australia, pp. 146-7.

[15] The Commissions did not use this term but spoke of the importance of letters home to Europe.

[16] Debates on Mines Regulation Act Amendment Bill, 6, 12 Dec. 1912, W.A. Parl. Deb., vol. xlv (N.S.), especially speeches by Phillip Collier, Minister for Mines, and S. W. Munsie, M.P. for the Boulder-Kalgoorlie area. I am indebted to Mr Ian Turner, of The Australian National University, for information in connection with the debates and activities of 1912 and 1916.

who were suffering from the pro-German policy of King Constantine. The first strike on the gold-fields took place in January 1916, one of the points at issue being the miners' demand that the government intern all enemy aliens. This strike took place during conditions of great economic activity and acute labour shortage, several of the mines remaining closed for a month or more. In the event, though the Federal government refused to intern Slav miners, several mine employers bowed to union pressure and, despite their desperate need of labour, refused for some time to re-employ their former Dalmatian miners; some Dalmatian families remained in considerable distress for many months.

After the war, with the return of British-Australian soldiers from overseas and the intensely pro-assimilation feelings engendered in the services, southern Europeans had a bad time. Hostility came to a head in August 1918 when returned soldiers were so incensed at the death of a comrade during a brawl with North Italian wood-cutters and miners that they demanded the deportation of all Italians from the gold-fields, forcibly deported a number of Italians and Slavs, frightened numerous others into the bush, and displayed particular enmity against Greek, Italian, and Slav clubs, shops, and hotels by looting or damaging a considerable number. Though in the end they were forced to abandon their objectives, they maintained their stand against the 'b—— dagoes' for quite some time, flatly telling the authorities that neither they nor 'Hell itself would bluff them'.[17] On this occasion trade union officials strongly opposed the returned soldiers and demanded immediate government action to protect southern Europeans and return those who had been compelled to flee.[18]

The 'anti-dago' riots of January 1934 at Boulder-Kalgoorlie were even more serious. These started after a prominent British-Australian footballer refused to pay for his beer at an Italian-owned hotel in Kalgoorlie, was forcibly ejected by the North Italian bar-tender, waited outside until the bar-tender emerged, challenged the latter to a fight, received a blow under the chin that knocked him flat on the pavement, and next morning died of concussion. That evening a mob of British-Australian miners, after overpowering the police resisting them, looted more than half a dozen southern European shops and burnt to the ground no less than five Italian, Greek, and Slav

17 See *West Australian*, 13-22, 27 Aug., 5 Sept. 1919.
18 Ibid., 15 Aug. 1919.

P

hotels or clubs. Next day, after absenting themselves from work, demanding that mine-owners dismiss all southern European miners and employees, and fortifying themselves with grog, they attacked the southern European residential area; after gunfire on both sides they drove many southern Europeans and their children into the bush—where some stayed panic-stricken for several days—and burnt down over fifty houses. At the height of the riots not even the British-Australian wives of southern European miners were exempt: the mob merely ordered them from home before destruction began.[19] Though the government and the rest of the state, and many British-Australians in Kalgoorlie, were horrified at this violence, the miners for long maintained an intransigent attitude, returning to work only when the government agreed to strict enforcement of the laws requiring all mine employees to have an adequate knowledge of English.

On this occasion, again, though the riots were triggered off by brawling and larrikinism, important underlying factors were general economic difficulties, resentment at southern European slowness in learning English, and suspicion at southern European persistence in forming residential blocs and organizing their own societies, clubs, and hotels. That the refusal of many British-Australians to have dealings with the southern European population may have encouraged this state of affairs did not occur forcibly to anyone at the time.

In Australian history, mining communities have been notoriously quick to break out into violence—as the story of Chinese miners in the 1850s and 1860s shows—and it would be wrong to assume automatically that these two outbreaks in Boulder-Kalgoorlie were typical of British-Australian behaviour to southern Europeans elsewhere in the continent. Nevertheless, though demonstrations elsewhere were less violent, much the same views and feelings prevailed in many places. Antagonism to southern Europeans became quite acute in north Queensland during the period before the Ferry Report and also in such places as the horticultural districts of the Murray-Murrumbidgee

19 Two men, one British and one Slav, were killed in the fighting and many others wounded. Damage was assessed at £65,000 or more, and over eighty persons prosecuted, about one-quarter of whom received terms of imprisonment. The *West Australian* launched an appeal throughout the state to help the homeless, and the government helped to replace destroyed buildings and homes. Cauldio Mattaboni, the Italian barman, was tried for manslaughter and acquitted. For details see the local press, court reports, and the *West Australian*, 30 Jan.-30 Apr. 1934.

rivers where southern Europeans—mainly northern Italians from the Venetian Alps, southern Italians from Calabria, Albanians from Korçë, and Croatians from the Medjumurje—entered from the mid-twenties onwards. Friction in farming areas such as these arose partly from economic factors—especially when southern Europeans rapidly accumulated enough capital to purchase their own properties and convert a predominantly British-Australian-owned district into one under the control of southern European proprietors. Both in north Queensland and in some horticultural districts farther south attempts were made, first to stop southern Europeans entering the farming districts, and then to prevent them leasing or purchasing land. Despite many indignation meetings and considerable political pressure these produced little more than occasional directions to enforce the laws requiring all persons owning real property to be natural born or naturalized British subjects.[20] On the Murrumbidgee Irrigation Area, for instance, some British-Australian farmers held heated meetings to bring pressure on the authorities to prevent Italians from settling in the Area; finally the motion was lost by 39 votes to 41.[21] After World War II the same farming interests persuaded the Water Conservation and Irrigation Commission to refuse transfer of farms to Italians, whether naturalized or not; the case was taken to the Supreme Court, which ruled that the Commission could prevent an Italian taking a farm if he did not measure up to the Commission's requirements concerning character and efficiency but could not discriminate against anyone on grounds of nationality or race.[22]

The reason for failure to achieve more lies in the nature of southern European competition in these areas. As labourers, southern Europeans were in contact with British-Australians already organized into powerful trade unions capable of enforcing conformity with wage regulations and of putting pressure on governments and employers to limit the engagement of

[20] These laws came into existence with the development of the White Australia Policy in the nineteenth century and with the determination of colonial legislatures to stop Asiatics buying land. They were not really directed against Europeans and it was only on occasion that they were so used.

[21] *Murrumbidgee Irrigator*, 29 July 1927; T. Langford-Smith, Land Forms, Land Settlement and Irrigation on the Murrumbidgee, New South Wales, pp. 243-4.

[22] *Murrumbidgee Irrigator*, 29 Apr. 1947; T. Langford-Smith, loc. cit. In north Queensland similar attempts to stop southern Europeans entering farming districts all failed.

immigrants sufficiently to ensure that the British-Australian labourers were in no danger of large-scale replacement by the southern Europeans; apart from a few cases of wage-cutting agreements, and a more frequent ignoring of restrictions on working hours, southern European labourers seem to have accepted the trade union system relatively quickly.[23] The real competition, however, was not in the field of wage-labour but in that of farm tenancy and proprietorship, into which southern Europeans entered as rapidly as they could, first by share farming or partnership and then by individual proprietorship.[24] This meant that southern European farmers were competing with British-Australian farmers on the home and overseas markets—a much more difficult thing for legislation to control. If southern Europeans and their families were prepared to work long hours and live relatively inexpensively, then they, and their compatriots working for them, could accumulate capital more rapidly than many of their British-Australian neighbours and yet not be competing so directly that legislators could take effective action. Furthermore, this kind of living, plus the traditional peasant economy of considerable self-sufficiency, enabled many southern Europeans to weather recession more easily than British-Australian farmers. Indeed, these two factors led Australian banks and creditors to regard southern European farmers very favourably and to advance them money to establish themselves as independent proprietors. In many cases this did not involve buying out a British-Australian farmer who was otherwise maintaining himself quite comfortably: often it meant the opening up of virgin land, the occupying of properties deserted as derelict, or the taking over of a property from some incompetent British-Australian farmer who was so much in debt that his creditors were on the point of foreclosing in any event. This was particularly true of the Murrumbidgee Irrigation Area and the horticultural zones of Berri and Barmera in South Australia, where returned soldiers were settled after World War I.[25] Some of these returned soldiers not only had almost no

---

[23] Borrie, *Italians and Germans in Australia*, pp. 108-16; J. M. Bertei, Innisfail, pp. 38 ff.

[24] Borrie, *Italians and Germans in Australia*, p. 105. The land records of the Murrumbidgee Irrigation Authority show exactly the same progress as in Queensland.

[25] Some of the now most successful horticultural farms on the M.I.A. were derelict or run-down properties taken over by southern Europeans with support from the Rural Bank (field survey, 1954-5); see also Borrie, op. cit., p. 106.

conception of farming but considered the country should support them no matter how lazy and wasteful they chose to be; neither their creditors nor the government felt very strongly that campaigns organized against southern Europeans by persons such as these need be taken seriously for very long. Furthermore, it was relatively more difficult in such circumstances to organize wholesale acts of violence, and though feelings at times ran very high, action seems to have been limited to shunning, insults, brawls, petty assaults, and resolutions against the use of languages other than English.[26]

Economic envy, then, goes far to explain why feeling often ran high in certain farming areas where British-Australians were well established by the time southern Europeans arrived. But also very much to the fore were the same attitudes and feelings that sparked off the Boulder-Kalgoorlie riots: dislike of hearing southern European languages, resentment at southern European clubs and businesses, distrust of southern Europeans for forming separate ethnic groups. These are all clear in the north Queensland friction, in the Murray-Murrumbidgee disputes, and elsewhere. They are also clear in zones where economic friction has been at a minimum: market-gardening zones in which British-Australians have never shown much interest; small retail businesses, where British-Australians gladly made use of southern European enterprises; deep-sea fishing businesses developed by southern Europeans in the absence of much British-Australian activity. The Molfettese fishing communities at Port Pirie and Fremantle, for example, rarely trod on the toes of Australian economic interests yet evoked very much the same feelings as those elsewhere.[27]

Much the same thing seems to have happened in the metropolitan areas. The small business activities of most southern European settlers do not seem to have cut across any strong

26 Field surveys in Griffith, Berri, and Mildura (1954-6) and local papers such as the *Murrumbidgee Irrigator*: 6 Feb. 1942 (resolution to intern those speaking any foreign language in a public place); 16 Aug. 1946 (brawls); 28 Feb. 1933 (describing Italians who took over run-down farms as having 'blocks that white men would not take').

27 Bromley, The Italians of Port Pirie, pp. 210 ff., and Gamba, *The Italian Fishermen of Fremantle*, Chapter 1. Gamba states that Italian fishermen at Fremantle often received showers of dung, stones, and abuse as they rowed beneath the bridge (p. 6). Ferry, in his bitter remarks about Greek restaurant-keepers (see pp. 2, 205 above), was clearly reflecting the dislike of many British-Australians for persons whose economic activities cut very little across their own but whose way of life was completely different. For Queenslanders' dislike of Italian clubs see Bertei, Innisfail, p. 41.

British-Australian interests, yet the same attitudes of condescension, suspicion, and resentment at southern European separateness sometimes appeared.[28] Unfortunately, very little detailed information is available at present about the day-to-day relationships between British-Australians and southern Europeans in the metropolitan areas, and much work remains to be done before any firm generalizations are possible.

Complicating the whole story have been the ultra-patriotic activities of many British-Australians—especially some members of the Returned Soldiers and Sailors' League—who were often quite ready to press matters to extremes. Much of the trouble at Griffith after World War I, as at Kalgoorlie and in north Queensland, derived from the activities of extreme sections of the R.S.S.A.I.L.A.[29] During World War II ultra-patriotic feelings again boiled to the surface and led to large-scale internment of Italians in most states of the Commonwealth. While wholesale incarceration was quite understandable in the early days of the Japanese invasion threat, continued internment later on arose very largely from suspicion of unassimilated alien groups and failure to understand the process of immigration, more especially the way in which Italian consuls abroad had forced Italians in Australia during the thirties to sign membership papers of the Overseas Fascist Party before they would recommend that a settler's wife and family be allowed to leave Italy to join her husband in Australia.[30]

Clearly, then, friction and mistrust between southern Europeans and British-Australians existed in many places and on numerous occasions. At times it had odd results. The majority of British-Australians in an area might grow quite hostile but a few, who knew and understood the southern Europeans well, stood out in their defence and consequently became most unpopular with other British-Australians. At times these earned

[28] In the Hindley Street area of Adelaide, for example—especially during war-time—and in parts of Sydney and Melbourne. Occasionally it produced window-breaking, damage to furniture and assault. One bad outbreak in Melbourne occurred between British-Australian and southern European labourers when Italians were used to break a wharf strike and suffered reprisals, including bomb-damage, as a result. For insults to Lipari islanders in Sydney see McDonald, Migration from Italy, p. 335.

[29] The Queensland returned soldiers enthusiastically supported the Kalgoorlie returned soldiers in the 1919 riots (West Australian, 21 Aug. 1919), as well as taking a leading part in the events leading up to the Ferry Commission. For further details see Bertei, Innisfail, pp. 33 ff.

[30] Borrie, Italians and Germans in Australia, p. 116; interviews with Italians interned during the war; and other sources.

the curious title of 'white dagoes'.[31] When feelings quietened down these 'renegades' acted as a bridge between southern Europeans and British-Australians and often led to greatly increased tolerance and understanding. Even so, many British-Australians have remained remarkably ignorant of their southern European neighbours and very much cut off from them. In 1954 at Griffith, for instance, one British-Australian official who had been born in the district, educated at schools containing numerous second-generation Italian children, and grown accustomed to playing football and tennis alongside persons of Italian descent, confessed that he had never once set foot inside an Italian home and was very surprised to find that the writer—at the time staying with an Italian family—could tolerate the filth and unhygienic conditions in which he imagined they lived; he was excessively surprised to hear that Italian homes were, on the whole, as modern and hygienic as his own.

The attitudes and feelings of British-Australians in direct contact with southern Europeans, then, varied considerably from year to year and place to place. It is noticeable, however, that such persons did not always resort to sophisticated doctrines of race superiority or press the distinction drawn by so many Australian newspapers and public men between settlers from the north and south of Italy; indeed, it was often the North Italian that aroused local feelings to a fever pitch of hostility, as in the troubles at Boulder-Kalgoorlie, the Murrumbidgee Irrigation Area and in many parts of Queensland. The most that British-Australians in these areas did was to assert, despite all evidence to the contrary, that the majority of 'dagoes' offending them came from southern Italy.[32] This particular distortion, however, does not seem to have appeared much at Boulder-Kalgoorlie, where southern Italians between 1895 and 1940 never made up more than 5 per cent of the total Italian population.[33]

Another point at which local British-Australian opinion often parted from official opinion was social intermixture and intermarriage. Men in public life might talk about the need for assimilation by this means. But British-Australians in close contact with southern European settlers sometimes showed great

[31] The term was still in use at Griffith, M.I.A., in 1954.

[32] During the Griffith troubles of 1927 the proportion of southern Italians to the total adult male Italian population was less than 15%: C. A. Price, Italian Population of Griffith.

[33] Naturalization records—annual movement charts.

reluctance to have social dealings with Mediterranean families and did not at all relish the prospect of their daughters marrying a 'b—— greasy dago'.[34] In short, in many places British-Australian opinion was quite ambivalent: southern Europeans should assimilate themselves to the local conditions and people; but local British-Australians could quite properly leave newcomers to become assimilated without assistance and, indeed, take steps to make one of the most important agents of assimilation virtually inoperative.

For the rest, local opinion matched very well the official. First, assimilation should take place rapidly, within a few years of arrival. Second, assimilation should cover several important areas of social life: adoption of local standards of economic behaviour; adoption of local standards of housing and hygiene; use of the English language; avoidance of groups and organizations confined to southern Europeans.

Economic Assimilation

It is sometimes suggested that, for British-Australians, the most important of all these factors was economic behaviour: the readiness or not of immigrants to accept Australian wage regulations and refuse all attempts by employers to use them as a source of cheap labour. There is no point in covering again ground other writers have already covered well.[35] But it is quite plain, from the particular instances of friction already mentioned, that sometimes economic factors have been much less important than social. Furthermore, these instances give some clue to the reasons. In the first place, outright economic competition between British-Australians and southern Europeans has not been very common. The entry of southern Europeans into independent businesses such as catering or fishing, or small farming activities such as market-gardening, involved relatively little friction with local British-Australians, few of whom were sufficiently interested in these things to become embittered at southern European success. Though the motives for southern European entry into these occupations

[34] This does not emerge very clearly in documentary material but does emerge quite definitely in field-work and interviews.

[35] See especially M. Willard, *History of the White Australia Policy*; A. H. Charteris, 'Australian Immigration Policy' in P. D. Phillips and G. L. Wood (eds.), *The Peopling of Australia*; Borrie, *Italians and Germans in Australia*; N. B. Nairn, 'A Survey of the History of the White Australia Policy in the 19th Century', *Australian Quarterly*, Sept. 1956.

sprang largely from their European background and traditions (see pp. 43-4 above), their actions undoubtedly eased greatly their accommodation with British-Australian neighbours. In this respect they took up the mantle of the Chinese settlers of the nineteenth century, who, after the gold-rushes petered out, adopted market-gardening and catering as the most profitable fields for economic endeavour until the time came for them to return to their families in Asia.[36]

In the second place, when working in direct association with British-Australian labourers southern Europeans were relatively quick to adopt trade union practices and abide by awards relating to minimum wages. Furthermore, when economic conditions became difficult and employment more scarce, a very large number of southern Europeans withdrew from active competition with British-Australian labourers. Either they bought their own properties or businesses and became employers rather than employees—as so many did during the great depression in north Queensland and the Murrumbidgee Irrigation Area[37]—or else they moved away from the district altogether and endeavoured to realize their ambition of investing savings in an independent business or farm—as did those Albanian and Dalmatian bush-clearers and miners who between 1929 and 1933 joined their compatriots engaged in market-gardening, poultry-farming, and so forth in the outer metropolitan areas.[38] Or else they accelerated the rate at which they left Australia and re-migrated to their country of origin.[39] In any event, the danger

36 This does not mean that southern Europeans simply stepped into the market-gardens and restaurants vacated by Chinese returning to Asia. Sometimes this happened, as with the early Bulgarian market-gardeners at Fulham, Adelaide, but the majority—certainly the majority of those interviewed—seem to have opened up new premises or cleared and converted ground for themselves.

37 On the Wade Shire portion of the M.I.A. Italian-owned farms increased from 46 in 1928 to 138 in 1934 (M.I.A. land records, Griffith).

38 In the western Sydney local government areas of Blacktown, Holroyd, Fairfield, Liverpool, and Camden the Dalmatian and Albanian population more than doubled between 1929 and 1933, as did the Dalmatian and Italian market-gardening population of Osborne Park, Perth in the same period (naturalization records, annual movement charts); see also p. 173 above.

39 Table VI shows the excess of male departures over arrivals in 1929-30. The rise in male departures as between 1926-8 and 1929-31 was: Greeks 941-1,422 (151·1%); Italians 4,009-5,807 (144·8%); Yugoslavs 1,117-1,485 (132·9%); Maltese 558-566 (101·4%); Spanish 128-155 (121·1%); average 6,753-9,435 (139·7%).

of outright competition between southern European and British-Australian labourers for scarce jobs was substantially reduced.

The principal arena from which southern Europeans refused to withdraw was small farming in places where British-Australians were already established or establishing themselves—notably various sugar and horticultural areas. Here British-Australians confronted the southern European desire for independence, a passionate wish to realize the peasant ambition of proprietorship; and here the British-Australian met his match. But even then the southern European often assimilated himself very quickly, in the economic sense of adopting the agricultural and marketing techniques of the British-Australians about him. To some extent this was enforced by legislation. Sugar quotas, the Federal government's purchase of sugar at a fixed price, various state agricultural regulations, all tended to force southern European sugar-farmers towards a standard economic behaviour.[40] Likewise in one or two horticultural areas certain techniques were at times imposed by administrative authorities with complete control over land tenure and irrigation water supplies and with the means to ensure that farmers were obeying various agricultural regulations.[41]

On the other hand, Australian economic techniques were very often voluntarily adapted, sometimes as the outcome of imitating the best British-Australian farmers in the vicinity. Numerous horticulturalists, for instance, have said that during their first one or two years they occasionally worked for a good British-Australian horticulturalist and so learnt the best methods of pruning, cultivating, manuring, irrigating, and farm management.[42] Sometimes new techniques, mechanized farm equipment, suggestions made by federal or state research institutes, and advice put forward in extension service lectures and papers on improved farm management were purposefully adopted; in this respect southern European farmers—once over their initial language difficulties and early problems of settlement—have often proved as quick and progressive as British-Australian farmers.[43] Though they may have come from a part of the world where,

---

[40] Borrie, *Italians and Germans in Australia*, p. 103; F. C. P. Curlewis, 'Some Industrial and National Aspects of the Australian Sugar Cane Industry' (lecture to University of Queensland, 20 July 1939).

[41] Field Survey in the M.I.A., 1954-5: T. Langford-Smith, Land Forms.

[42] Interviews at Griffith, Berri, Barmera, Mildura.

[43] Report on the Agricultural Extension Services in the Murrumbidgee Irrigation Area, Department of Commerce and Agriculture, Canberra, 1952; interviews with farmers and officials at Griffith, Berri, and Mildura.

at the time they left, agricultural equipment was rudimentary and knowledge of scientific farming limited, and though they may originally have entered small-scale farming because their traditional garden agriculture led them to seek openings in this particular field, they have showed after some years in the country that they can grasp and implement advanced methods of agriculture as well as anyone.

Here and there, of course, there are relics of the Mediterranean background: an occasional preference for organic manures instead of artifical fertilizers, for intensive utilization of existing farm acreage rather than increasing farm size to enlarge output, and so forth. But by and large, in the areas investigated, southern European farmers have assimilated themselves to Australian farming conditions relatively quickly. A great deal more work remains to be done, however, before we can generalize with safety about southern European farmers throughout Australia as a whole.

In other fields of economic activity, also, much research is needed before a clear picture of economic assimilation will emerge. From what is known the story seems to be very like that of agriculture. With fishing and catering, too, legislation went some way in compelling conformity to British-Australian practice: state fisheries regulations concerning size and type of net, or health regulations concerning methods of storing and processing food. Yet some conformity arose from imitation, as in the size and type of fishing boats.[44] Perhaps the starkest form of economic imitation has been the way southern European caterers before World War II usually adopted, often quite unnecessarily, the least inspired British-Australian dishes and methods of cooking; the local 'Greek' or 'grill' rarely rose beyond fish and chips or grilled steak, sausages and eggs. Indeed, in general terms it seems true to say that the great broadening of Australian diet and food came with the immigrants of 1947 and later—some of them admittedly from southern Europe— and that this broadening, at first confined to new catering establishments, is only slowly making its influence felt upon older catering establishments, southern European and British-Australian alike.

44 Gamba, *The Italian Fishermen of Fremantle*; Bromley, Italians of Port Pirie, pp. 75-6; McDonald, Migration from Italy, p. 303. These authorities are speaking of the Sicilian-Molfettese fishermen at Fremantle and the Molfettese at Pt Pirie. The same thing appears to be true of the Greek fishermen at Thevenard, S.A.

Some European techniques and customs survive, of course, particularly in special crafts such as the terrazzo work undertaken by many Friulani settlers in Sydney. Even here, however, there has been considerable adaptation to Australian conditions and adoption of new and improved techniques.[45]

To some extent this assimilation to Australian economic techniques—whether by imitation or by adoption of new and improved methods worked out by government agencies—is an expression of the pressure that novel geographical conditions have imposed on all newcomers to the country. Though many parts of Australia have a Mediterranean climate, the physical environment—especially the aridity, areas of flat country, or ocean tides and currents—is sufficiently different from the Mediterranean to make newcomers realize that European methods are not always relevant to Australia. In this respect southern Europeans have adapted themselves not so much to British-Australian methods as to the same geographical conditions that had earlier forced British settlers to modify the traditional techniques they brought with them to the southern hemisphere. Consequently, what appears to be part of the process of social and economic assimilation is really part of the more general process whereby both Britishers and Europeans have, willy nilly, moved closer to each other under the compulsion of a novel but common environment. This aspect of assimilation frequently receives less attention than it deserves; it is important because migrant 'assimilation' to the economic customs of the host society may not represent any real movement of the peoples towards each other, and may in fact distract attention from the less conspicuous aspects of social life where differences may continue for many decades and provide much better evidence of the speed or slowness of the assimilation process.

This point suggests another reason for the need to be wary of overstating the importance of economic activity at the expense of other elements in the assimilation process, particularly of those elements stressed in the official British-Australian view of assimilation: friendly intermixture and the speaking of English, family life and intermarriage, community life and the formation or not of separate ethnic clubs, churches, and schools. These aspects of social life have sometimes, indeed, determined the extent of economic assimilation. The area of economic life

45 McDonald, Migration from Italy, pp. 287-8, 339.

where southern Europeans have stood conspicuously apart from British-Australians has been in their approach to communal and family labour. In the early stages of settlement it was very common for groups to lease or purchase enterprises and to work together for longer hours than the average British-Australians in similar enterprises. Later, as the partnership accumulated capital, one would buy out the others, these then obtaining their own farms, boats, or shops.[46] A family once separately established often took in relatives and compatriots as labourers and assistants, requiring every person—father, mother, children, relatives, and assistants—to work long hours and with little relaxation (pp. 185-7 above). Not infrequently adult children worked without wages, or turned in their outside earnings to the father or mother, on the understanding that when the time came the family would set them up on their own.[47]

Again, facility in English has often considerably affected economic assimilation. Some surveys in farming areas of Australia show that migrants who arrived at an age too old to acquire a new language easily have often given up any effort to learn English but have set up as independent farmers using bilingual friends to conduct their business transactions. These have been far more resistant to modern methods of agriculture, and have retained the traditional European methods of cultivation far more persistently, than bilingual compatriots more closely in touch with British-Australian neighbours and agricultural officers.[48]

Now this situation presupposes that persons ignorant of English are living in close juxtaposition with bilingual friends and relatives, and that it is only this closeness that enables such arrangements to obtain. In turn, this closeness means that some kind of ethnic group exists from which the language situation derives. Indeed, it may be asserted that the existence of ethnic groups also underlay the prolonged continuation of

---

[46] For fishing see Bromley, Italians of Port Pirie, pp. 74-6, Gamba, *The Italian Fishermen of Fremantle*, pp. 33-4; for farming, Borrie, *Italians and Germans in Australia*, pp. 94, 105; McDonald, Migration from Italy, p. 339; Land Records of the M.I.A. (these show that about 41% of those leasing or purchasing farms by 1933 first started in partnership); for catering, interviews with various restaurant-keepers.

[47] From interviews with Greeks, Dalmatians, and Italians; also Bromley, op. cit., p. 77.

[48] Report on the Agricultural Extension Services in the M.I.A., p. 29.

European family habits and dislike of intermarriage; even more clearly it underlay those ethnic clubs and societies so disliked by British-Australians. At this point, then, we arrive at the heart of the assimilation problem: the immigrant ethnic group.

THE VARIETIES OF ETHNIC GROUPS

It must be said at once that we are not concerned here with all the kinds of ethnic groups that exist. There are groups of immigrants, and of the descendants of immigrants, that are essentially associations for the preservation of one or two traditional customs: the occasional tartan meeting of a Scottish clan abroad or the colourful activity of a European folk-dancing society. Such associations may claim the loyalty of numerous immigrant families but they play only a small part in the lives of members and may have little to do with the process of assimilation.

Nor are we necessarily concerned with ethnic groups that are essentially political or intellectual in character. A small number of intellectual refugees scattered in towns here and there over a continent may form a society for the preservation of some political policy in Europe, may create the whole apparatus of headquarters, officers, and records, and may at times publish special newspapers and periodicals. Numerous organizations of this kind have appeared in America and Australia, but unless they arise from the needs of, or have considerable influence on, the majority of settlers, they have little to do with the problems of assimilation under discussion. Such activities may, of course, profoundly affect the assimilation of the persons concerned, and in all subsequent discussion it must be remembered that every migrant group contained a number of families whose problems of assimilation were quite unlike those of the remainder. At this point, however, we are concerned less with the minority than with the majority of settlers, and can take into account only those institutions and organizations that affected the relationship between the main body of settlers and their British-Australian neighbours. Our primary concern, then, is with the localities where a mass of settlers were facing assimilation and with those problems that affected them most acutely—acquisition of the English language; preservation of European family values and customs; the vitality of informal and formal social clubs and societies; in short, essentially with those ethnic groups that are influential in the principal places of settlement and cover a very great part of the social, cultural and—at times—economic life of the majority of immigrant families.

This kind of group is best covered by the term 'group settle-ment'. The term has sometimes been used in a somewhat different sense from that implicit here, in an administrative sense, referring to the results of action by public or private organizations in collecting venturesome families, arranging their passages from Europe, and placing them in a relatively short space of time in rural settlements carved out of the forest, prairie, or bush.[49] In this sense, though a group settlement usually contains persons of the same background and traditions, it may in fact be no more than a collection of families from all over one or more countries of origin, families who may have little in common except their sponsorship by the same organi-zation and their life together in the new settlement.

The other meaning of group settlement comes from sociology, with its emphasis on the 'group' as a collectivity that has an established pattern of psychological relationship and is recog-nized as a distinct entity both by members and outsiders.[50] It consists of persons who already have some relationship, who are in some sense an entity, before they ever reach their new home. For some sociologists these previous relationships must be as close as those prevailing amongst a swarm of bees that breaks away from its old hive to set up a new home; the move-ment of a considerable section of the population of a village or district in Europe to one particular place abroad is a case in point.[51] For other sociologists, the previous relationships need not be so close; even so, the concept does imply the settling together of persons who already have much in common—language, religion, social customs. Whether the narrower or wider meaning is adopted, plainly the term can refer to communities that come into being by the unorganized processes of chain migration as

[49] E.g. The Western Australian Group Settlement Scheme of the early 1920s—see G. F. Plant, *Oversea Settlement*, p. 98.

[50] *Dictionary of Sociology*, p. 133.

[51] T. Lynn Smith, 'When in the settlement or colonization of new lands a new colony or community is established as an offshoot from an older one, similar to the swarming of a hive of bees, the process is known as group settlement' (*Dictionary of Sociology*, p. 137). This 'swarming' concept is particularly apt to describe movement within, say, a new world settlement (see Lynn Smith, *Brazil—People and Institutions*), but it is equally relevant to international migration.

well as to organized settlements established in one or two years.[52]

The history of migration shows that a great many settlements satisfy both the administrative and the sociological definitions—for example, the bodily transfer of Lutheran peasants from Klemzig and other villages of south-eastern Germany to South Australia in 1838-9,[53] or the recent agreements between the governments of Brazil and the Netherlands transferring selected farming families to agricultural colonies in Brazil.[54] But the number of settlements coming into being through the processes of chain migration, without the organized settling of even an original nucleus, have been so numerous that this work adopts the sociological usage rather than the administrative. Communities arising from organized schemes of development are here called 'organized settlements', and may or may not be group settlements.

The term has yet another complexity. In earlier years it referred to persons who planted themselves very close to one another, either in relatively compact rural villages or hamlets—as did members of those ethnic and religious settlements that played so important a part in opening up America—or else in one solid city bloc, as did those Neapolitan immigrants who monopolized whole sections of Mulberry Street, New York, at the turn of the century.[55] Almost there was the implication that members of the group settlement occupied nearly all the space available in a restricted area and were thereby enabled to have close personal and social relationships, to spend most of their leisure activities together, to marry freely amongst themselves but not with others, and at times to act together for purposes of organizing local administration, education, and the like.

This implication was quite valid before the days of telephones, automobiles, and the apparatus of modern communications, and

[52] Lynn Smith, when describing group settlements or colonies in Brazil, gives examples that reveal considerable chain activity, as does H. Hack, in his *Dutch Group Settlement in Brazil*. Hack's preliminary definitions suggest he is speaking of organized settlements only, but his descriptions of particular places, e.g. description of Carambey colony, pp. 13-14, make it plain that he is speaking of chain settlements as well. See also C. A. Price, 'Immigration and Group Settlement', in Borrie (ed.) *The Cultural Integration of Immigrants*.

[53] T. Hebart, *The United Evangelical Lutheran Church in Australia*, Chapters 1-3.

[54] Hack, op. cit.

[55] Park and Miller, *Old World Traits*, p. 146.

before the days of highly complex governments that leave relatively little to local organizations. Now, however, rural and suburban families need have practically no dealings with their immediate neighbours but may confine their administrative dealings to impersonal representatives of government and their social and leisure-time contacts to families who, though in the same general area, are not immediate neighbours. Thus immigrants of the same ethnic, political, or religious background may be dispersed over a considerable area yet maintain societies, clubs, churches, informal social relationships, and all the other things that go to make a group settlement work as a closely-knit social entity. The Dalmatian small-farming group settlement of outer west Sydney, for instance, is dispersed over a strip of country nearly twenty miles in length; though here, perhaps, it might be safer to speak of three closely connected group settlements since there are three halls and community centres.

There have been cases where chain immigrants from one village or district of origin have dispersed over a very large area but have still managed to maintain close contact with one another. A number of Kytheran settlers, despite their wide dispersal over New South Wales and southern Queensland, kept closely in touch by numerous visits to the Kytheran nucleus in Sydney, by punctilious attendance at ceremonial functions such as weddings and funerals, by ensuring that their children stayed with relatives sufficiently often to keep them in touch with the rest of the community, and by retiring to live near each other in Sydney. The area involved is too great for us to speak of the Kytherans of eastern Australia as members of a single group settlement. Nonetheless the tenacity with which many of these first-generation Kytherans maintained close contact with each other illustrates the strength of the forces that kept persons of the same origin settled in an area twenty to thirty miles long so closely connected that we can confidently speak of a single ethnic group settlement.

This situation makes it very easy to misinterpret documentary and statistical material. First-generation settlers dispersed throughout a locality may have formed a very strong group settlement but their children, more in contact with families outside the ethnic group through schools, sports clubs, and so on, may have very much weaker ties with the ethnic community. When grown up these second-generation persons may still live in the same general area as their parents but have few contacts with each other; as has happened, it seems, with the Molfettese

Italians settled in the suburbs around Port Adelaide, South Australia.[56] The fact that persons of one ethnic origin live in the same area does not, then, necessarily imply the existence of an ethnic group settlement, so that a group settlement must be distinguished from a mere concentration or agglomeration. The former presupposes the latter, but the existence of an ethnic concentration or agglomeration does not necessarily presuppose an ethnic group settlement, at any rate if the majority of persons are of the second generation.

With first-generation settlers the problem is somewhat different: here the evidence suggests that ethnic concentration is almost always a sign of group settlement, simply because migrants coming under the system of chain migration, and confronted by a strange environment and society, nearly always stayed or gathered together in closely-knit social groups. With first-generation settlers, however, there is a difficulty of quite another kind: the difficulty of deciding, when examining any given ethnic concentration, exactly what kind or kinds of group settlements it contained. And here we reach a matter of considerable importance in understanding the process of assimilation.

So far we have been considering problems of migration and settlement in terms of migration chains, of the way in which, after periods of great restlessness and mobility, numbers of families from various areas of origin settled down in some particular place and occupation. Furthermore, the narrative has given the impression that, except for a few who went off permanently by themselves, the majority of migrants remained attached to a group of friends and compatriots; or, if they did go off by themselves, it was not long before they were either joined by others or returned to the group they had left. In other words, the implication has been that the primary unit of settlement was a village or district chain and that, *ipso facto,* a village or district group was the settlement unit principally involved in the process of assimilation.

In practice the situation was much more complex. During the process of settlement and movement, village or district chains—or sections of them—found themselves in the same place as chains from another district of the same region of origin, or from another region of the same Folk, or from another Folk with whom they had close religious or linguistic affinities.

56 Bromley, Italians, pp. 17 and 18.

It then sometimes happened—especially if the chain units were in themselves too small to provide all the institutions and social life required by families settling abroad, or if British-Australian hostility drove the chain groups together for comfort and support—that the cultural things common to all these different migrants overrode purely village and district ties and welded the chains into ethnic group settlements wherein the greater part of ethnic group life was dominated by regional interests, Folk interests, or even supra-Folk interests (as when a spirit of Yugoslav state-nationalism subdued the regional and Folk loyalties of a mixed concentration of Serbs, Croats, and Slovenes). Where regional forces dominated, we may speak of a regional group settlement; where Folk forces dominated, of a Folk group settlement; where supra-Folk forces dominated, of a supra-Folk group settlement.

It must not be supposed that larger interests always subdued the lesser; that an ethnic concentration of families from several villages, districts, and regions inevitably grew into a Folk group settlement. Sometimes, because of the separatist tendencies of strong local chains and loyalties larger interests never produced anything more than the occasional Folk or supra-Folk society sponsored by a few devoted but uninfluential ethnic intellectuals and politicians. Even when they did predominate, these larger interests sometimes lost ground, especially when British-Australian hostility eased or a district chain became so active that it brought to the one place in Australia sufficient families to provide all the social organizations and activities required by immigrant life. Against this breaking-down process regional group settlements have usually seemed secure—for reasons that will appear later—though clearly there have been exceptional cases. But in Folk and supra-Folk group settlements there has been a quite noticeable tendency to break down into group settlements based on lesser ties, or at least into a kind of federation of district or regional groups.

This, however, is not the end of the complexity. The difficulty is greater than that of simply deciding whereabouts an ethnic concentration lay along the series running from the simple village group settlement to the supra-Folk group settlement: in many cases an ethnic concentration did not fit this particular scheme at all. There were cases where district or even village groups and interests found themselves face to face with Folk or supra-Folk interests with no regional concentration intervening; or where regional groups confronted supra-Folk interests with no Folk concentration intervening; or where village and district groups faced British-Australian society alone, unsheltered from the direct forces of assimilation by any regional, Folk, or supra-Folk concentration: only 39 per cent or so of southern European settlement occurred in areas where village, district, regional, and Folk concentrations existed contemporaneously.[57]

Nor is it easy to generalize about the various chains themselves. It is difficult to see in the statistics for Australia as a whole any system or order in the way the chains settled in one or another kind of ethnic concentration. Further, when one delves beneath the ethnic concentration into the group settlement structure, it is often impossible to detect much system or order in the behaviour of similar chains. District chains from two nearby Greek islands, for instance, might settle in the same ethnic concentration and in much the same numerical strength; yet one might retain a predominantly district group character until gradually assimilated direct into British-Australian society, while the other allowed its district loyalties to become rapidly submerged in the growing Greek community. Some general trends there were, but the irregularities are so numerous that overmuch generalization becomes highly dangerous.

Possibly the detection of an underlying pattern of behaviour falls more within the province of an anthropologist; certainly only anthropological techniques, including detailed and extensive field inquiries, can determine whether in any given concentration there exists a district group settlement, or a regional group settlement, or a Folk group settlement. Possibly, then, social historians or demographers, because of the methods they use, should confine themselves to surveying ethnic concentrations and refrain from talking about group settlement structure. Yet even in a general work such as this it is possible to reach some conclusion by combining impressions gained during periods of field-work with the information emerging from detailed analysis of demographic and documentary records such as the marriage records, these being particularly helpful since they reveal the extent and direction of intermarriage between various groupings and, consequently, the relative strength of district, regional, Folk, supra-Folk and British-Australian forces. In short, the conclusions of a social historian, though necessarily more tentative than those of an anthropologist, can

[57] For this and other figures see Appendix 3:25-6.

be sufficiently reliable to show that several different kinds of group settlement existed in a variety of ethnic concentrations. They may then be extended to all ethnic concentrations revealed by surveys of statistical material, not to define rigidly the group structure of all southern European concentrations in Australia, but simply to show that in certain kinds of ethnic concentration it was possible to have one of a number of varieties of group settlement, and which of these was likely to be most common.

Certainly any general work on assimilation must make the effort, since it is clearly in group settlement structure that the core of the assimilation problem lies. For this work the final test is whether settlers have, as measured by the indices and impressions mentioned, allowed themselves to be drawn towards the British-Australian culture and environment primarily as members of district and regional groups, or whether they have clung to Folk and supra-Folk institutions, or even created them, as a preferable alternative to assimilation into, or utter neglect by, the British-Australian culture. Whenever Folk or supra-Folk interests appear to have pressed more strongly on district and regional loyalties than have British-Australian forces, we can sense the underlying change in social organization and speak of a Folk or supra-Folk group settlement, either unitary or federal: whenever British-Australian pressures appear to have been stronger than Folk or supra-Folk pressures, then we can speak of a collection of district or regional group settlements with relatively unimportant or non-existent Folk links between them.

Further than this, on present evidence, we cannot go. The pattern that emerges from the material and methods available will delineate itself more clearly by way of illustration and example. Let us start, then, with the simplest group settlement of all—the village or district.

Village and District Group Settlements

It is unnecessary here to treat village and district group settlements separately, principally because pure village concentrations (consisting entirely of families from the one village or town) and simple district concentrations (consisting entirely of families from villages in the one district) have been relatively rare in Australia—well under 10 per cent of all southern European settlement (see Appendix 3:26). The important thing about these concentrations is that they always seemed to have been organized as genuine village or district group settlements.

On *a priori* grounds this is to be expected: as preceding chapters
show, family, village, and locality loyalties were exceedingly
strong in most villages and districts of southern Europe; indeed,
it was these loyalties and interests that lay behind the whole
process of chain migration and settlement—both primary and
secondary. It is not unreasonable to assume, therefore, that
forces strong enough to bring settlers from one village or district
of origin to one place of settlement in Australia were also strong
enough to keep such immigrants, when in that place, associated
together in the full life of a village or district group settlement.
Experience with many settlements in the field confirms this
assumption and suggests that statistics showing concentrations
of first-generation settlers from the same village or district of
origin are a reliable guide to the existence of village or district
group settlements.[58]

Regional Group Settlements

With regional concentrations the position has been somewhat
different. Family ties, personal friendships, knowledge of small
local events and careers, these were much less important where
regions were concerned and played only a minor part in the
course of chain migration. Consequently there are no *a priori*
grounds for assuming that a concentration of persons from the
same region of origin usually resulted in a regional group
settlement. Nevertheless, field investigations suggest that
regional interests, though quite unimportant in the process of
migration, were often sufficiently strong during the process
of settlement to weld diverse chain groups into a unified
regional group settlement. In such cases regional interests and
loyalties gradually became so important that village and district
ties became quite subordinate, families from different parts of
the region intermarried, formal and informal social activities
took place through regional organizations and groups, regional
festivals became more important than village and district
festivals, and so on. Occasionally a local village or district
society remained active—the Lumbarda society in the Dalmatian
and Croatian concentration of Oakland, California, has remained as a social and mutual benefit society for families from
the little town of Lumbarda on the central Dalmatian island
of Korčula—but its activities were restricted to one or two special
functions and embraced nothing like that general range of
social activities necessary for an ethnic group settlement. In

[58] Appendix 1:9 and p. 248 below

short, village and district relationships may have survived for a specific purpose, but the more general social relationships operated on a regional basis. This held even when active village and district chains eventually brought sufficient families to provide the full life of a group settlement on a village or district basis.

This phenomenon is amply illustrated both in Australia and in the Americas. The Bulgarians started settling as market-gardeners during the 1920s at Fulham and adjacent districts west of Adelaide; to this area came migrants from thirty or more villages in the districts covered by the north-eastern corner of Tirnova province, the south-eastern corner of Russe province, and the western end of Sumen province. Together they formed a group settlement based essentially on the fact that they all came from the north-eastern region of Bulgaria; here regional interests apparently forced village and district relationships into quite a subordinate position. Similarly, in the western market-gardening areas of Sydney, migrants from numerous villages in the Dalmatian districts of Korčula, Hvar, Pelješac, Makarska, Kotor and Zadar, during the 1920s formed what can best be described as an extended group settlement based on their common origin in the region of coastal Dalmatia. (This group settlement resembles the Dalmatian settlement in the Pajaro valley of Santa Cruz county, California, where, however, there are relatively more families from Brač island and from the southern Dalmatian districts of Dubrovnik and the Konovali.)[59] Another illustration is the Calabrian settlement at Griffith, N.S.W., where migrants from a number of villages in districts centred on Ardore, Oppido, Cinquefrondi, and Gioiosa Ionica have subordinated their village and district loyalties to their common interests as families from the one region of central Reggio Calabria.[60]

Amongst Greek settlers much the same thing is visible. Settlers from mainland regions such as Arcadia, Laconia, Egypt, and north-western Macedonia have generally subordinated their small village and district loyalties to their loyalties to their common region of origin. The same is true for those islands—

[59] Field survey in Santa Cruz county, 1959.

[60] Several Americans discuss district and regional factors in group settlement, but they are more concerned with district and regional loyalties in relation to Folk and native American loyalties than to each other; e.g. C. A. Galitzi, *A Study of Assimilation among the Rumanians in the United States*, p. 88; Blegen, *Norwegian Migration to America*, vol. II, p. 74.

Crete and Cyprus—that are large enough to be counted as regions in their own right—hence the quite powerful Cretan, Cypriot, and Greek-Macedonian organizations in Sydney or Melbourne and the gradual appearance of Arcadian, Laconian, and other associations meeting the needs of many newly-arrived migrants from those regions of the Greek mainland.

This tendency for regional interests to override village and district relationships is not surprising. Regional dialects, history, and customs have been an important element in the history of southern Europe and, especially where a strong Folk, or state-nationalist spirit was relatively late in appearing, have been much more important than Folk relationship (see pp. 6, 55-8, 73 above). Regional relationships have been equally important amongst migrants abroad, partly because they carried their regional selfconsciousness with them and partly because persons from the same region could share the more intimate aspects of social life: use the same phrases and inflexions, understand the same jokes, play the same games, appreciate references to regional events and personalities, hold the same views about family life and upbringing, and worry together about the resistance of the second generation abroad to traditional family values and customs. These forces operated most strongly at the village and district level but they were still very strong at the regional level. Consequently, when migrants from different districts of the same region found themselves settling in the same place abroad they quickly discovered their common dialect and interests and rapidly built up a regional group settlement: sometimes scattered families from several districts came together for general social activities; sometimes scattered families from other districts attached themselves to an already existing village or district group and slowly converted it into a regional group settlement.

Sometimes these group settlements, formed almost fortuitously during the course of chain settlement, grew so large, and became so well known, that they began to attract from elsewhere in Australia persons from the same region who were lonely without the company of families using the same dialect and capable of sharing the same social interests and customs. This was the reason given by one or two migrants from the Venetian provinces (during interviews in Griffith in 1955-6) for leaving their jobs in Queensland and South Australia and moving to Griffith to join the big chain settlement of farmers from the foothills of the Veneto.

The phenomenon of regional attraction, however, lies outside the chain process altogether: it belongs to the realm of 'gravitation' group settlement, whereby persons who had no connexion before coming to Australia were attracted to each other by their need for the company of congenial souls and customs. In the history of southern European peoples in Australia gravitation processes have been much less important than chain forces, primarily because the greater part of gravitation settlement seems to have occurred when large chain settlements attracted from elsewhere in Australia a relatively small number of families hailing from villages scattered through other parts of the region of origin. Even when a regional group was formed through the coming together of southern European pioneers in the early years of settlement, before long some started to bring out friends and relatives and swell the group settlement by chain migration. The Calabrian settlement at Griffith is a very good illustration of this.[61]

In any case it is important to distinguish gravitation settlement from secondary chain migration (see pp. 174, 182 above). The great bulk of movement into Griffith from other parts of Australia arose from secondary chain migration, as is clear from interviews and from the fact that so many later arrivals were related to, or derived from the same district as, those families already established there.[62] Even so, this qualification of the relative importance of chain and gravitation forces in no way alters the fact that, by whatever means families from the same region came together in Australia, the tendency was for regional interests and loyalties to subordinate village and district interests, no matter how active village and districts chains became later on.

There were, inevitably, exceptions to this tendency. They were not, however, as common as might appear at first sight. It could be argued that a clear exception existed amongst the Greek-Macedonians of Toronto where heavy chain migration since World War II has been accompanied by decay in the old Macedonian regional organizations and by the appearance

[61] Interviews in Griffith area, 1955-6; also birth, death, marriage, land, naturalization, and alien registration records relating to the area. Some American writers have not always distinguished between gravitation and chain processes and have attributed to gravitation forces ethnic concentrations that were in origin primarily chain settlements, e.g. Blegen, loc. cit., Galitzi, loc. cit.

[62] C. A. Price, Italian Population of Griffith.

of new and active local societies formed by settlers from townships such as Florina, Kastoria, Vevi, and Antarktikon. Regional disintegration is possible in this case, but it is by no means certain. The decay of the older organizations has been largely due to personal bickering while the new local societies are frequently mutual benefit societies with strictly limited functions. The test comes when one applies measures such as the rate of group out-marriage, which measure the degree to which such local organizations represent a fundamental breaking-up of Greek-Macedonian regional life. So far these measures suggest that no such breaking-up is occurring.[63] The same may well be true of the newly-formed Florina society in Melbourne, though here it is too early to state anything with certainty.

There is, however, another and much more important set of apparent exceptions that are not really exceptions: the smaller Greek islands. Statistics indicate impressively that large regional concentrations of Greek islanders exist in parts of Australia; field-work reveals, however, that these regional concentrations contain virtually no regional group settlements. Indeed regional values and loyalties are not only subordinate, they are practically non-existent. The reason quickly becomes apparent, however, for the so-called regional groupings of Greek islands are not, for the most part, genuine regional groupings at all: the Ionian isles, the Cyclades, and the Sporades represent convenient cartographic or administrative ways of grouping a great number of islands scattered about the Ionian, Aegean, and Candian seas; in terms of ethnic realities these regional divisions have seldom meant much at all.

The Ionian isles of Corfu, Paxos, Levkas, Ithaca, Cephalonia, Zante, and Kythera were in classical days inhabited by different varieties of Greek peoples, took different sides during the Peloponnesian War, were each subjected to different kinds of pressure during the Norman, Venetian, and British occupations, and after their incorporation into the Greek state in the 1860s were included in different administrative divisions, Levkas eventually being incorporated in the mainland nomarchy of Preveza, and Kythera in the south Peloponnesian nomarchy of Argolis and subsequently of Attica. Geographical propinquity explains why Kythera has usually had very close relationships with the southern Peloponnesian areas around Vatika Bay, Levkas with the

---

[63] From field-work and marriage record surveys conducted by the author in Toronto in 1958. For the general use of intermarriage ratios see below pp. 265-8. For further details on the Macedonians see pp. 310-24.

mainland towns of southern Epirus, and Corfu with those of northern Epirus. In these circumstances, a sense of regional unity or loyalty had difficulty in emerging. What did emerge was a very strong island (district) loyalty which, when transported abroad, proved quite strong enough to subordinate village ties and relationships and which then stood directly confronting Folk interests and loyalties with little or no regional interests intervening. The same may be said of the Cyclades and other island groupings. Hence the very strong Kytheran, Ithacan, Levkan, Kastellorizan, and other communities of Sydney and Melbourne.[64]

All this means that statistics relating to district and regional concentrations of settlers (see, e.g., Appendix 3:31-2) from smaller Greek islands must be examined with particular care. With the exception of Kythera, the few islands there given show a very high regional concentration, but this means little more than a fortuitous collection of settlers from islands in the same somewhat artificial regional grouping.

The only genuine exception to the general tendency for regional forces to override village and district interests is the occasional village or district that is so different from adjacent towns or districts (both in its own and their eyes) that its sons and daughters abroad found themselves, voluntarily or otherwise, putting village and district loyalties before regional loyalties. Migrants from the central Dalmatian island of Brač sometimes did this. Though, throughout the period under review, they spoke the same Čakavian dialect of Serbo-Croat as those from the neighbouring islands of Hvar, Vis and Korčula (and as did those from the mainland port of Split ten miles away), they retained many archaisms in their speech and were felt by other Dalmatians to be a somewhat backward, peculiar, and clannish lot of people. Stories concerning their peculiarities and stupidities were legion, both in Dalmatia and abroad, and to them was attributed the story of a Bračani ship passing another ship on the way to Split: 'Good-day, gentlemen', hailed the passing captain, a courteous seaman from elsewhere in Dalmatia. With one irri-

---

64 The Dodecanese islands may prove to be exceptional here—cf. the present co-operation amongst the various Dodecanese groups in Melbourne. This may, however, be a temporary phenomenon and disappear when each island group reaches a substantial size. Thus in Sydney the smaller groups —Kalymnos, for example—give rights of full membership to all Dodecanese islanders but the larger groups—Kastellorizo and Rhodes—confine such rights to persons of Kastellorizan or Rhodian descent.

tated and bewildered voice the Bračani crew cried back: 'We are not gentlemen, we are Bračani.'

Another popular story related how the Bračani once upon a time felt mildly conscious that they were, perhaps, less quick in the uptake than other folk and decided to import some intelligence into the island. Not wishing to be mocked in nearby ports and islands they sent secretly to the Doge of Venice, who, after some perplexity and much discussion with his fellow oligarchs, decided to give them a mouse, telling them that in his opinion this little animal was the highest embodiment of intelligence in the world. Great was the jubilation when the mouse arrived in Brač but loud were the lamentations of horror when a few days later it escaped to a nearby islet. Determined to regain their intelligence, the islanders, after much mental travail and pain, at length conceived the idea of tying hundreds of long ropes around the islet and dragging it and its precious burden by brute force across the sea so that it should never more be separated from them.[65]

Such stories may sound good simple fun, but like the myths discussed earlier (p. 127 above) they express deep social truths and illustrate the strength of the forces that have sometimes kept Bračani overseas more aloof from regional and Folk groups than other Dalmatian settlers. As one old Bračani settler in California remarked when asked to join one of the new 'Yugoslav' societies formed in the early 1920s: 'It has taken me forty years in California to stop thinking of myself as a Bračani and to start thinking of myself as a Dalmatian; it would take quite another forty for me to learn to be a Yugoslav, and that is too much. No, definitely no!' Certainly the Bračani societies seem to be more numerous and powerful than other district societies in California, yet, as pointed out by other Dalmatians who have liked and respected the Bračani and have felt impelled to defend them against criticism and condescension, some of them at least did noble work in helping organize some of the early pan-Slav mutual benefit societies.[66]

Bračani settlers in Australia were not nearly so numerous as in California—see Table II; consequently, unable to build up strong self-sufficient communities, they were forced to mix more with other Dalmatians. Even so, certain Bračani characteristics appear to have survived for some time in Boulder-Kalgoorlie

[65] For these two stories I am indebted to Professor Kadich of the University of California.

[66] John Tadich, 'Reminiscences'; also my field-work in California, 1958-9.

and Osborne Park, Perth, where over three-quarters of the pre-war Bračani population settled. Much more detailed field-work is required, however, before it will be possible to say how far these characteristics have survived to the present and to what extent Bračani clannishness still influences relationships with other Dalmatians in these areas. Certainly Bračani settlers seem to have intermarried less with British-Australians than have many other Dalmatian islanders, and this may possibly be evidence of strong clannishness (see Appendix 18).

At this point it is convenient to summarize what has been said about regional group settlements. With the exception of one or two unusual places such as Brač, and remembering the caveat about the deceptive character of Greek island groupings, it is possible to take statistics of regional concentration as fairly good evidence of regional group settlement. Unfortunately, this statement applies without qualification to only a relatively small proportion of settlement, for only 10 per cent or so of settlement took place in conditions where regional concentrations were not associated with concentrations of migrants from other regions of the same Folk. The presence of these other families, though in no way altering the power of the forces described, did sometimes modify their effects, thus further complicating the pattern of settlement and assimilation.

Folk Group Settlements

Folk concentrations and groups are extremely complex to analyse and assess. In the first place one has to reckon with the fact that gravitation processes (which are more difficult to study than chain processes)[67] were more important in Folk settlements than in any other. There are many reasons for this, but they all centre round the fact that a Folk group was the settlement unit normally producing the larger social institutions: newspapers, political societies, schools, churches, and so on. The larger district and regional groups in Australia, as in America, produced numerous social and mutual benefit organizations. They occasionally produced festivals and religious ceremonies—as evidence the re-creation by the Molfettese Italians at Port Pirie of the

[67] Primarily because documentary material—birth, death, marriage, naturalization, alien registration and other records—can establish family relationships and a common village or district of origin; and these are very strong evidence for chain migration. Statistics establishing a common region or Folk, however, say nothing about how or why the families concerned came to that particular place, on which only field-work can throw any light.

traditional Molfettese festival of Our Lady of Martyrs.[68] But they rarely, if ever, produced a separate newspaper, church, or school—partly because they lacked resources but primarily because newspapers and schools cannot be founded on the basis of an unwritten regional or district dialect but require a written Folk language and literature.[69] Likewise a separate church requires at least a Folk, if not an international, liturgy and hierarchy. Furthermore, politically-minded immigrants anxious to express themselves find it much easier to manage on a Folk-nationalist or state-nationalist basis than on the basis of less formal district and regional organizations.

As a result, the various Folk interests produced the more formal institutions, and it was these that exercised considerable attraction for dispersed members of the Folk anxious to benefit from institutional facilities. This does not mean, however, that Folk institutions sprang into existence wherever sufficient members of a Folk found themselves together in the one place. With Greek immigrants, and with many other Orthodox peoples, this was often so: in Australia large numbers of settlers gave scope for the strong Folk nationalist feelings associated with autonomous Orthodox churches (see pp. 70-2 above), and resulted in the formation of Greek communities—often with dependent schools, societies or newspapers—in large cities such as Newcastle, in every capital city, and in country towns such as Bunbury and Innisfail. With Catholic Folk, however, this particular force has been lacking.[70] Consequently, mere juxtaposition of different col-

[68] Bromley, Italians of Port Pirie, pp. 143-4.

[69] Those newspapers produced by the larger district or regional societies —e.g. the *Kastoriana Nea*, published in New York by the Greek Macedonian community from Kastoria town—are really local newsletters giving news of events in the home district and of careers of its sons and daughters abroad. They do not pretend to give the general coverage of a fully-fledged ethnic newspaper and, in any case, are printed in the Folk language.

[70] The contrast here between Catholic and Orthodox settlers has been greater in Australia than in the Americas, primarily because Australian Catholicism, unlike American, has never really developed the system of national parishes. The history of this system is too complex for elaboration here but in effect it gave much greater scope for Poles, Italians, Croats, and others to obtain their own national priests, build their own churches and schools, and win some measure of independence from the Irish, French, and Spanish hierarchies of the new world. The system has often lost its power by the second and third generation but, at its height, exerted an influence on the settlement pattern somewhere between that of Australian Catholicism and Orthodoxy. A good account is in E. C. and H. M. Hughes, *Where Peoples Meet: Racial and Ethnic Frontiers.*

lections of Italians, Croats, and the like—juxtaposition brought about by the movement and splitting of migration chains during the process of settlement—did not always produce Folk institutions, let alone a Folk group settlement. This was the case with those Venetian and Molfettese (south) Italians who lived for years at Port Pirie with very little contact.[71] Other cases existed in the larger cities and in various small farming areas.

At other times Catholic Folk did subordinate district and regional loyalties to form a Folk group settlement; and here the forces were most complex. One important force was British-Australian indifference and hostility, which occasionally reached such proportions that district and regional groups settled in the one area felt impelled to join together for mutual assistance and protection or, at least, to recognize their common Folk origin in the face of persistent indifference and condescension. Italian Folk loyalties in the Murrumbidgee Irrigation Area and in north Queensland were fostered very largely in this way.

Forces such as these—which for convenience we may term forces of 'compression'—were also prominent in those supra-Folk group settlements based on major ethnic distinctions such as language (see p. 7 above). And here it may be as well to postpone discussion of Folk group settlements in order to digress briefly upon the subject of supra-Folk settlements generally: the forces leading to the formation—and occasional disintegration—of both kinds of settlement were so similar that it will be easier subsequently to make a general assessment of both forms at once.

Supra-Folk Settlements

Forces of compression, then, were important in the formation of supra-Folk groups. This was clearly visible in the Murrumbidgee Irrigation Area where British-Australian hostility to all 'dagoes' brought a few of the old Catalan Spanish families there into touch with Venetian Italian settlers. British-Australian indifference and hostility in Boulder-Kalgoorlie brought Croats from central Dalmatia, Serbs from Herzegovina and coastal Montenegro, Macedonians from Florina, and Bulgarians from Tirnova together into a Slavonic group during the years before 1920. 'Those b—— Slavs', as they were known to many British-Australian diggers—a lumping together that became reality, for

71 Bromley, op. cit.

a time at least, when migrants found that after some linguistic and religious compromises they could understand each other's speech and attitudes quite readily.

Another important force encouraging co-operation between different Folk was religion. It has been said that, however strong religious affiliation may have been in Europe, it became very weak in Australia; freedom from traditional religious controls and customs, the novel spectacle of numerous competing denominations, and the urgent and absorbing business of finding economic security temporarily diverted migrants' attention from their historic faiths.[72] Certainly this seems true of some migrants: one robust and vigorous lady from central Dalmatia, for instance, was reared as a Catholic Croatian, adopted Orthodoxy when she married a Serb Dalmatian from Kotor, but re-embraced Catholicism when her first husband died and she married a settler from one of the islands near her own birthplace; what she did when, still vigorous and hearty in her seventies, she buried her second husband and took yet another Serb Dalmatian for partner is somewhat obscure.

On the other hand common religious background definitely did influence some immigrants. In Adelaide there were not enough Bulgarians or Macedo-Slavs to form separate Bulgarian or Macedonian Orthodox Communities; so these immigrants joined together to support the Russian Orthodox church in Adelaide. (This is rather different from the co-operation between Greek, Syrian, and Lebanese pioneers in Sydney to build a church that could be variously used for Greek or Syrian liturgies. It was a purely temporary arrangement that produced no lasting contact between the Folk groups concerned.[73])

Political forces, too, were influential in bringing together members of supra-Folk divisions. The dream of a united South Slav kingdom, liberating all these South Slavonic peoples subject to the Hapsburg and Ottoman empires and embracing all South Slav peoples from Slovenes to Bulgarians, was relatively strong amongst migrants to America and Australia in the second half of the nineteenth century. This factor in addition to linguistic similarity and desire for mutual assistance, lay behind the formation of the Slavonic Illyrian Mutual Benefit Society of California in 1857, the oldest surviving Slav organization in

[72] Interview with Serb settler in Sydney, 1957. The same theme appears in some of the American literature.

[73] Article by D. M. Galanis in *Krikos*, July-Aug. 1957.

the United States.[74] Something of the same spirit lay behind South Slav co-operation in the early days of mining at Broken Hill and in the gold-fields of Western Australia.

A similar force was peasant radicalism (see p. 81 above), which laid hold of many Slav migrants before and after arrival in Australia and helped to ensure co-operation between various South Slav peoples. An interesting and important product of this radical spirit was the 'Workers' Fighting Movement', established in Broken Hill in 1928 and later extended to South Slav concentrations elsewhere in Australia. The majority of leaders and members were Croatian Dalmatians, but the movement also included a number of Serbs, Slovenes, inland Croatians, and an occasional Macedonian and Bulgarian. Most of the leaders were radical and Communist in outlook and made their views forcibly known through the organization's Serbo-Croatian paper *Napredak*. Furthermore, for a long time these radicals were the most active persons in the Slav groups at Perth, Osborne Park, Spearwood, Swan, and Boulder-Kalgoorlie in Western Australia, at Blacktown, Leppington, Cabramatta, Warriewood, Sydney, and Broken Hill in New South Wales, and at Tully and Cairns in northern Queensland; here they pushed settlers towards building local halls and clubs, organized social and sporting functions, arranged political lectures, or raised funds for friends in Europe. The split between Stalin and Tito greatly weakened this radical element and enabled a number of the more Catholic-minded Dalmatians to win control of some of the local communities.[75]

The interesting point here, however, is that the Catholic Dalmatians, whose interests had apparently hitherto been regional rather than state-nationalist, were to some extent impelled by their indignation at radical policy to subordinate regional loyalties and co-operate as Yugoslavs on a state-nationalist basis. In other words, it is not at all clear whether the supra-Folk group settlement that was coming into being

[74] An interesting history and survey of this organization is in Meler, *The Slavonic Pioneers of California.*

[75] From interviews with radical and non-radical Slavs in Perth and Sydney and from the pages of *Napredak* (the name was adopted from the name of the Broken Hill branch). The above account is very sketchy, as a full history of the organization, including an explanation of all the changes of policy and nomenclature (at different times it was known as the 'Progressive Federation of Yugoslav Immigrants', the 'Union of Yugoslav Immigrants' and the 'Association of Yugoslav Immigrants'), is yet to be written.

R

under radical leadership is now being counter-attacked by a revival of district and regional interests or is being split along ideological lines. Ideological divisions need not have the same disruptive power as territorial divisions because the possibility of conversion is always strong; it is much easier for a Yugoslav to change from mild radicalism to mild Catholic anti-radicalism than for a person reared in central Dalmatia, and very much tied to his territorial heritage, to suddenly identify himself as a Serb or a Slovene. In short, the tension amongst Yugoslavs of outer western Sydney may well express a struggle for power to control an embryonic supra-Folk group settlement rather than the destruction of such a settlement by regional and district interests.

This point, however, brings us back to the general nature of the forces controlling both Folk and supra-Folk settlements, and to the need for re-emphasizing two matters touched on at the beginning of this analysis of ethnic groups.

Folk and Supra-Folk Settlements—General

The first point needing re-emphasis is that the existence of Folk or supra-Folk interests did not, amongst Australia's pre-war southern European settlers, necessarily mean a true Folk or supra-Folk group settlement. A group settlement, as already defined, implies the active intermixture of families through informal social relations, clubs, churches, schools, marriages, and so forth. The appearance of one Folk or supra-Folk organization did not necessarily bring all these other relationships into being. The formation, for instance, of one Slavonic society in an area containing numbers of Slovenes, Croats, Serbs, Macedo-Slavs, and Bulgarians did not mean that district, regional, or Folk group settlements were becoming welded into one Slav group settlement unless the emergence of that society expressed important social changes in the area: changes whereby other relationships became subordinated to supra-Folk relationships; the Slavonic society became more important than district, regional, and Folk clubs; informal social life and marriage between Slav families became as easy and frequent on a Slavonic basis as on a district, regional, or Folk basis; a Slavonic newspaper became widely read and influential throughout the area; and so on. Similarly, the appearance of an Italian nationalist society and newspaper in an area containing groups of Piedmontesi, Tuscans, and Sicilians did not necessarily mean that regional groups were becoming welded into an Italian Folk group settlement. Vocal nationalist societies and newspapers were often the creation of an active but small minority and had little influence on the great majority of settlers; as happened, it seems, in some of the mixed Piedmontese and Sicilian areas of North Queensland.

This restriction of political activity to a vocal minority is one reason why state-nationalism has been relatively unimportant in the history of southern European settlement in Australia. In the days when immigrants started to come in significant numbers to the southern seas, Spanish and Yugoslav state-nationalism was non-existent or else so weak that it no more than brushed the surface of immigrant life. For a time, during the 1920s, a few 'Yugoslav' societies sprang up in the capital cities of Australia, but they had little influence on immigrant life generally and have become even less important in recent years with the arrival of large numbers of fiercely patriotic Serb and Croat refugees who have formed their own quite intransigent Folk-nationalist groups and societies.[76] The 'Yugoslav Society' of Sydney, for instance, had some short-lived importance in the late 1920s but rapidly dwindled into a Serb royalist club and has for long been of little significance.[77] Only amongst small-farming areas such as those near Sydney and Perth—where peasant radicalism was relatively strong—did anything like a true South Slav supra-Folk settlement show signs of coming into being.

The second point needing re-emphasis is that both Folk and supra-Folk settlements were far more liable than district or regional group settlements to be undermined by changes in the process of migration. It not infrequently happened, for instance, that a number of Italian, Greek, or South Slav pioneers from widely separated regions were thrown together in the early years of settlement and formed small but lively Folk or supra-Folk group settlements. Then the pioneers started to bring out friends and relatives, chain migration got well under way, and before long the one area contained large numbers of families from diverse villages, districts, and regions of origin. This rapid growth in numbers—particularly in the numbers of wives

[76] The arrival in Australia late in 1960 of ex-King Peter of Yugoslavia gave scope for these refugees to display their full rancour with Yugoslav state-nationalism.

[77] Interviews with members and non-members of the society in Sydney, 1956-7.

and children, many of whom were illiterate and quite uninterested in political or literary affairs—greatly strengthened village and district interests. It also brought to the surface regional differences in family values and social customs—differences that unattached pioneers had tended to overlook in the turmoil of finding a living but were more disposed to heed when their womenfolk joined them.

Sometimes this rapid growth of local interests completely shattered the original Folk or supra-Folk group settlement and replaced it by a number of lesser group settlements linked only by odd ties of pioneer friendship and the occasional Folk or supra-Folk organization or newspaper. The Slavonic group settlement of San Francisco, really very strong from the 1850s to the 1880s, gradually broke up in this way during later decades. Admittedly supra-Folk organizations, such as the American Yugoslav Women's Club and the Sokol societies, grew quite strong during the 1920s and have survived until the present, but the general impression conveyed by newspapers, books and interviews is that Folk and regional interests grew steadily stronger—especially Folk churches, newspapers, mutual benefit societies, and informal social activities—until the South Slav peoples of northern California, in so far as they can still be separated out from the American people as a whole, can only be described as a collection of Folk groups linked by a minority of enthusiastic families prepared to carry on the old traditions.[78]

At other times the growth of local interests, though not strong enough to shatter the original group settlement completely, did prove strong enough to convert it into a kind of federation of lesser groups. In central Sydney, for instance, the old Greek Community of the decades before 1914 was

[78] This somewhat broad generalization about South Slav history in California is undoubtedly open to challenge, especially by those involved in the work of 'Yugoslav' and other supra-Folk organizations. My general impression comes from two months' interviewing in northern California in 1959; from a study of the marriage and naturalization records of Santa Cruz and Santa Clara counties, and of the marriage records of the Church of the Nativity, San Francisco; from an examination of newspapers such as *Sokol, Jadran, Glasnik* and the *Watsonville Register*; also from books such as the county histories of California; V. Meler, op. cit.; *Narodni Adresar*; S. N. Sestanovich (ed.), *The Slavs of California*, and Milla Logan, *Bring Along Laughter*. The last is particularly valuable in showing the strength of district, regional, and Folk ties amongst ordinary families as opposed to Slavonic, Yugoslav, and other supra-Folk interests.

essentially the co-operative work of a few pioneers from the islands of Kythera, Ithaca, Samos, and the Cyclades, and from the mainland areas of Athens, Volos, and the Peloponnesus. From the 1920s onwards, when the second stage of settlement for most chains was well advanced and was bringing out increasing numbers of women and children, there appeared some very active district and regional communities, each expressing itself through an incorporated or unincorporated club or association. At present there are over twenty district and regional societies as opposed to half a dozen Pan-Hellenic organizations (see n. 80 below).[79]

In some cases these associations are little more than mutual benefit societies working as subdivisions of the Greek Community and using Community premises and facilities. In other cases they are large and wealthy organizations with club premises sufficiently attractive to monopolize almost completely the social life of member families and to focus the activities of numerous informal groups and cliques. Since many of these organizations confine full membership to persons who were born in the district or region concerned, or to descendants of such persons, they have been an understandably important agency in keeping settlers from one particular part of Greece closely tied to one another, in preserving local words, customs, and idiosyncrasies, and in slowing up intermarriage with other groups.[80]

[79] For the reason why Greek mainlanders tended to form regional communities and Greek islanders district communities, see p. 234 above.

[80] For evidence concerning intermarriage see p. 259 below. The Kastellorizan society of Sydney—formed in 1924 and eventually incorporated in 1948 as the Castellorizian Association of New South Wales—illustrates the aims and membership clauses of such organizations. Its Articles of Association limit ordinary membership to persons 'who, being natives of the island of Castellorizo, or natives of a district within 15 miles of the island of Castellorizo [to cover islanders who bought farms and other property on the Turkish mainland opposite the island], or descendants of such natives, or married to such natives, are residing in the Commonwealth of Australia'. The Articles also provide for associate and honorary members, who have no voting rights and are sometimes persons temporarily in Sydney; relatively few non-Castellorizans have been granted such membership. The preliminary memorandum states that one of the objects of the association is 'to provide facilities which will tend to strengthen the bonds of kinship between natives of the island of Castellorizo and their descendants resident in the Commonwealth of Australia, and by entertainments, lectures and otherwise to foster the cultural and historical social customs of the people of that island'. In recent years the association has had its premises in Oxford Street, Sydney and a membership of 600 or so, some three-quarters being pre-war families.

So strong have some of these district and regional societies grown, and so much influence have they exerted over immigrants, that some leaders of the Greek Community and other pan-Hellenic organizations have criticized them for encouraging settlers to confine their interest to district concerns, to abstain from participating in pan-Hellenic activities or mixing with other Greeks, and to undermine, in fact if not in intention, the Folk life of the Greek group settlement; instead of recognizing that they are branches of the Folk tree, the district and regional groups have wrongly taken the view that they are independent seedlings or suckers.[81] Other Greek leaders have examined the tortuous history of ancient Greece, with all its antagonism and rivalry between the various city-states, and have apparently concluded that local societies and groups will always command greater loyalty amongst the *hoi polloi* than Folk organizations;[82] consequently they have concentrated on keeping the leaders of each district group loyal to the Community as a whole so that the work of the church and the pan-Hellenic organizations will not suffer through lack of influential support.

So far, because of the strong traditional veneration for the Greek church, the desire of many parents to have their children taught Greek in the language schools organized by the Community in the evenings and on Saturdays, the love of educated Greeks for pan-Hellenic culture and history, and the activities of royalist, radical, and other organizations that cut across

[81] This botanical metaphor has also been much used in Toronto, Canada, where Greek district societies have been growing very strong since World War II, especially those representing immigrants from Florina, Kastoria, and other places in Greek Macedonia. Some leaders of district societies say they have been forced to develop active local groups since the Community was doing next to nothing to help new arrivals find jobs, cope with sickness, provide adequate social facilities, etc. (field-work in Toronto, 1958).

[82] D. G. Galanis, after surveying the Australian scene, states in his *Krikos* article 'The First Greek Immigrants', 'it is noticeable that while the smaller Greek Communities have become very active i.e. the new Communities formed in smaller towns, the larger Communities have undergone some kind of slackness; this must be ascribed to the many small societies that exist in the big cities; these, instead of co-operating with the Communities, often function independently or even in opposition. Why is not the Sydney Community, the biggest and oldest, permitted to have a worthy and impressive building with offices, library, assembly hall and theatre? The answer must be found in the natural lack of cohesion amongst Greek peoples. Greeks have always been individualists, which is the reason why in ancient Greece we had separate kingdoms of Thebes, Athens, Sparta, Ithaca, and so on.' (Translation.)

district interests, Greek Folk loyalties have preserved sufficient unity to enable one to speak of a Greek Community in Sydney that is a federation of district and regional groups.[83] Much the same situation has developed in cities such as Melbourne and Perth.

Forces of separation have been even stronger in a number of Italian Folk concentrations. In Griffith, N.S.W., there were relatively few pioneer Italians during the 1920s and these tended to co-operate against British-Australian indifference and hostility; at that time one could possibly have spoken of an Italian Folk group settlement. Since then chain migration has brought so many new families that for many years migration streams from six very different areas of origin have been discernible: the Monferrato hills of Piedmont; the plateaux and slopes of the Veneto; the slopes and higher plains of Friuli; the limestone basins of Abruzzi-Molise; the hills and coasts of central Reggio Calabria; and the Mount Etna region of Sicily. Admittedly Italian Folk loyalties and institutions are still in existence, many families subscribing to an Italian newspaper, listening to Italian broadcasts, working together to build a church that caters primarily for Italians, and meeting each other in the Yoogali club—a British-Italian club with a predominantly Italian membership.

Nevertheless, these Folk institutions and activities have not, it seems, been nearly as important for most families—except for those prominent in Folk institutions—as less formal activities based on family, district, and regional ties. Even at the Yoogali club, settlers from the various areas of origin—at any rate from the two more important ones, Reggio Calabria and the Veneto— often sit and play in regional groups, using their own particular dialect. The scorn with which many Venetians regard Calabrian social customs and farming methods, and the low degree of intermarriage between the different groups, provides further evidence of this separation.[84] In short, so far as first-generation settlers from the two major areas of origin are concerned, we are not even dealing with a federation of district or regional group settlements. Folk ties have been much weaker than in

83 In Sydney now there are societies representing the islands of Ithaca, Kythera, Lesbos, Chios, Samos, Lemnos, Kastellorizo, Symi, Rhodes, Kalymnos, Karpathos, Crete, and Cyprus; also the mainland districts or regions of Athens, Arcadia, Vatica, etc.

84 C. A. Price, Italian Population of Griffith; see also pp. 260-1 below.

Orthodox concentrations, such as the Sydney Greeks, and we can do little more than speak of a collection of regional group settlements with relatively unimportant Folk ties and connections between them.

ETHNIC GROUP SETTLEMENTS—STATISTICS

All this makes interpretation of Folk and supra-Folk statistics very difficult. For instance, almost two-thirds (65·5 per cent) of the total of southern European settlers in Australia between 1890 and 1940 spent some or all of their time in areas where village, district, or regional concentrations were associated with Folk concentrations; yet without field-work in each area it is impossible to say definitely whether Folk group settlements existed there, let alone what kind of settlements they were.

From the viewpoint of assimilation to British-Australian culture this does not matter very much. Even if Folk ties were weak, the settlers concerned were nevertheless protected from British-Australian influences by the village, district, or regional concentrations existing there at the same time; and with these, as we have seen, the probability of group settlement was very high. Indeed, if we add to this 65·5 per cent all those who settled in village, district, or regional concentrations without association with Folk agglomerations, some 83·3 per cent of southern European settlement seems to have occurred in ethnic concentrations where the probability of group settlement was very high indeed.[85]

The remaining 16·7 per cent may be divided into two. Settlement in places containing no ethnic concentration of any kind accounts for 8·8 per cent; this may be termed 'solitary settlement'—settlement where immigrants were exposed directly to British-Australian influences without any ethnic concentration which might act as shield or filter. The remaining 7·9 per cent represent settlement in areas where concentrations of persons from the same Folk were unaccompanied by village, district,

85 For statistics see Appendix 3:28, items D1 and D6. We can here ignore Greek islanders for, though their regional ties were weak and the probability of regional group settlement low, only 8·2% of Greek islanders—i.e. 1·1% of total southern Europeans—settled in regional concentrations unaccompanied by district concentrations or village concentrations. Furthermore, over nine-tenths of this 1·1% is accounted for by areas where regional concentrations coincided with Folk concentrations; and with Orthodox Greeks the probability of Folk group settlements existing in areas of Folk concentration is much higher than with most other southern European peoples.

or regional concentrations. This may be termed 'potentially solitary settlement'—settlement where immigrants might have been exposed direct to the full force of British-Australian culture or might have been protected by Folk group settlements (Appendix 3:28 (D4)).

There were of course a few members of village, district, and regional concentrations who, without moving from their place of settlement, gradually withdrew from the local group settlement and severed connections with the friends and fellow ethnics amongst whom they lived; to this extent these concentrations also were areas of potentially solitary settlement. From the statistics available, however, this phenomenon is quite impossible to assess; that requires detailed field-work. Furthermore, the phenomenon changed rapidly over time as families dropped, and then picked up once more, the threads tying them to their friends and compatriots. All one can properly say is that field-work already completed suggests that southern Europeans living cheek by jowl with families from the same village, district, or region rarely let go their ethnic connections permanently, at least in the first generation. Moreover, when this did happen the person involved was often cantankerous, or a man who found life in his new country so difficult that he withdrew into a protective cloud of cussedness, alcohol, or eccentricity; the dropping of ethnic ties then involved not substituting British-Australian contacts for ethnic contacts but a gradual shedding of all normal social relationships.[86] In the circumstances we can do no more than use the extent of solitary settlement as a known measure of direct exposure to the British-Australian environment, and the extent of Folk group settlement as a rough measure of potentially direct exposure.[87]

Quite clearly, then, the ethnic group settlement, whatever its form, has been of the greatest importance to the whole process of migration and assimilation. This is no new discovery. The vast mass of North American, South American, European, and other literature on the subject has always emphasized this aspect of the problem; to say nothing of those writings concerning

[86] I found two or three such cases in field-work at Griffith; see also McDonald, op. cit.

[87] For a full discussion of these terms, of the methods adopted in calculating the amount of settlement in the various types of ethnic concentration and in conditions of ethnic solitude, and of the merits and defects of these methods, see Appendix 3:14-32.

culture contacts between ethnic groups long settled in the same country: American whites and Negroes, Jewish communities in various parts of the world, Tamils and Sinhalese in Ceylon, and so on. Much of this writing is, however, based on an anthropological form of inquiry that examines the workings and importance of various ethnic communities; this, though fascinating and illuminating in its own way, cannot say how many such communities there were and what proportion of migrants came under their influence. Other writers, with greater interest in demographic aspects of the subject, have tried to assess the extent of ethnic concentration but have been severely handicapped by inadequate statistics and documents; on the whole they have been forced to make do with census and migration statistics, with all their drawbacks, and have therefore been able to do little more than point to the agglomeration of persons of this particular nationality or that particular birthplace in this or that part of the country.

Australia is very fortunate in possessing in its naturalization records documentary material that enables an estimation of the extent of the various kinds of group settlement and of the proportion of immigrants that have reacted to assimilative forces through the medium of such groups. And here it is plain that the common British-Australian opinion—that most southern Europeans tended to form ethnic communities and remain isolated from the main streams of Australian life—was well founded. Whether the hostility aroused by these communities was equally well founded, or whether it was no more than an irrational feeling compounded of suspicion of the unusual and ignorance of the facts of immigration, is another matter altogether. Before venturing on to this much more treacherous ground, however, we must dwell for a moment on one or two other matters that should be considered.

Earlier (p. 226) it was asserted that though it is difficult to detect any consistency or order about the various kinds of group settlement in general, it is very much more difficult to detect any order or consistency in the behaviour of chains which, in terms of origin and settlement, are otherwise quite alike. This is at once clear from the statistics (see Appendix 3:31, 32). Thus the proportion of migrants settling in solitary conditions varied between different chains: less than 2 per cent for Ithacan Greeks but 23·7 per cent for Akratan Greeks; less than 5 per cent for migrants from the Venetian mountains and foothills of Treviso but over 20 per cent for migrants from the Friuli foothills a

few miles to the north-east; 6 per cent for settlers from the
Mount Etna region of Catania province, Sicily, but 22 per cent
for migrants from Iblei mountains fifty miles or so away in the
southern end of the province.

The same kind of variations appear in the statistics of village,
district, regional, and Folk concentration. All that may safely
be said here is that most southern Italian chains showed a
relatively high rate of concentration in village groups whereas
northern Italian chains tended to prefer district and regional
concentrations. Otherwise the statistics show few consistent
differences between the various areas of origin. In this particular
aspect of migration and settlement, then, as in so many others,
we must beware of the dangers of generalizing about the
behaviour of statistical groupings such as Italians, Yugoslavs,
and Greeks. We must certainly beware of misleading and
inaccurate generalizations such as Ferry's assertion that southern
Italians were more disposed to form immigrant groups than
were northern Italians (p. 205 above).

Dual and Triple Assimilation

The second significant matter in the statistics is the rarity
of 'pure' ethnic concentrations—a village concentration existing
alone in a British-Australian environment, or a regional concentration existing without any gathering of migrants into
village or district concentrations within it or a Folk agglomeration around it. Pure village, district, regional Folk, and supra-
Folk concentrations accounted for less than one-fifth of all
southern European settlement in Australia whereas mixed
concentrations of one kind or another accounted for over three-
quarters.[88] Furthermore, only a few of these mixed concentrations were simple compounds of village, district, and regional
groups—that is, concentrations where settlers had to do no
more than make the relatively simple adjustment of living
with families from other parts of the same district or region.
The great majority of mixed concentrations, some two-thirds of
all settlement, were agglomerations of persons from different

[88] Pure concentrations, excluding supra-Folk = 16·1% (from Appendix
3:26, items (a)1, (b)1, (c)1, (d)1). Mixed concentrations = 100·0% less
16·1% pure concentrations and 8·8% solitary, i.e. 75·1%. If all supra-Folk
concentrations were taken into account the proportion of pure concentrations would fall a little from 16·1% and the proportion of mixed concentrations rise above 75·1%.

districts, regions, and Folk.[89] Here, often without a common dialect, frequently without common social customs and values, often lacking a common history and tradition, settlers found it necessary to make considerable adjustments towards each other's way of life.

At this point we are not discussing the establishment of those close and far-reaching social relationships requisite for group settlement, but simply those minimal relationships necessary for ordinary life in areas containing families of widely different background: the observance of laws concerning nuisance and trespass; the knowledge of local shopping and drinking customs; the understanding of local schooling requirements or conventions concerning children's clothing and playing in the streets. In this sense families living in mixed concentrations, even though largely sheltered by some kind of group settlement, might have to accommodate themselves to living in the same locality as families from other regions of the same Folk, families from other southern European Folk, and families of British-Australian origin.[90] In other words, for two-thirds of southern European settlers the process of assimilation—through all its stages of accommodation, integration, amalgamation and final assimilation—was a highly complex matter involving several languages and several sets of social customs.

Dual, triple, even quadruple assimilation, then, was a very common phenomenon. Yet it was frequently misunderstood or deliberately misinterpreted. For example, an Italian consul might visit an area of northern Queensland containing families from Monferrato in the north-west, from Friuli in the northeast, from Catania in Sicily, and from Malta and Dalmatia. There he might deliver a lecture implying the need for every Italian, and for those Maltese and Dalmatians reared in the

89 65·5% (excluding supra-Folk concentrations), see Appendix 3:28, column D1. Much the most common grouping was that combining district, regional and Folk concentrations, 48·5%. District-Folk combinations made up only 7·4% and regional-Folk groupings 9·7%. Apart from these Folk combinations the most important were varieties of district-regional concentration, 7·8% (from Appendix 3:26, cols. a, b). For these calculations village concentrations unaccompanied by a district concentration count as a district concentration, on the grounds that persons from one village represent the values of their district in a general regional or Folk concentration.

90 For the purposes of this discussion it is unnecessary to further complicate the story by adding relationships with people from northern and eastern Europe. Mixed areas of this kind occasionally become important, as with the Jewish-Greek-Italian area of Carlton-Collingwood-Fitzroy in Melbourne.

Italian tradition, to study the great writers of Italian history and literature, preserve the Italian culture, and support Italian nationalist aspirations. But in such an area it might well have been that settlers from Friuli or Catania, organized as regional groups, more familiar with their own dialect than with official Italian, much more concerned with their own regional customs than with Italian nationalist aspirations and values, were assimilating themselves far more rapidly to the language and customs of their British-Australian neighbours than to the Italian Folk values put forward by the occasional Italian newspaper or Folk society. Even more, it was only the odd Dalmatian or Maltese who had been so influenced by pro-Italian forces home in Europe that he felt himself part of the Italian cultural tradition and obliged to take an active interest in Italian papers, societies, and nationalist aspirations. The great majority of Maltese and Dalmatian settlers were indifferent or hostile to Italian culture and aspirations, and responded to the forces of British-Australian culture as Maltese and Dalmatians rather than as Italians.

In the days of Mussolini, Italian consuls sometimes stirred up Italian nationalist sentiments quite deliberately, despite their knowledge of the true position in Malta and Dalmatia and of the fact that many Italian settlers of the twenties and thirties were assimilating themselves to British-Australian surroundings as members of regional groups rather than of Italian Folk group settlements. A consul might occasionally remind settlers that their first duty was to their new country, but frequently this reminder was no more than superficial verbiage to disguise the fascist policy of ensuring, both at home and abroad, that Italian Folk nationalism dominated regional differences and eventually absorbed Malta and Dalmatia.[91]

Since the end of World War II Italian consuls have sometimes indulged in similar activities. These, however, have apparently arisen not from deliberate policy on the part of the Italian

---

[91] The full history of the *Fascio dall estero* (the Overseas Branch of the Fascist Party), and its activities in Australia has yet to be written. Interviews and documents now available make Fascist policy clear enough to support the argument above; e.g. public displays of Fascist papers and insignia by Security Service in Adelaide during the war and interviews with Italians in Port Pirie and Adelaide. The Queensland evidence is also considerable. For general works see N. O. P. Pyke, 'An Outline History of Italian Immigration into Australia', *Australian Quarterly*, xx (1948), iii; Borrie, *Italians and Germans in Australia*, pp. 122 ff.

Republic but from a failure on the part of newly-arrived consuls—reared in an Italy where Italian Folk sentiments had become much stronger and more widespread than in earlier decades—to realize the great strength of regional loyalties and dialects amongst Australia's older Italian settlements.[92] Furthermore, there is little evidence to suggest that in recent years consuls, newspapers, and other Italian Folk agencies have not meant exactly what they said when reminding Italians in Australia that their first duty is to their new country. Nevertheless, any encouragement of Italian Folk loyalties helps to increase the complexity of assimilation by strengthening languages and loyalties other than those inherent in the original migration chains, and by adding more problems to those already existing between chain groups and their British-Australian environment. Italians, of course, are by no means the only Folk involved here.

ASSIMILATION AND INTERMARRIAGE

Be all this as it may, there can be no doubt that forces of double or triple assimilation have been at work amongst many of Australia's pre-war settlers, affecting language, religion, politics, family customs, and many other aspects of life in southern European group settlements. Perhaps the best measure of all these forces is intermarriage, that is, marriage outside one's own group. One can argue indefinitely, and passionately, about the strength and significance of this or that nationalist aspiration, this or that dialect or language, this or that family custom or gathering, this or that attitude of condescension by one set of southern Europeans towards another. (At Griffith some Venetians were far more open and violent about their alleged superiority over southern Italians from Calabria than were local British-Australians.) But the cold hard statistics of intermarriage cannot be ignored or their significance denied. Where, in some particular chain group, intermarriage took place frequently with British-Australians but rarely with other southern European families in the Folk or supra-Folk concentration, then clearly those concerned were organized primarily as district or regional groups, were little influenced by Folk or supra-Folk interests, and were losing their group coherence before the direct pressure of British-Australian forces. Conversely, where intermarriage occurred frequently with

92 One such incident occurred during the author's field-work in Griffith.

families of another region or Folk and rarely with British-Australians, it is manifest that the chain group was becoming subordinated to a Folk or supra-Folk group settlement and that direct exposure to British-Australian influences was relatively slight.

Again, where members of a chain group rarely intermarried, either with British-Australians or with families from other regions or Folk, they were clearly members of a relatively strong village, district, or regional group settlement, and faced all outside influences as members of that settlement. This does not mean that such a group settlement was necessarily strongly *resistant* to all outside forces: there is a clear difference between facing novel conditions and resisting every one of such conditions. The German-Lutheran settlements of South Australia, or the Pennsylvania-German settlements of Pennsylvania, Virginia, and Maryland, adopted other languages as well as their own, other forms of dress, other economic habits, and other social customs; yet they have married relatively little outside their own people. Indeed, this phenomenon has occurred so often that some scholars have challenged the notion that intermarriage is a useful measure of assimilation. Simon Marcson, for instance, has pointed out that American groups such as the Scots-Irish—whose pioneer ancestors arrived very early in North American history and who have played no small part in building the American society and culture of today—have married outsiders less than have some of the second- and third-generation persons whose parents or grandparents arrived from southern and eastern Europe a mere half-century or so ago; he argues from this that factors such as religion and occupational status often exert more influence on intermarriage than does ethnic origin, that 'a group may become assimilated without showing a high rate of intermarriage', and that 'intermarriage is . . . therefore not an index of assimilation'.[93]

There is much in this view, particularly as it emphasizes the importance of occupational status and religion in intermarriage. But it makes things unnecessarily complicated by confusing assimilation with integration. The fact that a particular ethnic grouping may have long been settled in the new world does not necessarily mean that it has become assimilated in the fullest sense for, as here defined (pp. 200-3), complete assimilation implies that descendants of immigrant families have become

[93] 'A Theory of Intermarriage and Assimilation', *Social Forces*, xxix (1950-1), 78.

so mixed up with the descendants of other immigrant stocks that they are virtually indistinguishable, at any rate in ethnic terms. A people may have arrived centuries before in pioneering days and may, by constant in-marriage, have remained clearly distinct from the rest of the population—whether for religious or occupational reasons or for reasons more directly connected with ethnic background is here immaterial. Such a people may be well integrated into society but they are certainly not well assimilated. For complete assimilation intermarriage is still a most reliable test, as it is likewise still a most reliable index of group cohesion. In this respect the views set forth by Julius Drachsler in his classic study of 1921 still hold.[94]

In short, there can be little doubt that a high rate of inter-marriage involves destruction of the original migrant group and is, to that extent, a useful index of assimilation. Furthermore, the partners chosen by those who do intermarry reveal the direction in which assimilation is taking place, whether towards a Folk concentration, a supra-Folk concentration, or into the various groups of native society. Here again, the British-Australian notion of assimilation, with its emphasis on marriage between European and British stock, was patently well-founded—even if somewhat inconsistently expressed.

The foregoing paragraphs show the importance of intermar-riage statistics as an index of assimilation and integration. But they say nothing about the considerable technical difficulties involved in such statistics. Briefly, one must, if possible, separate the first generation (adult settlers or I's), not only from second-generation persons born in Australia (IIb's), but from second-generation persons born in Europe and brought to Australia when children (IIa's); in most intermarriage statistics the IIa's are included with the I's, yet their marriage pattern can be very different. Where possible one must also separate the third and later generations from other elements in the Australian-born population. Only after this can one decide whether an ethnic group is maintaining coherence by marrying within itself

---

94 *Intermarriage in New York City*: 'Intermarriage, as such, is perhaps the severest test of group cohesion' (p. 18); 'it is evident that the higher the proportion of intermarriage . . . the higher is the degree of assimilation with other groups' (p. 19). See also John Kolehmainen, 'A Study of Marriage in a Finnish Community', *American Journal of Sociology*, XLII (1936-7), 379; James H. S. Bossard, 'Nationality and Nativity as Factors in Marriage', *American Sociological Review*, IV (1939), 792; Ruby J. R. Kennedy, 'Single or Triple Melting-Pot?', *American Journal of Sociology*, XXXVI (1943-4), 331; Kiser, 'Cultural Pluralism', p. 126.

generation after generation or is amalgamating with other ethnic stocks.[95]

After isolating the different generations within the various district, regional, and Folk groupings, we can then look at intermarriage from two points of view. First, one may think of those who intermarry as persons who either escape from the ethnic group altogether or else introduce alien and novel influences into it. The strength of this alien or escaping element may be measured by taking intermarried persons as a proportion of all married persons in the group, whether the latter have married in Australia or in Europe before migrating. The ratio obtained—Intermarriage Ratio A—is a useful measure of the degree of group solidarity and group coherence.

Intermarriage may also be looked at from another point of view—that of all those members of an immigrant group who were born in Australia, reared in Australia, or came out as adults but lived in Australia as single persons long enough to become familiar with at least some Australian customs and people or with the customs and members of other immigrant groups; that is, from the standpoint of all those who had some opportunity to marry outside their own ethnic grouping. When taken as a proportion of all these persons, those who inter-married represent that element that was in touch with British-Australian or other European families and did not resist the opportunity to marry into such families. This ratio, Intermar-riage Ratio B, is a very useful measure of the long-term trends that control ethnic group solidarity. A group, such as the Macedonians from Florina or Kastoria, showed Intermarriage Ratios A of only 5 per cent or so, primarily because some three-quarters of the settlers were married when they arrived; yet the Intermarriage Ratios B showed that 50 per cent or more of Macedonians with an opportunity to marry British-Australians did so, and that these groups, unless reinforced with further immigration, were confronted with relatively rapid disintegration and assimilation.

Intermarriage Ratio B is the ratio normally used in inter-marriage inquiries in the Americas and elsewhere. But to use it properly one must make sure one is dealing with those persons, and only those persons, who had some opportunity to

[95] For a full discussion of these categories, and of the measurement of intermarriage generally, see C. A. Price and J. Zubrzycki, 'The Use of Inter-marriage Statistics as an Index of Assimilation', *Population Studies*, xvi (July 1962), i, 58-69.

S

intermarry. 'Wharf-side brides'—girls who came to Australia, were met by their fiancées and married, if not in the church nearest the wharf, at least within a few weeks of arrival— cannot legitimately be included, since they had no opportunity to marry outside their own ethnic grouping. Yet these are normally included when calculating Ratio B; conversely, all single male settlers who lived for some time in Australia and then either married by proxy or paid a short visit to Europe to marry should be included, yet such marriages, being registered in Europe and not in Australia, are not usually included when calculating Ratio B.

In practical terms it is impossible to obtain a reliable B ratio unless one undertakes special surveys, such as have occasionally been undertaken in the United States and Australia.[96] The naturalization records, however, go a long way to help, especially in separating out the IIa's and the various ethnic groups. From these records, and from one or two special surveys, it is plain that in the years 1890-1940 there were in operation several general forces that affected all southern European groups. Other things being equal, chains bringing relatively large numbers of young settlers showed a higher rate of intermarriage with British-Australians than those bringing more older men; apparently the younger a southern European on arrival, the less fixed he was in habits of thought and behaviour, the easier he found it to adopt the customs of his new neighbours, and the more likely he was to marry outside his own ethnic stock (Appendix 4:14). Likewise chains with a longer duration of residence showed a higher proportion of intermarriages than those more recently arrived (Appendix 4:13). The special surveys also suggested that occupation played some part in intermarriage—settlers engaged in skilled trades and other occupations bringing them into relatively frequent personal contact with others showed a higher rate of intermarriage than those engaged in farming or catering, which permitted a higher degree of isolation (Appendix 4:40).

Another important general factor was the size of the group settlement. Lacking wide opportunities to mix with young people of their own ethnic origin, without sufficient human

---

[96] Kolehmainen, op. cit.; Ray Baber, 'A Study of 325 mixed marriages', *American Sociological Review*, II (1937); J. S. Slotkin, 'Jewish-gentile intermarriage in Chicago', *American Sociological Review*, VII (1942). I have also conducted two such surveys, at Griffith, N.S.W., and amongst the Greeks of Sydney, N.S.W.

resources to organize large-scale social activities, lacking financial resources for building their own clubs and halls, the smaller district and regional groups often found themselves drawn into the orbit of larger groups or else into general Folk or British-Australian activities. The effect on marriage patterns was noticeable for, other things being equal, the smaller groups showed a much higher proportion of out-marriages. In Griffith, for instance, the smaller groups from Piedmont, Lombardy, Friuli, Catania, and the Abruzzi had, by 1954, much the same age and sex structure, and about the same proportion of I's, IIa's and IIb's, as the two large groups from the Veneto and Calabria. Yet these small groups together showed an Inter-marriage Ratio B for men of well over 50 per cent, compared with 20 per cent or so for the Venetians and Calabrians (Appendix 4:26). Similarly in Sydney the smaller Greek island groups together showed an Intermarriage Ratio B of more than 70 per cent, compared with 50 per cent and less for larger groups such as the Kytherans and Kastellorizans (Appendix 4:21).

Within these general trends, however, there existed consider-able diversity. Groups of the same order of size, settled in much the same environment, having been in Australia for much the same length of time, displayed very different marriage patterns. In Sydney, Kytheran Greek settlers married much more outside their own group than did Kastellorizan settlers; moreover, most of these Kytheran intermarriages were with British-Australians rather than with Greek girls, suggesting that the Kytheran district group was losing its coherence more rapidly than the Kastellorizan and was assimilating itself not so much to the Greek Folk community as to British-Australian society in general (Appendix 4:21, 22). On the other hand, the male statistics suggest that the Cypriot group was losing its coherence at much the same rate as the Kytheran, but to the Greek Folk community rather than to British-Australian society (Appendix 4:21, 23).

In Griffith, too, the various Italian groups behaved very differently. Of the two large groups the Calabrian showed a higher proportion of intermarriages than the Venetian, both for males and females, and a significantly higher proportion of intermarriage with British-Australian girls. Whatever the reasons for this, it is plain that many British-Australian girls at Griffith were not at all affected by theoretical talk about the compatibility of 'tall, fair northern Italians' and the complete unsuitability of 'short, dark southern Italians' (Appendix 4:26-7).

Another very important difference between the various district and regional groups lies in the way their marriage pattern changed with fluctuations in chain migration. With the Kytherans of New South Wales the early stages of settlement—when unattached men formed the great majority of settlers—saw a relatively low proportion of in-group marriages (38·5 per cent) and a relatively high proportion of intermarriages with British-Australians (42·3 per cent). Then, during the third stage, with the coming of women and children from Kythera and the strengthening of local customs and habits, intermarriage with British-Australians became less acceptable (16·0 per cent) and in-group marriages increased considerably (74·0 per cent). Finally, with the growing to maturity of the IIa's and IIb's during the fourth stage, despite some heavy post-war immigration, in-group marriages fell away (53·9 per cent) and intermarriage with British-Australian girls increased again (33·3 per cent). Throughout, intermarriage with other Greeks was relatively unimportant (see Appendix 4:32-5).

Kastellorizan Greeks in Sydney, however, did not react in this way, apparently because more of them had brides sent out to Australia. In the early stages of settlement Kastellorizan Greeks had a much higher proportion of in-group marriages than Kytherans (66·7 per cent: 38·5 per cent), and this fell only a little in the second stage. Furthermore, when it did fall a bit during the fourth stage it reflected the growing tendency of Kastellorizans to marry other Greeks; the proportion marrying British remained low throughout.[97] In short, the Kastellorizan group resisted assimilation more strongly than other groups but when it did assimilate it did so to the Greek Folk community rather than to British-Australian society.

Quite different again was the Venetian group at Griffith. Here in-group marriages by men were very high during the early stages of settlement (90·4 per cent), primarily because of marriage by proxy, re-migration to Italy for brides, and the sending of fiancées to Australia. During the third stage in-group marriage actually fell away (66·7 per cent), only to rise again as a result of heavy chain migration in the late forties and early fifties (72·8 per cent). It is interesting to note that what suffered here were not intermarriages with British-Australians—

---

[97] Fourth stage (males): in-group, 41·7%; British-Australian, 8·3%; other Greek 50·0%.

which relatively increased—but marriages with other Italians. Precisely the same thing happened with the Calabrian group.[98]

This change in the male marriage patterns of the two largest groups at Griffith was even more pronounced in female marriages and reflected the trend noticeable in other ways: a fairly sharp line between the two groups once pioneering days were over, then some intermixture and blurring of distinctions during World War II, followed by heavy chain migration and a deepening of the lines of division. This high rate of in-group marriages—very much higher than amongst the Sydney Greeks—is one reason for preferring to think of the Griffith Italians as a number of regional group settlements with certain Folk interests in common rather than as a federation of regional groups in an Italian Folk group settlement (see pp. 247-8 above).

All this means that with large groups such as the Kytherans of Sydney and the Venetians and Calabrians of Griffith, assimilation was taking place at least as much into British-Australian society as into Greek and Italian Folk society. On the other hand, the smaller Greek groups in Sydney were being assimilated primarily into the Greek Folk community and the smaller Italian groups at Griffith into one or other of the two large regional groups. The problem of dual or triple assimilation— the clash of assimilative forces exerted by regional, Folk, and British-Australian influences—was certainly very prominent in these areas.

Likewise, these special surveys show that assimilation, whether into Folk, supra-Folk, or British-Australian society, was taking place much more slowly with some groups than others. First, there were groups such as the Sydney Kastellorizans, who maintained a high proportion of in-group marriages for the fifty years or so of their sojourn in Australia; much higher than with some other groups. Second, there were groups that developed a high rate of intermarriage—especially with the coming to maturity of the IIa's and IIb's (Appendix 4:32-9)— only to find it forced down again by prolonged periods of heavy chain immigration.

In these circumstances it is very difficult to generalize, either about the extent of dual or triple assimilation or about the speed at which southern European groups in general were losing their group coherence in the years under review. In any case, outside the special surveys, the evidence is meagre. Official statistics help very little (Appendix 4:12). Even the naturaliza-

98 Appendix 4:26 and C. A. Price, Italian Population of Griffith.

tion records are comparatively useless, primarily because they show only marriages between male I's and British-Australian girls (or girls of other nationalities), not marriages between the different generations, or between members of different regions in the same Folk; nor do they give any information about marriages of single southern European women.

For what they are worth, however, these records suggest that, if we take an average duration of ten years in Australia, some 30 per cent of southern European settlers married British-Australian girls. This, of course, is Intermarriage Ratio B—intermarrying settlers as a proportion of all settlers who had lived in Australia long enough to intermix with families outside their own ethnic stock. Intermarriage Ratio A—intermarrying settlers as a proportion of all married settlers—was very much lower, 10 per cent or less. The addition of the single men reduces the intermarried element still further, to about 5 per cent.[99] Compared with other countries these seem fairly normal rates of intermarriage and group disintegration. But further and more definitive statements must await more detailed studies.

Assimilation and Intermarriage—the Second Generation

The intermarriage ratios, then, confirm the central thesis of this section: that there did exist general forces influencing all ethnic group settlements but that these forces were often so modified by the particular circumstances surrounding the origins and settlement of each immigrant group that it is difficult to discern a simple general pattern of group behaviour. Nevertheless, one general point is quite clear: however a particular group eventually responded to the challenges of single, dual, or triple assimilation, it was in the arena of marriage that it felt the challenges most severely; primarily because intermarriage cut so drastically and quickly at the central citadel of group values and group coherence. Economic assimilation, or absorption, took place comparatively rapidly—despite the hostility shown by British-Australians when they felt their economic interests endangered. Acculturation to some superficial characteristics often proceeded apace, too; adoption of Australian dress is an example, despite the occasional retention of articles of clothing

[99] From Intermarriage Ratios A and B in Appendixes 8-21, adjusted for estimated exaggeration, and each group brought to a common duration of residence of ten years—this being very close to the average duration of residence between arrival and naturalization.

that southern Europeans felt to be more suitable for Australian conditions than the normal British-Australian garb.[1] But over family values, domestic customs, local religious beliefs and superstitions, dialect and social habits—the things most affected by intermarriage—many southern Europeans fought a strong, and at times quite bitter, rearguard action. To them inter-marriage represented either the loss of a loved one from the fold or else the introduction of alien influences into the home, into the very place where they felt most secure, most cushioned against the strangenesses of British-Australian life, most able to relax happily and gently in the atmosphere of their old world life.

It was bad enough when an adult settler married outside his group; though with such unsettled conditions in the early stages of settlement, with such a surplus of men, with so few complete families to guide and comfort, it was understandable and for-givable; indeed, at times it gave a struggling chain a certain prestige value. But in the case of intermarriage by a second-generation boy or girl, reared in a settled home, cherished by a complete array of parents, uncles, aunts, and god-parents all well aware of the proper way of doing things, the matter was very different.

Take the case of a Venetian or Kastellorizan mother watching her eldest son fall in love with a British-Australian girl and hearing him announce his intention of marrying her. To the mother this was often a heartbreak, something about which she felt so strongly that she did not mind pouring it all out to a comparative stranger like the writer. She saw entering the inner fold someone who would one day be the elder lady of the family —yet someone who could not speak the local dialect and for that reason alone could never reach terms of easy intimacy and con-fidence with womenfolk expressing their domestic thoughts naturally and easily in dialect rather than in stilted English; someone who, worst of all, might feel no need to make her infants learn the dialect well enough to converse with their grandmother and receive her loving advice and affection. Again, she saw in such a marriage the entry of a person who had been brought up in the relatively restrained atmosphere of a British-Australian nuclear family and had little understanding of—and probably little sympathy for—the wider loyalties of southern

[1] Many Italian farmers still insist on wearing heavy flannel shirts while at work because they feel that flannel absorbs sweat better than other materials and protects the wearer against chills (field-work on M.I.A. etc.).

European family and local life: the duties and pleasures involved in travelling long distances to attend weddings and funerals of far-flung relatives and friends, in helping impoverished relatives and fellow-villagers to come to Australia, in finding work and accommodation for them, in allowing them to invade home and kitchen with noise and song and laughter. Again, she could see the entry of someone whose upbringing would inevitably strike at the traditional lines of authority in so many southern European families; someone who would feel no obligation to defer to her mother-in-law on matters of child care or household management; someone who, worse still, might undermine the eldest son's respect for his father and reliance on his judgment and advice. Finally, she saw entering the family a girl who might well expect her husband to help with household chores such as washing-up, who would spend quite a lot of her time at tennis or surfing or parties instead of being dutiful about the house.

Small wonder that mothers and fathers would advise their Australian-born son to enjoy the company of a British-Australian girl at dances and parties if he must, but to think very carefully before marrying her. A model conversation, based on talks with Greek, Italian, Albanian, Dalmatian and Maltese families, could well run:

> No, my son, she would not know how to look after you in the way you have been accustomed to; she would not wait on you while you sat at table or do the wash-up by herself while you smoked and talked with your men-friends after dinner; she would want to go to parties and sports and spend far more money on clothes and make-up than I—content with my dark sober clothes, the proper garb for a matron of our people—have ever done in all my life. If you must marry a girl whose parents are from a family and district we do not know, then at least marry a girl whose family come from our part of the world [region or Folk]. She at least will have some idea of how to look after you and of her duties as a wife and mother.

So strongly did many parents feel on such matters that they were often prepared to surrender other values in order to preserve this central point. Peloponnesian Greek parents in Toronto, for example, told the writer how they found that, in energetically practising their traditional custom of strict chaperonage over daughters, they were collectively encouraging their sons to marry British-Canadian girls. Sons, always allowed more freedom than daughters, enjoyed attending dances, hikes, and skiing parties where British-Canadian girls were present, and they often preferred this kind of social life to the formal call upon a Greek girl at her home, or the more formal Greek dances where dark-clad matrons sat like crows upon chairs around the walls, their dark beady eyes fixed upon every move the young Greek girl made. (This simile has been used by second-generation Greeks in both Toronto and Melbourne.) Not unnaturally many Greek-Canadian boys fell in love with British-Canadian girls and refused to heed their parents' advice about marrying outside their own regional or Folk group. The Greek parents then found to their great dismay that they were not only losing their sons but that their homes were full of well brought-up but unwanted daughters, rapidly growing past the usual age of marriage.

Some parents tried to retrieve what they could of the damage by taking their daughters on a grand tour of the 'old country'— to see if they could find some suitable relative for a bridegroom. Occasionally this succeeded, but Greek-Canadian girls, educated to a much higher level than their relatives in Greece and used to far more elegant conditions of life, did not always wish to pair off with an ill-educated cousin from a peasant's home in the Arcadian mountains. Other parents encouraged the attentions of young immigrants fresh from Greece. This also worked at times, but only, it seems, when the young man was bright enough to adopt Greek-Canadian ways fairly rapidly and become acceptable to the girl concerned. (From his point of view, of course, alliance with a wealthy and influential Greek family in Toronto helped his own career greatly, and it is noticeable that several of the young men now prominent in Community affairs have married in this way. So much so, indeed, that envious new immigrants—often at loggerheads with the old régime over Community affairs and conditions of employment (see pp. 196-9 above)—have accused the 'old guard' of seducing their natural leaders by dangling forth the bait of a wealthy bride.)

Even these measures, however, have not solved the problem completely and there is still, it appears, a surplus of Greek-Canadian girls; some say the phenomenon is common throughout all North America.[2] Whether such measures succeeded or failed with the daughters, however, they did not undo the damage done by the intermarriage of the sons. Consequently parents slowly saw that they could only stave off intermarriage by modifying traditional methods of bringing up daughters. Many parents have now greatly relaxed their strict control of daughters and give them much more freedom to attend unchaperoned dances, ski-parties, and so forth.

[2] From information given the writer in 1958 by Professor Triantis, University of Toronto, and by members of the Greek community.

The same predicament has confronted southern European families in Australia. The 'Olympic' Society in Melbourne was started in 1942 by a small number of second-generation Greeks who were tired of being called 'dagoes' by British-Australian schoolmates. They decided to form an organization that would show everyone that Greek boys could play football and cricket as well as any Australians, and could behave with even more dignity on the field than most British-Australian teams. Having achieved considerable success here—winning the respect of many British-Australians—they widened their activities to include dances and social evenings. Finding their families still strict about daughters' behaviour, these young Greek-Australians refused to give way but carried on their social activities with British-Australian girls—some of whom they had met at general sports socials and for whom they had considerable liking. After a number of Greek-Australian boys married British-Australian girls—including four of the five foundation members of the 'Olympic'—parents realized they were in the same position as their compatriots in Toronto. Eventually the parents, after much discussion and in their anxiety to encourage their sons to marry Greek-Australian girls, agreed to a compromise whereby Greek-Australian girls could attend dances and parties without adult chaperonage provided brothers or cousins escorted the girls there and back, and provided those organizing the society guaranteed there would be no 'funny business' during the evening such as couples slinking away to cars.[3]

Other southern European families have adopted similar expedients. At Griffith, for instance, brothers often chaperone their sisters to young people's dances while daughters are sometimes allowed to play tennis and join other social and sporting organizations.

On present evidence it is very difficult to determine how far these parental concessions have been successful in holding back the rate at which second-generation children marry outside their group. In those groups investigated it is plain that second-generation men have had a much higher intermarriage rate with British-Australian girls than have the first generation.[4] But

[3] Information from members of the 'Olympic' Society.

[4] Appendix 4:7, 11 show the intermarriage proportions for Griffith Italians, 1920-54, were 6·8% for I's and 33·3% for II's. The corresponding proportions for Sydney Greeks, 1920-56, were 24·3% for I's (certainly too high since this includes a number of IIa's), and 54·0% for IIb's. The Toronto Greek figures 1927-57 were 18·1% for I's, and 47·4% for II's.

these relatively high second-generation intermarriage rates include all those marrying before parents gradually modified their policy concerning daughters' upbringing. There is insufficient evidence at present to assess intermarriage rates since that time, especially as the matter is complicated by recent heavy chain migration and a large surplus of fresh young immigrant males seeking wives amongst second-generation girls.

In some individual cases the policy has clearly been very successful. Typical here is the case of a second-generation Peloponnesian Greek girl whom I interviewed in Toronto in 1958. Her eldest brother married a British-Canadian girl, left the family restaurant to become a skilled tradesman, and went to live in a suburb so remote that he saw his family only on rare occasions. When the daughter grew up she was allowed far more liberty than usual and in many ways behaved like a British-Canadian girl, freely attending young peoples' parties, hikes, and skiing expeditions. Nevertheless she was quite determined to marry no one but a second-generation Greek boy. The new immigrant Greek boys didn't understand Canadian ways, she said: the British-Canadian boys did not understand all that was good in those Greek family values and customs of which she approved; in any case she was quite determined to avoid giving her family all the pain that her elder brother had given by marrying right outside the group. Consequently she was very active in the Canadian section of the Greek Orthodox Youth Association (Goya) and hoped to find her husband therein. Had her parents not modified their policy, though, she might easily have reacted as had her elder brother and left the family fold completely.

Whatever the outcome of all this there can be no doubt that the second generation have played, and will play, the key part in the fight to preserve southern European family values and group coherence. Herein they have been acting as the bridge between the old world and the new. Straining away from old world values they often cause much worry to their parents and render themselves quite unpopular with their cousins and acquaintances more recently arrived. The latter, though in many ways out of accord with earlier first-generation settlers, have often had much difficulty in understanding the social activities of their second-generation cousins. One good illustration here (from Leeton, in 1956) is a Sicilian-Australian girl who had been reared relatively freely and had become accustomed to attend dances where, chaperoned by an adult, she had been able to dance with her brothers and their friends. Later she became affianced to a relative newly arrived from Sicily and was most amazed and distressed when, attending a dance with her fiancé and agreeing to have one dance with another close relative, she saw her future spouse bounce furiously out into the middle of the room and smite her partner in the face for this breach of local Catanian custom.

Another illustration is the difficulty members of essentially second-generation societies, such as the 'Olympic' or 'Canadian Goya', have in maintaining uniformly amicable relationships with organizations formed by their first-generation cousins recently arrived. There have sometimes been misunderstandings between the Olympic—with its emphasis on Australian sports such as cricket and Australian football—and the Aeas and Hellenicos clubs with their emphasis on European sports such as soccer.[5] Likewise, 'Canadian Goya' in Toronto has been interested in Canadian skiing and dancing and much less so in Greek sports and dances. (The Greek Orthodox Church in North America has frowned upon this division in Goya, asserting that an Orthodox youth organization is essentially religious in character and purpose and should not be divided. Those behind 'Canadian Goya' have hitherto replied (mid-1958) that the church had to choose between having both a Canadian and a Greek Goya and losing the second-generation Greek-Canadians altogether; the divided society was preferable and could become one for religious discussions and education.)[6]

On the other hand the second generation often find it quite impossible to identify themselves completely with the values of the host society. One intelligent second-generation Dalmatian girl in her early twenties put this clearly and vividly when discussing with the author her life at an Australian state school, her faultless Australian accent and idiom, and her happy relations with several British-Australian friends. But, she added,

the fact that I read and write Dalmatian well and enjoy Dalmatian books and music, plus the ideas my family have instilled into me through my childhood, make me feel as if suspended between two worlds; or rather, like someone who has left home to look at an attractive spectacle in a shop-window—the British-Australian life

5 For a summary of 'Aeas' and 'Hellenicos' see J. A. Petrolias, Post-War Greek and Italian Migrants in Melbourne, p. 115.

6 In all these second-generation societies there are a few first-generation immigrants—usually bright and well-educated persons from towns like Athens—who feel somewhat strange with less educated migrants direct from the Greek villages.

around me. I have left home to see the bright world glittering in
the shop but can never get closer than staring through the glass.[7]

This peculiar 'bridge' position of the second generation comes
out in all sorts of ways; especially where parental pressure has
not driven their children to violent reaction against the old
world culture: fluency in both dialect and English; ability to
enjoy both the British-Australian food served in the homes of
British-Australian friends and the traditional dishes of their own
homes; enjoyment of British-Australian dance music and songs
yet love of the traditional dances and songs of their parents'
region of origin; amused or irritated contempt with the involved
religious customs and liturgies of their parents yet a wistful feeling that perhaps minor superstitions or long liturgical chantings
have a point and appeal all their own. There is also evidence to
suggest the second generation have sometimes adopted a mid-
way position between their parents and British-Australian society
in matters such as average age of marriage and size of family.[8]

The formation of second-generation societies such as 'Olympic'
and 'Canadian Goya' is, of course, the consequence of the peculiar position of the second generation. Not that they always cut
themselves off from the group life of their parents. Some second-
generation individuals entered wholeheartedly into the district
and regional associations formed by the first generation, especially when the societies were well established, wealthy, and with
multifarious business interests; others have taken an active part
in Folk or supra-Folk organizations. But it is clear that the activities of these essentially first-generation organizations have not
been enough to satisfy the needs of many second-generation
southern Europeans: they have had to form special organizations
to express their own attitudes to the problems of assimilation.

Difference of interest between first and second generation, of
course, varied much from place to place and group to group.

[7] Interview in Sydney in 1956. There are, of course, numerous similar
illustrations, both in Australia and other countries, e.g. H. G. Duncan,
Immigration and Assimilation, Pt VIII.

[8] C. A. Price, Italian Population of Griffith. Here we must remember the
difficulty of assessing British-Australian behaviour in the particular areas
concerned; also the need to relate age of marriage and size of family to the
age structure of the ethnic group at any given time. Even so it is interesting
to see such statistics as those showing that average size of Calabrian families
in Griffith was, for almost every five-year period, $4x$ for those who had had
their children in Calabria, $3x$ for Calabrian II's in Griffith, $2x$ for British-
Australians. (x is variable according to each five-year period of marriage
duration.)

Field-work and special surveys give the impression that tension was least in areas where ethnic concentration was dense and the ethnic group relatively self-contained. In a village such as Hanwood, on the Murrumbidgee Irrigation Area, about 90 per cent of primary school children in 1954 were of Italian parentage and had very little dealings with British-Australian persons or the English language, except when in class with the teacher. In such cases it was not until entering high schools at about thirteen —when many ethnic group opinions and views were strong and well formed—that southern European children had much to do with British-Australian children; and, for all those going straight on to the land when they left school between fourteen and sixteen, this lasted only a year or two.

Tension has been more obvious in areas where, though the first-generation group settlement was well-knit and strong, it was intermixed with other ethnic groups or with many British-Australian families. Here the second generation, attending school with children of other origins from the impressionable infant ages onwards, could not help but adopt many British-Australian customs and attitudes and see basic differences between their parents' views and those of neighbouring families. Such was the background of many of those second-generation Greeks in Sydney and Melbourne who formed typically second-generation clubs such as the 'Olympic'.

The position might have been very different here had the ethnic school been at all common; that is, an institution drawing children from families all over the ethnic group area. In the early days of Australian history such schools did exist, more particularly those schools organized by German Lutheran settlers in the rural areas of South Australia and the eastern states. From the 1850s onwards, however, the colonial governments struck a series of blows at such institutions: first, by withdrawing financial aid to all church and other private schools; second, by refusing to permit non-English-speaking state schools; third, during World War I, by forbidding all church and other private schools to teach in any language except English (the ethnic language could be taught only for a limited period of time as an ordinary subject in the school curriculum);[9] finally, by ensuring that all

9 The Australian states, especially South Australia, show interesting parallels here with American states such as Pennsylvania, where the state government likewise put steadily increasing pressure on the ethnic school from the 1850s onwards. In the United States, however, enforcement of teaching in English in private ethnic schools was not as severe as in Australia.

private schools taught a curriculum approved by the state educational authorities.

As a result, by the time southern Europeans began to settle in Australia in any number they found the true ethnic school—a full-time institution teaching in the ethnic language—quite impossible to form. Admittedly, they could have formed a modified ethnic establishment, one where children of the one ethnic origin were kept together in the one institution, where an hour was squeezed in here and there on ethnic history and literature, and where students were permitted to use the ethnic language in play-time and after hours; one, in short, which created in dispersed group settlements the kind of establishment that could fulfil the role of the state primary school situated in dense ethnic areas. But here the poverty of most southern European arrivals, together with the fact that family loyalty led them to save for the passages of friends and relatives or to support elderly relatives in Europe, virtually prevented them financing private institutions that could survive without state aid. As state law insisted upon compulsory education, southern European settlers had little alternative but to send their children to the existing state or private schools and there mix with children of other origins.

The one thing the ethnic groups could do was to form small Saturday, Sunday, or evening schools where children could spend a few hours a week learning the ethnic language and literature. Orthodox communities have been particularly prone to do this, although Catholic groups have occasionally done so. But the results have not always been ethnically satisfactory. Children, tired after a day's work at school, or envious of the freedom their British-Australian friends enjoy on Saturdays, have often resented parental pressure to learn a sometimes difficult European language and literature. Too much pressure has sometimes led to children reacting against their parents' culture and withdrawing from the ethnic group as soon as possible.

Unfortunately there are no available statistics showing the prevalence of such schools or the numbers that have attended them. Nor is it possible to calculate exactly how many second-generation children have been educated in areas of dispersed group settlements and in areas where group settlements have been concentrated enough to dominate primary, and even secondary, schools run by the state. What seems plain at present is that many of the second generation living in dispersed groups found it necessary to form special organizations. In this sense the second generation—except for some of those who married out of their ethnic group at an early age and became rapidly absorbed into British-Australian society—had as much ethnic group life as their first-generation parents. Their group organization may have been somewhat different but they, too, faced the challenges of dual and triple assimilation within groups and associations rather than as separate individuals.[10]

Assimilation—Conclusion

In the preceding sections we have been surveying a great variety of forces at work in the process of assimilation; or rather of dual and triple assimilation, for such it was for the majority of settlers. At this point it is unnecessary to review these forces —family values, district and regional customs, dialect, religion, Folk-nationalism, peasant radicalism, British-Australian attitudes, and so forth—as they will receive more attention when the whole field of migration, settlement and assimilation comes under general review. The point at issue here is that, whatever force or combination of forces controlled the assimilation of any particular migrant chain, the challenge for probably 90 per cent of settlers was met through the medium of an ethnic group settlement. These were the fortresses erected by immigrants in their fight to adapt themselves to Australian conditions. These were the guardians of the European dialect or language, the source of the numerous ethnic clubs and organizations, the centre of the struggle over in-marriage or out-marriage. They were, in short, the heart of the movement to preserve those things that British-Australians so disliked about southern European settlement, whether such dislike found expression officially in parliamentary speeches and reports of Commissioners such as Ferry or in the hostility of British-Australians living in those areas where southern Europeans settled in numbers.

In one sense the British-Australians were right. The southern European fight to retain their customs and institutions did not spring primarily from the hostility and indifference of British-Australian society but from the very nature of southern European migration and settlement. Had British-Australians invari-

[10] There is virtually no Australian statistical data concerning the second generation (see Appendix 4:6-8); one is therefore unable to construct any map of second-generation concentrations or to assess their numbers in district, regional Folk and supra-Folk groupings. The above sketch is based entirely on field-work. There is considerable American literature on the second generation, e.g. bibliographical note on p. 493 of M. R. Davie's *World Immigration*.

ably welcomed southern Europeans with open arms the same separatist forces would still have been at work. What pre-war British-Australians failed to realize—and in many instances still do not realize—is that ethnic group settlements were not directed against British-Australian culture but were an inevitable and necessary accompaniment of migration to a new land. Necessary, because arrivals in a strange land cannot strip themselves of their old world culture overnight: they need companionship with people of their own kind, people who speak the same language, people who can come into the home with understanding and help when there is trouble, people who have the same background and experience and can therefore appreciate reminiscences, jokes, and familiar hospitality. Such companionship is quite essential to the normal immigrants' sense of security and happiness; any attempt to interfere with it will, in the opinions of competent psychiatrists and in the experience of other countries of immigration, add to the difficulties of adjustment and increase the dangers of mental instability, alcoholism, and even suicide.[11] Moreover, such groups often act as a very useful half-way stage in the process of assimilation: in these groups new arrivals meet 'old hands', persons who have been in Australia some time and can act as interpreters and guides or explain the 'oddities' of Australian behaviour.

Furthermore, British-Australians before the war rarely realized that, in the presence of these quite inevitable tendencies to form immigrant groups, every act of hostility on their part made the situation so much the worse, drove southern Europeans to reinforce their fortresses the more vigorously, and simply slowed up the process of assimilation. Such activities as those of the miners at Boulder-Kalgoorlie, of the horticulturalists on the Murrumbidgee Irrigation Area, of the sugar-farmers and returned soldiers in northern Queensland reinforced southern group life so strongly that the walls will not disintegrate for

[11] There is a mass of American literature on these topics but little Australian. Research is at present being conducted on the extent of mental breakdown amongst migrants—e.g. I. A. Listwan, 'Paranoid States: Social and Cultural Aspects', *Medical Journal of Australia*, May 1956; I. A. Listwan, 'Mental Disorders in Migrants: Further Study', *Medical Journal of Australia*, April 1959; and I. A. Listwan and Sir Harry Wunderley in *Proceedings of the Second Conference on Immigration*, Australian National University, Canberra, 1960. So far there is little work started on alcoholism and suicide. My own research amongst the well-integrated Italian farming groups at Griffith—based largely on death registrations—suggested that suicide was very rare (as could be expected amongst such groups) and that maladjustment more frequently appeared through alcoholism.

T

many years. Indifference and condescension have had much the same effect, though not so pronounced.

In short, the great majority of British-Australians took that course of action most designed to achieve the opposite of what they wanted. Even in conditions of amity and interest, assimilation is at least a three-generation process. The first generation need, and must create, ethnic groups in which they can preserve the old world culture that alone they understand and feel secure in. The second generation need, and must create, particular groups where they preserve a cultural life somewhere between that of their first-generation parents and British-Australian school-friends—a curious limbo that they alone can understand and appreciate. Only with the third generation is there any likelihood of complete assimilation; and for some groups—depending on size, conditions of isolation, and many other factors—that is much too soon. Economic absorption and social integration may, with amity and understanding on both sides, arrive in the first generation. But full amalgamation, acculturation, and assimilation are rarely achieved in less than three generations and have often taken longer.

Third-generation southern Europeans, however, except in one or two of the older chains, are only just reaching maturity, and their behaviour is beyond the scope of this book. It is time now to return to their grandparents—the southern European settlers of pre-war days—and review what has emerged in previous chapters about their life and work in Australia generally.

CHAPTER VII

CONCLUSION

My task is done, my song hath ceased, my theme
Has died into an echo; it is fit
The spell should break of this protracted dream.
The torch shall be extinguish'd which hath lit
My midnight lamp—and what is writ, is writ.

Childe Harold's Pilgrimage, IV, 185

THE social historian, alas, is not in the same position as the poet. In 'what is writ' here he must bring his argument into focus to show that generalizations are often risky; that in the particular area of migration and settlement they can be very dangerous; and that the only safe way to achieve greater understanding is to dwell in detail on the careers of individual southern European pioneers and in the histories of particular southern European groups and societies. Generalizations reached after such a discipline—if, indeed, it is a discipline to examine material so fascinating and absorbing—may prove valuable for further research or for framing public policy. Without it, understanding is shallow, opinions are out of context, the picture—lacking natural colour and vitality—is grey and uninspired. Therefore, some of the main conclusions of this work are set out in preceding pages, alongside the detailed material from which they derive: the general conclusions on the assimilation of southern Europeans in Australia, on the reasons why some nine-tenths of them formed closely-knit social groups through which they met the challenges of assimilation, the reasons for their strong resistance to intermarriage, the way in which British-Australian hostility and indifference made assimilation so much more difficult and slow—all these appear after the evidence from which they rise. They will not be repeated here.

The purpose of this chapter, then, is to bring into review, not so much the various steps in the narrative or argument—which stand or fall with their own evidence in the text—but those general themes that have been running through the whole story and can now be seen in their entirety. From the historian's viewpoint there is certainly one advantage in this kind of conclusion: it enables him to depart a little from the rigorous standard he has endeavoured to apply in the body of the work and to provoke the crystallization of readers' reactions by venturing certain subjective opinions and by bringing in further impressionistic material, more especially incidents and careers that are not necessarily typical but are certainly interesting and may point to matters that subsequent enquiry may show to be of great importance. This chapter, then, though it refers mainly to things already discussed, will occasionally bring in new material and suggestions, and give opinions not warranted in the strict scientific sense—primarily to draw attention to gaps in our knowledge that could be usefully filled by future research.

THE NEED FOR DISTRICT AND REGIONAL ANALYSIS

The first thread running through this work is the difficulty of discussing southern European settlers in general categories of nationality and birthplace. Conditions of settlement in Australia varied from locality to locality, so that one set of southern Europeans found different conditions from their compatriots settled elsewhere, and therefore behaved somewhat differently. Then, too, over 90 per cent of Australia's pre-war settlers came not as a broad scatter from southern Europe as a whole but in concentrated streams from relatively small and restricted areas of origin often differing considerably in geography, dialect, religion, social customs, family habits, and political traditions. Consequently, although four-fifths were migrants from 'peasant' villages and towns and had much in common in economic background, type of training, and ambition to own independent farms or businesses—this common peasant background, indeed, to some extent controlled their marked preference for certain occupations and areas of settlement and their avoidance of the pastoral and cereal-sheep zones of the continent—the differences in origin were nevertheless such that migration streams, or chains, seldom behaved in the same way. They differed as to the reasons why migrants felt dissatisfied with their homes, why some streams started to Australia before others, why some contained a relatively high proportion of persons who had lived in America, Africa, or New Zealand before coming to Australia. Again, they differed in the way they reacted to wars, depressions, or government controls on migration, in the numbers leaving Australia to return to Europe or settle elsewhere, in their choice of occupations to follow and places to settle in, in the way they formed various kinds of ethnic group settlement through which to meet the challenges of assimilation.

With such marked differences between migrants from the various areas of origin in Italy or Spain, the islands of Greece, the valleys of Albania and Yugoslavia, it is clearly misleading to speak in general terms of 'Italians' or 'Greeks' or 'Yugoslavs'. When adequate data are lacking there is, of course, no alternative; indeed, the major pioneering works in this field have been based largely on census categories of this kind.[1] When better material becomes available, however, we must grapple with particular villages and districts of origin and particular places of settlement in Australia, and reinterpret the migration process in their light. Sometimes it is important to distinguish more general groupings: regions of origin, based essentially on dialect and social customs; Folk groupings (Serbs, say, or Croats or Slovenes) based essentially on language, literature, political aspirations, and religious traditions; supra-Folk groupings (such as the South Slav or Latin peoples) based on similar languages or religions. Even when dealing with these larger groupings, however, official categories of nationality or birthplace are not very helpful: a Folk does not always coincide with a nation or country of birth, as witness all those ethnically Greek migrants who have come to Australia from Rumania, Turkey, Cyprus, and Egypt.

On a field as vast as southern Europe on the one side and the continent of Australia on the other, it is clearly impossible to do enough field-work to construct a complete detailed picture. But Australia is fortunate in possessing records that now enable the scholar to dig much more deeply than the census and migration statistics permitted. In naturalization records, alien registration records, and vital records there is enough information to show which village and district streams were active at what times, in what places, and in what occupations; they also permit identification of the various regional, Folk, and supra-Folk ethnic concentrations. When to this information is added the evidence of selected interviews and field observation, southern European settlement in Australia can be surveyed much more thoroughly than the census and migration records can be. Though complete explanation of group differences does not emerge from this survey, the picture discernible takes us very much further in understanding the whole process.

1 See Foreword, also Chapter I.

CHAIN MIGRATION

The second theme running through this book is chain migration and settlement. This process does not explain the whole story of southern European settlement in Australia, nor the whole story of ethnic group formation: the attraction of regional and Folk customs produced 'gravitational' forces encouraging ethnic concentration while British-Australian hostility sometimes 'compressed' some southern Europeans—who otherwise had little in common—into permanent or temporary 'compression' groups. But the fact that over 90 per cent of Australia's pre-war southern Europeans came to their new land under the system of chain migration had much to do with the character of the various migration streams and the way group settlements appeared during the course of settlement.

Chain migration has been treated in detail earlier and needs no further treatment here. There is, however, one important element in it that deserves fuller consideration: the fact that it is a dynamic process, starting from small beginnings and passing through many stages before it appears in one of its many varieties of full development. From this have followed several important results which, even though precise effects varied from group to group, can be discussed in fairly general terms.

Accidental Character

First, the whole process has seemed almost accidental, depending largely on the character and career of the pioneer who started it: if he became a successful fish-restaurant-keeper in Melbourne or a prosperous sugar-farmer or market-gardener in northern Queensland, then so did many of his fellow-villagers and compatriots. Herein lies the importance, and fascination, of pioneer careers. Herein also lies the reason for the scant references to unproductive chain pioneers—those who failed as settlers and returned to Europe or those who, while succeeding in establishing themselves in Australia, did not attract many friends to join them. There have been some failures and also considerable wastages—between one-third and one-half of pre-war southern European male immigrants either returned permanently to Europe or else left Australia to settle in some other country (p. 101)—but on the whole the story of chain migration must be treated as a success story, for in a long-term survey of southern European settlements we must examine the chains that succeeded rather than those that failed: the latter are not here to be examined.

Pre-War and Post-War Chain Migration

The successful pre-war chain settlements have been the foundation-stones upon which much of the great post-war migration from southern Europe to Australia has been laid. Since the end of World War II well over 300,000 southern Europeans have settled in Australia and not much more than one-third of these have received government assistance. The remainder have come out on private resources, sometimes provided by organizations such as the resettlement services of the Roman Catholic Church and the World Council of Churches, but more commonly with the assistance and encouragement of fellow-countrymen who were either established in Australia before the war or else arrived after the war but themselves received help from some successful pre-war settler.

The pattern of southern European migration to Australia since the war has been far from identical with that before it, nor is Australia still receiving the same proportion of settlers from each of the same restricted areas of origin. The one-third or more migrants assisted by the Australian government, and those assisted by church and other organizations, have included families from central Italy, the Peloponnesus, Trieste, and other areas not well represented in Australia before the war; these in turn have started their own chain processes. More important, the dynamic nature of chain migration itself produces a constantly changing pattern. Older chains become quiescent while other chains, equally old, regain new leases of life; younger chains die away while others, equally young, increase their activity. These changes, without altering the districts of origin, may greatly alter the numerical balance of the district streams; as evidence the decline during post-war years of migration from Kastellorizo—which was practically denuded of inhabitants by 1947 and became incapable of sending more than a trickle each year—compared with the great increase of migration from Lesbos, Chios, Samos, Crete, Tripolis, Epirus, and other islands and districts of Greece. All of these had small chain settlements in Australia before the war and on these have built up substantial post-war colonies.

Chain Migration as a World Movement

These changes in chain migration have not always arisen from events in the particular districts of origin in Europe or places of settlement in Australia; sometimes they have been due to events elsewhere in the world. Changes in government policy or in economic prosperity—the quota laws restricting southern European immigration to the United States in 1924 or the economic recession afflicting North America in the early twentieth century—have diverted migration streams from one part of the world to another, building up chains in one place that might otherwise have built up elsewhere. Moreover, the fact that in 1901, say, a pioneer from a little Bračani village was doing better as a restaurant-keeper in San Francisco or as a nitrate dealer in Antofogasta than his pioneer brother on the gold-fields of Western Australia not only encouraged persons from that village to go to San Francisco or Antofogasta rather than to Coolgardie but sometimes drew the Australian pioneers across the Pacific to California or Chile, so killing any prospect of that village chain developing into anything important to Australian history. Conversely, a successful Ithacan restaurant-keeper in Melbourne or Korčulan cane-cutter in North Queensland could draw fellow-villagers from the Ithacan colony at Johannesburg or from the Korčulan colony in northern New Zealand and greatly curtail chain development in those areas. In this sense chain migration is a world-wide phenomenon and cannot be understood if chopped up into discrete migration chains running to various places of settlement.

International and Internal Migration

Nor can chain migration be understood if chopped up into such artificial divisions as 'international' and 'internal' migration. The discussions on the first three stages of chain settlement (see Chapter V) showed how movement about Australia was an inevitable part of chain settlement—especially in the early stages when young male migrants wandered together from place to place looking for lucrative employment before settling permanently into some farm or business. This movement about the country of settlement, however, cannot properly be divorced from movement about the world as a whole. Take, for instance, two eighteen-year-old cousins who left their little township on the Dalmatian coast in 1890. John went to Johannesburg and after eighteen months worked his way across the Indian Ocean to Adelaide (1891) where he worked as a coastal sailor until deciding to join a friend in a restaurant in Sydney (1893). Meanwhile Peter went straight to New Orleans to join an uncle oyster-farming (1890), moved to the Dalmatian fishing colony in San Francisco (1892), staying there until John wrote of his success in Sydney and persuaded Peter to join him (1894). Some time later they heard of the good luck of friends gold-digging at Kalgoorlie so worked their way by coastal vessel to Western Australia (1896). After a while chasing the elusive gold they concluded that restaurant work was more profitable and enduring, though less exciting, so joined a fellow Dalmatian who, having struck it lucky and decided to retire from the gold-fields to open a restaurant in Melbourne, asked the two cousins to go with him as cook and waiter (1898). After a year or so the cousins became restless at not having their own business and decided on a change, John going to join some relatives gum-digging in northern New Zealand and Peter travelling to the cane-cutting areas of northern Queensland (1900). Peter spent a few years rapidly moving about the cane townships of Queensland and then paid a deposit on his own farm (1903), where he did so well that he persuaded John and some of his New Zealand friends to come and do likewise (1906). Meanwhile John had married a Dalmatian lass in New Zealand and when they arrived Peter became even more aware of the loneliness of single life; he decided to leave John to run the farm while he took a fifteen-month trip home to Europe to see his family and choose a bride. Having successfully courted and wedded someone selected by his family he then organized the sale of his family's less lucrative holdings and contributed some money to consolidate the little estate. Finally, having talked glowingly of Australian life, he persuaded his younger brother Stephen to come back with himself and his bride to Queensland (1907). There the little family nucleus stayed, eventually becoming highly successful farmers and the pioneers upon which a large-scale chain settlement was subsequently built.[2]

Clearly, the cousins' movements across international boundaries and about South Africa, America, Australia, and New Zealand were all part of a single process of migration and settlement that started when they left Dalmatia in 1890 and finished, for them, when they became permanently settled with their

2 Based on the careers of several Dalmatians whose families the writer interviewed in Australia and California.

wives and relatives in Queensland in 1907. To split the phenomenon into 'international' and 'internal' movements destroys the unity of the whole process and gives rise to the misleading notion that there is something intrinsically different about international and internal migration. There is obviously the difference that international migration involves changes of law and allegiance, but this distinction can be much over-stressed. Chain migration can produce well-established colonies of fellow-townsmen overseas that may socially and linguistically be very similar to the town of origin—much more similar, in fact, than the town of origin is to another town in the same European country. Calabrian farmers, for example, have some-times said that coming to a Calabrian farming settlement in Australia is less of a social upheaval than going to work as an industrial labourer in Milan where dialect and customs are so very different; the fact that they come to a different legal and political system upsets them very little as long as they are within a Calabrian group settlement.

There is, of course, an advantage in splitting international and internal migration when the scholar is concerned simply to study the way economic and social changes give rise to movements of population from one part of the same country to another. This has become of all-absorbing interest to many American scholars and—because of the highly complex state of United States social organization and the relatively low rate of recent immigration from overseas—rightly so. But even here there is always the danger of forgetting that a shift in popula-tion, such as that from the east coast to California, may not be explicable entirely in terms of events within the United States itself; for some families at least such movement, and the motives for it, may be a continuation in America of chain processes originating overseas; and must be explained in those terms.

That the danger is not remote is evident from a sometimes over-rigid insistence on describing persons crossing international lines as 'immigrants' or 'emigrants', and persons moving inside a country as 'migrants'. (Some American scholars adopt a more precise usage and divide internal migrants into 'in-migrants' and 'out-migrants', leaving the term 'migration' free to cover all migratory processes.)

Another illustration comes from *Population Index*, which inserts all references to migration under one of two major divisions—International Migration and Internal Migration.

There is no proper place in such an index for works covering such general topics as chain migration and settlement; for the *Volkwanderung*, the journeyings of Polynesian islanders about the Pacific, the wanderings of Vlach shepherd tribes about the countries of southern Europe, or for any other movement that finds international boundaries irrelevant or incidental; for such fascinating and important topics as the gold discoveries in California and New South Wales in the mid-nineteenth century— discoveries which drew migrants from all over the world as well as from other parts of the United States and Australia. Above all there is no proper place for studies on migration, as such, on the temperamental and psychological conditions that encourage some families to migrate and others to stay, on the basic economic and social conditions that push or pull people from one place to another: yet these matters underlie the whole process of migration, international and internal, and cannot be divorced from either. A better division for such an index would be: *Migration in General* (to cover works on the general phenomenon of migration and works covering both international and internal movement); *International Migration; Internal Migration*—the last two to cover works dealing with internal or international movements.

Rising Living Standards : Ecological Succession

Another important consequence of treating chain migration as a dynamic process is the clear realization that the character of settlement changes greatly with the passage of time; in particular, numbers of hard-working and unhygienic peasants gradually transform themselves into well-to-do persons saving money for investment, children's education, or bringing out friends from the old country, and eventually into prosperous farmers or businessmen with homes as hygienically kept and comfortably furnished as those of British-Australians about them. This is something British-Australians seldom realized before the war. On the whole they tended to judge southern European settlers as they first saw them, in the stage of greatest impoverishment and least attractiveness. Moreover, when those early batches of southern European immigrants raised themselves out of the mire the attention of British-Australian neighbours was diverted to a fresh influx of chain settlers, as dirty and impoverished as their forerunners had been. Consequently British-Australians found it difficult to think of southern Europeans as anything else but persons content forever with low living standards and primitive and unhygienic conditions: hence the British-Australian stereotype of the 'dago' immigrant 'living perpetually on the smell of an oily rag'.

Nor have post-war conditions and the greater tolerance displayed towards New Australians invariably changed this attitude. This is quite plain from remarks made to the writer during his travels and from questions asked of him and his colleagues after lectures and meetings. One man, for instance, read a report of a lecture by the writer on this very topic—the gradual evolution of southern European settlers from conditions of poverty and their eventual adoption of British-Australian standards—and wrote from Sydney in August 1960.

Dear Sir,

Undoubtedly you are a man of academic standing, which makes it very hard to believe you could write such trash. You apparently never fought these chaps during the war when we were paid a few shillings to kill them; and we are now forced to pay their fares out here so that they may lower our standards of living, as they are making a very good job of doing.

After the war I bought a block of land and built my own home. A couple of years after I had completed my house some southern Europeans built shacks (which I would only keep cattle in) opposite and alongside my house. Although at a very conservative estimate I would say there is £60 a week coming into the shacks, which have been up for twelve years, and the occupants own two cars, including a new one, and have TV etc., they have not laid one brick for the foundation of their home.

These are actually the better class dwellings they live in.

I could go on for pages giving you detailed *facts* of how these people are lowering our standard of living, which is anti-Christ, and yet us Australians donate thousands of pounds each year to help these backward countries raise their standard of living.

I hope you will have a look at the facts before writing such articles next time.

Yours faithfully.

The dismay of this British-Australian at seeing his neighbourhood turn so unexpectedly into something other than he expected is understandable. Yet should he stay in his home long enough he will almost certainly see a gradual improvement of the area and a distinct rise in the standard of housing.

Similar sentiments have been expressed as recently as 1962, as instance the letter of Franco Battistessa of Leichhardt, Sydney, in the *Sun-Herald* of 16 September 1962. Here the writer quotes from an anonymous letter sent to him by someone signing himself 'Dago-Hater'. This letter includes the sentences 'You come out to our decent country with your greasy unwashed faces, long hair and jabbering. Why don't you go back to your own horrible Latin countries'.

Associated with this topic is that of ecological succession, here meaning the way in which immigrant families start in the cheap slums and apartments of inner city areas, move off when prosperous to better housing in suburban areas, and are replaced in the inner city by new arrivals anxious to live cheaply and save quickly. This work has made little reference to ecological succession, except in the case of Greek restaurant-keepers who eventually let their cheap quarters over their inner city shops while they themselves bought good homes in the suburbs. One reason for this is that only a minority of pre-war southern Europeans settled in such places;[3] the majority lived in rural areas or metropolitan market-gardening zones, where the problem was not of ecological succession but of gradual improvement to houses on existing holdings. A second reason is lack of reliable information covering all groups. The pre-war census statistics, for instance, do not make clear whether those in inner city areas were newcomers replacing older settlers or were the older settlers themselves. What detailed information is available shows that this kind of ecological succession sometimes operated, but by no means always. With the Kytherans, for instance, there was a pronounced tendency for older settlers to improve their businesses in the city and for newcomers, after a year or so learning the business, to move into smaller country restaurants. Likewise some older Lipari islanders have remained in Italian city concentrations where they own prosperous businesses and sometimes act as patriarchs to newer arrivals.[4] In these circumstances the lively problem of ecological succession

3 Some 14% if we count all inner city zones as slums or cheap living areas and 28% if we include all inner suburbs as well. Since not all such zones were cheap living areas these statistics—for the 1947 Census local government area figures—exaggerate the picture.

4 Writer's field-work in Sydney, 1955-7. J. Zubrzycki, in *Immigrants in Australia* and in *Immigration*, a commentary prepared for the *Atlas of Australian Resources*, discusses the matter generally in relation to post-war immigrants; see especially his sections on Metropolitan Concentration and Metropolitan Segregation. Here again, however, the fact that the census does not cross-classify birthplace by duration of residence in Australia by particular local government area prevents any thorough examination of ecological succession in the post-war period; this must await the results of further detailed field studies.

awaits further study—though slum clearance programmes, and the replacement of cheap inner city homes by large blocks of flats and apartments (as at Carlton, Melbourne), render the task of the investigator increasingly difficult.

Old and New Settlers

Ecological succession, and the question of how far new arrivals take up the way of life of earlier settlers, leads on to the next major effect of the dynamic processes of chain migration—the curious tension that appeared in some groups between older and newer settlers, comments on which have, so far, been confined almost entirely to the economic aspects. The disparity between what the older settlers expected from the younger relatives they helped and what they received, and the attitude of the youngsters to their elders set up a tension that has already been discussed (pp. 196-9).

But tension has appeared in other fields as well. New clubs have sometimes come into being as expressions of dissatisfaction felt by recent arrivals with the clubs of their elders. In a sense this is understandable. The older Folk, regional, and district societies were formed by the first generation of settlers to meet the needs of men who worked hard and long, had little time for outdoor sports, and who required some organization to act as a mutual benefit association and a centre for social life. Arrivals of twenty and thirty years later, coming to more settled conditions, feeling the need perhaps for less mutual benefit activities but more outdoor recreation, found these older clubs inadequate except for evening recreation. Hence the appearance of clubs catering for soccer, athletics, cycling, and other sports of interest to adult European migrants.

More important still is the struggle that has sometimes taken place between old and new settlers for control of existing organizations. This is particularly true of well-established Folk societies where schism would be impracticable and the formation of a rival organization inconceivable—the various Orthodox Communities, for instance. On the surface the struggle often appears as complaints by newcomers that the society does not do enough to help new arrivals or keeps its membership fees far above the newcomer's purse; or, on the other side, as complaints by older settlers that green young men are trying to force the organization to abandon a well-tried policy that has been hammered out over the years in the light of Australian conditions. It is quite clear, however, that in some cases these complaints are surface expressions of a deep-seated struggle for power. Not unnaturally some of the older men wish to remain in control of the organizations they founded, and which (because they were either unwilling or unable to enter British-Australian organizations) have been a means of satisfying their desire for positions of responsibility. Not unnaturally, those new arrivals anxious for responsibility and power resent their exclusion from office and endeavour to overthrow the 'old gang'. Hence their fury when the old gang 'seduces' one of their leaders by marrying him off to a wealthy daughter and gradually converting him to the 'established' point of view (p. 265). In this sense, these struggles—which occasionally reach quite bitter levels in ethnic press and radio programmes—are a sign of non-assimilation. Few of the older settlers and even fewer of the newcomers feel able to satisfy their desire for responsibility and power in the larger, more numerous, and more variegated British-Australian organizations; consequently social energy builds up in the ethnic clubs, and there have sometimes been the most incredible manoeuvres, counter-manoeuvres, 'party platforms', whispering campaigns, and all the other techniques and apparatus of a singularly bitter general election.

There is another factor, too, behind this rivalry. In the twenty-year interval, say, between the arrival of the founders of the society and that of their young relatives, considerable changes took place in many areas of origin. The standard of education has risen somewhat in Greece and Italy between 1925 and 1945; in particular the national tongue and literature has driven dialect further into the background and young men have become more conscious of their Folk-nationalist heritage. Consequently, when they arrived in Australia they often looked down on their older peasant relatives who were still speaking dialect and were still far more interested in district and regional matters than in nationalist affairs. Although often less well educated than their second-generation cousins reared in the new world, they nevertheless sometimes could not help despising their uncles and becoming very impatient with their ideas and policies.

The same kind of tension lies behind some of the rivalry for control of ethnic newspapers—and the appearance of new ones—though here additional factors are at work, such as the need felt by an anti-clerical or non-clerical faction to start a newspaper in competition with an official Roman Catholic or Orthodox paper.[5] This struggle between earlier and later arrivals must not be exaggerated, however, because, with some exceptions (as when newcomers arrived with no connexions with previous settlers), it took place in the general context of chain migration and of all the family and district loyalties involved therein. Divergence of interest and outlook did not prevent most older arrivals from fulfilling their 'obligations', from giving new arrivals accommodation and employment, and from lending them money to set up on their own when they had satisfactorily passed their apprenticeship. Nor did divergence of outlook prevent many new arrivals from accepting their relatives' help with gratitude, and from heeding their opinions and advice about Australian customs. Consequently the processes of chain settlement continued on; squeaking and grating somewhat here and there, but basically continuing their task of building up the ethnic groups and organizations through which the various levels of first-generation settlers faced the problems of their new home.

First and Second Generation

This underlying sense of unity must be remembered when reviewing relations between first- and second-generation settlers, and care taken to set inter-generation tension in the general context of deep-seated family loyalties. We have seen it in connexion with the entry of the second generation into novel occupations and homes—sometimes with parental approval and sometimes in the teeth of intense parental hostility (pp. 193-5), and again in the curious compromise over ethnic societies and customs reached by those members of the first and second generation who were anxious to make every effort in order to retain family and ethnic group solidarity (p. 266). The tension that did exist, however, was of quite a different kind from that discussed above. It was not conflict of opinion between an older and younger generation of adult immigrants with differing economic interests and differing views on the best way to organize ethnic groups in a strange land: rather was it profound difference of opinion about the role of ethnic groups and ethnic customs in a society where the younger generation had been reared amongst, and much influenced by, the customs and attitudes of British-Australian society (see pp. 262-72).

[5] *Il Corriere d'Australia* is an Italian paper that has recently started up in rivalry to the church-controlled paper *La Fiamma*.

Further, relationships between first and second generation have rarely evolved in isolation; they have been constantly influenced by the arrival of fresh batches of first-generation immigrants under the dynamic processes of chain migration. Where these fresh batches are large and numerous—as in the case of some chain groups since the war—the second-generation viewpoint tends to be swamped and the process of assimilation retarded.

THE IMPORTANCE OF THE EUROPEAN BACKGROUND

The third major theme running through this book is the desirability of examining southern European settlement in Australia in the light of the European background. Indeed the evidence on which it is based confirms the conclusion of so many American works: it is not only desirable but entirely necessary to resist the still common practice of treating immigrants as though they come from a cultural vacuum. Clearly the background to each little area of origin has had tremendous influence on the way migrants have settled in Australia, as well as on the process of emigration itself.

Geographical Background

Geographical background has obviously been important. This is not, perhaps, so true of climate as of other things. Evidence from Tasmania (p. 151) suggests that factors other than climate explain the failure of pre-war migrants from the Mediterranean to settle in Australia's coldest region. Likewise the north Queensland story suggests that factors other than climate controlled southern European settlement in the sub-tropical regions of Australia; especially as a very large proportion of settlers came from the cold valleys and slopes of the Pyrenees and Alps and from the Monferrato hills of northern Italy. The question, however, is still open; further research may reveal that those southern Europeans who built up successful sugar-farms in north Queensland and who later moved south to avoid the north Queensland humidity have nearly all derived from colder parts of southern Europe, whereas those who have remained have been mainly families from the warmer regions of coastal Sicily and Dalmatia and from warm island archipelagos such as Malta and the Dodecanese.

There can be no dispute at all, however, about the importance of geological background. First, terrain has greatly influenced southern European settlement in Australia, and, indeed,

U

in other parts of the world. It has meant that the areas of origin of the great majority of Australia's southern Europeans were restricted areas of fertility, that the possibilities of rationalizing farming were limited, that habitation districts quickly reached a population maximum, and that families had little alternative but to exist in Malthusian misery or migrate elsewhere. For centuries, even millennia, the people of such districts have been emigrating and colonizing as they could; in the nineteenth century some turned their attention to the southern seas and the pioneering movement to Australia began, bringing with it the strong sense of village or district identity that had been encouraged by these restricted areas of habitation. This, in turn, played a part both in the process of chain emigration and in the formation of strong district group settlements overseas.

Second, the great pre-historic earth movements left lines of weakness in the surface of southern Europe resulting in shattering earthquakes and devastating eruptions. These, too, encouraged pioneers to emigrate and eased the task of successful settlers in persuading others to join them.

Third, the long indented coastlines encouraged both coastal trading between the villages and townships of the Mediterranean and the occasional appearance of some great port such as Barcelona, Naples, Valetta or the Piraeus. From these coastal villages and towns came those seafaring southern Europeans who started the movement to Australia; it was they who, without government assistance or cheap passages, determined that well over half of Australia's pre-war southern Europeans should come from coastal districts.

Fourth, the geological background has left its mark on the way southern Europeans have adapted themselves to Australian conditions. One example, from the Italian settlements in the horticultural zones of the Murrumbidgee Irrigation Area of New South Wales, will suffice. Some settlers there came from parts of the Friuli foothills where permanent springs have enabled farmers to irrigate, but where difficult soils and lack of natural drainage have made them only too well aware of the ease with which irrigated ground is waterlogged and salted; hence the traditional deep drainage techniques of parts of Friuli—usually the simple technique of digging deep trenches and filling them with stones and gravel. Others, however, came from the rain-fed shales of the Monferrato hills, benign and fertile slopes where farmers found the more it rained the more the soil produced; hence the old Monferrato saying—'you can't have too much water'. Not surprisingly, the Friulani farmers on the Murrumbidgee Irrigation Area early realized the dangers of waterlogging and salting and were amongst the first to put deep drainage on their properties: some Monferratan farmers found it much more difficult to adapt themselves.

Garden Agriculture and Subdivision of Property

Finally, the awkward plots and terracing that were necessitated by the rugged terrain, together with the system of subdividing property between heirs, had much to do with the evolution of both garden techniques of agriculture and the fierce peasant desire to consolidate holdings into an independent self-sufficiency. These forces greatly influenced the occupations chosen by southern European settlers in Australia and their concentration in intensive farming activities such as horticulture and market-gardening. At the same time, the fact that so much garden farming was combined with herding, poultry-keeping, fishing, or petty trading often encouraged immigrants to turn their minds, successfully, to those activities instead of farming.

One thing here is not yet clear. Minute subdivision of property in Europe arose largely because fertile land became so quickly occupied and because parents felt obliged to deal justly with all sons equally, rather than leave one son a consolidated estate and force the rest into other occupations or into a subordinate status. What southern European settlers will do when confronted with a similar situation in Australia is not yet clear. So far the existence of unused land and the steady growth of industry have allowed them to escape this dilemma. Furthermore, in some areas of close settlement, subdivision of farming land is prohibited by law, as on the Murrumbidgee Irrigation Area where the authorities hold that one family needs 15-30 acres of horticultural land, and that only one working family may reside on one farm.

One interesting feature of this garden background is the scope it gave for a nostalgic yearning for Mediterranean trees and animals. A southern European restaurant-keeper or trades-man in inner Sydney or Melbourne had little chance to satisfy himself here. But a small-scale farmer, though concentrating on poultry or fruit or vegetables, often could not resist the desire to create a little bit of his old world for himself by way of planting a few olive trees, fig trees or grapevines, or by keeping a few tame goats. One Dalmatian vegetable farmer west of Sydney was so determined to grow some of his beloved Adriatic grapes that he kept on planting them time and time again; only when he lost one cherished planting through waterlogged soil, and two more through bush-fires, did he finally give up.

Nuclear Settlement and Overcrowding

Another background factor of importance has been nuclear settlement (see p. 38), from which about three-quarters of Australia's pre-war southern European population derived. There is no doubt that the local customs and loyalties involved not only reinforced the system of family migration but acted as a powerful force encouraging southern Europeans to settle in areas of intensive farming, and in the compact residential areas of the inner cities and suburbs. Here to some extent they could re-create the colourful noisy conditions of their home villages and towns: the crowd of women gathered together in vegetable markets, combining the business of haggling with the delights of gossip; the little cafés and clubs where the menfolk could relax and refresh themselves without having to travel long distances from home; the singing and laughter in streets and yards. Some Calabrians have said that Australian suburbs— where so many houses have relatively large grounds and gardens—were so unlike their home towns in Calabria that they felt completely lost and strange. Another Calabrian asserted that Canberra, which is residentially almost all suburban, was not a good place for Calabrians to live in as there was no communal centre for them to practise their old customs or express their emotions in noise and song and laughter. It often took many years for settlers to become used to Australian conditions here.

Much more work is required before one can be dogmatic on this matter or assess the way the different chains and groups reacted to the problem. It is interesting to note, however, the considerable difference between such peoples as Kytherans and Ithacans. Ithacans, coming from an area of relatively high nucleation, concentrated from the very beginning in certain parts of Melbourne, Sydney, Newcastle, and other metropolitan centres; less than 15 per cent of Ithacan settlement—even including those temporarily settled in mining towns such as Kalgoorlie—took place elsewhere (see Appendix 19). Kytherans, on the other hand, who came from an island where the majority of inhabitants live in small scattered hamlets, dispersed quite

quickly in twos and threes amongst the country towns of
southern Queensland, New South Wales, and northern Victoria;
nearly two-thirds of Kytheran settlement took place in this
way (see Appendix 19). It is impossible to assert definitely
that this difference between the pattern of Kytheran and
Ithacan settlement in Australia directly reflects the difference
of settlement patterns in Europe; but the contrast is striking,
and the European background seems a likely explanation of
some of the difference.

The other relevant feature of nuclear settlement is crowded
living conditions: a family of six or eight or ten often squeezed
into one or two rooms or shared them with close relatives.
Many immigrants gladly continued this system in the early
stages of settlement in Australia, since it gave them much
needed companionship, enabled them to save money relatively
quickly, and solved the problem of finding accommodation for
the friends and relatives they brought to Australia. More
interesting, though much more difficult to assess, is the degree
to which the system modified itself with the lapse of time, with
increased familiarity with English-Australian customs, and with
the family's growing financial security and desire for comfort.
Field-work shows that some families eventually adopted the
common British-Australian habit of expecting each nuclear
family to have its own home. Others, however, compromised
by modernizing the home, buying comfortable furniture, in-
stalling good plumbing and cooking facilities, and then added
sufficient rooms to accommodate a number of relatives or enable
subdivision into several semi-independent apartments; in such
cases there was usually a large enough kitchen-living room for
everyone to have meals together. Yet others, particularly in
farming areas, erected small cottages a few yards from the
main house to cater either for elderly parents or married
relatives.

Some British-Australians, convinced that a multi-family home
is necessarily equated with unhygienic habits and low living
standards, have resented the survival of this European custom.
Certainly such homes often have a definite Mediterranean
atmosphere, encouraging much noise and singing, the 'strange
odours' of continental cooking, and the 'disgraceful' sound of
Mediterranean dialects and languages. This resentment, when
allied to disgust with the low living standards of migrants in
the early stages of settlement, has led many British-Australians
first to resist southern European infiltration into their residen-

tial area and then to evacuate it speedily. This phenomenon is well known elsewhere.[6] Part of its interest lies in judging the 'tipping point'—that point of time when British-Australians realized that their resistance to infiltration was useless, that southern Europeans were simply going to continue buying large British-Australian homes and subdivide them, and that the best thing to do was to sell out as quickly as possible and go elsewhere. Since the only people willing to buy were southern Europeans anxious to enter the area, the process accelerated by leaps and bounds. It has been clearly visible in various city areas as well as in some zones of intensive farming, and is still very pronounced in the post-war era.[7]

What British-Australians have not always realized is the role of the second generation here. In groups that adopted the single family home, of course, the second generation grew accustomed to British-Australian ways from the start. In groups continuing the multi-family home, however, the second generation sometimes found themselves at loggerheads with their relatives when they announced their preference for the single family home. Hence the anger and dismay of parents who saw their children setting up independent establishments when they expected them to bring their brides to the family home to look after their seniors in old age (pp. 194-5). This remark, however, takes us away from nuclear settlement as such and on to another of the major background factors.

The Family

At this point there is no need to stress the very great effect of southern European family life and customs on the course of migration and settlement. Running throughout this whole work is the thread of kinship, the strength of family authority, and the prevalence of wider family loyalties, which had so much to do with chain migration, with the choice of occupations, with the decision on where to settle. These stood at the heart of the battle over assimilation and the efforts of the first generation to discourage their children from marrying outside the ethnic group. There are, however, other important aspects

[6] Writers on Negro infiltration into certain American cities quote similar examples.

[7] The rapid consolidation of Italian horticultural farms since 1945 in the Murrumbidgee Irrigation Area emerges clearly from the land maps. This consolidation, of course, derived from factors other than the tipping point—so also in north Queensland, south-west Western Australia, etc.

of southern European family life in Australia—size of family, age of marriage, and the like—about which there is very little information. Indeed the whole matter of southern European family life in Australia, and the extent to which the family customs and loyalties of each particular group survived amongst the second and third generations, requires considerably more research—if possible by anthropologists trained in matters of kinship and of family customs and values. It may well be that southern European notions of family obligation and morality are beginning to make themselves felt in Australian society at large and will become increasingly important in matters of public morality.

Dialect and Language

Closely connected with family customs and values is the problem of dialect, primarily because the intimate concerns of family life are expressed naturally in local dialect and because through it the second generation imbibed parental opinions.[8] Local dialect, especially amongst Spaniards, Italians and Yugoslavs, has contributed to the formation and preservation of ethnic group settlements: by encouraging established settlers to sponsor, accommodate, and employ persons with whom they had no problem of communication; by drawing lonely and scattered settlers into district and regional concentrations; by providing a clear process of distinguishing those who belonged to the district or regional group from those who did not. In this sense local dialect was of great importance in the process of dual and triple assimilation; its survival amongst the second and third generation is an index of group coherence and a sign of strong resistance to Folk, nationalist, and British-Australian ways.

Unfortunately there are no adequate statistics for assessing how widely southern European dialects have spread or survived in Australia as a whole. There have been no census questions concerning mother-tongue in Australia, and even if there had been—as in Canada and the United States—the various local dialects are not always distinguishable. Field-work completed so far simply reveals great variation between different migrant groups and between different places of settlement. One general point does, however, seem clear: local dialect was a dwindling force in many parts of southern Europe during the 1920s and

8 For definition of dialect see Chapter III, n. 19.

1930s. This has already been mentioned in connexion with relations between pre-war and post-war settlers; its importance here is to remind us that those interested in post-war southern European immigrants will probably have to pay more attention to Folk-nationalist languages, and less attention to local dialect, than those interested in pre-war settlements. Even with post-war arrivals, however, local dialect is at times important enough to warrant special attention.

Since there are no statistics concerning mother-tongue, it is equally impossible to assess the importance and durability of Folk-nationalist languages throughout Australia as a whole. Judging by the activities and circulation of Folk newspapers such as *La Fiamma* or the *Hellenic Herald*,[9] by the existence of ethnic language evening and Saturday schools, and by the circulation of Folk-nationalist periodicals published in Europe,[10] Folk-nationalist languages have weathered the storms of assimilation better than local dialects.

Such judgment, however, is certainly superficial and probably false. A number of pre-war settlers interviewed subscribe to ethnic papers published in Australia in order to obtain news of marriages, births, tennis competitions, bargain sales, and other items of interest in particular places of settlement; they subscribe to overseas periodicals such as *Matica* very largely to obtain news about domestic events in their own region of origin or about ethnic settlements in America, Africa, and other parts of the world. They frequently pass lightly over articles dealing with political activities in the country of origin, or articles lauding Folk-nationalist culture and literature, or many of those things that interest immigrants recently arrived from Europe. The second generation often merely glances at pictures and headings and then puts the paper away.

In this sense local dialect has had greater survival power than Folk language: it is the language of the home and, for the second generation and sometimes the third, comes easily and quickly to the tongue; moreover, it is essentially a spoken language requiring none of the effort involved in learning to read and write a literary language.

9 Founded in Sydney in 1947 and 1926 respectively; there are now numerous foreign-language papers in Australia.

10 E.g., *Matica*, a Croatian periodical published in Zagreb and containing much news of Croatians overseas, is visible in the homes of many pre-war Dalmatian settlers in Australia.

On the other hand some of those second-generation children who did acquire the Folk language and literature, which required considerable effort and was of little practical use, became much more Folk conscious than their parents. The pressure of radio, films, television and comics has been so great in recent decades that any second-generation person prepared to keep up with the Folk literature and culture of his ancestors has been emotionally committed, to some extent ,at least. Some-times he has been reacting against the hostility of British-Australian school-mates towards 'dago' children; sometimes he has become fascinated by the history and literature of his ancestors, and by the Folk values they embody—on occasions so fascinated that he has slipped almost unconsciously into the role of an evangelist, committed to an intense missionary campaign amongst his weaker brethren. In such cases the Folk language has been far more important than local dialect, and has survived more successfully.

In sum, though there is no evidence for Australia as a whole, field-work amongst a number of immigrant groups suggests that for the generality of southern European settlers ,and their children local dialect or the spoken tongue of the home has been more important and has survived longer than the Folk language: where, however, the Folk language (and literature) has been influential ,it has survived more effectively than local dialect and has been a major factor in building up and pre-serving strong Folk organizations and group settlements. (These remarks refer, of course, to those peoples whose local dialect and Folk language substantially differed—see pp. 54-8.)

Folk-Nationalism

This assessment of dialect and language has gradually turned into an assessment of Folk-nationalism and its importance in rela-tion to district and regional customs and values. At this point there is no need to repeat the evidence concerning the part played by Folk forces—or supra-Folk forces—in creating ethnic institu-tions and attracting scattered settlers desirous of using those institutions, in welding heterogeneous masses of village, district and regional groups into relatively ,compact Folk or supra-Folk group settlements, and in creating the intricate but fascinating problem of dual or triple assimilation (see Chapter VI). It is suf-ficient here to emphasize the impossibility of elucidating from any current statistics just how many of those southern European

settlers who were in mixed district, regional and Folk concentrations—two-thirds of the total—maintained district or regional
group settlements, and how many of them subordinated local
loyalties to Folk and supra-Folk interests. Detailed inquiries in
particular areas suggest that regional loyalties often predominated over Folk interests but that this was more pronounced with
Catholic immigrants (71 per cent of all southern European
settlers) than with Orthodox (25 per cent), who in their efforts
to form their own Folk-nationalist Orthodox communities had
an additional inducement for allowing district and regional
values to take second place.

As a cause of emigration, however, and as a factor in the
course of chain migration, Folk interests were equally important
—or unimportant—as between Catholic and Orthodox. Occasionally Folk conflicts in Europe, and the economic chaos and un-
certainty associated with them, were influential in forcing people
away from Europe: the Bulgarian, Greek, Serb, Macedonian, and
Turkish struggle from 1870 onwards is an example of this; the
Basque and Catalan struggle against Castilian central government in Spain is another. But, by and large, Folk antagonism in
Europe was less important to chain migration than family and
district loyalties: it was during the course of settlement, and the
formation of ethnic groups, that Folk forces became of considerable importance.

Religion

Mention of the difference between Catholic and Orthodox
settlers leads to the difficult matter of religious affiliation. Again
we are concerned with something of secondary importance in
the origins and course of chain migration—though here also
there are exceptions, especially in the Balkans where religious
factors have been so entwined with Folk factors that conflicts
between different Folk were often associated with religious persecution and expulsion. But, speaking generally, religion was far
less important in the process of migration than family and village values.

In the course of settlement, however, religious factors became
quite as important as family and local loyalties. Indeed, they
are often difficult to separate from local customs and ceremonies,
which have so often had a religious basis or at any rate a religious sanction. For instance, a mother supervising her son's
baptism has often been quite unable to distinguish between

the religious and secular elements in the ceremonies she arranges: it is no less important to her that the church be decorated in a manner befitting her son's status than that the priest perform the service with liturgical correctness and proper chanting; it is no less important to her that the godfather make his speech at the proper moment during the post-baptismal meal than that he be aware of his religious duties as godparent.

It is very largely this impossibility of separating religious custom from family and social custom that has rendered religious assimilation somewhat difficult for southern Europeans in Australia. Roman Catholic immigrants, for instance, soon became aware that beneath the familiar Latin rite there lay very great socio-religious differences between themselves and the predominantly Irish-Australian population of the Roman church in Australia. Even if they found a priest who spoke their Folk tongue they soon realized he could not hear their confessions in dialect, that he was unfamiliar with their local customs at baptisms, funerals, and weddings, that he rarely understood, or sympathized with, many of those superstitions associated with family and village life in their district of origin (see p. 68). Moreover, they found that the Roman church in Australia was comparatively strict over such matters as meatless Fridays or attending Mass every Sunday.[11]

As a result many Catholic immigrants dropped what interest they had had in church life in Europe and concentrated more and more on the business of achieving worldly prosperity or of maintaining social contact with fellow-settlers. Others, more concerned to keep in touch with their church, made sure that at least their children attended a Roman Catholic school and went to church regularly. These families, however, were sometimes most upset when their children came home full of the need for maintaining religious standards in the home, severely criticized their father for failing to attend Mass, and sharply rebuked him for sitting down to a Friday evening meal of spiced meat balls and spaghetti. Sometimes the parents gave way; sometimes the two generations reached an amiable though uneasy compromise; sometimes the father or mother insisted that the child leave the church school and go to a state school instead. In this general situation, the absence of a real national parish system in Australia (see Chapter VI, n. 70) made things more

11 Basques, Maltese and some other southern European Catholics have been very strict on such things but other Spaniards and many Italians were accustomed to a much less strict system.

difficult for the first generation and for the maintenance of real understanding between first and second generation.[12] On the other hand, it made for easier relationships between the second generation and British-Australian Roman Catholics, so acting in favour of assimilation by the third generation.

With Orthodox settlers the situation was even more difficult. In addition to the profound differences in socio-religious customs and traditions there existed a basic difference between all the Orthodox churches and the British-Australian churches already established in the continent. Immigrants might ask an Anglican priest to perform the actual ceremony of baptism, marriage, or burial, while one or two—realizing the closeness of Orthodox and Anglican doctrine and the moves for intercommunion between the churches—might even attend the Anglican Eucharist and assist as altar servers. But many Orthodox settlers cling to the feeling that long services with much chanting are the only proper form of sacramental worship. This, when added to the strong Folk traditions enshrined in each Orthodox church, led most Orthodox settlers to form an Orthodox community as soon as numbers permitted.

The coming into being of separate Orthodox churches—in Australia there are now Syrian, Greek, Russian, Ukrainian, Serbian, Bulgarian, and Macedonian Orthodox churches—has certainly made life easier for the first generation and, by re-creating the familiar conditions of Europe, has undoubtedly aided contented settlement.[13] But it has occasionally made things more difficult for the second and third generations. Some second-generation Greeks, for instance, have said that they go to church only for the sake of family unity at Christmas or Easter, or for family ceremonies such as baptisms and weddings, that the long strange liturgies merely bore them, and that they feel such routine concentration on rites and ceremonies takes people's minds away from the proper business of living a good moral life. As no scholar has yet made a complete survey of the church life of the second-generation members of any Orthodox group in Aus-

[12] One Roman Catholic priest of Irish origin, who has long been interested in immigration and familiar with the system in both America and Australia, strongly defended—to the writer—the Australian hierarchy's refusal to introduce the national parish system fully into Australia. Rapidity of assimilation was one of the main grounds for his defence.

[13] This point has been made repeatedly in the general literature; see, e.g. L. Benyei, 'Greek and South Slav Immigrants in Melbourne'; *The Study of Immigrants in Australia*.

tralia, it is impossible to say how typical these opinions are; but interviews with second-generation Greeks in Melbourne and Sydney indicate that they are very common.

There is here one noticeable and important difference between Australia and the United States. The great Orthodox immigration to America was so drastically reduced after 1924 that first-generation settlers subsequently received little reinforcement and were gradually overtaken by the second generation.[14] In the last few decades, therefore, second-generation persons have been numerically influential in the Orthodox churches and have felt strong enough to organize campaigns for certain liturgical changes and for a greater use of English in the services. Likewise the recent moves to unite the various Orthodox churches into one Orthodox church of America—in which English would have a much larger place—have received much impetus from second-generation persons who are less interested in the Folk antagonisms of their parents and grandparents and see no reason why the Orthodox church should not become a typically American church. In Australia, however, immigration from the Orthodox world has been increasing slowly ever since the turn of the century and since World War II has been running at a comparatively high level. Consequently first-generation settlers still exceed second-generation children (see Appendix 4:8), and are still able to insist on the full Greek and Slavonic liturgies. Possibly this situation lies behind the feelings of those second-generation persons who have become dissatisfied with or disinterested in the churches founded by their parents.

The predicament of Moslem settlers in Australia—mainly Albanian settlers in Western Australia and near Shepparton, Victoria—has been even more acute than that of Orthodox migrants, primarily because some sections of their religious code are prohibited by law. The Moslem communities of Australia await further investigation, but there have apparently been the same rifts between the second generation and those first-generation parents anxious to keep as much as is possible of their European faith.

All these remarks about first-generation reactions to church life in Australia refer, of course, only to those who had an interest in religion in Europe and retained it for at least some of their sojourn in Australia. They do not refer to that unknown number of atheistic or rationalist migrants; nor to that unknown

14 Hutchinson, *Immigrants and their Children*, Table VI.

number of persons whose cultural and religious heritage received such a shaking during the rapid mobility and hard living conditions of the early years of settlement that they did not pick up the threads again when conditions improved and religious life became better organized.

Politics

Difficult as assessing the importance of religious organizations amongst Australia's pre-war southern European settlers is, it is very much more difficult to assess the importance of southern European political organizations and opinions (here referring to royalist, conservative, radical, or Communist opinions, not to Folk-nationalist or state-nationalist opinions, which concern the very existence of a people, not the way it conducts its political affairs). The difficulty arises partly from the marathon work involved in locating all the political organizations and papers. Churches and religious communities, once formed, are comparatively conspicuous and have rarely disappeared. But numbers of little political organizations have sprung into existence, sometimes to deal with a particular issue, and have then disappeared. So have some ethnic newspapers and those odd broadsheets and circulars that have been produced for some special occasion. More important still, much of the political life of southern European settlers has taken place in district and regional clubs, or in the Folk churches, and there is little documentary material available about it.

In such circumstances it has been quite impossible to conduct a complete and all-embracing inquiry into the political life and thought of southern European settlers to incorporate in this work. At this stage it is possible to discuss only the situation in the ethnic political organizations so far examined or the political discussions overheard in ethnic social clubs. Nor, for the purposes of this book, is any complete and general survey necessary. The main emphasis here has been on the basic ethnic groups and loyalties that lay behind the course of migration and that very largely controlled the process of settlement and assimilation. Only rarely have ethnic political organizations or political ambitions, as such, become important in Australia—normally they were the by-product of a group life that covered all manner of activities and purposes besides politics. One noticeable exception was the peasant radicalism of many Dalmatian settlers, which at one time seemed to have won complete control of several Dalmatian settlements, converted them from regional to supra-Folk groups, and brought many settlers into close touch with British-Australian radical, socialist, and Communist organizations (p. 241). Another possible exception was the Australian branch of the Macedonian Revolutionary Organization—a movement that will be referred to in more detail later.

Nevertheless, even though primarily a by-product of ethnic group life, these political organizations and activities performed a useful function. In a sense they represented miniature political systems within relatively self-sufficient ethnic settlements and thereby enabled many politically-minded southern Europeans, who either would not or could not obtain positions of importance in the established political parties of Australia, to liberate their energies and satisfy their urge for political argument and debate. (This is, of course, a special aspect of the general struggle for power within ethnic organizations that has been mentioned earlier.)

At this point we reach one of the most fascinating questions in the study of ethnic activities: were those who expressed political opinions simply transferring to Australia the arguments and political thought forms prevalent in their European homeland? Or had they come to understand the arguments and political thought forms of Australia so well that they simply used the ethnic language and societies as vehicles for discussing the politics of their new land—a situation presupposing a fairly high degree of assimilation? Or were they manoeuvring in a curious in-between world where the political policies and thought forms derived from Europe mixed in more or less uneasy terms with Australian?

Unfortunately very little is as yet known on this matter.[15] What information is available suggests that Communist supporters had the least trouble in welding European and Australian viewpoints, primarily because Communists in both countries used no other thought forms, and advocated no other policies, than those laid down by the Third International in Moscow; *Napredak* and *Makedonska Iskra* (*Macedonian Spark*) illustrate this very clearly.

Numbers of industrial labourers, miners, and other southern Europeans connected with the trade union system also came to terms with Australian customs fairly quickly, though the difference between the various European brands of socialism and Australian socialism sometimes caused confusion.

15 Petrolias has done some useful pioneering work in his study, Post-War Greek and Italian Migrants in Melbourne.

Settlers having much difficulty in grasping Australian political terms, or else making little effort to move away from European concepts, included numbers of peasant radicals from Dalmatia, Macedonia, and Bulgaria, who did not come under direct Communist influence. Political conversations with this type of pre-war settler—even as late as the early 1960s—sometimes progressed no further than the iniquities of those who opposed Stephan Radich in Croatia in the early 1920s and the paramount importance of implementing the policies that Radich advocated. Perhaps the absence of any true peasant class in Australia, and the very great difference that existed between peasant holdings in southern Europe and small-scale horticultural or market-gardening farms in Australia, encouraged this failure to adopt an Australian political viewpoint. This predicament was not, of course, confined to Slav peasants, and it is perhaps significant that a number of first- and second-generation Italians and others have become active in the Australian National Catholic Rural Movement, a movement that has been attempting, amongst other things, to foster some aspects of European peasant life in Australia.

Another class of immigrants is illustrated by those Bulgarian market-gardeners who were interested in peasant radicalism when they came to Australia between 1900 and 1930, were suspected of sympathizing with Bulgarian Communism in the early years of World War II, and after the war became active supporters of the Liberal Party of Australia. In some cases the suspicion of Communist sympathies was never well founded; in others it is not plain whether those concerned eventually became genuine converts to an Australian political viewpoint or whether they wished to remove the stigma of Russian Communist sympathies by joining the most conservative Australian party they could find.

Greek islanders provide another interesting example. Discussions in their clubs and on informal social occasions varied, of course, from group to group and with the local problems confronting each area of origin. Even so, political discussions often revealed a fascinating mixture of notions about Greek and Australian affairs: heated arguments about the domestic policies of Venizelos or Metaxas were rapidly succeeded by arguments about Liberal Party-Labour Party policies in Australia; prolonged discussion on the wisdom of the local authorities at home in Europe in putting a new water-fountain in the middle of the village square were succeeded by a debate on whether the local government authorities of New South Wales should have been softer or firmer with attempts to open up the 'green belt' for building.

Despite the warmth of feeling displayed, however, and the vigour with which points were emphasized by rattling the little coffee tables or thumping down glasses of liqueur, there is no doubt that the issues that stirred Greek islanders most deeply were the best way to tackle Yugoslavia and Albania about those Greeks still left in Yugoslavia, Macedonia or Albanian-Epirus, or the proper time and method for Greek Cypriots to obtain union with Greece. In other words, the issues about which they felt most strongly, at times to the point of tears, were Folk-nationalist aspirations on which persons of all political opinions were basically agreed, but about the best methods of achieving which policies differed. The same was also true of Catalan settlers in Melbourne concerned with the policy of the Franco government towards Catalonian independence, of Maltese settlers when discussing the relative merits of the pro-Italian Mizzi government or the pro-British Strickland party, and sometimes of Venetian settlers whose homes lay close to areas where the Italian state was grappling with Tyrolean-German or Slovene minorities. In this sense the amount of time, or heat, expended arguing about Folk aspirations, as compared with that spent on other political issues, is a useful, though difficult, measure of assimilation. Settlers who felt they had become so Australian that Folk conflicts in Europe seemed all rather petty and irrelevant may have spent less time arguing politics, even Australian politics, than some of their compatriots: but they had achieved a much greater degree of assimilation.

The general phenomenon we have been considering—the process whereby political life and discussion of a more or less mixed European and Australian character took place inside ethnic institutions—very largely explains why so few pre-war southern European settlers took part in the work of British-Australian political organizations. Another important reason is the absorption of so many settlers with the business of living: persons primarily concerned with establishing themselves and their families are rarely willing to spend time and energy in the political life of a new country.[16] Sometimes, of course, migrants were forced into Australian politics to preserve the very existence of their migration system—as were those Italians in North Queensland who organized themselves during the great depression to resist

---

16 Borrie, *Italians and Germans in Australia*, p. 122

V

the attempt of the British Preference League to restrict Italian settlement in the sugar districts.[17]

These remarks, of course, apply only to the mass of southern European settlers. There have always been those occasional first-generation southern Europeans who took a leading part in British-Australian politics; at any rate ever since the Eureka Stockade in 1854 when an Italian ex-schoolteacher named Raffaele Carboni was one of the main persons concerned in arousing the miners to active resistance.[18] On the whole, however, participation in Australian political life has been left for the second and third generation.

Law and Order

Consideration of political life leads naturally into a consideration of the way southern Europeans reacted to the system of law and conventions of social order prevalent in Australia—in many ways so different from the system and conventions in which they had been reared (p. 79). It has already been suggested that the shaking-up processes involved in migration, and the consequent stripping away of European cultural, social, and religious customs, have sometimes proved too great a strain and that some immigrants broke down in lunacy, alcoholism, suicide, and crime. Material on the first three topics is scanty at present (p. 272); all that can usefully be said here is that had British-Australians felt the problems to be serious they would almost certainly have initiated public inquiries. The fact that, in all the hostility and suspicion aroused by pre-war southern Europeans in various parts of Australia, demands for such inquiries never became pronounced is evidence that the problems were not acute.

The same argument may be applied to crime in general. British-Australian awareness of immigrant crime has been relatively sharp since the war, partly because of the much greater number of new arrivals, partly because some post-war arrivals have been 'displaced persons' with tragic histories and disorganized personalities that break down under the strain of adjusting to the quite novel conditions of life in Australia, and partly because foreign names stand out in newspaper reports so much more sharply than British-Australians. Before the war, however, British-Australian attention was seldom drawn to immigrant crime except where it concerned types of crime well known in

17 Bertei, Innisfail, pp. 38 ff.
18 Lyng, *Non-Britishers in Australia*, p. 94.

southern Europe but rare in Australia: settling disputes amongst
Calabrians or Sicilians by using knives; the attitude of some
southern Europeans that a husband is justified in starting a feud
if his spouse falls victim to the wiles of an expert seducer; the
tendency for some southern Europeans to abduct young women
instead of asking them to leave their families and come respectably to the nearest Registry Office.

What British-Australians have not always realized is that these
crimes reflected recognized ways of solving difficulties in southern
Europe; that to southern European eyes the tendency of some
British-Australians to jab broken bottles in their opponent's eye
is much more reprehensible than the quick clean thrust of a
knife; that a system resulting in the occasional feud or occasional
abduction—the recognized means (sometimes secretly approved
by the girl) of breaking through a rigid chaperonage system,
when all else has failed—is very much better to many southern Europeans than the loose moral code of many British-
Australian families and the much greater rates of fornification,
adultery, and illegitimacy.

British-Australians have also often failed to realize that older
settlers put very great pressure on newcomers to abandon southern European conventions such as these (the writer has heard
one old-established Calabrian family explaining to newcomers
that they must abandon the habit of carrying knives as soon as
they arrive in Australia); further these crimes have usually been
confined to persons of the same ethnic group. Occasionally a
southern European has knifed a British-Australian when in fear
of a beating-up—as in the incident that started the Kalgoorlie
riot of 1919 (p. 209). But it is significant that the Kalgoorlie riots
of 1934 were triggered off when an old-established Italian used
British-Australian techniques of fisticuffs in dealing with an unpleasant British-Australian customer (p. 209).

To some extent the same considerations apply to the other
class of crime that British-Australians asserted had been imported direct to Australia from various southern European districts of origin—that arising from the bandit tradition of parts
of southern Europe, notably the underground activities of
Sicilian societies such as the Mafia and the Black Hand. Unquestionably, these societies did operate in parts of northern
Queensland, although their power has probably been exaggerated.[19] Here again, however, activities were confined mainly to

19 Bertei, Innisfail, p. 41; Borrie, *Italians and Germans in Australia*, p. 115;
J. R. Harvey, *Black Hand of Vengeance*.

members of the same ethnic group; also it is significant that British-Australians only made much of them when attacking Sicilians on other grounds—their economic success during the great depression, and their danger to Australia as enemy aliens during World War II.

Speaking generally, then, it appears that some southern European types of crime definitely came to Australia with pre-war immigrants—especially those arising from the historical fact that long centuries of misgovernment in southern Italy and Sicily had forced people to rely upon feuding, banditry, and secret societies to obtain any degree of social justice, and that even the more orderly and enlightened governments of more recent decades had not succeeded in completely eradicating these customs by 1940. On the other hand, it is equally clear that these crimes were not widespread or conspicuous—nothing like the extent they were in North America. In short, southern Europeans adapted themselves relatively quickly to the legal system and conventions of their new land.

Here again the influence of chain migration was important. For most groups of southern Europeans, chain migration continued over relatively long periods of time and on a scale insufficient to bring enormous numbers of new migrants to the same place at the same time; rather did chain groups build up steadily and surely, always containing a relatively large proportion of older settlers knowledgeable in Australian ways. In these circumstances the likelihood of gang activities was very much less than amongst the great concentrations of North America. Moreover the bulk of Sicilian and Calabrian migrants to pre-war Australia settled in rural areas, not in great urban concentrations like New York or Chicago, where it was relatively easy to organize crime and racketeering. Whether the greater influx of Sicilians, Calabrians, and others to Australia since the war will change the story it is too early to say. The reports that have appeared so far show that, in general terms, the post-war southern European crime rate has been very much lower than that of the Australian average—but as these reports have not cross-classified southern European immigrants by type of crime it is impossible to say anything definite about the type of crime particularly associated with the various groups of southern Europeans.[20]

20 Reports of the committee established to investigate the conduct of migrants, Commonwealth Immigration Advisory Council.

Race

Some British-Australians still express the opinion that Sicilians, Calabrians, Greeks, and Albanians indulged in these 'un-Australian' crimes because they came from 'inferior races', or from racial stocks that suffered degeneration through mixture with Negro, Arab, and other strains. Mediterranean immigrants, they argued, were less satisfactory than northern and central Europeans, intermarried and intermixed less easily with British-Australians than did northerners, and formed racial cliques and groups far more difficult to assimilate.

The evidence set out in previous chapters suggests there is no sound foundation for this opinion. Ethnic group formation arose inevitably out of the processes of migration and settlement and was as conspicuous amongst northern Italians, Dalmatians, and Bulgarians as amongst Sicilians, Calabrians, Albanians, or Greeks. Likewise the marriage rates (see Appendixes 8-21, 4:26-7) suggest that migrants from the Mediterranean coast and islands were every bit as willing to marry British-Australian girls as were migrants from farther north; furthermore, that British-Australian girls were equally ready to marry them. Some of the highest intermarriage rates are among peoples such as the Lipari islanders. There are, it is true, great variations in the rates of intermarriage, but these quite clearly vary from chain to chain rather than from racial zone to racial zone—if such zones can, in fact, be defined.

General Assessment of Background Factors

These, then, are the principal factors. It is of interest now to consider which have been the more important in the process of migration and settlement as a whole. Clearly some have had little relevance—physical type or historic traditions of feuding and banditry. Some—political alignments and opinions as to the proper way to order political affairs—have been important on occasion. Others, however—particularly the geographical and economic background, traditions of nuclear settlement, family structure, village and district loyalties, dialect, religious organization, and Folk-nationalist aspirations—have had very great influence. Which of these has been of greatest significance it is quite impossible to say. For one thing the various forces operated in different ways on different groups at different times. But of even more moment is the very great difficulty involved in disentangling the forces when at work, of isolating one particular force for examination when in reality it was acting upon

other forces and being acted upon by them throughout the
duration of a highly intricate social process. The story becomes
still more intricate when we remember the large part played
by accident and chance—the arrival of a particular pioneer of a
particular character at a particular place at a particular moment
of time; on this casual basis so much of the story of chain migration has hung, and in this sense separate examination of the
main forces at work can be misleading. In other words, discussion
may help to crystallize thought about the operation of this or
that general force, but these forces can be understood only when
seen within the context of the complex histories of numerous
migrant groups. It is these complex and continuous 'stories'
that give meaning to all the rest.

THE STORY : A MACEDONIAN ILLUSTRATION

Ideally the 'story' aspect should be illustrated by tracing one
comprehensive and continuous history from each of the main
groups of migrants. Space and time make such a fascinating
task, alas, impossible. But we can at least illustrate the complexity
of the major background factors and the colourful and intricate
way in which they are interwoven with other forces at work in
Europe and Australia by briefly tracing the history of a single
group. The illustration chosen is that of migrants from the adjacent districts of Bitola in south-western Yugoslav Macedonia
and of Kastoria and Florina in the north-west corner of Greek
Macedonia; partly because they are one of the most interesting
of all migrant peoples, and partly because the intense regional,
religious, and Folk-nationalist rivalries in the area have produced a spate of highly partisan and misleading literature on
these people and on their settlements abroad.

(The Macedonian story may seem disproportionately long
and involved, yet it is just these elements that stress the main
point of this work: only through an understanding of the vast-
ness and complexity of the background material can we arrive
at an understanding of the problems of assimilation faced by the
migrants.)

Before Marshal Tito created the autonomous republic of
Macedonia within the federation of the new Yugoslavia, Macedonia did not exist in any legal or administrative sense:[21] the
name simply indicated an area in the central Balkans, the precise

[21] We are not here concerned with legal and administrative boundaries in
classical and Byzantine days—though the boundaries then also were somewhat vague.

boundaries of which varied according to each writer and speaker but which were generally agreed to include the region running from Lake Ohrid south to Grevena, north-east through Salonica to Kavalla, north-west along the Rhodope Mountains to Bansko, and back via Skopje and Gostivar to Ohrid. The people of this region have been the subject of prolonged and often furious argument. In classical days, though they spoke a variety of Greek, sent their kings to the Olympic games, and founded the greatest of all Hellenic empires, they were thought of as remote and somewhat odd relatives of Greeks proper, a cut above the 'Barbarians' but not really true Hellenes.[22] In later centuries the population changed considerably, the area being subjected to large-scale invasions by Albanian, Germanic, Bulgar, and other Slav tribes—the last becoming so important that the language eventually spoken by the majority of the people consisted of a series of Slav dialects transitional between Serbian and Bulgarian. Furthermore, the region became a battleground of rival political ambitions, falling variously under the control of the Roman, Byzantine, Serbian, Bulgarian, and eventually Ottoman empires. When under Byzantine and Turkish control, Greek was usually considered to be the official language, religion, and culture of the Christian population: Greek then made considerable headway, more particularly in the towns, amongst commercial, official, and literary families, and amongst the inhabitants of densely settled grape-growing rural districts. When under Serbian and Bulgarian political and ecclesiastical control Greek influences declined, the Slavonic liturgy and culture became much more influential, and the Slav dialects and customs of the villagers received much fortification. Perhaps the most important of these cultural upheavals occurred in the eighteenth century when the Ottoman authorities permitted the Greek *Phanariot* Patriarch and officials at Constantinople to revert to the Greek ecclesiastical supremacy of the Byzantine period, suppress a number of Slav episcopacies, expel Slav bishops and clergy, replace the Old Slavonic rites by Greek, and convert all schools to Greek institutions. Against this policy of Hellenization Slav feeling slowly mounted and in 1870 became sufficiently strong to force the Sultan to permit the establishment of a Bulgarian Orthodox Exarchy—with authority over central and eastern Macedonia as well as Bulgaria—and to allow most dioceses of

[22] See Pierre Jouguet, *Macedonian Imperialism and the Hellenization of the East*, pp. 66-9.

southern Macedonia to place themselves under this exarchy or, at least, to establish rival churches and schools.

From this time on the modern Macedonian problem became acute and drew crowds of peripatetic scholars, journalists, and politicians, all anxious to decide just who the Macedonians were and to what political state they should belong. Most observers agreed that pockets of Turks, Pomaks (Moslem Bulgarians) and Vlach Rumanians were scattered throughout the whole area, but that Albanians predominated on the western edge, Bulgarians in the east, and Greeks in the south; also that in and near many large towns there were still some businessmen, officials, and vine-growers who, whatever their racial origin may have been, had identified themselves with the Greek civilization and considered themselves to be true Hellenes. Over the rest of the population, however, controversy raged furious: Greeks argued that they were genuine Greeks who had unfortunately fallen under Slav linguistic influences; Bulgarians, that they were true Bulgarians; Serbs declared them to be a species of Serb; other observers decided they were a distinctive people—the Slav Macedonians or Macedo-Slavs—who ought to be the backbone of an independent Macedonian state. The villagers themselves rarely thought beyond family, village, and district contexts, but those that did usually regarded themselves as having closer affinities with Bulgarians than with any other people and favoured either incorporation into a new Bulgaria or else an independent Macedonian state. Certainly most of them welcomed the gradual spread of the Bulgarian Slavonic church, the most bitter opponents being those city families who identified themselves with the Greek civilization and were most dismayed when the *Phanariot* policy of Hellenizing the Slav-speaking population was reversed and the new Slav churches and schools attracted away many Macedonian villagers and townsfolk.

Into this medley of conflicting forces came Russia's attempt to have most of Macedonia incorporated in an independent Bulgaria (1877-8), the decision of the other great powers to leave Macedonia as part of the Ottoman Empire, the institution of a violent and savage policy of oppression by Ottoman officials, the appearance of Greek, Albanian, and Bulgarian guerrilla forces, and the outbreak of various rebellions whereby temporary combinations of Albanians, Vlachs, Greeks, and Slavs tried unsuccessfully to establish some sort of autonomy through the Internal Macedonian Revolutionary Organization (I.M.R.O.). Whether those Slavs interested in the I.M.R.O. were sincerely in favour of independence, or whether they simply hoped to create a state that would eventually be absorbed into Bulgaria without re-arousing the great-power hostility of 1878, is still a matter of fierce debate. Certainly pro-Bulgarian influence increased in later years. The truth appears to be, however, that Slav interests in the I.M.R.O. were at first predominantly in favour of autonomy and that only when Greece and Serbia came out forcibly in favour of partitioning Macedonia did Bulgarian sympathizers begin to attain ascendancy over I.M.R.O. policy;[23] even then Slav Macedonians favouring independence still remained a very in-fluential element.

In the event the programmes for independence or for incor-poration into Bulgaria failed. At the end of the wars wresting Macedonia from Turkey the Treaty of Bucharest divided the region between Serbia, Greece, and Bulgaria (1913); Bulgaria received little more than the undisputedly Bulgarian areas; Serbia won most of north Macedonia and the disputed districts around Bitola and Lake Ohrid; Greece gained not only the clearly Greek areas of south-west Macedonia and the Chalcidice but also much of the disputed territory in southern Macedonia, including the districts of Florina and Kastoria. Serbia and Greece at once proceeded to implement policies designed to abolish all Slav Macedonian and Bulgarian influences, imposing Serbian or Greek churches and schools, making it very difficult for those speaking only Macedo-Slav to obtain official positions or econ-omic advancement. The Greeks at times went so far as to force the adult population—grandmothers included—to learn Greek at night-classes, prosecuted persons heard speaking Slavonic in public, compelled families to adopt Greek names, and generally took vigorous action to 're-convert' their misguided subjects to the Hellenic culture.[24]

During these troublous times many Macedonians—both towns-folk and villagers—started to leave home and found chain settle-ments overseas. Some pioneers left because Turkish estate hold-ers in the better settled areas enforced heavy extra burdens on the peasantry, more particularly the giving of much unpaid time

23 Hugh Seton-Watson, *Eastern Europe Between the Wars, 1918-1941*, pp. 312-19. The Greek view, that the I.M.R.O. was never more than a Bulgarian 'lure', is expressed in such works as C. J. Christides, *The Macedonian Camouflage*, pp. 30-6.

24 Some of this derives from secondary sources, but all the more personal details in this and later passages come from interviews with Greek and Slav Macedonians in Canada and Australia.

to the landlord's own property and free timber, transport, and food for his retainers; some of these pioneers, in fact, started leaving Macedonia early in the nineteenth century and founded the quite substantial Macedonian gardening and dairying colony at Constantinople. Mountain peasants, including many families who had moved from the plains to remote mountainous districts in order to escape Turkish burdens, found their small mountain habitation districts becoming rapidly overcrowded and their properties minutely subdivided between heirs. Yet other migrants were Greeks from towns such as Kastoria and Kozani who found their businesses affected by the general insecurity of the times.

A very large number of families, however, left as a direct consequence of political upheaval and guerrilla fighting: the pioneer from Florina district mentioned on p. 104 was hurried out of the country by his uncle after the boy, then aged eleven, had witnessed Greek guerrillas slit his father's throat—because in his capacity as a skin and wine merchant he had had dealings with Turkish officials—and then kill his mother through administering an over-generous dose of burning fat to her naked stomach in an attempt to extort from her the whereabouts of her husband's alleged hoard of 'ill-gotten' money. Yet others left because of political and cultural pressure: one Toronto pioneer from the predominantly Greek town of Kastoria was a schoolteacher who left home when Kastoria came under Bulgarian control and all teaching in Greek was forbidden; conversely, one Macedo-Slav family from Florina came to Australia because they had been trained as Slav Macedonian teachers before Greece annexed the district, and felt that the new Greek policy gave them no hope of any occupation except that of agricultural labouring. These pioneers then proceeded to contact those still at home and the chain movement gathered impetus; it received additional impetus from the fact that family and village loyalties in Macedonia were very strong and the pioneer task of founding chains was therefore made so much the easier.

At first the greater number of emigrants settled in the Macedonian colony at Constantinople, but after the rebellion of 1903 the Ottoman government started to discriminate against Macedonians in their capital town, so forcing would-be migrants to look elsewhere.[25] Many thousands then moved to North America,

[25] In his *La Macedoine et les Macedoniens*, Dragonoff estimated there were in Constantinople about 2,500 persons from Florina and nearly 2,000 from Kastoria—see Balikci, *Macedonians and Bulgarians*, p. 39.

but from the turn of the century onwards Australia also received small trickles, which increased rapidly after the new Serb and Greek policies of the early 1920s (see Appendix 16 and Table I). Some derived from the Greek district of Kozani in southern Macedonia and settled as restaurant-keepers and businessmen in Melbourne. A much greater number came from the villages in the mountain area of Bitola, Florina and Kastoria: most settled as market-gardeners in the Werribee district of outer Melbourne and the Fulham district of west Adelaide, as dairy-farmers and horticulturalists in Gippsland, as small-scale farmers and timber-cutters in the south-west of Western Australia; a small proportion of them, however, settled in rural parts of New South Wales as timber-cutters and eucalyptus-burners or as unskilled labourers or caterers in Sydney, Newcastle, Melbourne, and various country towns (Appendix 16). The settlement pattern of these migrants differed sharply from that of their cousins and brothers in Toronto, where Macedonian pioneers from the villages around Florina and Kastoria, after some years of experiment in different occupations, entered the restaurant business in such large numbers that by World War II about two-thirds of them were so engaged.[26] In this sense pre-war Macedonians in Australia kept more closely to the occupations of their country of origin than those in Toronto and other cities of North America, thus following the general difference between southern European settlement in Australia and North America (see Chapter V).

When forming their group settlements abroad these Macedonian migrants of the early twentieth century showed a curious combination of district, regional, and Folk-nationalist forces. Largely because family, village, and district loyalties were so strong, the tendency was for families from the same village or district to form, as soon as numbers were adequate, closely-knit societies providing mutual-benefit facilities for members and a closely contained and active social life; hence the dozen or so societies in Toronto representing different villages in Kastoria district. At the same time a number of Macedonian regional societies came into existence—the 'Ion Dragoumis' Society of Toronto or the 'Hellenic Macedonian Legion' of Melbourne—and these tended to maintain regional dialects and interests. On the other hand the bitter Folk-nationalist conflicts at work often led to a sharp rift between immigrants; some identified themselves as Greeks

26 Balikci, op. cit., and my own work on Toronto Macedonian marriage records in 1958.

and joined Greek communities abroad: others, as Macedo-Slavs and joined Macedo-Bulgarian communities. Where these Macedo-Bulgarian groups reached any substantial size they became highly Folk-nationalist in outlook, bitterly opposed to all things Serbian and Greek and, in the absence of a separate Macedonian Orthodox church, were content to draw their priests from the Bulgarian church. For this, and for many social purposes, pro-Bulgarian and pro-independence Macedonians were content to work together with Bulgarians proper, though they retained clear differences of opinion as to the proper future of their country.

During the 1940s the situation changed. The harsh overlordship of the Bulgarian government when acting as agent for the Axis conquerors led to considerable friction between Slav Macedonians and Bulgarians proper and greatly strengthened the hands of those who claimed that the Macedo-Slav dialects and customs were so different from Bulgarian that independence was the only proper course. Amongst settlers abroad this was reflected in a growing tendency to assert that, though Bulgarians proper were welcome to Slav Macedonian communities, they must realize the communities were generally committed to the cause of Macedonian independence and the creation of a Macedonian Orthodox church. Later still the creation of a new republic of Macedonia within post-war Yugoslavia, and the appearance of an autonomous Macedonian Orthodox church within that republic, undermined much of the earlier suspicion against the Serbs. Admittedly, the new system has had to overcome the anti-Communist sentiments of many Macedonians abroad—made much easier by the Tito-Stalin split—and also the feeling that Tito's move was no more than a cunning attempt to cut the ground from under an independent Macedonia. On the whole, however, Slav Macedonians abroad appear to have become much more friendly to Yugoslavia, many of them welcoming Macedonian literature produced in Skopje and the travelling representatives of the Macedonian Orthodox church. The principal enemy, therefore, is still Greece, and here feelings have grown steadily more bitter since the 1920s, largely because the Greek government's policy of moving Greek refugees from Asia Minor into parts of Macedonia in the early 1920s has greatly strengthened the Greek element in the area embraced by the proposed Macedonian state, and also because the Greek policy of rapid Hellenization succeeded in convincing some Slav-speaking villagers that they had always been part of the Greek civilization.

This latter phenomenon, indeed, caused tremendous rifts, frequently through the one village and sometimes through the same family. For instance, since 1890 or so the village of Antarktikon (Zheleva), near Florina (Lerin), has sent several thousand settlers to Toronto. These have split into two groups, each with its own quite powerful village organization: one, identified with the Greek community, bears the Greek name Antarktikon and the other, identified with the Macedo-Bulgarian community, bears the Slav name Zheleva. One member of a prosperous Antarktikon family was for long the enthusiastic president of the Greek society; his brother made an equally zealous leader in the other group.

It is usually very difficult to assess what proportion of migrants from these disputed areas have identified themselves with one or other of the two Folk groups. Ardent phil-Hellenes usually take the line that, apart from a number of old pro-Bulgarian diehards and a few more recent cranks, all immigrants from Greek Macedonia have been true Greeks and join Greek communities; they may speak Slav as a second language but they are Greeks at heart and that is all that matters. The vocal Macedo-Slavs at once retort that all this is false and that Slav-speaking Macedonians—whether they have been forced to acquire Greek as a second language or not—have been true Macedo-Slavs at heart. The only reason for Macedo-Slavs joining the Greek community, they say, is that the Greek government has consistently made it difficult for members of Macedonian Orthodox communities abroad to assist their relatives to leave Greece or to lighten their economic difficulties in Greece itself; consequently, they continue, many true Macedo-Slavs have joined the Greek Orthodox Community and Greek Macedonian societies to keep the road clear for bringing relatives overseas, or to preserve them from harsh treatment in Greek Macedonia itself.[27] Once all their near relatives are safe abroad, however, the whole family

27 One family, who took their boy for baptism at the Macedo-Bulgarian church of St Cyril and Methodosius, later received letters from relatives in Greece saying that news of this had been sent to the Greek government by Greek-Macedonian 'spies' in Toronto and that the family were being watched by the police, ostracized socially, and discriminated against in employment; they begged their relative in Toronto not to do such a thing again. Similar cases have been mentioned by Slav Macedonians in Melbourne. The Greek government, of course, has been even more watchful of Macedo-Slav sympathizers in Greece since the civil war and the danger they feel exists on their northern frontier; see also Benyei, 'Greek and South Slav Immigrants in Australia', p. 81.

reverts—so it is said—to Slav Macedonian connexions, both religious and social. The Macedo-Slav point here has some substance—especially as it has been admitted privately by prominent
Greeks—and it is wiser, when assessing numbers in each Folk
group, to concentrate on those who have been abroad for some
years and who have no close relatives left in Europe.

Another difficulty is the tendency of some Macedonians
abroad to keep a foot in both camps for business reasons. One
very wealthy businessman in Toronto has for long subscribed
to both Greek and Slav churches, while others—those engaged
in skilled trades or commercial printing—have been forced to
maintain good relations with both sides since the patronage of
one group only would be inadequate to maintain business
prosperity. This was also visible in Australian townships such
as Queanbeyan, where Macedonian settlers were for long only a
handful and found it useful to have business and marketing
relations with southern Greeks. Furthermore, where there have
been too few Macedo-Slavs and Bulgarians to form a Macedo-
Bulgarian church, the Macedo-Slavs, because of their basic loyalty
to the Orthodox doctrine and liturgy, have often attended the
Greek Orthodox church—at any rate for baptisms, weddings,
funerals, Christmas, and Easter. (On occasions they also attended
the Syrian Orthodox and Anglican churches.)

Even so, these families have often retained a deep-seated
loyalty to the basic cause of 'Macedonia for the Macedonians';
they are very familiar with the complexities of Balkan history
and politics, keep themselves up to date by reading literature
published by Macedonian organizations in America and, in one
case at least, so convert their southern Greek wives that the
latter become more ardent supporters of Macedonian independence than their husbands. Moreover, the independent Macedonia
they want is not a small state covering present Macedo-Slav
districts but a full-blown Macedonia that would include not
only Yugoslav and Bulgarian Macedonia, and the disputed
areas around Florina and Kastoria, but also the traditionally
Greek areas of Grevena and Kozani, the port of Salonica, and
all those areas settled by Greek refugees from Asia Minor.
Having themselves been for so long a minority people within an
artificial Greek state, a little reversal of roles, they argue, would
do no harm; certainly they say, with their close business and
religious ties with Greek people, they would treat the Greek
minority in an independent Macedonia far more kindly than
the Greeks have treated them.

The important point here is not the justice or practicability of these political ambitions in Europe, nor the truth or falsity of the mass of literature put out by the various Folk-nationalist organizations and governments.[28] It is to assess how many persons migrating from the disputed areas of Macedonia identified themselves with the various Folk viewpoints, and how far this affected their pattern of settlement. Here generalization without adequate field-work is dangerous. From places investigated, however, together with an examination of marriage records and the literature, it would appear that migrants from Grevena, Kozani, and other clearly Greek areas in southern Macedonia have been little influenced by Bulgarian, Serbian, or Macedo-Slav Folk views; an example here are those settlers from Pentafilion and other villages near Kozani who came to Melbourne from the end of World War I onwards, formed themselves and others into a Greek Macedonian society subsequently called 'Alexander the Great', and became a district group within the federal structure of the Greek Folk community. Equally little affected, it seems, were the traditionally Greek element in wholly or partially Hellenized towns set within predominantly Slav districts—Salonica, Kastoria, Florina, Bitola, for instance. Illustration are those migrants from the fur-trading and fur-processing town of Kastoria, who settled in New York, Toronto and other American cities from the turn of the century onwards; they spoke almost no Slav at all and formed very strong village organizations within the local Greek communities.

Far harder to assess are those from bilingual and Slavophone villages and towns—and these made up the majority of emigrants to Australia (Table II and Appendix 16). Those who have been settled abroad for several years and feel no threat of Greek official discrimination, and who are part of chain communities

28 Besides C. J. Christides, *The Macedonian Camouflage*, the Greek view appears in V. Coloctronis, *La Macedoine et L'Hellenisme*, G. B. Zotiades, *The Macedonian Controversy*, and S. P. Kyriakides, *The Northern Ethnological Boundaries of Hellenism*. The pre-war Serb view appears in the Serbian census maps of 1924. Amongst prolific Bulgarian writers have been J. Ivanov; a more moderate pro-Bulgarian view appears in H. N. Brailsford, *Macedonia: Its Races and their Future*. The notion of a distinct Macedo-Slav people—first argued by P. D. Dragonoff in the mid-1880s—was given widespread publicity by J. Cvijic's map of 1913 and R. W. Seton-Watson's *The Rise of Nationality in the Balkans*. Typical of recent literature favouring Macedonian independence is G. Anastasoff, *Autonomous Macedonia*, published by the very active Macedonian Political Organization, Indianapolis. A very good objective account is H. R. Wilkinson, *Maps and Politics*; see also E. Barker, *Macedonia*.

large enough to enable some degree of social and religious self-sufficiency, have often leant more heavily to the Slav cause than the Greek. In Toronto, for instance, there had appeared by 1958 only one Greek organization for villages in the district of Kastoria, compared with ten for the Macedonian-Bulgarian community. Likewise, where a single village chain gave rise to both a Greek and a Slav organization, the Slav society usually had more members and greater financial resources; the Zheleva society of Toronto, for instance, has been larger and wealthier than the Antarktikon. Finally there have long been many more Macedonian families associated with the two Macedo-Bulgarian churches than with the one Greek church in Toronto (1958), a fact that appears not only from church records but from marriage records also. Greek Macedonians in Toronto admit the size and strength of Slav Macedonian societies, but assert that they consist almost entirely of older pro-Bulgarian settlers and their children, and that 80 per cent of post-war arrivals, adequately educated as to their true Greek heritage, at once join Greek societies. When pressed, however, they admit that many new arrivals join Greek societies only temporarily, to facilitate the bringing out of relatives; also they reveal, by their anger at the success which the Slav societies have had in using their better halls and social facilities to 'seduce' new arrivals, that the problem is more serious than they admit; furthermore some reluctantly agree that, whereas many so-called Greek Macedonians go to Slav functions and clubs, few avowedly Macedo-Slavs attend Greek functions. On balance, and as a rough estimate only, it would appear that at least three-quarters of Toronto's pre-war Macedonian settlers identified themselves with the Macedo-Bulgarian communities and that at least one-half of post-war Macedonian arrivals eventually find their way there.

Analogous situations have developed in Melbourne and Perth. In Melbourne, for instance, migrants from Florina district split into those organized into the Hellenic Macedonian League—affiliated with the Greek Orthodox community—and those belonging eventually to the Slav Macedonian people's community. In the twenties and thirties, again very largely because of the smallness of numbers and the desirability of maintaining business relationships with other Greeks, the majority of Florina settlers apparently associated with the Greek community. Since the large post-war migration to Melbourne from both Greek and Yugoslav Macedonia, the autonomous Macedo-Slav group in Melbourne itself has grown much stronger and the Slav churches more powerful.[29] Recent field-work in Melbourne suggests that Kastorian and Florinan families now identified with the Macedo-Slav movement make up at least half, and probably more, of immigrant families from Greek Macedonia. More field-work in Melbourne will be necessary, however, before this highly complex situation becomes clear.

In Adelaide events evolved somewhat differently because of the presence of the relatively large Bulgarian population in the market-gardening areas near Fulham. Consequently, migrants from Florina district, who started arriving from the 1920s onwards and nearly all settled in the Fulham area as market-gardeners, tended to become part of the Bulgarian community. With the Bulgarians they attended the Russian Orthodox church of Adelaide and formed the 'Balkan (Macedonian) Club' of pre-war days. A number also became interested in I.M.R.O. literature and in the Macedonian organizations and papers published in America. The post-war influx has complicated this pattern and it is at present somewhat difficult to tell how many recent arrivals from Greek Macedonia are joining their relatives and compatriots in the Macedo-Bulgarian community and how many have broken away altogether to join the Greek Orthodox church.

Such metropolitan families, however, accounted for well under half Australia's pre-war immigrants from the districts of Bitola, Florina, and Kastoria, and even here the majority were engaged in market-gardening in the outer suburbs rather than in inner city occupations. Those in the rural districts of New South Wales, Victoria, and Western Australia were scattered about in small concentrations, apparently with few connexions with southern Greeks or eastern Bulgarians, and with still slenderer ties with the Greek or Bulgarian churches. Yet many kept alive the tradition of Macedonian independence. Some subscribed to pamphlets and papers published by the Macedonian Political Organization in America and became fiercely Folk-nationalist; others seem to have retained only a gentle interest in the matter, being more concerned to keep alive the dialect and customs of their villages and districts of origin. Here also

---

[29] About 1952 a Macedonian Bulgarian priest succeeded in obtaining enough support to build one church, but that did not satisfy everyone and a second community has been started recently with a priest from the Macedonian Orthodox Church of Yugoslavia (Benyei, 'Greek and South Slav Immigrants in Australia', pp. 79-81).

W

heavy post-war immigration has increased Slav Macedonian
loyalties and there are now active communities in Queanbeyan,
Manjimup, Shepparton and elsewhere. (Since World War II
there has been some tendency for Macedonians to leave rural
areas and settle in metropolitan areas such as Melbourne,
Canberra, and Newcastle.)

From this brief survey of migration from the Macedonian
districts of Kastoria, Florina, and Bitola to Canada and Australia
emerge one or two important points. First, although Folk-
nationalist and religious feeling was fierce and bitter, splitting
most settlers into sharply separated cultural groups abroad, this
did not greatly affect the character of their settlement. In
Australia the chain system worked in such a way that the great
majority of early migrants from the villages—whether ultimately
identifying themselves as Greeks or as Slav Macedonians—settled
in small clusters as market-gardeners, dairy-farmers, small
farmers and so on; herein they showed a very different settlement pattern from that of southern and island Greeks.[30]
Conversely, in Toronto, the chains operated in such a way that
the great majority of settlers—whether ultimately identifying
themselves as Greeks or Slavs—settled as restaurant-keepers;
again showing a somewhat different settlement pattern from
southern and island Greeks who were more involved in other
kinds of retail and commercial activity.[31]

Secondly, it seems that these settlers—whether thinking of
themselves as Slavs or Greeks—were often much more at home
with their local district dialect of Slavonic than with Greek:
even for many of those recent arrivals reared under an extreme
Hellenizing programme Greek was the language of the school
and of business, not the language of the home. Consequently
even ardent pro-Greek Macedonians found themselves slipping
into the odd Slav phrase here and there; this easy facility in
Slav, of course, was one reason why Greek-minded settlers found
themselves drawn more to the large Slav-Macedonian communities than Macedo-Slavs in the same position were to the Greek.

Language raises the third point—the attitude of southern and

[30] Appendix 16. Post-war arrivals may be concentrating more in metropolitan areas (Benyei, op. cit.), though the rural settlements have not yet been
studied.

[31] For the high proportion of Slav Macedonian restaurant-keepers see
Balikci, *Macedonians and Bulgarians.* My own research on marriage and
other records in Toronto showed that during the period 1926-54 over two-
thirds of Greek Macedonians were engaged in catering compared with
slightly less than half of southern and island Greeks.

island Greeks to the Macedonians. The Macedo-Slavs, of course, they feared and despised. But they also displayed a very patronizing attitude to even the most pro-Greek of settlers from Florina or Kastoria. Their attitude to the occasional Slav word overheard at the Greek church was symptomatic here: it reminded them perpetually that Macedonians were somewhat different beings, migrants from the far north of their realm, tangled up with all sorts of unpleasant creatures such as Serbs and Bulgarians, at best the descendants of those ancient Macedonians whom they had never really admitted to be true Hellenes. As one old southern Greek (Peloponnesian) lady said: 'Oh, those Macedonian Greeks are Greek in sentiment, certainly, but they aren't proper Greeks and can't even speak the language properly; I wouldn't want my daughter to marry one of those.' Conversely, one intelligent fur-merchant from Kastoria town said: 'We Kastorian fur-traders have been Greeks for millennia and have always been ardent supporters of the Greek church; but the southern Greeks still call us "Bulgarians"; we shall never live it down.' Certainly the marriage statistics for Toronto confirm this: only a fifth or so of those second-generation Greek Macedonians marrying within the Greek community married into families of southern and island origin.[32]

It is possible that the furious way in which some migrants call themselves Greek, and fiercely defend their Greek heritage, arises from this feeling that southern Greeks still do not accept them fully. It is very interesting to note that in the middle of an ardent defence of the Greek church one of these settlers might say: 'Of course the Orthodox Youth Organization isn't for us, it's for the Greeks'—while a moment later another would describe in detail the way in which his district organization threatened to withdraw completely from the Greek Community because of the high-handed action by some of 'those southern Greeks'.

All this means that while Folk-nationalist and religious forces were strong enough to keep most Greek Macedonians away from their Macedo-Slav relatives, they were not strong enough to weld them fully into the Greek Folk community.

District and regional customs, together with regional differences in language, seem to have been more important than Folk values here. They, together with strong family loyalties and a somewhat unusual mountain peasant background, played the decisive role in the way the chains reacted to assimilation.

32 Analysis of marriage records, Toronto, 1958.

It is possible that this inability of the Greek Folk community to accept Macedonians on equal terms partly explains the very high rate of marriage between pre-war Macedonian settlers in Australia and British-Australian girls (Appendix 16, Ratio B (t)). Another reason is that given by the Slav-Macedonians themselves: so grateful are they for the freedom they have enjoyed in Australia as compared with Greece and Serbia that they have always been eager to become Australian citizens as soon as possible, to make English the second official language of their church, to allow their children to speak English in the home and make British-Australian friends.[33]

Conclusion

The power of family, district, and regional forces, and the way they interacted with all the other forces at work in the process of migration and settlement, brings us back to the point of this Macedonian illustration: the great complexity of the subject, and the need for understanding the operation of general forces by studying the detailed history of each immigrant group. Nor are the Macedonians so much more complex and interesting than any of the other chain groups. They all have their intricacies and colour, their vivid personalities, their moments of grandeur, and their periods of dull patient labour when submerged in establishing themselves in their new country. In Australia we have tended to think primarily of the dullness, the peasant background, the smells and dirt associated with the primitive background and a tradition of long hard toil. Or we have been captivated and amused by works such as Nino Culotta's *They're a Weird Mob*. But we must not forget that through this often squalid, and sometimes odd, pathetic, and amusing story there gleams the occasional gold of an heroic past. It may seem a far cry from an Ithacan dish-washer in Melbourne to the epic deeds of Ulysses, from the Maltese street-labourer to those courageous defenders of the Cross of Christendom against the Star of Islam, from the sweating Catanian or Calabrian farmer to those colourful Norman adventurers who wrested Sicily and southern Italy from Saracen

[33] Field-work in Melbourne and Queanbeyan in 1960 shows there is some truth in these statements: English has become the second official language in one of the two Macedonian churches and the duration of residence between arrival and naturalization has been shorter for Slav Macedonians than Greeks (nine years and thirteen years between 1900 and 1946)—see Appendixes 16, 19, 20.

and Byzantine overlords, from the patient Albanian market-gardener to the heroic and fantastic figure of Skanderbeg, from the Dalmatian poultry-keeper to those bold seamen who risked the unknown seas in frail wooden craft in search of profit and adventure. Yet Australia's southern European settlers have been reared in these traditions: they pass them on by word of mouth to their children and proudly show volumes of epic deeds to their visitor. The high Byronic theme of Childe Harold's pilgrimage contains a light and colour much too bright to use when interpreting southern European settlement in Australia: but it does no harm now and again to lift one's eyes to such a light, and then, turning again to the toil of peasant pioneers, catch the occasional reflection of gold and beauty in their own patient struggles and achievements.

BIBLIOGRAPHY

This bibliography lists only those works referred to in the text.

A. BOOKS AND ARTICLES

Agapitidis, S., *The Population of the Dodecanese Islands*, Athens, 1948.

Anastasoff, C., *Autonomous Macedonia*, Indianapolis, 1945.

Baber, Ray, 'A Study of 325 Mixed Marriages', *American Sociological Review*, 1937, Vol. 2.

Balch, Emily, *Our Slavic Fellow Citizens*, New York, 1910.

Barbagallo, C., *La Questione Meridionale*, Milan, 1948.

Barker, E., *Macedonia*, London, 1950.

Baron, Stanley (ed.), *Country Towns in the Future England*, London, 1944.

Benyei, L., 'Greek and South Slav Immigrants in Australia', in C. A. Price (ed.), *The Study of Immigrants in Australia*, Canberra, 1960.

Blegen, T. C., *Norwegian Migration to America: The American Transition* (2nd vol.), Minnesota, 1940.

Boniface VIII, Pope, Bull *Unam Sanctam*.

Borrie, W. D. (ed.), *The Cultural Integration of Immigrants*, UNESCO, Paris, 1959.

Borrie, W. D., *Italians and Germans in Australia*, Melbourne, 1954.

Bossard, James H. S., 'Nationality and Nativity as Factors in Marriage', *American Sociological Review*, IV (1939), 792.

Brailsford, H N., *Macedonia: Its Races and Their Future*, London, 1906.

Carpenter, Niles, *Immigrants and their Children*, Census Monograph VII (U.S.A. Census, 1920).

Charteris, A. H., 'Australian Immigration Policy', in P. D. Phillips and G. L. Wood (eds.), *The Peopling of Australia*, Melbourne, 1928.

Christides, C. J., *The Macedonian Camouflage*, Athens, 1940.

Clifford, F. C., *New Italy—a Brief Sketch of a New and Thriving Colony*, Sydney, 1889.

Coloctronis, V., *La Macédoine et L'Hellenisme*, Paris, 1919.

Cowdry, E. V. (ed.), *Human Biology and Racial Welfare*, New York, 1930.

Curlewis, F. C. P., *Some Industrial and National Aspects of the Australian Sugar Cane Industry* (Lecture to University of Queensland), Brisbane, 1939.

Davie, M. R., *World Immigration*, 2nd ed., New York, 1949.

Decesare, F. S., *Reports upon the Suitability of the British Colonies in Australasia as a Field of Maltese Emigration*, Malta Government Printing Office, 1883.

Dictionary of Sociology (ed. H. P. Fairchild), New York, 1944.

Douglas, Norman, *Old Calabria*, London, 1956.

Drachsler, Julius, *Intermarriage in New York City*, Columbia, 1921.

Dragonoff, P., *La Macédonie et les Macédoniens*, Paris, 1922.

Duncan, H. G., *Immigration and Assimilation*, New York, 1933.

Encyclopedia Italiana.

Fairchild, H. P. (ed.), *Dictionary of Sociology*, New York, 1944.

Fairchild, H. P., *Immigration*, New York, 1925.

Fairchild, H. P., *Greek Immigration to the United States*, Yale, 1911.

Ferry, T. A., *see* Australia, Queensland, *Parliamentary Papers*.

Firth, R., *Elements of Social Organization*, London, 1951.

Foerster, R. F., *The Italian Emigration of our Times*, Harvard, 1919.

Francis, E. K., 'Minority Groups—a Revision of Concepts', *British Journal of Sociology*, II (1951), iii, 219-29.

Galanis, D. M., 'The First Greek Migrants', *Krikos*, London, July-August 1957.

Geographical Handbook Series (Naval Intelligence Division), *Albania*, London, 1945; *Dodecanese Islands*, London, 1941; *Greece*, 3 vols., London, 1944-5; *Italy*, 3 vols., London, 1944-5; *Spain*, 3 vols., London, 1941-4; *Jugoslavia*, 3 vols., London, 1944-5.

Galitzi, C. A., *A Study of Assimilation among Roumanians in the United States*, Columbia, 1929.

Gamba, C., *The Italian Fishermen of Fremantle*, University of Western Australia, Dept of Economics Publications, Series A (Economics), No. 2, 1952.

Goldman, L. M., *Jews in Victoria in the Nineteenth Century*, Melbourne, 1954.

Hack, H., *Dutch Group Settlement in Brazil*, Research Group for European Migration Problems, *Bulletin*, Vol. 7, Supp. 4, The Hague, 1959.

Haedo, Diego de, *Topographia e historia de Argel*, 1612, reprinted, Madrid, 1927-9.

Halich, W., *Ukrainians in the United States*, Chicago, 1937.

Hansen, M. L., *The Atlantic Migration*, Harvard, 1945.

Harvey, J. R., *Black Hand of Vengeance*, Brisbane, 1948.

Hebart, T., *The United Evangelical Lutheran Church in Australia*, Adelaide, 1938.

Hempel, J. A., *Italians in Queensland*, Canberra, 1959.

Hughes, E. C. and H. M., *Where Peoples Meet: Racial and Ethnic Frontiers*, Glencoe, Ill., 1952.

Hurd, W. B., *Racial Origins and Nativity of the Canadian People*, Census Monograph No. 4 (Canada Census, 1931), Ottawa.

Hutchinson, E. P., *Immigrants and their Children 1850-1950*, Census Monograph (U.S.A. Census, 1950), New York, 1956.

International Union for the Scientific Study of Population, *Cultural Assimilation of Immigrants* (Supplement to *Population Studies*, March 1950), London, 1950.

Jerome, Harry, *Migration and Business Cycles*, New York, 1926.

Jouguet, Pierre, *Macedonian Imperialism and the Hellenization of the East*, London, 1928.

Kennedy, Ruby J. R., 'Single or Triple Melting-Pot?' *American Journal of Sociology*, XLIX (1943-4).

Kirkconnell, Watson (ed.), *Canadian Overtones*, Winnipeg, 1935.

Kiser, Clyde V., 'Cultural Pluralism', *Annals of the American Academy of Political and Social Science*, CCLXII (1949).

Kolehmainen, John, 'A Study of Marriage in a Finnish Community', *American Journal of Sociology*, XLII (1936-7), 371-82.

Kyriakides, S. P., *The Northern Ethnological Boundaries of Hellenism*, Salonika, 1955.

Lane-Poole, S., *The Barbary Corsairs*, London, 1890.

Laukas, Menas, 'Life History', MS. quoted in Park and Miller, *Old World Traits Transplanted*.

Lermer, Arthur, *The Evolution of Canadian Policy towards Cultural Pluralism*, Canadian Jewish Congress, Montreal, 1955.

Listwan, I. A., 'Mental Disorders in Migrants: Further Study', *Medical Journal of Australia*, I (1959), 566-8.

Listwan, I. A., 'Paranoid States: Social and Cultural Aspects', *Medical Journal of Australia*, I (1956), 776-8.

Listwan, I. A., and Wunderley, Sir Harry, 'Immigrants and Mental Health, Further Study', in C. A. Price (ed.), *The Study of Immigrants in Australia*, Canberra, 1960.

Lochore, R. A., *From Europe to New Zealand*, Wellington, New Zealand, 1951.

Logan, Milla, *Bring Along Laughter*, New York, 1947.

Loomis, C. P., and Beegle, J. A., *Rural Social Systems*, New York, 1950.

Lyng, J. S., *Non-Britishers in Australia*, Melbourne, 1935.

McDonald, J. S., 'Italy's Rural Social Structure and Emigration', *Occidente*, XII (1956), 437-56.

Malinowski, B., 'Myth in Primitive Psychology', in W. R. Dawson (ed.), *The Frazer Lectures 1922-1932*, London, 1932.

Marcson, Simon, 'A Theory of Intermarriage and Assimilation', *Social Forces*, XXIX (1950), 75-8.

Meler, Vjekoslav (ed.), *Slavonic Pioneers of California*, San Francisco, 1932.

Miller, W., *Greece*, London, 1928.

Moore, W. E., *Economic Demography of Eastern and Southern Europe*, Geneva, 1945.

Nairn, N. B., 'A Survey of the History of the White Australia Policy in the 19th Century', *Australian Quarterly*, September 1956.

Newbigin, M. I., *Southern Europe*, London, 1949.

Niau, J. H., *The Phantom Paradise—The Story of the Expedition of the Marquis de Ray*, Sydney, 1936.

Olivier, T., *Report on Lands in Cyprus for a Maltese Settlement 1879*, Malta Government Printing Office, 1880.

Panunzio, C. M., *The Soul of an Immigrant*, New York, 1937.

Park, R. E., *Human Communities*, Glencoe, Ill., 1952.

Park, R. E., *Race and Culture*, Glencoe, Ill., 1950.

Park, R. E., *Society*, Glencoe, Ill., 1955.

Park, R. E., and Miller, H. A., *Old World Traits Transplanted*, New York, 1921.

Peterson, William, *Planned Migration*, Berkeley, 1955.

Pisani, L. F., *The Italian in America*, New York, 1957.

Plant, G. F., *Oversea Settlement*, Oxford, 1951.

Polyzos, N. J., *Essai sur l'émigration grecque*, Paris, 1947.

Prestianni, Nunzio, *L'Economia Agraria della Sicilia*, Palermo, 1947.

Pribichevich, S., *Living Space*, London, 1940.

Price, A. Grenfell, *White Settlers in the Tropics*, New York, 1939.

Price, C. A., 'The Effects of Post-War Immigration', *Australian Quarterly*, XXIX (1957), 28-40.

Price, C. A., 'Immigration and Group Settlement', in W. D. Borrie (ed.), *The Cultural Integration of Immigrants*, UNESCO, Paris, 1959.

Price, C. A., *Malta and the Maltese*, Melbourne, 1954.

X

Pyke, N. O. P., 'An Outline History of Italian Emigration into Australia', *Australian Quarterly*, XX (1948), iii.

Redfield, R., *Peasant Society and Culture*, Chicago, 1956.

Re-Migration (Report to the Sixth International Conference on Non-Governmental Organizations interested in Migration), Geneva, 1957.

Roberts, Peter, *The New Immigration*, New York, 1912.

Sestanovich, S. N. (ed.), *The Slavs of California*, Oakland, 1937.

Seton-Watson, Hugh, *Eastern Europe between the Wars, 1918-1941*, Cambridge, 1945.

Seton-Watson, R. W., *The Rise of Nationality in the Balkans*, London, 1917.

Slotkin, J. S., 'Jewish-gentile intermarriage in Chicago', *American Sociological Review*, VII (1942).

Smith, T. Lynn, *Brazil—People and Institutions*, Baton Rouge, 1954.

Smith, T. Lynn, in *Dictionary of Sociology* (ed. H. P. Fairchild), New York, 1944.

Steiner, E. A., *The Immigrant Tide*, New York, 1909.

Steiner, E. A., *On the Trail of the Immigrant*, New York, 1906.

Sweet-Escott, B., *Greece: a Political and Economic Survey 1939-53*, London, 1954.

Tadich, John V., 'Reminiscences', in Vjekoslav Meler (ed.), *Slavonic Pioneers of California*, San Francisco, 1932.

Taylor, A. J. P., *The Hapsburg Monarchy*, London, 1948.

Thomas, W. I., and Znaniecki, F., *The Polish Peasant in Europe and America*, New York, 1927; 3rd ed., 1958.

Trouton, R., *Peasant Renaissance in Yugoslavia 1900-1950*, London, 1952.

Vlassis, G. D., *The Greeks in Canada*, Ottawa, 1953.

Voinovich, L., *Dalmatia and the Yugoslav Movement*, London, 1920.

Ware, Caroline, 'Ethnic Communities', *Encyclopaedia of Social Sciences*.

Wilkinson, H. R., *Maps and Politics*, Liverpool, 1951.

Willard, M., *History of the White Australia Policy*, Melbourne, 1923.

Willcox, W. F., *International Migrations*, 2 vols., New York, 1929-31.

Wunderley, Sir Harry, 'A Survey of Immigration and Mental Health in Australia', in C. A. Price (ed.), *The Study of Immigrants in Australia*, Canberra, 1960.

Zotiades, G. B., *The Macedonian Controversy*, Salonika, 1954.

Zubrzycki, J., *Immigration* (a Commentary prepared for the Atlas of Australian Resources, Department of National Development), Canberra, 1960.

Zubrzycki, J., *Immigrants in Australia*, Melbourne, 1960.

B. OFFICIAL DOCUMENTS

AUSTRALIA

Censuses.

Commonwealth, *Parliamentary Debates*, 1904-1940.

————, *Parliamentary Papers*: 'Royal Commission on Foreign Contract Labour in Western Australia', 1901-2 vol. 2, p. 871.

————, Bureau of Census and Statistics, Australian Demography (Annual Bulletins), 1908-current.

————, ————, *Official Year Book of the Commonwealth of Australia*, 1908-current.

————, Department of Commerce and Agriculture, *Report on the Agricultural Extension Services in the Murrumbidgee Irrigation Area*, Canberra, 1952.

————, Department of Immigration, *Statistical Bulletin* (Quarterly).

————, Federal Health Council of Australia, Report of Fifth Session, Canberra, 1931.

————, Immigration Advisory Council, *Reports of the Committee established to investigate conduct of Migrants*, Canberra, 1955, 1957.

Queensland: *Parliamentary Debates*, 1884-1940.

————, *Parliamentary Papers*: 'Report of the Royal Commission to investigate the Social and Economic Effect of Increase in Numbers of Aliens in North Queensland', 1925 vol. 3, Paper A28 (the 'Ferry Report').

Western Australia: *Parliamentary Debates*, 1902-40.

————, 'Report of the Royal Commission on the Immigration of Non-British Labour', *Votes and Proceedings of the Parliament*, 1904 vol. 2, Paper A7.

GREECE
Annuaire statistique de la Grèce, Athens.

Censuses.

International Labour Office, *Labour Problems in Greece* (Report of the Mission of the International Labour Office to Greece, October-November 1947), Geneva, 1949.

ITALY
Censuses.

Istituto Centrale di Statistica, Rome, *Annuario Statistico Italiano*.

————, *Movimento della Popolazione e cause di morte*.

Nuovo Dizionario de Comuni e Frazioni di Comune, Rome, 1954.

Statistica Guidiziaria Penale (Annual), Rome.

MALTA
Censuses.

Report on Emigration for the Fiscal Year 1922-3, Valetta, 1923.

Report on Emigration for the Fiscal Year 1923-4, Valetta, 1925.

UNITED STATES OF AMERICA
Censuses.

Congress, *Reports of the Immigration Commission, 1907-10*, Washington, 1911.

Report of the Commissioner General for Immigration, Washington, 1907.

YUGOSLAVIA
Censuses.

Emigration Commissariat of the Kingdom of Yugoslavia, *Report*, Zagreb, 1929.

C. NEWSPAPERS AND PERIODICALS

Il Corriere d'Australia (The Australian Courier), Sydney.
La Fiamma (The Flame), Sydney.
Gazeta Polska (Polish Gazette), Chicago.

Glasnik (American Yugoslav *Herald*), San Francisco.
Hellenic Herald, Sydney.
Jadran (Adriatic), California.
Kastoriana Nea (New Kastoria), New York.
Krikos (The Link), London and Athens.
Makedonska Glas (Macedonian Herald), Sydney.
Makedonska Iskra (Macedonian Spark), Melbourne.
Matica, Zagreb.
Murrumbidgee Irrigator, Leeton, N.S.W.
Napredak (Forward), Sydney.
Narodni Adresar (National Directory of Croat-Serb-Slovene organizations, etc., in U.S.A. and Canada).
Il Risveglio (Il Nuovo Risveglio) (The Awakening), Sydney.
Sokol (The Falcon), San Jose, California.
Watsonville Register, Santa Clara county, California.
West Australian, Perth, W.A.

D. UNPUBLISHED MATERIAL

Balikci, Asen, Remarques sur la Structure du Groupe Ethnique Bulgare et Macédonien de Toronto. National Museum of Canada, Ottawa.

Bertei, J. M., Innisfail, University of Queensland Library.

Bromley, John, The Italians of Port Pirie. Thesis, 1955, in Australian National University Library, Canberra.

Langford-Smith, Trevor, Land Forms, Land Settlement and Irrigation on the Murrumbidgee, N.S.W. Thesis, 1958, in Australian National University Library, Canberra.

McDonald, J. S., Migration from Italy to Australia. Thesis, 1958, in Australian National University Library, Canberra.

Petrolias, J. A., Post-War Greek and Italian Migrants in Melbourne. Thesis, 1959, University of Melbourne.

Price, C. A., The Italian Population of Griffith. Australian National University Report, 1955.

INDEX